Ethical Intuitionsim

# Ethical Intuitionism

Michael Huemer

First published 2005
This paperback edition first published 2008 by
PALGRAVE MACMILLAN
Houndmills, Basingstoke, Hampshire RG21 6XS and
175 Fifth Avenue, New York, N. Y. 10010
Companies and representatives throughout the world

PALGRAVE MACMILLAN is the global academic imprint of the Palgrave
Macmillan division of St. Martin's Press, LLC and of Palgrave Macmillan Ltd.
Macmillan® is a registered trademark in the United States, United Kingdom
and other countries. Palgrave is a registered trademark in the European
Union and other countries.

ISBN-13: 978–0–230–57374–1 paperback

This book is printed on paper suitable for recycling and made from fully
managed and sustained forest sources. Logging, pulping and manufacturing
processes are expected to conform to the environmental regulations of the
country of origin.

A catalogue record for this book is available from the British Library.

Library of Congress Cataloging-in-publication Data
Huemer, Michael, 1969–
    Ethical intuitionism/Michael Huemer.
        p.cm.
    Includes bibliographical references (p.) and index.


    1. Ethical intuitionism. 2.Ethics. 3. Intuition. I. Title.

BJ1472.H84 2005
170'.42–dc22

                                                        2005052289


10    9    8    7    6    5    4    3    2    1
17    16    15    14    13    12    11    10    09    08

Transferred to digital printing 2008

*For my students*

The only real valuable thing is intuition.

ALBERT EINSTEIN

# Contents

# Analytical Contents

PART I: ALTERNATIVE METAETHICAL THEORIES

non-moral properties can achieve the same advantage.

## PART II: ETHICAL INTUITIONISM

# Preface

We all make value judgments, but hardly any of us understand what we are doing when we do. Through conversations and debates that I have had over a number of years, I have come to the conclusion that nearly all intellectuals in our society think that morality is somehow unreal. I have come to expect, whenever the subject of the nature of values arises, to be told blithely that morality is all a matter of emotions or conventions, that it is all an illusion created by our genes, or that it is a myth sponsored by religion. This seems to be the sophisticated and 'scientific' view. I recently surveyed a class of about forty undergraduates on the subject. After explaining the terms 'subjective' and 'objective', I asked how many of them believed that 'morality is subjective'. *Every single* person in the room raised their hands, save two—those two were myself and my graduate student teaching assistant. This is all the more remarkable for the fact that it is usually all but impossible to attain universal agreement, in a philosophy class, on anything. Professors of philosophy, whose job it is to study such things as the nature of values, are less united—objectivism remains a respectable minority position in the field. Yet most experts seem to agree that morality is in some sense unreal.

None of this seems to stop anyone—whether students, professors, or other intellectuals—from making moral judgments, arguing about what the correct moral views are, or trying to get others to obey the correct moral principles. Even those who declare morality an illusion will often proceed to hold forth on the wrongness of the war in Iraq, or of human cloning, or at least of their boyfriend's cheating on them. And they seem to expect their arguments to be taken as reasons for other people to act in certain ways. This strikes me as odd. If I thought that the giant rabbit standing in the corner of the room was a hallucination, I don't think I would hold forth in public about what his favorite food was, plan my actions around his schedule, or expect others to alter their behavior in the light of my claims about him. If morality is an illusion, it is equally unclear why anyone should care about its hallucinatory dictates. And those who regard morality as a matter of conventions or of emotions do not seem in practice to treat it accordingly. They do not argue about what is moral as one would be expected to argue about what the social conventions are or what emotions people feel. They seem to treat their moral claims as having some kind of force greater than assertions about conventions or emotions. If abortion fails to cohere with American social conventions, or if it stimulates negative emotions in certain observers, exactly why is that supposed to convince a pregnant woman who does not want a baby to carry the child to term anyway?

Perhaps my questions are naive, and perhaps the moral anti-realists have some sort of sophisticated answers to them. I only report how things seem to me at first glance. At first glance, one would think that modern philosophy's discovery—if that is what it is—that morality is subjective, illusory, or otherwise non-objective would have a profound impact on how we think and talk about moral issues; yet those who embrace the alleged discovery in one instant seem to forget about it the next, devoting almost no thought to what the implications might be for the practice of moral argument, exhortation, and so forth. A simple explanation suggests itself: perhaps most avowals of anti-realism are fundamentally *insincere*. In the context of an abstract philosophy discussion, we *say* morality is unreal, and we may even tell ourselves that we believe that. But what we really believe is revealed more by the way we talk about morality in concrete situations and by the way we order our lives according to moral principles than by what we say in the philosophy room.

But it is not as simple as that. Sometimes moral anti-realism *does* affect how we talk about moral issues. People will argue that the government should not 'legislate morality' because morality is subjective. Or that we should not try to prevent female circumcision because morality is culturally relative. Or that we should refrain from judging others, or that a teacher should not presume to teach moral principles, because no objective moral truths are known. Of course, most professional philosophers would be embarrassed to hear such arguments. If morality is subjective, it does not follow that the government should not legislate it; what follows is that the government should legislate morality if doing so accords with the legislators' subjective preferences. If morality is culturally relative, it does not follow that we should not interfere with the customs of other cultures; what follows is that we should interfere with other cultures if doing so accords with our customs. If no objective moral truths are known, it does not follow that we should refrain from judging others or from teaching moral principles; what follows is that we do not know whether it is objectively true that we should judge others or teach moral principles. All three arguments mentioned at the beginning of this paragraph seem to proceed by unconsciously exempting some moral principle from the general anti-realism they assume: the principle that one *should not* make laws based on mere subjective preferences; that one should not impose parochial conventions on other societies; that one should not make judgments one does not know to be objectively correct; that one should not teach things one does not know to be objectively correct.

I therefore favor a different account of our culture's attitudes towards morality: I suggest that they are incoherent; indeed, blatantly so. Whatever thoughts most individuals have about the nature of value would not withstand a minute of scrutiny. We think that values are subjective but that the Iraq war was objectively wrong; we think that morality is an illusion but that we should all act morally; we think that, because there are no objective values, it is objectively wrong to impose our values on others.

The question is, which of our conflicting beliefs are false, and which if any are correct?

Most who deny the existence of objective values will concede that, at least at first glance, it *seems* natural to suppose there are objective values. Nearly every society throughout history has taken the objectivity of values for granted. And as I've suggested, even members of our own cynical society appear to assume the objectivity of values in their ordinary thinking about particular moral questions. If there really are no objective values, then this must be the most significant discovery of modern philosophy, and perhaps the first time the discipline of philosophy has managed to convince large numbers of people to embrace a massive revision of common sense. If, on the other hand, there *are* objective values, then the widespread opinion to the contrary must be among the greatest errors of modern philosophy, and of modern intellectual culture generally.

The latter is what I believe. I have written this book to defend a thoroughly objectivist, rationalist account of the nature of morality and moral knowledge. The view I defend is known, somewhat misleadingly given the connotations of the term 'intuition' in popular culture, as *ethical intuitionism*. It holds that there are objective evaluative facts—facts such as that it is wrong to cause gratuitous suffering to others—over and above the natural, non-evaluative facts; that we have a kind of intellectual insight into some of these evaluative facts; and that they provide us with reasons for behaving in certain ways, irrespective of what we desire. This position is widely viewed as naive and indefensible. I believe on the contrary that the common objections to it are far weaker than they have been taken to be and could not have moved any reasonably reflective intuitionist to abandon her position.

The first part of the book, following the introductory chapter, is negative: it endeavors to refute three alternative theories about value. The second part explains and defends my own views about value: chapter 5 explains how we know moral truths; chapter 6 deals with the problem of moral disagreement and error; chapter 7 explains how values provide reasons for action; and chapter 8 responds to numerous objections. Finally, chapter 9 offers a review of the main arguments of the book, along with some speculation about why the conclusions I defend are unpopular and why the issues are important.

Who should read this book? I have sought to write a book that could be read with profit by other professors—but I did not seek to write one that could *only* be read by professors. The nature of morality and value is everybody's business. The problems of moral relativism and skepticism, if indeed they are problems, affect students and lay people as much as professional philosophers. So I have aimed my work at both professional and amateur philosophers. This is a difficult undertaking, and doubtless opinions will differ on how successfully I have pursued it. I have sought to advance the state of the field, but I have also explained classic arguments that students new to the field should hear. Some of my colleagues may occasionally be bored by the repetition of old arguments, while some lay people may be confused by technical points. To minimize the latter difficulty, I have marked with asterisks ('\*') the more technical sections of the book, including some sections responding to views put forward by specific individuals in the contemporary academic world. The non-specialist can skip these sections without losing the thread of argument.

This book has benefitted from the comments of a number of friends and colleagues, including Elinor Mason, Doug Husak, Ari Armstrong, Bryan Caplan, Robin Hanson, Tyler Cowen, Ananda Gupta, and two anonymous reviewers at Oxford University Press. Stuart Rachels and Richard Fumerton merit special recognition for their extensive, invaluable comments on the manuscript. I am grateful to all of these individuals, without whom the book would be much less satisfactory than it is.

M.H.

# 1
# Introduction

## 1.1 The field of metaethics

The field of *ethics* addresses evaluative questions: these are questions about what is good or bad, or what should or should not be done. An evaluative question calls for an *evaluative statement* as an answer: this is a statement that inherently makes a positive or negative evaluation of something.[1] The following are examples of evaluative statements: 'One should keep one's promises'; 'Happiness is good'; 'Pol Pot is evil'; 'Honesty is a virtue'. The last is evaluative because it is part of the meaning of 'virtue' that virtues are good.

*Metaethics*, on the other hand, is the branch of philosophy that addresses questions about *the nature of* values and evaluative statements. These questions are generally not themselves evaluative; that is, they do not call for evaluative statements as answers. Here are some examples.

First, there are semantic questions: When I say, 'It is wrong to eat your pet dog', what does that mean?[2] Can 'wrong' be defined? Does it refer to a property that dog-eating allegedly has? Does 'good' refer to a property that life, happiness, and so on have, and can it be defined?

Second, there are epistemological questions: How, if at all, do we *know* that it is wrong to eat your dog? Can we justify our evaluative beliefs by arguments? Do we need to? Do we have some way of 'perceiving' moral values?

Third, there is at least one important metaphysical question: Are there objective values? Or: Are some evaluative statements objectively true?

1

Fourth, there are questions about moral psychology and rational action: What motivates us to (usually) act in the ways we consider moral? What good reasons, if any, do we have to be moral?

All these are metaethical questions, not ethical questions. Notice that, while they are all *about value* in one way or another, they are generally not *evaluative questions*. When I ask, 'Are there objective values?' the answer is either 'There are objective values' or 'There are no objective values'. Neither of these answers is itself an evaluative statement; neither expresses a positive or negative judgment about something. When I ask, 'Do we have some way of "perceiving" moral values?' the answer is either that we have such an ability or that we do not; neither of these answers is itself a value judgment.

This book is about those sorts of questions. My aim is to show that there are objective values, to explain how we know about them and how they give us reasons for action, and to refute the main competitors to my own views in metaethics.

## 1.2  What is objectivity?

The most discussed metaethical question is that of whether value is 'objective'. What does it mean for a phenomenon to be 'objective'?

When a person is aware of something, we call the person a 'subject' of awareness. The thing he is aware of we call the 'object' of awareness.[3] For a feature of something to be 'objective' means, roughly, that it is *in the object*. A 'subjective' feature is one that is *in the subject*.[4] But what does it mean to be 'in the subject'? I propose this definition:

*F*-ness is subjective = Whether something is *F* constitutively depends at least in part on the psychological
attitude or response that observers have or
would have towards that thing.

I define an 'objective' feature as one that is not subjective.[5] Consider some examples:

*Funniness* is subjective, because whether a joke is funny depends on whether people would be amused by it. If no one would find it amusing, then it isn't funny. This is a point about the meaning of 'funny'—'funny' means something like 'has a tendency to amuse audiences'.

Similarly, *sexiness* is subjective, because what is sexy depends on what people would feel attracted to. This, again, is a matter of the meaning of 'sexy'.

On the other hand, *squareness* is objective: whether an object is square has nothing to do with observers' reactions to it. To be square, a figure just has to have four equal sides and equal angles. No one has to feel any way about it, think anything about it, or even see it.

What about psychological traits, such as happiness—are they subjective? Not in the sense I intend. Whether a person is happy depends on the attitudes of someone—namely, the person himself— but it does not depend upon the attitudes of *observers towards* him. Whether you are happy does not depend upon how someone observing you feels.

Another notion to clarify is that of *constitutive dependence*. Consider this example. It is widely believed that for some diseases, a patient's chances of recovery are affected by his attitude—if a patient takes a positive attitude, this has a beneficial effect on his body, making him more likely to recover. Imagine a disease that is unusually subject to the power of positive thinking: *anyone* who believes he will recover from the disease does so, and anyone who believes he will not recover does not recover. Should we then say that a given individual's recovery or non-recovery from the disease is 'subjective', because whether he recovers depends on whether he believes he will?

No; that is a case of *causal* dependence (the patient's positive attitude causes his recovery), not constitutive dependence. A subjective property is one that is at least partly *constituted* by its tendency to elicit a certain reaction from observers. In other words, if *F*-ness is 'subjective', then part of *what it is* for a thing to be *F* is for observers to have or be disposed to have some particular sort of reaction to it. In the above example, there happens to be a causal connection between positive thinking and recovery; it is not that part of what constitutes one's recovery from the disease is one's positive attitude (what would constitute recovery is cessation of whatever the symptoms of the disease are). In contrast, the ability to amuse people is (all or part of) what constitutes being funny. That is why funniness is a subjective property in my sense, while the 'property' of recovering from our hypothetical illness is not.

There are controversial cases. Some philosophers think colors are subjective. Some think, for example, that for a thing to be blue is just for it to be disposed to cause a certain sensation (the 'blue sensation') in normal humans viewing it in normal conditions. It doesn't matter for our purposes whether this is right or not. What matters is to understand what is meant by a subjectivist theory. This is a subjectivist theory of color, since it makes the color of a physical object constitutively dependent on observers' psychological responses to it (counting sensations as 'psychological responses').

## 1.3   Five metaethical theories

Is *goodness* objective? *Moral realists* say yes; *moral anti-realists* say no. There are three forms of anti-realism:

1   *Subjectivism* (which includes relativism) holds that moral properties are subjective in the sense just defined: for a thing to be good is for some individual or group to (be disposed to) take some attitude towards it. The simplest form of subjectivism states that '*x* is good' means 'I approve of *x*'. Notice that since on this analysis, 'good' applies to whatever the speaker approves of, one person could truthfully say, 'Polygamy is good', while another truthfully says, 'Polygamy is not good'. Their statements do not logically conflict, any more than they would if the first had said, 'I like pickles' and the other said, 'I don't like pickles'.

Other forms of subjectivism substitute other attitudes for approval and other persons or groups for the speaker. Thus, the view that to be good is to be approved by society is a form of subjectivism, as is the view that to be obligatory is to be commanded by God.

2   *Non-cognitivism* holds that evaluative predicates do not even purportedly refer to any sort of property,[6] nor do evaluative statements assert propositions. Evaluative statements do not make claims about how the world is, not even about the part of the world that includes human observers. What do they do instead? Some say that they just express speakers' emotions. Thus, 'Stalin was evil' is like 'Boo on Stalin!' Notice that 'Boo!' is not an assertion (it does not say the world is a certain way), not even an assertion about the speaker's feelings, though it can be used to *express* one's feelings. That is why 'Boo!' is neither true nor false. Similarly, non-cognitivists have traditionally denied that evaluative statements can be true or false.[7]

Another variant of non-cognitivism holds that evaluative statements are more like imperatives. 'Stealing is wrong' is like 'Don't steal!' Notice that, again, 'Don't steal!' is not an assertion and is neither true nor false.

3   *Nihilism* (a.k.a. 'the error theory') holds that evaluative statements are generally false.[8] Why? Because evaluative statements assert that things have objective value properties, but in reality there are no such properties. When we say, 'Stalin was evil', we don't just

mean that we don't like Stalin, nor are we just trying to express our hostile feelings about him. We think that there is this property of 'evilness' out there, and he had it, and that's what moral language is about. However, says the nihilist, we are mistaken: there really aren't any properties like that. So our statement is just false. Nothing is either good or evil.

In subsequent chapters we will look at why philosophers have held these views. Right now, it is important to see why the above three positions are the only possible forms of anti-realism. Either 'good' purports to refer to a property—that is, '*x* is good' asserts that *x* has a certain property—or it does not. If it does, then either some things have the property or nothing does, and either the property depends on observers or it doesn't. If we say 'good' doesn't purport to refer to a property at all, then we have ethical non-cognitivism. If we say 'good' purports to refer to a property but nothing has that property, then we have nihilism. If we say 'good' purports to refer to a property, some things have that property, but the property depends on observers, then we have subjectivism. Lastly, if we say 'good' purports to refer to a property, some things have that property, and the property does not depend on observers, then we have moral realism. Those are the only possibilities.

We can make the same point—that there are exactly three possible anti-realist positions—by considering the question of 'objective moral truths'. A statement is objectively true if and only if: it is true and what makes it true is not even partly the attitudes or psychological reactions of observers towards the things the statement is about. Thus, 'Mosquitos have 47 teeth' is objectively true, because it is true and what makes it true is not even partly my or anyone else's reaction to the things (mosquitos) that the statement is about. But 'Jon Stewart is funny' is not objectively true: it is true, but what makes it true is partly the reaction people have towards the thing (Jon Stewart) that the statement is about.

Anti-realists deny the existence of objective moral truths. If a moral statement is not objectively true, then there are just three possibilities: either it is non-objectively (subjectively) true, or it is false, or it is neither true nor false. Hence, we have the subjectivist, nihilist, and non-cognitivist positions, again.[9]

The fact that these are the only three possible forms of anti-realism is important, since it means that if we can refute all of them, we will have established moral realism.

Moral realism comes in two main varieties:

1 *Ethical Naturalism* holds that there are objective moral properties but that they are *reducible*. Traditionally, naturalists thought that one could define (that is, explain the meaning of) terms like 'good' using wholly non-evaluative terms. For example, perhaps the good can be defined as whatever most promotes human survival, health, and happiness.

In the late twentieth century, another form of naturalism gained favor, a form which does not claim that the *meaning* of the word 'good' can be explained in non-evaluative terms, but nevertheless holds that *what goodness is* can be explained in non-evaluative terms. These modern naturalists compare their view of evaluative properties to scientific theories about the nature of heat, sound, or water. The word 'water' does not mean the same as 'chemical compound each of whose molecules contain two hydrogen atoms and one oxygen atom'. You can see this from the fact that people understood remarks like 'I'd like a glass of water' long before anyone knew modern chemistry. Nevertheless, $H_2O$ is in fact what water is. Similarly, the modern naturalists hold, it will be possible to explain what goodness is using non-evaluative language, although the correctness of this explanation will not follow merely from the meaning of the word 'good'.

In addition to the claim that moral properties are reducible, naturalists typically advance a second important thesis: that moral statements can be justified empirically; that is, they can be justified ultimately on the basis of observation.

2 *Ethical Intuitionism* holds that moral properties are objective and irreducible. Thus, 'good' refers to a property that some things (perhaps actions, states of affairs, and so on) have, independently of our attitudes towards those things, and one cannot say what this property is except using evaluative language ('good', 'desirable', 'should', 'valuable', and the like).

Intuitionists also have an epistemological thesis, from which their doctrine gets its name: that at least some moral truths are known intuitively. The notion of 'intuition' is subject to interpretation, but at least this much is generally meant: some moral truths are known directly, rather than on the basis of other truths, but not by the five senses (we do not see moral value with our eyes, hear it with our ears, and so on).

Naturalism and intuitionism differ, then, on two fronts: they differ metaphysically, over the issue of whether evaluative properties are reducible; and they differ epistemologically, over the issue of whether moral knowledge is empirical. It would be possible to hold other forms of realism by combining the naturalist view on one issue with the intuitionist view on the other. But no actual philosopher I know of has held such a view, so I won't discuss it in this book. The philosophers who have held that value is an irreducible property have always appealed to intuition to account for our awareness of this property, and those who have taken value to be reducible to natural (that is, non-evaluative) properties have always tried to account for moral knowledge empirically.

## 1.4 An alternative taxonomy of metaethical views

As the preceding section suggests, metaethical theories are traditionally divided first into realist and anti-realist views, and then into two forms of realism and three forms of anti-realism:

This is not the most illuminating way of classifying positions. It implies that the most fundamental division in metaethics is between realists and anti-realists over the question of objectivity. The dispute between naturalism and intuitionism is then seen as relatively minor, with the naturalists being much closer to the intuitionists than they are, say, to the subjectivists. That isn't how I see things. As I see it, the most fundamental division in metaethics is between the intuitionists, on the one hand, and everyone else, on the other. I would classify the positions as follows:

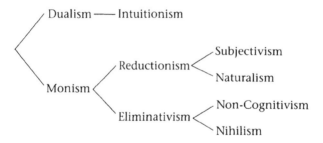

(I have borrowed terminology from the philosophy of mind literature.) Here, dualism is the idea that there are two fundamentally different kinds of facts (or properties) in the world: evaluative facts (properties) and non-evaluative facts (properties). Only the intuitionists embrace this.

Everyone else is a monist: they say there is only one fundamental kind of fact in the world, and it is the non-evaluative kind; there aren't any value facts *over and above* the other facts. This implies that either there are no value facts at all (eliminativism), or value facts are entirely explicable in terms of non-evaluative facts (reductionism). Subjectivism and naturalism are thus seen as siblings engaged in a family squabble: they agree that we can reduce goodness to something else; they just disagree over whether that something should include psychological reactions of observers.

Why is my taxonomy more illuminating than the traditional one? Because it puts the question of what exists in the world front and center. Intuitionists differ fundamentally from everyone else in their view of the world. Subjectivists, naturalists, non-cognitivists, and nihilists all agree in their basic view of *the world*, for they have no significant disagreements about what the non-evaluative facts are, and they all agree that there are no further facts over and above those.[10] They agree, for example, on the non-evaluative properties of the act of stealing, and they agree, contra the intuitionists, that there is no further, distinctively evaluative property of the act.

Then what sort of dispute do the four monistic theories have? I believe that, though this is not generally recognized, their disputes with each other are merely *semantic*. Once the nature of the world 'out there' has been agreed upon, semantic disputes are all that is left.

Admittedly, I am using 'semantic dispute' in a slightly broader sense than usual. I don't mean that the four monistic theories are notational variants on each other, or that it is only their partisans' different use of words makes them seem to disagree. What I mean is that their disagreement is fundamentally not about what the facts in the world are, but about the *mapping* between facts in the world and our language and thoughts. This is most obvious in the case of the non-cognitivists, who differ from the other monists over the issue of whether evaluative statements make factual claims. One might say that the subjectivists and naturalists differ over what goodness is—but since they don't disagree over what the non-evaluative facts are—this is really only a dispute over which of the non-evaluative features of things the word (or concept) 'good' denotes. Even the nihilists differ from the reductionists purely on semantic grounds—they differ over whether the commonly accepted non-evaluative facts *make evaluative statements true*. Nihilists think that nothing is good because they believe that the meaning of the word 'good' is such as to preclude its denoting any natural or psychological property, while the reductionists disagree with this semantic claim.

The traditional classification initially *seems* to put the metaphysical question first. The question of whether there are objective values seems to be a metaphysical one—and it would be, if the analysis of 'value' were agreed upon by all parties. But given the views held by many philosophers, the question is partly metaphysical and partly semantic. It turns on (a) whether moral statements assert the existence of objective values, and (b) whether these statements are sometimes true.

None of this bears on the cogency of my central arguments in this book; the plausibility of any of the five metaethical views in no way turns on what one regards as the 'most illuminating' way of classifying them. It does, however, bear on how *interesting* my central claims are. The fact that intuitionism differs radically from all other theories in metaethics makes it a particularly interesting view, if it can be defended.

## 1.5   A rationalist intuitionism

My position is a form of ethical intuitionism. It is not the only possible form—some intuitionists would disagree with some of what I have to say, though all would agree with the core of it. Here I list the main tenets of my form of rationalistic intuitionism, along with a very brief indication of how I intend to argue for each of them.

First, there is a semantic thesis: Evaluative predicates like 'good' function to attribute objective features to things. This is solely a point about the meanings of words—the semantic thesis does not entail that things *have* objective value properties; it just states that, when we call a thing 'good', we are *saying*, whether correctly or not, that it has an objective value property.

This thesis can be established by looking at how we use evaluative language. For instance, we can say, 'If adultery is wrong, then Clinton should be punished'. But we would never say something like, 'If adultery—boo!, then punishing Clinton—yay!' or, 'If don't commit adultery, then punish Clinton!', as the two forms of non-cognitivism mentioned earlier would encourage us to interpret the statement. Nor do we, intuitively, find the inference 'Our society accepts eating animals; therefore, eating animals is not wrong' logically compelling, as one form of subjectivism would lead one to expect. These are just two of many examples that can be given to illustrate that we in fact use evaluative language in exactly the way that we would if we were attributing objective properties to things.

Second, there is a metaphysical thesis: We are not always wrong when we make value judgments; some things are good and some things are bad. So there are objective values. The justification for this turns on the next point.

Third, there is an epistemological thesis: We are justified in believing some evaluative statements on the basis of rational intuitions. Our knowledge of moral truths is not wholly derived from sensory perception, nor are moral truths all derived from non-moral truths. At least some moral truths are self-evident.

Intuitions, in my sense, are a sort of mental state or experience, distinct from and normally prior to belief, that we often have when thinking about certain sorts of propositions, including some moral propositions. They are the experiences we report when we say a thing is 'obvious' or 'seems true'. Why are we justified in believing propositions on the basis of such experiences? I argue that, in general, it makes sense to assume things are the way they appear, until proven otherwise. All reasoning and judgment proceed upon this principle, and even the arguments of the moral anti-realists rest upon intuitions. I also argue that many of the objections to the use of ethical intuitions would, if consistently applied, require abandoning sensory perception as well and renouncing all knowledge of the world.

Fourth, there are two, closely related theses about the nature of reasons for action: When we have justified evaluative beliefs, those beliefs may constitute good reasons for action, reasons that we have independent of our desires. If I justifiably believe that stealing is wrong, then I have a good reason not to steal my nephew's candy, regardless of how much I might want to, whether I could get away with it, and so on. Furthermore, not only do moral beliefs constitute *good reasons* for or against certain actions, but they also sometimes constitute our actual *motives* for action, motives that are qualitatively different from our desires.

These claims conflict with the popular Humean theory of practical reasons, according to which all reasons or motives for action depend upon desires. Suppose I have a desire for coffee ice cream, and I think that going to the store will help me to get some coffee ice cream. Then I have both a good reason and a motivation for going to the store. According to Humeans, all practical reasons and motivations involve desires in that way. So when I decide not to steal the candy because I think stealing is wrong, that also involves some desire of mine. Perhaps I have a desire not to break society's rules, or a desire not to see my nephew cry, or just a desire not to be a thief. Consequently, if I had different desires, then I would have no reason not to steal—and I *could* have had different desires while still being perfectly rational.

The Humean theory of practical reasons is my main opponent. But the Humean theory is supported by no good arguments and is implausible in its treatment even of cases not involving morality. I shall argue that Humeans can offer no plausible understanding of the phenomenon of weakness of will, nor can they explain why it is rational to forego immediate satisfactions for the sake of greater long-term benefits, nor can they plausibly explain why morality has the importance for us that it does and why it is rational to act morally.

I shall explain and defend all these points in the succeeding chapters. But many philosophers consider intuitionism incredible on its face. As David Lewis says, I cannot refute an incredulous stare;[11] however, I will confront all of the major objections leveled against intuitionism. On examination, these objections prove far weaker than is generally supposed. To take one case, the most popular 'refutation' of intuitionism cites the prevalence of moral disputes as evidence against either the objectivity or the knowability of moral claims. The assumption seems to be that if there were objective moral truths and we had a way of knowing them, then there would be little moral disagreement. Yet our experience with other matters whose objectivity is hardly in dispute provides no support for that prediction. There is, regrettably, quite a bit of dispute about the efficacy of astrology, about whether gun control laws reduce crime, and about who is likely to win the next Super Bowl; yet hardly anyone denies that these matters are 'objective' or that it is possible to have justified beliefs about them. Nor do proponents of the argument from disagreement, as I call it, have a ready explanation for why the mechanisms that lead to disagreements about these issues should not operate in moral matters. Indeed, such proponents seem to operate with a simplistic picture of human psychology in which the unreality of a subject matter is the only possible explanation for a failure of consensus about it.

## 1.6 Background assumptions

There remains one preliminary matter to discuss before proceeding to the case for ethical intuitionism. That is the matter of the general philosophical assumptions I take for granted in this book.

Imagine a pair of scientists debating the merits of the General Theory of Relativity. Scientist *A* cites Eddington's 1919 observation of the gravitational bending of light around the sun as evidence in favor of the theory. Scientist *B* then asks how Eddington knew he wasn't dreaming—or, indeed, how any of us know the senses are a reliable source of information about external reality at all. Does *A* have to answer this?

No; *B*'s questions are not a fair move in a debate about physics. One reason for this is pragmatic: if we accept *B*'s dialectical demands, then nearly every discussion can be derailed into a debate about philosophical skepticism. It is not that I consider that issue unworthy of discussion; indeed, at another time, I should be happy to discuss it.[12] But a physics discussion is not the place to raise it. If one is worried by general skeptical considerations, one ought to take that up with an epistemologist, and even then only in certain conversational contexts. Of course, if skepticism is actually true, then General Relativity is not justified, by Eddington's observations or anything else. But when we are talking about physics, we tacitly assume the falsity of skepticism. Without that, we would never make any progress.

Going beyond pragmatic considerations, many responses to philosophical skepticism have been articulated and defended. It is reasonable, even without having examined the issue in detail, to think that *some* response to skepticism in epistemology is correct, one that enables us to have at least reasonable beliefs about the physical world, and it probably doesn't matter for the purposes of doing physics exactly what that response is.

I expect the reader to agree so far. After all, hardly anyone in real life would think to argue in the way I imagined scientist *B* arguing. A similar rule applies in metaethical discussions. We should not consider it a fair move, for example, for someone arguing against ethical intuitionism to deploy *general* skeptical arguments. In other words, in this discussion, I may assume that we are justified in believing most of the things we normally take ourselves to be justified in believing, outside the area of ethics. I may assume that we are justified in believing that rocks exist, that we are conscious, that the earth will continue to exist next week, that $4+1=5$, and that no object can be both completely red and completely blue. Thus, if some particular argument against intuitionism can be shown to be merely a special case of a more general argument impugning our knowledge of those sorts of things, then I may set that argument aside as not relevant to the current discussion.

What holds for general philosophical skepticism holds equally for general ('metaphysical') *anti-realism*. That is, just as I don't need, in defending the possibility of moral knowledge, to answer arguments against the possibility of knowledge in general, I don't need, in defending the objectivity of value, to answer arguments against the possibility of objective reality in general.

Readers afflicted with general skeptical or anti-realist sentiments may, then, wish to regard the main theses of this book as conditional: if there is, in general, an objective reality, and we can know things about it, then there are also objective evaluative truths, which we can know something about. That is, there is no *special* problem for moral objectivity and knowledge.

# Part I

# Alternative Metaethical Theories

# 2
# Non-Cognitivism

## 2.1 Classical non-cognitivism

Pleasure is good.

How should we understand that statement? The most straightforward answer is the cognitivist one. *Ethical cognitivism* is the view that evaluative statements like 'Pleasure is good' assert propositions, which can be either true or false, just like the statements 'The sky is red' and 'Weasels are mammals'. Given this, the most straightforward account of what the word 'good' is doing in the sentence is this: there is a property, *goodness*, which the word refers to, and the sentence ascribes that property to pleasure.[1]

*Non-cognitivists* deny that 'good' denotes a property, and they deny that 'Pleasure is good' asserts anything in the way that 'Weasels are mammals' does. It is thus up to them to give us an alternative account of the meaning of 'Pleasure is good'. Two main non-cognitivist accounts have arisen: emotivism and prescriptivism.

*Emotivism* holds that the primary function of '*x* is good' is to express a positive emotion or attitude (not a belief) that the speaker has about *x*. Thus, '*x* is good' is like, 'Hooray for *x*!' When one says, 'Pleasure is good', one is not *asserting* that one has this feeling; one is just expressing the feeling. Compare: when one says 'Ow!', one is not *asserting that* one feels pain; one is just expressing one's pain. One difference between assertion and expression is that an assertion, such as 'I am in pain', is either true or false, whereas a mere expression, such as 'Ow!', is neither true nor false. Thus, emotivists have traditionally denied that '*x* is good' is either true or false.[2]

*Prescriptivism* holds that the function of '*x* is good' is, roughly, to tell people what to do. Thus, it is like 'Pursue *x*!' or 'Approve of *x*!' Note that 'Pursue *x*!' is not an assertion and is neither true nor false. Similarly, '*x* is good' is neither true nor false on a simple prescriptivist view.[3] Admittedly, moral statements differ from other imperatives in some important ways, so '*x* is good' is not *exactly* like 'Pursue *x*'. For instance, it seems that moral imperatives have a kind of universality: in putting forward a moral imperative, one endorses some sort of general rule applicable to all people, including oneself, which is not true of ordinary, non-moral imperatives.[4]

Other, more subtle forms of non-cognitivism exist. Perhaps evaluative statements have both emotive and prescriptive functions. Perhaps they serve as much to influence the audience's feelings as to express the speaker's.[5] Perhaps they express some other non-cognitive mental state, besides emotion and desire.[6] What is common to all the non-cognitivist views is, again, that they hold that the primary function of evaluative statements is something other than asserting propositions.[7] The arguments of this chapter will support cognitivism against any form of non-cognitivism.

## 2.2   How can we tell if cognitivism is true?

I begin with a simple but crucial observation for the debate about ethical cognitivism. The observation is that the issue at hand is empirical. Cognitivism and non-cognitivism are competing claims about the current meaning and function of evaluative language. Non-cognitivists are not advocating a *change* in how we use language—that would just amount to an effort to change the subject. They are trying to describe how evaluative language actually works. And claims of this sort are empirical. Imagine someone maintaining that the word 'duck' means 'four-legged animal'. This hypothesis has testable predictions: for example, that typical English speakers (competent in the use of these words) would not call anything a 'four-legged animal' unless they would also call it a 'duck'. We can test this prediction by, for example, asking some competent speakers whether they would call a cat a 'four-legged animal', and also whether they would call it a 'duck'.

That is a simple example. Refuting non-cognitivism will not be so simple, for non-cognitivism is a more abstract thesis which need not involve the claim that 'good' is synonymous with any other expression. Nevertheless, the point remains that cognitivism and non-cognitivism, as claims about meanings, ought to have testable predictions about the way we use evaluative language. We can see whether people use evaluative statements more like how they use typical proposition-expressing sentences, or more like how they use typical non-proposition-expressing sentences. We will consider this in the next section.

Not everyone frames the issue this way. And admittedly there are other considerations relevant to assessing ethical non-cognitivism besides that of whether we treat ethical statements like assertions. Usually, philosophers rely on broader theoretical considerations, such as the supposed desirability, in general, of maintaining a 'naturalistic worldview' (avoiding 'weird' things that scientists don't talk about), the alleged untenability of alternative metaethical theories, and the ability of non-cognitivism to explain why we are *motivated* to act in the ways we consider moral.

The appeal to these broad theoretical considerations is methodologically inferior to the kind of appeal I shall make to how we use ethical language. Why? Because the linguistic evidence is by far the more *objective* evidence. Here I am using 'objective' in an epistemological sense (not the sense discussed in section 1.1): objective evidence is, roughly, evidence whose *existence* and *relevance* can be ascertained in a relatively straightforward manner; it does not require difficult exercises of judgment, weighing of competing considerations, resolution of complex philosophical issues, or the establishment of an overall worldview, to determine whether the evidence exists or what conclusion it supports.

For example, A. J. Ayer argued for non-cognitivism by appealing to the premises (1) that ethical statements are unverifiable, and (2) that a statement has cognitive meaning only if it can be verified. In short, Ayer cited the unverifiability of ethical statements as evidence against cognitivism.[8] This evidence is highly subjective, for in order to determine whether ethical statements are really unverifiable, we must first resolve such philosophical questions as whether intuition counts as a means of knowledge, whether facts about our attitudes and conventions count as verification for evaluative statements, and whether evaluative statements ever help explain non-evaluative facts. Furthermore, in order to accept the unverifiability of evaluative statements as evidence for non-cognitivism, one must first accept Ayer's logical positivist philosophy about what 'meaning' is. All of these are highly contentious, complex, philosophical issues. My point is not that these issues cannot be resolved, nor that arguments involving controversial philosophical claims are never appropriate. My point is that it would be foolish to rely on evidence of that kind when straightforward, objective tests of a thesis are available.

My methodology is roughly this. There are some sentences that are *uncontroversially* assertive—sentences that ethical cognitivists and non-cognitivists alike would take to assert propositions. There are other sentences that are uncontroversially non-assertive. We can identify features of the former that do not belong to the latter, and see whether evaluative statements have those features. The evidence I shall cite is straightforwardly available to any competent English speaker. Nor can its relevance be easily disputed. Doubtless some will dispute whether the evidence is *sufficient* to reject non-cognitivism, but even non-cognitivists admit that it counts against their theory.[9]

## 2.3   The linguistic evidence for cognitivism

There are several features characteristic of proposition-expressing sentences, all of which evaluative statements have:[10]

(a) Evaluative statements take the form of declarative sentences, rather than, say, imperatives, questions, or interjections. 'Pleasure is good' has the same grammatical form as 'Weasels are mammals'. Sentences of this form are normally used to make factual assertions.[11] In contrast, the paradigms of non-cognitive utterances, such as 'Hurray for *x*' and 'Pursue *x*', are not declarative sentences.

(b) Moral predicates can be transformed into abstract nouns, suggesting that they are intended to refer to properties; we talk about 'goodness', 'rightness', and so on, as in 'I am not questioning the act's prudence, but its rightness'.

(c) We ascribe to evaluations the same sort of properties as other propositions. You can say, 'It is true that I have done some wrong things in the past', 'It is false that contraception is murder', and 'It is possible that abortion is wrong'. 'True', 'false', and 'possible' are predicates that we apply only to propositions. No one would say, 'It is true that ouch', 'It is false that shut the door', or 'It is possible that hurray'.

(d) All the propositional attitude verbs can be prefixed to evaluative statements. We can say, 'Jon believes that the war was just', 'I hope I did the right thing', 'I wish we had a better President', and 'I wonder whether I did the right thing'. In contrast, no one would say, 'Jon believes that ouch', 'I hope that hurray for the Broncos', 'I wish that shut the door', or 'I wonder whether please pass the salt'. The obvious explanation is that such mental states as believing, hoping, wishing, and wondering are by their nature propositional: To hope is to hope *that something is the case*, to wonder is to wonder *whether something is the case*, and so on. That is why one cannot hope that one did the right thing unless there is a proposition—something that might be the case—corresponding to the expression 'one did the right thing'.

(e) Evaluative statements can be transformed into yes/no questions: One can assert 'Cinnamon ice cream is good', but one can also ask, 'Is cinnamon ice cream good?' No analogous questions can be formed from imperatives or emotional expressions: 'Shut the door?' and 'Hurray for the Broncos?' lack clear meaning. The obvious explanation is that a yes/no question requires a proposition; it asks whether something is the case.

A prescriptivist non-cognitivist might interpret some evaluative yes/no questions as requests for instruction, as in 'Should I shut off the oven now?' But other questions would defy interpretation along these lines, including evaluative questions about other people's behavior or about the past—'Was it wrong for Emperor Nero to kill Agrippina?' is not a request for instruction.

(f) One can issue imperatives and emotional expressions directed at things that are characterized morally. If non-cognitivism is true, what do these mean: 'Do the right thing.' 'Hurray for virtue!' Even more puzzlingly for the non-cognitivist, you can imagine appropriate contexts for such remarks as, 'We shouldn't be doing this, but I don't care; let's do it anyway'. This is perfectly intelligible, but it would be unintelligible if 'We shouldn't be doing this' either expressed an aversive emotion towards the proposed action or issued an imperative not to do it.

(g) In some sentences, evaluative terms appear without the speaker's either endorsing or impugning anything, yet the terms are used in their normal senses. This is known as the *Frege-Geach problem* and forms the basis for perhaps the best-known objection to non-cognitivism.[12] Consider two examples.

*Example 1:*
'If adultery is wrong, then God will punish Clinton.' This sentence delivers no verdict on adultery; it says neither that adultery is wrong nor that it is not. So 'wrong' is not used there to express a negative psychological reaction to adultery, nor is it used to issue an anti-adultery imperative, nor to influence the audience's feelings against adultery. It is difficult to see how the non-cognitivist could explain the meaning of 'adultery is wrong' in this context. Indeed, since a statement of the form 'If *p* then *q*' generally requires a *proposition* to be plugged in for *p*, it seems that if 'adultery is wrong' expresses no proposition, then the whole sentence is nonsense—like 'If please pass the salt, then the potatoes need more salt' or 'If hurray for the Broncos, then the Broncos are going to win'.[13]

*Example 2:*

Aboard the sinking *Titanic*, the captain says: 'There's a right way to handle this situation'. Since he doesn't say *what* the right way to handle the situation is, he is not expressing a positive emotion towards anything, trying to influence anyone's attitudes, or telling anyone to do anything. Yet 'right' is evidently being used in its normal sense nonetheless. This is shown by the fact that the captain could sensibly continue as follows: 'And that way is to draw straws to see who may get on the life boats'. Although he has now endorsed drawing straws, he obviously has not changed the meaning of his initial use of 'right'.

A tempting move is to let evaluative terms refer to emotions or acts of issuing commands when they appear in these contexts. For instance, we might read 'If adultery is wrong, then God will punish Clinton' as meaning something like, 'If adultery conflicts with God's commands, then God will punish Clinton'. Here is why that won't help the non-cognitivist: Does the sentence 'Adultery is wrong', when stated by itself, mean that adultery conflicts with God's will?

Suppose the non-cognitivist says 'yes'. Then 'Adultery is wrong' expresses a proposition, which is either true or false: it is either true or false that adultery conflicts with God's commands. Our erstwhile non-cognitivist has thus abandoned non-cognitivism in favor of *subjectivism*: it is subjectivists who say that evaluative statements express propositions about someone's attitudes. We will critique subjectivism in the following chapter; for now, the important point is that this is not a way of preserving non-cognitivism.

Suppose, then, that the non-cognitivist says 'no'. Now consider the following deductive inference that someone might make:

If adultery is wrong, God will punish Clinton.
Adultery is wrong.
Therefore, God will punish Clinton.

Our non-cognitivist is now committed to claiming that 'adultery is wrong' has a *different meaning* in the first premise from its meaning in the second. For he has said that in the *first* premise, 'adultery is wrong' means that adultery conflicts with God's commands. But in the *second* premise it does not mean this; instead, it just expresses some non-cognitive attitude. If so, the above argument should strike us as illogical, as committing an equivocation. But this is not the case—we can see that the first two statements entail the third. This can only be the case if 'wrong' has the same meaning in both premises.[14]

The same applies to any other attempt to save non-cognitivism by letting evaluative terms refer to someone's emotions or commands. Thus, suppose the non-cognitivist says 'There's a right way to handle this situation' means 'There's a way to handle this situation that I would approve of'. Now ask: Does '*x* is right', by itself, mean 'I would approve of *x*'? If the non-cognitivist says 'yes', then he has abandoned non-cognitivism in favor of subjectivism. 'I would approve of *x*' is a factual claim, which is either true or false, not a non-cognitive utterance.

If the non-cognitivist says 'no', then he must say that 'right' shifts its meaning between the following two sentences—

There is a right way to handle this situation.
The right way to handle this situation is to draw straws to decide who gets on the lifeboats.

—since 'right way' in the *first* sentence means 'way that I would approve of', but 'right way' in the *second* sentence does not mean this but instead functions to express a non-cognitive emotional attitude towards the drawing of straws. If so, then the second statement does not entail the first. But that's false: 'right' obviously has the same meaning in both sentences, and the latter sentence obviously entails the first.

Let us summarize the arguments given under points (b)-(g) above. Here is a strong reading of the argument against non-cognitivism:

1. Each of the following sentences makes sense:

    I am questioning the act's rightness.
    It is true that pleasure is good.
    I hope I did the right thing.
    Is abortion wrong?
    Do the right thing.
    If pleasure is good, then chocolate is good.
    Something is good.

2. None of those sentences would make sense if non-cognitivism were true.
3. Therefore, non-cognitivism is false.

Each of the sentences listed in premise (1) creates a distinct objection to non-cognitivism; the non-cognitivist must deal with *all* of the examples in order to defend his position.

The justification for premise (1) is that the sentences listed, and others like them, would strike any ordinary English speaker as making sense; indeed, they are not even slightly odd. Some sentences of these kinds would even be regarded as indisputably true by nearly everyone. Virtually no one would dispute the truth of my claim that *I believe pleasure is good*, or that *If abortion is wrong, then fetuses have rights*. The *prima facie* case for holding each of those sentences to be intelligible is about as strong as that for holding anything to be intelligible.

Premise (2) seems plausible given the non-cognitivist's thesis that 'Pleasure is good' means something like 'Hurray for pleasure' or 'Pursue pleasure'; neither of these views provides a basis for any straightforward understanding of any of the sentences mentioned in (1). In some cases (as in 'I hope I did the right thing'), it is hard to even think of a first-pass paraphrase of the sentences based on the non-cognitivist's theory. In other cases, one can think of a first-pass paraphrase, but it is evidently a nonsense sentence (like 'If hurray for pleasure, then hurray for chocolate').

(3) follows from (1) and (2). I assume the non-cognitivist would want to attack premise (2), since attacking (1) seems hopeless. We will consider attacks on premise (2), at least for some of the kinds of sentences listed, in the following sections of this chapter.

Now, here is a weaker interpretation of the problem for non-cognitivism. On this interpretation, the argument does not conclusively refute non-cognitivism; however, it has force against non-cognitivism even if the non-cognitivist can find a way to make sense of the sentences listed under premise (1) above.

4. If non-cognitivism were true, then it would be more likely that the following sentences would strike us odd, malformed, or confused, than it would be if cognitivism were true:

> I am questioning the act's rightness.
> It is true that pleasure is good.
> I hope I did the right thing.
> Is abortion wrong?
> Do the right thing.
> If pleasure is good, then chocolate is good.
> Something is good.

5. None of those sentences strike us as odd, malformed, or confused.

6. Therefore, our reaction to those sentences is evidence in favor of cognitivism over non-cognitivism.

We can see that (4) is true by contrasting paradigmatically non-cognitive utterances. There is, to my knowledge, no uncontroversially non-cognitive expression or sentence from which one could form sentences analogous to any of those listed under (4). 'Hurray for the Broncos' and 'Pass the salt' do not give rise to sentences like those. So we must at least say that, if non-cognitivism does not entail that we should find the listed sentences unintelligible, it at least leads one to expect this. Imagine how things would stand if the sentences listed *did* strike us as odd, malformed, or confused. If most competent English speakers found 'I believe pleasure is good' unintelligible, just as we in fact find 'I believe please pass the salt' unintelligible, then obviously non-cognitivists could and would cite this as powerful evidence for their thesis. Conversely, if we do not find 'I believe pleasure is good' to be unintelligible, then this fact is evidence against non-cognitivism.[15]

Nor should one underestimate the strength of this evidence. The non-cognitivist makes a claim about actual meanings, but all of the reasonably direct and objective evidence, drawn from the way we use ethical language, points towards cognitivism. Every linguistic test that would differentiate uncontroversial examples of cognitive utterances from uncontroversial examples of non-cognitive utterances delivers the result that evaluative statements fit in with the cognitive. Evaluative statements act in every way like factual claims.

Hitherto, non-cognitivists have rested their case on the sorts of broad philosophical arguments that I have previously argued to be methodologically inferior to the reliance on linguistic intuitions and facts about language usage. Despite my methodological objection, I do not plan to ignore their arguments; they will be taken up in later chapters. They can generally be viewed as arguments against the workability of other metaethical positions, particularly moral realism. If the other metaethical positions should really prove to be unworkable, then we would have reason to revisit non-cognitivism. But for now we should reject it.

## *2.4 Hare on moral truth

Most of the arguments discussed in the preceding section have been known in some form to philosophers for over 40 years, yet there remain non-cognitivist philosophers. In this and the following two sections, I consider how some prominent non-cognitivists respond to some of these problems.

To begin with, R. M. Hare has addressed the problem of moral truth, endeavoring to show that his version of prescriptivism can preserve a notion of truth and falsity for moral statements. How? Two distinct proposals can be found in his work. First, Hare proposes that moral statements have a descriptive, proposition-expressing meaning *in addition to* their prescriptive meaning. It is this descriptive meaning that enables them to be true or false. Hare seems to think of the descriptive meaning of a moral statement as equivalent to that of a statement of the non-moral facts that are the speaker's *reasons* for making the moral judgment.[16] For example, suppose Jon has a comprehensive moral theory, according to which the morally right action in any situation is always the action that produces the greatest amount of happiness in the world. Jon says, 'Eating meat is wrong'. According to Hare, Jon's statement has a descriptive meaning and a prescriptive meaning. The descriptive meaning is, 'Meat-eating decreases the amount of happiness in the world'. The prescriptive meaning is something like, 'Don't eat meat'.[17] The original statement, 'Eating meat is wrong', can be assessed as true or false by reference to whether eating meat in fact decreases the amount of happiness in the world.

I think this is a false conception of meaning. When one makes a moral claim, the *meaning* of the claim is one thing; one's *reason* for it is another, and the latter is generally not part of the former. For example, suppose that George favors invading Iraq. His reason is that he thinks Iraq has weapons of mass destruction, and he thinks this an adequate justification for invasion.[18] A second individual, Tony, also thinks we should invade Iraq. But Tony does not believe Iraq has weapons of mass destruction. Tony's reason for favoring invasion is that Saddam Hussein is a cruel dictator who has caused much suffering for the people of Iraq. George and Tony have the following exchange:

*George:* We should invade Iraq.
*Tony:* I agree. We should invade Iraq.

On Hare's view, Tony is confused in thinking that he agrees with what George said. For though Tony may be said to agree with George's plan of action, part of the meaning of George's statement was that Iraq has weapons of mass destruction, which Tony does not believe. So Tony actually doesn't agree with the statement as a whole. But this is obviously false. While George may have been *thinking* that

Iraq has weapons of mass destruction, and while this may be part of the *reason* why he said what he did, George did not, in the above exchange, actually *say* that Iraq has weapons of mass destruction, nor did he say anything which implies this.

I do not know whether Hare would actually consider 'Iraq has weapons of mass destruction' to be part of the meaning of George's statement. Perhaps Hare would instead require us to formulate George's overall, comprehensive ethical theory. Unfortunately, most people have no such theory. But suppose we are lucky in this case and George has a comprehensive ethical theory. Let us say his theory is utilitarianism. Then, Hare might say, the descriptive meaning of George's statement is, 'Invading Iraq would maximize total happiness in the world'. While this might seem less absurd than the previous suggestion, it is still false: in saying merely that we should invade Iraq, George does not say that doing so would maximize happiness, nor does he say anything which implies this; he simply has not said *anything*, so far, about why he thinks we should invade Iraq. And if Tony should have a competing ethical theory, this would not preclude him from agreeing with George's conclusion by saying, 'Yes, we should invade Iraq'.

Consider a second example, even more damaging for Hare's conception of moral truth. As in the first case, George thinks we should invade Iraq because Iraq has weapons of mass destruction. Jean-Pierre also believes that Iraq has weapons of mass destruction and agrees with George on all other non-moral matters. But Jean-Pierre and George have different fundamental moral values, as a result of which Jean-Pierre does not take these facts to justify invasion. George says, 'We should invade Iraq'. According to Hare, Jean-Pierre should judge that statement to be *true*.[19] For it is the descriptive meaning of the statement that determines truth or falsity, and Jean-Pierre agrees with George on descriptive matters.

Thus far, I have been talking as though Hare would rely on the speaker's moral standards to determine what the descriptive meaning of a moral statement is. In fact, however, Hare adverts to the 'commonly accepted' standards 'within a given society'.[20] Thus, if George and Tony belong to the same society, they would wind up (thankfully) meaning the same thing by 'We should invade Iraq'. But it is easy enough to revive the above problems by simply supposing George to belong to a different society from Tony or Jean-Pierre. And the reliance on socially accepted standards just creates a further problem for Hare's account, that of how to deal with people who disagree with their society's moral standards. Such people would, on Hare's view, be forced to call moral judgments made on the basis of the prevailing moral standards 'true'. And when such moral dissidents called something 'good', part of what they would be saying would be that the thing satisfied society's moral standards. It seems clear that, if anyone's moral standards are involved in determining the descriptive meaning of a moral claim, it ought to be the speaker's standards.

I take it that Hare's first effort to secure truth and falsity for moral statements fails. It is, in fact, the product of an unfortunately common fallacy to which philosophers have yet to be fully immunized: that of confusing a speaker's substantive background beliefs with the *meanings* of his words. A special case of this is confusing a person's reasons for saying something with the meaning of the statement. When we express a moral judgment, we are not thereby reporting the factual grounds we have for the judgment.

Hare makes a second attempt to secure moral truth, using a non-cognitivist analysis of 'true'. Hare suggests that in some cases, we might call a moral statement 'true', meaning thereby simply to endorse it: 'it will not be a *statement that* we endorse it, but an *expression of* endorsement'.[21]

One problem with this suggestion is that the word 'true' is not used this way in English. In English, 'true' is only applied to (things expressing) propositions. Thus, I cannot say, 'It is true that please pass the salt', even if I endorse the imperative to pass the salt. I cannot say, 'It is true that hurray for the Broncos', even if I endorse the sentiment behind the sentence 'Hurray for the Broncos'. Hare would thus have to claim that evaluative statements work differently from all the paradigmatic non-cognitive utterances in that, for some reason, one *can* apply 'true' to them.

In addition, Hare's proposed non-cognitivist interpretation of 'true' faces many of the same problems as a non-cognitivist analysis of 'good'. The sentence '*x* is true' bears all the linguistic marks of a factual assertion. We can speak of 'the proposition that *x* is true' and 'the truth of my claim'; we can say, 'I believe *x* is true', 'I hope *x* is true', 'I wonder whether *x* is true', 'If *x* is true, then so is *y*', 'Do you swear to tell the truth?' and 'There is many a true word spoken in jest'.[22] All of these are hard to make sense of on a non-cognitivist construal of 'true'. And the considerations usually adduced in support of non-cognitivism about 'good'—such as the alleged unworkability of alternative theories and the action-guiding character of moral judgments—will not aid the non-cognitivist about 'truth'.

A better proposal, perhaps closer to what Hare intended, is the redundancy theory of 'truth': 'it is true that' is simply redundant. 'It is true that pleasure is good' just means 'Pleasure is good', just as 'It is true that cows have four stomachs' just means 'Cows have four stomachs'. This gives us a principled reason for holding 'It is true that pleasure is good' to be non-cognitive and 'It is true that cows have four stomachs' to be cognitive, without having to say that 'true' shifts its meaning.

The problem with this suggestion is that it can make no sense of statements in which 'true' or 'truth' is used without specifying *what* is or might be true, such as 'Do you swear to tell the truth?' and 'Many a true word is spoken in jest'. Neither a redundancy theory nor an endorsement theory of 'true' handles these examples. Nor can we interpret these statements along the lines of 'Do you swear to say what you endorse?' and 'Many a word endorsed by the speaker is spoken in jest', since either of these interpretations would abandon the non-cognitivist treatment of truth for a subjectivist theory, treating truth merely as the property of being endorsed by the speaker.[23] Note that sentences of this kind may just as well advert to moral truths as non-moral ones—'Jon spoke the truth' may be said in the same sense when Jon's salient remark was 'Cats have teeth' as when his salient remark was 'Burning cats is wrong'.

Some of Hare's own statements constitute counter-examples to non-cognitivism both about ethics and about truth. Immediately following Hare's proposal of the endorsement theory of moral 'truth', we find these remarks:

> So we cannot make standards acceptable simply by accepting them; rather, in saying that they are acceptable we are expressing our acceptance of them; and whether we should accept them is a matter for rational thought. . . .

> We have to do this thinking, and there are ways . . . of doing it well.

> If we do it well, we shall attain *knowledge* of the *truth* of moral statements. . . .[24]

'Acceptable', 'should', 'have to', and 'well' are all evaluative expressions. It is unclear what any of the above statements are supposed to mean on a non-cognitivist construal of evaluative expressions. Nor can I understand what 'We shall attain knowledge of the truth of moral statements' is supposed to mean if 'truth' is a non-cognitive term serving only to express endorsement of a given statement. It is tempting, particularly in view of the rest of Hare's views, to interpret this as meaning something like, 'We shall attain knowledge of which moral statements would be endorsed by all rational beings after sufficient reflection'. But to accept this interpretation would be to drop the proposed non-cognitivist theory of truth in favor of a cognitivist one in which 'true', applied to evaluative statements, means 'would be endorsed by all rational beings after sufficient reflection'. But if those are the truth-conditions for evaluative statements, then we might as well just analyze moral terms as referring to what rational beings would endorse, and abandon non-cognitivism for subjectivism. I conclude that Hare has failed to articulate a legitimate sense of moral truth consistent with his metaethics.

## *2.5   Gibbard's factual-normative worlds

The latest in anti-realist technology, Allan Gibbard's 'factual-normative worlds' are abstract objects designed to help explain the meanings both of simple evaluative statements and of complex sentences with evaluative components. A factual-normative world is a combination of a complete specification of the way the world is, $w$, with a complete set of rules for acting and for approving/disapproving of things, $n$. We can represent a factual-normative world as an ordered pair, $\langle w, n \rangle$.[25]

The meaning of an ordinary factual statement with no evaluative terms can be represented by a set of possible worlds—roughly, the set of all ways the world might be that would make the statement true.[26] Similarly, Gibbard thinks, we can represent the meaning of a statement containing evaluative terms by a set of factual-normative worlds—the set of all factual-normative worlds in which the statement holds. A statement 'holds' in a factual-normative world $\langle w, n \rangle$ if, roughly, someone who thought the world was like $w$ and who endorsed norms $n$ would accept the statement. For example, suppose you have just stolen a piece of candy from an infant, and a friend says: 'If stealing that candy was wrong, God will punish you'. Now imagine two possible worlds, $w_1$ and $w_2$, and two possible complete sets of norms, $n_1$ and $n_2$, where:

In $w_1$, God punishes you.
In $w_2$, God does not punish you.
$n_1$ permits the candy theft.
$n_2$ forbids the candy theft.

From these worlds and these norm-sets, four factual-normative worlds can be formed: $\langle w_1, n_1 \rangle$, $\langle w_1, n_2 \rangle$, $\langle w_2, n_1 \rangle$, and $\langle w_2, n_2 \rangle$. The statement 'If stealing the candy was wrong, then God will punish you' holds in $\langle w_1, n_1 \rangle$, $\langle w_1, n_2 \rangle$, and $\langle w_2, n_1 \rangle$; it does not hold in $\langle w_2, n_2 \rangle$.[27] So $\langle w_2, n_2 \rangle$ is the only one of the four worlds that the speaker's statement rules out. Gibbard's view can be applied equally well to more complex statements and more general statements about wrongful actions (for instance, 'If it is wrong to do something, then it is wrong to get your little brother to do it').

What does the device of factual-normative worlds accomplish? It gives Gibbard a way of saying that the sort of statements that worried us in section 2.3—such as 'If stealing is wrong, God will punish you'—are meaningful. Importantly, Gibbard need not posit any shift in the meaning of 'wrong' from 'Stealing is wrong' (asserted by itself) to 'If stealing is wrong, God will punish you'. Nor must he give separate theories of the meanings of different kinds of sentences containing evaluative terms; there will be general rules relating the meanings of complex sentences to those of their simpler parts, which are the same for evaluative and non-evaluative statements—for example, the non-cognitivist won't have to say that 'if . . . then' has different meanings depending upon whether an evaluative or a descriptive statement is plugged in for the antecedent.

To gain these appealing advantages, we need only draw the link between factual-normative worlds and *meanings*. What exactly does a set of factual-normative worlds have to do with what I mean when I make some statement containing 'wrong'? Gibbard thinks that to explain the meaning of a statement is to explain the state of mind that it expresses. His view is not, of course, that I actually have the relevant set of factual-normative worlds *in mind*—possible worlds are typically too complex for any human mind to fully conceive, to say nothing of the infinite *sets* of factual-normative worlds to which Gibbard's theory adverts. Rather, Gibbard's view is that we have two sorts of mental states, *beliefs* and attitudes of *norm-acceptance*, and mental states of each of these kinds can be said to *rule out* certain factual-normative worlds. This 'ruling out' is a matter of objective logical relations, so my beliefs and norms might rule out things that I don't realize they rule out (because I have not followed out all the logical consequences of my beliefs and norms). Here are a couple of examples: If I believe that it is going to snow tomorrow, then my belief rules out every factual-normative world in which it doesn't snow tomorrow. If I accept a norm of not killing people, then I rule out any factual-normative worlds in which killings of persons are permitted. Notice that this norm not only rules out some competing norms, but also rules out some fact-norm combinations. For instance, my no-killing-people norm rules out the following combination: the factual claim that selling cigarettes kills people + the norm of approving of cigarette sales. So any factual-normative world including both of those things would be ruled out; however, a factual-normative world that approves of cigarette sales but contains the factual claim that selling cigarettes does not kill people would not be ruled out.

When you make a statement, you express a state of mind—a set of beliefs and norm-acceptances—that rules out certain factual-normative worlds. The set of factual-normative worlds in which your statement *holds* is just the set of worlds that your mental state *does not rule out*. That is what the set of worlds we have been discussing has to do with meaning.

It may seem that all of this solves the Frege-Geach problem. Gibbard seems to think so. But in fact it does not touch the core problem.

Let us begin with a thought experiment in the philosophy of language. It is commonly (though not universally) accepted that there are things called 'propositions' that our beliefs are about. If you believe it will rain tomorrow, then your belief is directed at the proposition *that it will rain tomorrow*. If you believe that Snoopy will get wet, then your belief is directed at the proposition *that Snoopy will get wet*. Now imagine that we met a philosopher who held the interesting thesis that there are no compound propositions. For example, there is a proposition *that it will rain tomorrow* and a proposition *that Snoopy will get wet*, but there is no such thing as the proposition *that if it rains tomorrow, then Snoopy will get wet*. This philosopher would run into trouble, because there certainly *is* such a thing as *believing* that if it rains tomorrow then Snoopy will get wet. The philosopher would have a hard time accounting for this, since he would have available no proposition that this belief could be directed at. He admits the state of believing that it will rain tomorrow, as well as the state of believing that Snoopy will get wet. So he might try from those two beliefs to somehow construct the compound belief. But the person who believes that *if* it rains tomorrow Snoopy will get wet, need not believe either that it will rain tomorrow or that Snoopy will get wet. So it appears the philosopher would lack the resources to do what he needs.

Now consider a different (alleged) belief: the belief that *if it was wrong to steal the candy, then God will punish you*. With respect to this belief, the non-cognitivist is in the same position as the hypothetical philosopher of the last paragraph. The non-cognitivist recognizes a state of accepting an anti-candy-stealing norm, which corresponds to the expression 'it was wrong to steal the candy', and he recognizes a state of believing that God will punish you, which corresponds to the expression 'God will punish you'. But there can be no mental state that corresponds in a similar way to the whole sentence, 'If it was wrong to steal the candy, then God will punish you', because someone who sincerely asserts that sentence need neither accept the anti-candy-stealing norm, nor believe that God will punish you. Gibbard's only psychological resources are beliefs and norms, but there is no possible combination of beliefs and norms that can be taken as corresponding to the conditional.

To put the matter another way: Gibbard wants to explain the meaning of the conditional, 'If it was wrong to steal the candy, then God will punish you', by reference to the set of factual-normative worlds that the speaker's state of mind rules out. As we saw above, the correct set of worlds to rule out is just $\{\langle w_2, n_2 \rangle\}$. But there is no possible combination of mental states—using the resources at Gibbard's disposal—that rules out just this world. The relevant possible mental states, on Gibbard's theory, are:

Believing that God will punish you.
Believing that God will not punish you.
Having no opinion about whether God will punish you.
Approving of the candy-stealing.
Disapproving of the candy-stealing.
Being neutral towards the candy-stealing.

Nine consistent combinations of mental states can be formed from these. None of them has the desired result of ruling out just $\langle w_2, n_2 \rangle$. For example, suppose that I *believe God will punish you* and I *approve of the candy-stealing*. This doesn't work, since it rules out $\langle w_2, n_1 \rangle$. In fact, no combination that includes *believing that God will punish you* works, since any such combination rules out $\langle w_2, n_1 \rangle$. No combination that includes *believing that God will not punish you* works either, since it will rule out $\langle w_1, n_1 \rangle$. No combination that includes *approving of the candy-stealing* works, since it will rule out $\langle w_1, n_2 \rangle$. No combination that includes *disapproving of the candy-stealing* works, since it will rule out $\langle w_2, n_1 \rangle$. This leaves only the combination *having no opinion about whether God will punish you* and *being neutral towards the candy-stealing*. But this fails to rule out $\langle w_2, n_2 \rangle$.

The problem here is the *separation* between belief states and norm-acceptance states, which is made inevitable by their being different kinds of mental states with no common objects. It is not in general possible to construct an attitude towards a compound proposition from attitudes towards the separate components of the proposition.

This is why Gibbard cannot in general supply meanings for compound statements in which one component is evaluative and the other non-evaluative.

Notice that the cognitivist has no problem here. The cognitivist need not try to construct the belief that *if stealing the candy was wrong then God will punish you* out of separate opinions about the candy theft and about God's possible future punishment. Instead, the cognitivist has a single object, the proposition *that if stealing the candy was wrong, then God will punish you*, and a single mental state (a belief) that can be directed towards that proposition.

## *2.6  Blackburn's solutions

A suggestion due to Simon Blackburn might help Gibbard. However, if it does, it would render the discussion of factual-normative worlds unnecessary; hence, I will discuss this as a separate proposed solution to the Frege-Geach problem. Blackburn's suggestion is that in uttering a conditional statement, one expresses a dispositional mental state: a disposition to accept the consequent, if one were brought to accept the antecedent. So if I say, 'If stealing the candy was wrong, then God will punish you', I am expressing my disposition to believe that God will punish you, if I should come to disapprove of the theft.[28] Presumably, Blackburn would say the same about conditionals that don't contain evaluations (the ability to do so would be an important virtue of this theory). So 'If it rains tomorrow, Snoopy will get wet' expresses a disposition to accept that Snoopy will get wet, if one becomes convinced that it will rain tomorrow.

Here is a story to illustrate why that's wrong. A psychiatrist has a patient who thinks he (the patient) is dead. The shrink says to the patient: 'All right. You know that the blood of dead people coagulates, right?' Patient: 'Yes.' 'So if you're dead, then if I prick your finger, the blood will not flow out, right?' 'Yes.' The shrink produces a needle, pricks the patient's finger, and the blood flows out. Shrink: 'What do you say now?' Patient: 'Well, I guess I was wrong. I guess the blood of dead people *doesn't* coagulate.'

In this example, the psychiatrist attempts to engage the patient with the following inference:

> If Patient is dead, his blood has coagulated.
> Patient's blood has not coagulated.
> Therefore, he is not dead.

The patient initially accepts the first premise. He is brought to accept the second premise. But instead of thereupon accepting the conclusion, he simply revises his belief in the first premise.

Similarly, if a person accepts 'If $A$ then $B$', he need not be disposed to accept $B$ upon being convinced of $A$; he might instead be disposed, upon becoming convinced of $A$, to stop believing 'If $A$ then $B$'.[29] In some cases, this would be perfectly rational. For instance, suppose I believe that since Ann is a reliable moral judge, if Ann thinks a person is evil, then that person is evil. But when Ann unexpectedly declares that Mother Theresa was evil, I do not accept that Mother Theresa was evil; instead, I give up the belief that if Ann says someone is evil, then they are. This shows that we cannot interpret accepting a conditional as being disposed to accept the consequent if one should come to accept the antecedent.

A qualification that appears in Blackburn's statement of the theory might be thought to help here:

Suppose I hold that either John is to blame, or he didn't do the deed. Then I am in a state in which *if* one side is closed off to me, I am to switch to the other—*or withdraw the commitment*.[30]

The italicized phrase seems to let Blackburn escape from my counter-example. Blackburn could say that when one sincerely asserts a conditional, one is disposed, upon accepting the antecedent of the conditional, to either accept its consequent *or* withdraw one's commitment to the conditional. In the preceding two examples, it is the latter that happens.

Remember that the original point of Blackburn's proposal was to enable the non-cognitivist to *explain what it means* to accept a conditional statement with an evaluative antecedent. While it may be true that a person who accepts 'If $p$ then $q$' is disposed, upon being convinced of $p$, to either accept $q$ or give up 'If $p$ then $q$', this cannot be taken as an *explanation* of what 'If $p$ then $q$' *means*. The effect of including the phrase 'or withdraw the commitment' within the characterization of what the commitment is supposed to be a commitment to, is to empty the supposed commitment of content. It is as if I said, 'I hereby promise to either pay you $10,000 or go back on this promise'. A commitment to (either perform act $A$ or withdraw this commitment) is equivalent to a 'commitment' to (either perform $A$ or not), which is no commitment at all. Similarly, a disposition to (either accept $q$ or stop having this disposition) is hard to distinguish from a disposition to (either accept $q$ or not).

To put the problem differently, the claim that a person has some disposition ought to imply *some* predictions about what the person would be likely to do (in non-dispositional terms) in at least some circumstances; otherwise, having the disposition would be indistinguishable from not having it. That is, claims about one's dispositions must entail determinate predictions regarding actions apart from the 'actions' of acquiring and losing dispositions. Blackburn's hypothesized disposition violates this constraint. Once 'or withdraw the commitment' is added to the characterization of what one is disposed to do, there is no longer any prediction as to what (non-dispositional) states a person would be likely to go into in any circumstances. It is now perfectly consistent with Blackburn's analysis that a person having the supposed disposition would behave in exactly the same way (characterized non-dispositionally) in every possible circumstance as a person lacking the disposition. The reason why Blackburn's qualification lets him escape from my counter-example, then, is that it empties his analysis of content.

While the initial theory of the meaning of conditionals may seem plausible at first glance, Blackburn's view of disjunctions, as expressed in the above quotation, does not. He contends that to accept a disjunction is to be disposed to accept either disjunct if the other one should be closed off to you. For example, I accept the statement 'Either there are unicorns living on the planet Jupiter, *or* cows have four stomachs'. (This is true.) According to Blackburn, this means that I am disposed to accept that there are unicorns on Jupiter if I should find out that cows don't really have four stomachs. But nothing remotely like that is the case.

Blackburn earlier put forward a slightly different theory, before he came to the one we've been discussing.[31] He proposed that compound statements with evaluative components express a kind of second-order evaluation—roughly, they express approval towards the sort of dispositions we've been discussing. So 'If stealing the candy was wrong, God will punish you' expresses the speaker's approval towards the having of (a disposition to accept that God will punish you, if one comes to disapprove of the candy theft). The difference between Blackburn's earlier and later views is that in the earlier view, he says we express *approval towards* certain dispositions, while in the later view, he says simply that we express the dispositions themselves. Does this difference affect the force of my objections? No—in essence, the same two objections apply. First, accepting a conditional does not commit one to approving of (a disposition to accept the consequent if one accepts the antecedent). One might instead approve only of a disposition to give up the conditional upon adopting the antecedent. Second, Blackburn's account cannot handle disjunctions. 'Stealing is wrong' logically implies 'Stealing is wrong, or unicorns live on

Jupiter'. But surely my disapproval of theft does not commit me to approving of *a disposition to accept that unicorns live on Jupiter, if one should come to approve of theft.*

Even setting aside these points, Blackburn's proposals thus far could at most provide an account of what goes on in sentences like 'If pleasure is good, then cinnamon ice cream is good' and 'Either Simpson didn't kill Brown, or the verdict was unjust'. We still don't know how, on a non-cognitivist view, to understand such sentences as the following:

1. I believe that cinnamon ice cream is good.
2. I wonder whether abortion is wrong.
3. I hope that I did the right thing.
4. People don't always do what's right.
5. Don't reward people for doing bad things.

Let us discuss each of these five sentences in turn.

(1) 'I believe that cinnamon ice cream is good.' Blackburn offers: '[B]elieving that $X$ is good or right is roughly having an appropriately favorable valuation of $X$'.[32] Notice that this is not what 'believe' *normally* means. Blackburn is positing an ambiguity in the word 'believe': when I say I believe pleasure is good, according to Blackburn, I actually am not saying that I *believe* anything in the sense in which I would say I believe it's going to rain tomorrow.

Consider one way of testing for ambiguity; I call it the joke test. Someone says, 'Stephanie has very fair skin. Her skin is even lighter than a feather'. The second sentence sounds funny because it treats two meanings of 'light', light as opposed to dark and light as opposed to heavy, as if they were the same. Now contrast the remark, 'Jerry is very pro-life. He believes that abortion is wrong even more strongly than that 2+2 is 4'. This remark is not funny at all. But if 'believe' were ambiguous, such that one could not 'believe' that abortion is wrong in the same sense that one can 'believe' that 2+2 is 4, then the second example should sound funny in the same way as the first.

(2) 'I wonder whether abortion is wrong.' Blackburn says: '[W]ondering whether $X$ is good or right is wondering what to do/ what to admire or value'. But though I wonder whether abortion is wrong, I thankfully am not wondering whether to have an abortion. Am I wondering whether to condemn abortion? Perhaps, but that would be another matter: wondering whether to condemn abortion would be, if anything, wondering whether *condemning abortion* is right, not wondering whether *abortion* is right. Blackburn's proposal becomes still less plausible when applied to wonderings about the

past or about other people: if 'I wonder whether it is right for me to do *A*' means 'I wonder whether to do *A*', then 'I wonder whether it was right for Truman to bomb Hiroshima' means . . . what?

(3) 'I hope I did the right thing.' Blackburn offers no help on this one, and I see no interpretation of this sentence paralleling his treatments of the previous cases—nor any other non-cognitivist interpretation, for that matter.

(4) 'People don't always do what's right.' Blackburn does not discuss this one, but taking a cue from his treatments of (1) and (2), we might try this paraphrase: 'People don't always do what is *to do*'. But this makes no sense. We might say that the sentence expresses disapproval towards *some things* that people do, but it is hard to see someone expressing disapproval just towards 'some things' but not towards anything in particular.

(5) 'Don't reward people for doing bad things.' We might try interpreting this as expressing disapproval towards a practice of rewarding people for doing things that one disapproves of. But this would be to treat 'bad thing' as a descriptive term equivalent to 'thing that one disapproves of', which is to abandon non-cognitivism in favor of subjectivism. The proposal that the sentence expresses disapproval towards the practice of rewarding people for doing things that *the speaker* disapproves of, similarly reverts to subjectivism.

In contrast, the cognitivist view is simple and straightforward. It does not require one to posit any ambiguities in words like 'believe', nor to think up eccentric semantic theories for each of the 'problem' sentences. On the cognitivist story, all of these sentences are easily understandable and mean just what they appear to mean.

## *2.7  Timmons' assertoric non-descriptivism

Since its inception, non-cognitivism, in its efforts to evade objections, has developed ever more resemblance to moral realism. Simple non-cognitivists such as Ayer just said moral statements don't assert anything, don't express beliefs, and can be neither true nor false; nor are there any moral properties or facts. Later non-cognitivists, such as Hare and Blackburn, tried to soothe common sense by letting us apply the words 'true' and 'false' to moral statements and speak of valid arguments involving them, while still maintaining the rest of the doctrine—that is, that moral statements do not assert propositions or express beliefs, nor are there any moral properties or facts. This philosophical trick required some reinterpretation of 'true' and 'false', but that was considered acceptable. The object of the game, for many philosophers, is to devise interpretations of common English words and phrases that make most of the statements ordinary people would accept come out as true—or at least as appropriate things to say—while still holding on to one's preferred metaphysical views (in this case, the view that there are no objective values). One of the rules of the game is that you never call your interpretations *re*interpretations; you always say you are giving the current actual meanings of the relevant words. Bishop Berkeley inaugurated this practice, attempting to show that his denial of the existence of matter was perfectly consistent with common sense,[33] and contemporary philosophers have raised it to an art form.

Returning to the history of non-cognitivism, the theory was not yet reckoned successful, because ordinary people will accept such statements as, 'I believe eating cows is wrong', 'Jon asserted that eating cows is wrong', 'The fact that the war is unjust explains why people are protesting it', and 'Slavery has the property of injustice'. Non-cognitivism, even of the Hare-Blackburn variety, still had to regard those statements as false, if not nonsensical.

Mark Timmons has recently produced the next, and presumably last stage in the non-cognitivist assimilation to realist ways of talking. His 'assertoric non-descriptivism' repudiates—at least verbally—nearly all of the theses that traditionally defined non-cognitivism. He allows that moral statements are assertions, express beliefs, and can be true or false. There are moral properties and facts. Timmons even repudiates relativism: the moral truth does not depend on my or anyone else's attitudes. However—this is the part that makes Timmons an anti-realist—moral statements are *not descriptive*, but evaluative. 'Descriptive' assertions are ones that purport to describe states of affairs in the world, and so require for their truth that the world be a certain way; in contrast, 'evaluative assertions' function to guide action and to express a mental state that consists of 'taking a moral stance on some issue'.[34]

If this combination of theses strikes you as inconsistent, you may be laboring under misapprehensions concerning the meanings of some of the words in the preceding paragraph, such as 'true', 'assertion', 'belief', 'property', and 'fact'. Begin with 'true'. The traditional view of truth is the correspondence theory: for a statement to be True is for it to correspond to the Facts in a mind-independent, outside World. For convenience, let us adopt the notational convention of using all-caps when referring to the denizens of this mind-independent world; so OBJECTS, PROPERTIES, and FACTS are the sort of things that occupy the WORLD according to the correspondence view, and that our statements need to correspond to.[35]

Timmons, following some recent philosophical trends, prefers a 'minimalist' interpretation of truth. For a statement to be true, he says, is just for it to be 'correct' to assert it, according to whatever the norms are for the class of statements to which it belongs. For *some* kinds of statements, the rules we have for when they are correct include that the external WORLD must be a certain way. But the rules for other kinds of statements—including evaluative ones—do not make such demands on the WORLD. When I say, '*It is true that* eating meat is wrong', I am really just saying, 'Eating meat is wrong'—the latter statement does not make any demands on the WORLD (again, it just expresses my moral stance), so neither does the former.[36]

Next, 'assertion': for Timmons, any sentence that has all the linguistic markers of an assertion, of the sort discussed in section 2.3, is *ipso facto* an assertion; that is all there is to being an assertion. So moral statements are assertive. Likewise, there are moral beliefs, because any mental state that can be expressed by an assertion automatically counts as a 'belief'. There are moral facts, because all that is required for there to be a 'fact' (but not a FACT) is that there be a true assertion. There are moral properties (not PROPERTIES), because all that is required for there to be 'property' is that there should be an adjective that we correctly apply to things. Thus, Timmons gets to say nearly all the things that realists customarily say. His statements only differ from those of the moral realist when using block letters: then he says there are no moral FACTS or PROPERTIES, nor are any moral statements TRUE.

That is just an overview, but it suffices to set the stage for my criticisms. I think that the best way of understanding what is going on in Timmons' work also shows what is unsatisfying about it. In essence, Timmons' view comes to the same as that of the traditional non-cognitivists, but with the following stipulations about word usage: Timmons extends the word 'assertion' to cover both what *they* called 'assertions' and what they called 'emotive expressions'; he extends the word 'belief' to cover both what they called 'beliefs' and what they called 'moral attitudes'; and he extends the word 'true' to cover both what they called 'true beliefs' and what they called 'admirable attitudes'.[37] His view that there are genuine assertions that are not descriptive initially sounds radical, even paradoxical; but properly understood, he is not saying that moral statements are assertions in the sense that earlier theorists understood the word 'assertion'. Of course, he would say that earlier thinkers misunderstood the English word 'assertion', but let's leave that aside. If Assertoric Non-Descriptivism differs only verbally from traditional non-cognitivism, then it seems unlikely that it offers any real advance on the problems faced by non-cognitivism.

Indeed, it does not. Timmons' treatment of the Frege-Geach problem is sufficiently like Blackburn's, and his treatment of moral truth sufficiently like Hare's, that I won't discuss them separately here. Instead, I shall raise two objections specific to his views.

The first concerns moral error. Unless we are dogmatic, we all admit that some of our moral views could be wrong. Such statements as, 'I think cloning is good, but I might be mistaken' are often apposite. The realist understanding of that remark is straightforward, but how can an anti-realist understand it? How can I be mistaken, if there are no moral facts independent of my attitudes? Timmons views this as the most serious problem facing anti-realism. His solution is that an admission of moral fallibility expresses an attitude towards one's own moral attitudes, namely 'an attitude of openness to the possibility that [one's moral outlook] might evolve into a different moral outlook as a result of new and persuasive arguments, as well as new experiences'.[38]

This clearly is not right. What Timmons describes might be what is expressed by 'I may *come to believe* my current outlook to be mistaken', but not what is expressed by 'My current outlook may be mistaken'. Consider a slightly different remark: 'My moral views may be mistaken in ways I shall never discover'.[39] This, too, makes perfect sense, but it evidently does not express an attitude about the possibility of my changing my moral views in some way in the future. Or suppose I remark, 'I may *wrongly* come to adopt a different moral outlook as a result of new and persuasive arguments'. This makes sense, and it entails that my moral outlook may evolve in the way Timmons describes, but it does not imply that my current outlook may be mistaken. Thus, one can avow moral fallibility without expressing openness to the possibility of one's outlook evolving, and one can express openness to the possibility of one's outlook evolving without avowing moral fallibility.

Furthermore, compare the two sentences,

I think eating meat is wrong, but I might be mistaken.
I think Napoleon was defeated in 1815, but I might be mistaken.

The latter sentence, presumably, just talks about how the mind-independent world might be, rather than about possible future changes in my beliefs. So Timmons must think that 'might be mistaken' has different meanings in the two sentences. If so, then this should be nonsensical:

So there are two things I might be mistaken about: the moral status of meat-eating, and when Napoleon was defeated.

But that follows from the two preceding statements, and it isn't nonsensical.

My second objection to Timmons' account is more fundamental. Timmons wants to show that common sense is not committed to moral realism, by offering interpretations of how language works that allow us to say the things we normally say without being committed to the existence of evaluative FACTS. The ploy fails because his interpretations are simply not what we mean by 'truth', 'fact', and so on. I propose to show this by arguing that, if they were what we meant, then we could not understand Timmons' exposition of his own theory; in particular, we would see no distinction between assertoric non-descriptivism and moral realism.

Timmons has only the English language to use in explaining his theory. He can introduce new, technical terminology, but then he must explain, in English, what his technical terms mean. Now, the distinction he posits between properties and PROPERTIES is crucial to explaining his theory and how it differs from moral realism; roughly, Timmons isn't a realist because he believes in moral properties but not moral PROPERTIES. How does he explain this distinction? Here is the entire passage introducing it:

> According to the correspondence theory, truth is a matter of a direct correspondence between language (or thought) and a mind-independent world of entities, properties, relations, or, more simply, facts (construed as constellations of the former). For expository purposes, it will be convenient to adopt Putnam's method of capitalizing such words as 'world,' 'object,' 'property,' and 'fact' in order to make clear that when I am talking about the inhabitants of the mind and discourse-independent world it is part of the correspondence view. As we shall see later on, the moral irrealist can help herself to talk about moral properties, relations, and facts, but, of course, it is part of the irrealist's story that there are no moral PROPERTIES, RELATIONS, or FACTS. So, according to the correspondence view, the truth of any sentence is a matter of its corresponding to the WORLD of OBJECTS, PROPERTIES, RELATIONS, and (if one wants to speak this way) FACTS.[40]

Notice that all we are told about the nature of PROPERTIES is that they are mind- and language-independent properties.

Hereafter, I shall use the term 'Timmons-property' to mean what Mark Timmons means by the word 'property' when he puts it in lower case (it is an open question, so far, whether that is the same as what 'property' means in English). Now, I contend that there is no sense to be made of Timmons' views, *unless* he is misusing 'property'. Consider what 'property' means in standard English: does it mean PROPERTY, or does it mean Timmons-property?

*Case 1:* Suppose 'property' in English means PROPERTY. Then the above passage from Timmons gives a circular definition: in effect, it tells us that a PROPERTY is a mind-independent PROPERTY. More importantly, Timmons' central claim that there are moral properties but no moral PROPERTIES is a straightforward contradiction.

One might say that he is not contradicting himself, because when he says this, he is using 'properties' non-standardly (that is, to mean Timmons-properties). But in that case, his account of the meanings of words is incorrect, and he therefore fails in his effort to show that common sense isn't committed to moral realism.

*Case 2:* Suppose 'property' in English means Timmons-property. Then PROPERTIES, according to the above passage, comprise that *subset* of Timmons-properties that are mind-independent. Timmons does not define 'mind-independent', but here are two reasonable criteria:

a) $F$-ness is mind-independent, provided: If a thing is $F$, then it would still be $F$ even if we had entirely different attitudes about it.[41]
b) $F$-ness is mind-independent, provided: It is possible that a thing be $F$ even if no one thinks so.

Timmons would affirm the mind-independence of moral properties on both interpretations. He says we are entitled to avow moral fallibility, even of the most radical kinds, so he would accept that moral properties satisfy (b). He also stresses that his view is not relativistic, and that it does not hold that a moral assertion describes the speaker's attitudes. He thinks moral assertions are 'categorical', which implies among other things that the speaker must be able to support them with 'non-subjective reasons, in other words, reasons that do not appeal to matters of individual taste, personal preference, or the like'.[42] So it seems that on his view, the logic of moral discourse commits one to affirming that moral properties satisfy (a). Moreover, this is obvious in any case—it is false that 'slavery would not be wrong, if only we slavery-haters mellowed out a little'.[43] So it seems that, if a PROPERTY is just a Timmons-property that does not depend on the mind, then Timmons does indeed take there to be moral PROPERTIES. So he is a moral realist.

Now here is what I think is really going on. Of course Timmons isn't a realist. We understand what Timmons is saying, and we understand it to differ from realism, because 'property' in English means PROPERTY; capitalization adds nothing. We understand Timmons' real view to be that (a) there aren't actually any moral properties, but (b) we can still go around using the *word* 'property', because it's just one of the rules of moral language that you get to use that word even when there aren't any properties around for it to refer to. The reason why Timmons' view is initially hard to grasp and why it appears so late on the scene, is that the rules of philosophical discourse preclude his describing his view in the most perspicuous way. For if he describes his view as I have, its falsity is apparent: it is not the case that in English, you are allowed to say there are properties of some kind when in fact there aren't any.

If Timmons' semantic views were correct, then we could not understand what realism was. His views entitle him—indeed, require him—to affirm all the *sentences* characteristic of realism: 'There are moral facts', 'Moral facts are independent of our attitudes', 'Moral statements are true when they correspond to the facts',[44] and so on. If the block-letter terms were not the ordinary English terms—if they were technical terms, as Timmons must represent them as being—then he would have to explain in English what they mean. But none of his attempted explanations would succeed, because we would interpret all the expressions in those explanations minimalistically, so we would take the realist to be committed to no more than Timmons is committed to. When Timmons tried to tell us that realists believe in a MIND-INDEPENDENT WORLD, we would just think he meant a Timmons-mind-independent-world.

Recent versions of non-cognitivism are a kind of meta-linguistic trickery. They seek to embrace common sense in words but reject it in substance. No one but Berkeley was fooled when Berkeley claimed to be an anti-skeptic; nor should we be fooled by today's non-cognitivists.

## 2.8 The introspective evidence

I have characterized cognitivism and non-cognitivism as theses about the meanings of evaluative statements. Assuming that evaluative *statements* express value *judgments*, the semantic claims also imply psychological claims: Cognitivism implies that what we call value judgments are a species of belief, as the term 'judgment' suggests;

non-cognitivism implies that they are instead a species of emotion, desire, or other non-cognitive state. We might expect to be able to resolve this dispute by introspection. When we make value judgments, is the experience more like typical emotions, desires, or other non-cognitive attitudes; or is it more like typical experiences of forming beliefs?

The emotivist might cite the fact that we typically experience emotions when we make moral judgments. Indeed, disputes over such matters as the morality of abortion and the justice of capital punishment are among the most emotional of all disputes. This is *some* evidence for non-cognitivism; after all, if there generally were *no* emotions associated with moral judgments, I would certainly claim this as evidence for cognitivism. But before endorsing non-cognitivism on this ground, let us seek a more nuanced view of what the two theories predict about our psychology.

First, although non-cognitivism more clearly predicts an association between moral judgment and emotion than cognitivism does, this association is hardly inexplicable on a cognitivist view. It shows only that we care about moral issues, in some cases very strongly. There are many other issues that we also care about strongly. Debates over whether God exists, who shot JFK, and what a particular disputed clause in a contract means, can all call forth strong emotions. But this exerts little if any pressure towards regarding statements about those subjects as mere emotional expressions devoid of factual content.

Second, our emotions about some things are stronger than about other things. If the core explanation for the correlation between moral judgment and emotion is that 'good' and 'bad' are just emotion-expressing terms, then what should we predict about how the *strength* of moral emotions should vary? It seems that the strength of the emotions associated with moral judgments should be roughly proportional to the perceived level of goodness or badness of a thing and to the confidence of one's moral judgment: the worse one takes a bad thing to be, and the more confident one is in one's judgment, the more strongly one should feel about it. Is this true? In some cases, yes: I feel more strongly about the wrongness of murder than I do about the wrongness of jaywalking. In other cases, no: I feel more strongly about someone's stealing my stereo (and this is a moral emotion, indignation) than I do about Emperor Nero's execution of Octavia in 62 A.D. Truth be told, I have little if any feeling about Octavia's murder. But Nero's execution of Octavia was far more wrong than the stealing of my stereo, and I am quite certain of that. This suggests that the emotions often associated with moral beliefs have more to do with such things as our concern for our own interests, the social groups we like to associate with, and the self-images we like to maintain, than they do with an emotive meaning built into the term 'wrong'. Though I cannot catalog all the things that influence our emotions, it is unclear why the sorts of factors that explain why people are emotional about *other* matters cannot also account for our emotions about moral issues.

Third, we can distinguish between the degree of confidence of a moral judgment and the degree of rightness or wrongness that the moral judgment attributes. Imagine someone who thinks abortion is likely wrong but lacks confidence in that judgment. He sees that there are plausible arguments on the other side. However, he says, *if* abortion is wrong, it is very seriously wrong, since the only way it would be wrong would be by being akin to murder. Here, the perceived degree of wrongness is very high, but the confidence in the judgment is very low. On the emotivist theory, what could these two dimensions correspond to? On the emotivist theory, one simply experiences a feeling about abortion. This feeling could come in degrees of intensity—people can feel more or less strongly about something. But how could this give rise to our sense that there are *two* things here that come in degrees and that may have radically different degrees in a given case?

Fourth, many moral judgments are made dispassionately, with no evident emotion. Now, in the case of Nero's killing of Octavia, the emotivist might say that I have a general sentiment of disapproval towards murder, and this induces me to say Octavia's murder was wrong even though I have no feeling about Octavia in particular. But this leads to a puzzling (for emotivists) feature of moral emotions: the most fundamental of our moral principles tend to elicit the *least* feeling. Consider the following candidate fundamental moral principles:

> Enjoyment is good.
> One should treat others as one would wish to be treated.
> The right action is always the action that produces the most good.
> A being has a right to something only if it can desire that thing.

Whether or not these principles are correct, they are examples of the sort of thing that philosophers take, plausibly enough, to be fundamental moral principles. But few people feel particularly emotional about these sorts of statements. They tend to be far more emotional about certain derivative moral judgments: that Steve mistreated Alice, that the Simpson verdict was unjust, or that the boss' demands are unreasonable. This is unsurprising to the cognitivist, as it is just an instance of a general pattern: people are more emotional about concrete matters affecting their own interests and those of people they know than they are about abstract, theoretical questions. But for the emotivist the phenomenon is unexpected: if moral judgments are essentially emotional, then shouldn't the most fundamental moral judgments exhibit the clearest, purest moral emotions?

Notice an important asymmetry here. Cognitivism does not require that moral judgments are always dispassionate; we know that people can be influenced by emotions in forming their beliefs, just as their beliefs can in turn influence their emotions; there is nothing special about morality in this regard. But emotivism requires that moral judgments are *always* emotional—because that, according to the theory, is just what moral 'judgments' *are*. Introspection shows this to be false.

Fifth, the procedures whereby we at least *sometimes* form moral judgments—notably, in moral philosophy—are far more like the way we form beliefs than like the way we typically acquire emotions. I want to know whether abortion is really wrong. I go to the moral philosophy literature on the subject. I read Thomson's thought experiment about the violinist. I read Marquis' argument about the rights of potential persons. I read Tooley's argument about the criteria for having a right to life.[45] In all of this, my mental activity is indistinguishable from what it would normally be when I am trying to figure something out. I start in a state of suspended judgment. I weigh reasons for and against a conclusion. Of course, nothing inherently precludes this sort of activity from resulting in one's feeling some emotion. But this is not normally how emotion works. I don't normally go to the professional literature for the purpose of having an emotion about something. I don't normally carefully weigh arguments, looking out for logical errors, for the purpose of forming an emotion. I don't normally try to decide what emotions to have, still less worry about 'getting it right'. None of those things is characteristic of how I would come to be afraid of heights, or love my girlfriend, or be annoyed by Barney the dinosaur.

As in the case of the linguistic evidence, everything here seems to be exactly as it would be if a cognitive interpretation of moral language were correct. I conclude that ethical terms are cognitively meaningful, just as 'blue' and 'square' are, and that ethical statements are claims about an aspect of reality, just as 'The sky is blue' and 'Dogs are square' are.

# 3
# Subjectivism

## 3.1 What is subjectivism?

Subjectivists take moral properties to be reducible to psychological properties and relations. They think that for an object to be good is for some person or group to have (or be disposed to have) some psychological attitude or reaction towards it. Here are a few examples of subjectivist theories; in each case, the '=' sign indicates that the expression on the right explains *what it is* for the expression on the left hand side to be true:[1]

a) *x* is good = The speaker believes that *x* is good.
b) *x* is good = The speaker approves of *x*.
c) *x* is right = Society approves of *x*.
d) *x* is right = *x* accords with God's wishes.[2]

Theories (a) and (b) make morality relative to the individual; that is, they imply that two different individuals may correctly call different things 'good'. According to (a), when I say something is good, I mean that *I* believe it is good; when you say something is good, you mean that *you* believe it is good. Theory (c) makes morality relative to a culture; it implies that members of different societies may correctly call different things 'right', though two members of a *single* society may not.

Note that each of these theories is a theory about what it is to *be* good or right, not about what it is to be *taken to be* good or right. Thus, (b) does not hold that for a thing to be *taken to be* good is for

48

it to be approved of. It holds that for a thing to *be* good is for it to be approved of.

One should not confuse subjectivism with the idea that there are no moral truths or moral facts. Take theory (c): it is definitely true that our society disapproves of theft; therefore, a cultural relativist should say it is *definitely true* that stealing is wrong (in our society). What the relativist denies is that this truth is *objective*, that is, independent of observers in the sense defined in section 1.2. But since there certainly are facts about observers, there is no difficulty in recognizing moral facts.

Subjectivism is a form of reductionism about value. The arguments I deploy in the following chapter serve to refute ethical reductionism in general. Nevertheless, subjectivism is such a common view that it is worth giving it an extra chapter of its own. There are special problems for subjectivism that do not apply to other versions of reductionism. Let us discuss each of the above four versions of subjectivism in turn.

## 3.2  Individualist subjectivism

Begin with theory (a):

a)  *x* is good = The speaker believes that *x* is good.

Its main problem is one of circularity: to know what it is for a thing to be believed to be *F*, we must first know what *F* is. A related problem is the infinite regress: if [*x* is good] = [I believe *x* is good], then [I believe *x* is good] = [I believe (I believe *x* is good)], and so on. In general, it is incoherent to postulate a proposition whose truth would consist solely in your believing it. The same point applies to the view that to be good is to be believed to be good by society, or by God, or by anyone else, and the same applies if we substitute 'perceived', 'known', 'asserted', or any other verb for 'believed'. The word 'good' should not appear within the explanation of what it is for *x* to be good.

This point is worth bearing in mind when we come to theory (b):

b)  *x* is good = The speaker approves of *x*.

If—as seems plausible—'approving' of a thing is having a moral belief about it, such as the belief that the thing is good, then (b) collapses into the benighted theory (a) with all its attendant incoherence. So the subjectivist will have to say that 'approval' denotes some kind of attitude or emotion not analyzable in terms of moral beliefs. Even so, theory (b) faces serious problems.[3]

First, imagine we meet a neo-Nazi. He says:

1. I approve of killing Jews.
2. Killing Jews is good.

His first statement is true. But the second obviously is not. But theory (b) implies that both statements mean the same thing, so both are true; indeed, that we are committed by our admission that (1) was spoken truthfully to admitting that (2) was equally truthfully spoken. This seems absurd.

Of course, (b) does not commit *us* to saying 'Killing Jews is good'; since *we* disapprove of such killing, we may truthfully say it is evil. But in doing so, we do not contradict what the neo-Nazi said. We merely report that killing Jews is bad *for us*, but it is nevertheless good for Nazis. Theory (b) thus makes it impossible to disagree with anyone about morality—this is a second absurd consequence. In saying that killing Jews is evil, we obviously *are* intending to contradict, and are contradicting, the neo-Nazi's statement.

Theory (b)'s third absurd consequence is that my moral attitudes are infallible.[4] That is, I would be correct to assert, 'Anything that I approve of is automatically good'. Only a dogmatic egotist would think this, but theory (b) implies that this is necessarily true, since something's being good just consists in my approving of it. If so, I can find out what is good and bad by simply introspecting my own attitudes. Utterances like the following would thus be a mark of confusion: 'I approve of it, but is it really good?' Yet this does *not* seem to be a confused remark; just as I can know that I believe something but still have some doubts about whether it is true, I can know that I approve of something but still have some doubts about whether it is good.

Fourth, consider the question, *why* do I approve of the things I approve of? If there is some reason why I approve of things, then it would seem that that reason, and not the mere fact of my approval, explains why they are good. If I approve of *x* because of some feature *x* has that makes it desirable, admirable, etc., in some respect, then *x*'s desirability (etc.) would be an evaluative fact existing prior to my approval. On the other hand, if I approve of *x* for no reason, or for some reason that does *not* show *x* to be desirable (etc.) in any respect, then my approval is merely arbitrary. And why would someone's *arbitrarily* approving of something render that thing good?

These reasons may explain why few philosophers have embraced theory (b). Let us turn to the more popular theory (c).

## 3.3 Cultural relativism

Theories like (c) are called 'cultural relativism':

c) *x* is right = Society approves of *x*.

Cultural relativism faces essentially the same problems as individual subjectivism, with minor modifications.

First, imagine that you are a German citizen during World War II. A Nazi officer asserts, 'Killing Jews is right', and most of his and your society agrees.[5] You, however, are a resister: like Oscar Schindler, you are secretly engaged in trying to prevent as many Jews from being killed as possible. According to theory (c), the Nazi officer is correct and you are wrong, for he and not you is acting in accord with the prevailing social norms. Far from being a moral hero, the cultural relativist must say that Schindler was immoral. It is difficult to see the plausibility of this view.

Of course, the relativist may say that Schindler was a hero according to *our* moral standards. But a large part of the *point* of being a cultural relativist—perhaps the central motivation of relativism—has traditionally been that one opposes judging other cultures by our moral standards, or indeed judging other cultures at all. So the fact that the Final Solution was evil according to *our* standards was irrelevant for people living in Nazi society—it gave them no reason for acting in any particular way—and the cultural relativist has no criticism to make of the moral standards that allowed the Nazis to do what they did. Indeed, if our own society's conventions should one day change in such a way as to endorse the mass murder of some minority group, the cultural relativist can only advise us that, on that day, it will be morally right to partake of the bloodshed.

Second, how does theory (c) explain moral disagreements? If one person says 'Abortion is wrong' and another member of the same society says 'Abortion is not wrong', then they are disagreeing with each other. But, according to (c), they are only disagreeing about what the conventions of their society are—they are disputing whether abortion is in fact allowed in their society. It is odd to think that this is all that moral debates are about. Furthermore, if one person says '*x* is right' while a member of *another* society says '*x* is not right', then the cultural relativist must say that they are not disagreeing with each other, since each is only reporting the conventions of his own society.[6] Even if I say, 'No, I don't just mean that members of *my* society should not do *x*; I mean that people in *your* society should not do *x* either. Your society's practices are wrong'—I still do not thereby disagree with the foreigner who says *x* is right. For in saying the foreign society's practices are 'morally wrong', according to theory (c), all I could mean is that they conflict with my society's rules. But here again the relativist is wrong: when I say that Nazi actions were evil, I obviously am not merely saying that the Nazis had divergent conventions from ours, nor am I saying something unintelligible.

Third, although theory (c) does not imply that any individual is morally infallible, it does imply that *society* is morally infallible. According to (c), whatever society endorses is right, automatically. Thus, everyone should accept such remarks as the following:

If our society approves of abortion, then abortion is right.
If our society does not approve of feeding the homeless, then feeding the homeless is not right.
If our society approves of torturing babies, then torturing babies is right.

I don't think any of those statements are true, and neither should you. Even if you happen to be pro-choice, I don't think you should endorse the remark that if society approves of abortion, then, automatically, it is right.[7] Our ordinary moral conception does not treat social endorsement as decretory.

Fourth and finally, why should we obey social customs? Either there are *good reasons* for the customs—that is, reasons that show the customs or the behavior they endorse to be good in some way—or there are no such reasons. If there are such reasons, then at least some evaluative facts exist prior to the customs. If there are no such reasons, then the customs are merely arbitrary rules, and why should we obey arbitrary rules?

To illustrate the dilemma, suppose the relativist says that customs exist to promote the stability and survival of social groups. Well, is the stability and survival of social groups *good*? If so, then that is at least one evaluative fact that is independent of customs. But if not, then the existence of a custom so far creates no reason to act in the way the custom requires. One might say that customs create non-moral reasons for actions—perhaps you should obey them in order to avoid punishment by other people. But, unless one posits an obligation to avoid punishment, this would not show why a person is morally obligated to follow social customs, but only why it is prudent to do so. And one may very well be able to get away with violating customs on some occasions, in which case the present view gives us no reason to act 'morally'.

I now turn to two responses that relativists may make to some of these problems. The first response I call 'the Rigidifying Move'. Traditionally, cultural relativists have been charged with endorsing such statements as,

If society were to approve of eating children, then eating children would be good.

which is clearly false. The Rigidifying Move claims that the word 'good' at the end of the above sentence refers to what society *presently*, in fact, approves of (as opposed to what it would approve of in the hypothetical situation described in the beginning of the sentence).[8] Since society presently does not approve of eating children, the sentence as a whole is false. To illustrate the idea, imagine that I am in Boulder when I utter the following statement: 'If I had flown to Minneapolis today, then Minneapolis would have been here'. This sentence is false. Minneapolis would still have been where it is; it would not have somehow moved to Colorado. 'Here' at the end of the quoted sentence refers to the place where the speaker in fact is, not where he would have been in the hypothetical situation described. According to the Rigidifying Move, the word 'good' works like 'here'. Thus, the relativist is not committed to the absurd statement that if we approved of cannibalism, then cannibalism would be good.

My response is that the relativist is still committed to endorsing:

If society *approves* of eating children, then eating children *is* good.

This slight modification—converting the offending sentence from the subjunctive to the indicative mood—is enough to defeat the Rigidifying Move. Invoking the analogy to the word 'here' again, consider the sentence, 'If I have flown to Minneapolis (such that I am now in Minneapolis), then Minneapolis is here'. This sentence is true, wherever the speaker is when he says it. Thus, the proposal that 'good' works analogously to 'here' offers the relativist no comfort this time.[9]

The second response on behalf of relativism I call the 'Fundamental Values' response, and it applies to the Nazi and Fallibility problems. The Fundamental Values response maintains that *some* socially accepted practices might be morally wrong in virtue of their failure to cohere with *other*, more fundamental social practices. For instance, suppose that early American society accepted a general norm of respect for persons but that, due to false factual beliefs, it failed to classify black people as persons. In that case, the relativist can argue that slavery was wrong in early America, notwithstanding its social acceptance—it was wrong in virtue of its conflict with the more fundamental norm of respect for persons.[10]

This reply does little to reduce the unpalatability of relativism. The view still implies that a society is infallible in its *fundamental* values. Moreover, there is no reason to assume that past acceptance of slavery was due to factual (non-moral) errors. Perhaps, instead, past acceptance of slavery was due to a *fundamental* antipathy felt towards members of other races, for no reason other than that they belonged to other races. Perhaps arguments about the inferior intellectual abilities of Africans were disingenuous rationalizations for this underlying racist hostility. And perhaps this antipathy was so deep and intense that it would have overridden any other values that conflicted with it. I do not know whether this is the case. But it hardly seems that this being the case would place the institution of slavery in early America beyond reproach. If anything, this would make it even more reprehensible. Yet the Fundamental Values reply entails the reverse. According to the relativist, provided that racist attitudes are sufficiently fundamental, they escape all possible moral criticism.

## 3.4   The divine command theory

We often hear warnings to the effect that the decline of religious belief undermines morality. There is more than one way of interpreting this concern, but here I shall focus on the suggestion that there could be no moral truths if God did not exist—as Dostoyevsky says, if there is no God, everything is permitted.[11]

The Divine Command Theory of ethics holds that an action is morally right if and only if it is of a kind that God commands (or approves of, or wants us to perform).[12] The version of the theory I want to discuss holds a similar view about all other evaluative properties, including goodness, justice, and so on—that is, that all of these properties depend on God in such a way that nothing could have any evaluative property if God did not exist; however, in the following, I shall focus on the property of rightness. Since it takes rightness to be reducible and dependent on the attitudes of an observer (God), the Divine Command Theory is a form of subjectivism. This is worth pointing out, since the theory is often seen as the arch-nemesis of cultural relativism, whereas in fact the two are variants on the same basic metaethical approach.

Note that the theory is not merely that it is always right to obey God's commands, or that we can find out what is right by consulting God's commands. Those views would be consistent with the idea that right actions are right independently of God but that God (being all-knowing) always knows which actions are right and (being all-good) always approves of them. Rather, the Divine Command Theory holds that right actions are right only *because* God commands them.

Does the divine command theory face the same problems as other forms of subjectivism? The answer is that there are two problems that are peculiar to the Divine Command Theory; on the other hand, the theory avoids at least one problem afflicting secular subjectivism. Consider six potential problems.

*First*, does God exist? If there is no God, the divine command theory is unattractive. Other subjectivist theories avoid this problem, since there is no doubt that human individuals and societies exist. There are serious grounds for doubting God's existence; however, they are beyond the scope of this book.

*Second*, how do we know what God approves of? Again, this problem has no analog for secular forms of subjectivism, since it is easy to know what human beings approve of. According to Western religious tradition, we can know God's desires from such sacred texts as the Bible or the Koran. But in fact, this source of guidance is notoriously unreliable. The moral guidance to be found in the Bible includes the following imperatives (my paraphrases):

Kill anyone who curses their parents. (*Leviticus* 20:9)
Kill anyone who commits adultery. (*Leviticus* 20:10)
Kill homosexuals. (*Leviticus* 20:13)
Kill women who have premarital sex. (*Deuteronomy* 22:20–1)
Kill people who work on the Sabbath. (*Exodus* 35:2)
Make war on the people occupying the promised land. Show no mercy; kill every man, woman, and child. (*Deuteronomy* 7:1–2; 20:16–17)
Slavery is okay. (*Leviticus* 25:44–5)
It is okay to beat your slaves, as long as they don't die. (*Exodus* 21:20–1)

Not to be provincial, I note that the Koran advises us:

Make war on and kill those who don't accept Islam. (*Sura* 9.5, 9.29–31)

Anyone who dies fighting for Allah will go to heaven. (47.4–6)
Unbelievers are the vilest of all creatures. (8.55)
They will suffer gruesome torture in hell, forever. (22.19–22)
Appropriate punishments for opposing Islam include execution, crucifixion, the cutting off of hands and feet, and exile. (5.33)
Cut off the hands of thieves. (5.38)

Few today, even among believers, would defend the above ideas and precepts. An obvious alternative for some theists would be to hold that although there is a God, He did not inspire the Bible or the Koran. The problem is that this would leave it mysterious how we can know what God wants, thereby threatening our capacity for moral knowledge. But it seems clear that we have some moral knowledge, as nearly any theist would agree.

Another alternative, for a Christian or Jew, would be to hold that the Bible contains some errors introduced by human transmitters of God's word, who may have misunderstood parts of God's message, inserted some of their own prejudices, or made mistakes in transmitting the scriptures down the generations. This would enable one consistently to reject the precepts I have listed above while maintaining that the Bible contains much that is true, important, and inspired by God. I cannot refute this position (not here, at any rate), nor do I claim that there is nothing of value to be found in the Bible or the Koran. But notice that if one takes this position, one cannot simply appeal to the Bible to determine what is right and wrong. The Divine Command theorist would have to posit some sort of access to moral facts independent of our knowledge of God's will,[13] which would seem to surrender one of the major advantages of a Divine Command theory—namely, its ability to explain moral knowledge. For example, the Divine Command theorist might be driven to posit a faculty of moral intuition—but then it is unclear how his theory would be better than traditional ethical intuitionism. Or the theorist might adopt one of the proposals of recent ethical naturalists (see the following chapter, where these proposals are also criticized).

*Third*, the problem of Nazis does not afflict the Divine Command theorist as it afflicts other subjectivists—the divine command theorist need not grant the truth of Nazi moral assertions, since the Nazis did not act in accord with God's will. But a similar problem arises nonetheless. The divine command theorist must hold that if God were to command us, for no particular reason, to torture and murder our children, then such actions would be moral.

A defender of the theory might observe that, since God is morally perfect, he would never command such things.[14] But this does not engage the objection. Even if we know that someone would not do A, we can still ask what would follow *if* he *were* to do it. For instance, I am not going to drink an entire bottle of Everclear. However, we can still discuss what would follow if I were to do so; for instance, if I drank a bottle of Everclear, I should immediately call the hospital. Likewise, we can talk about what would follow if God were to command us to murder children, even if we are sure he will not do so. Furthermore, the reasoning for the claim that God would never make such a command is fallacious. According to the divine command theory, whatever God commands is right, so if God were to command murder, murder would be right. Therefore, God's moral perfection is no obstacle to his issuing such a command: a morally perfect being is not debarred from commanding people to do things that are morally correct as of the time he commands them.[15]

Robert Adams proposes another response to the problem. He says that the obligation to obey God's commands is contingent on there being a *loving* God. If God were to command the killing of children, this would show that He was not loving as Christians believe him in fact to be. Since the rightness of an action consists in its conforming to the will of a loving God, child killing would *not* be right in that situation.[16] But nor, on Adams' view, would it be wrong. Since on Adams' view, an act's being commanded (forbidden) by a loving God is a necessary condition on its being right (wrong), Adams must say that if God were not loving, if He refrained from forbidding the killing of children, or if He simply did not exist, then there would be *nothing wrong* with killing children. This is hardly more plausible than the position that God's commanding child murder would make it right.

*Fourth*, the divine command theory is less subject to the problem of disagreement than other forms of subjectivism are, because it is not absurd to suppose that people disagreeing about ethical questions are sometimes disagreeing about what God would approve of. It seems odd, nonetheless, to maintain that *everyone* who argues about moral questions, including atheists, agnostics, and polytheists, is arguing about what God would approve of.[17]

*Fifth*, there is one problem afflicting other forms of subjectivism that does *not* apply to the divine command theory. This is the problem that subjectivists must hold some individual or group to be morally infallible, which is implausible. But in the case of God, it is not implausible—indeed, it is true by definition—that he is infallible.

*Sixth*, and most importantly, even if there is a God, why should we do what He says? Someone's telling you to do something does not in general create a moral obligation to do it. If your next door neighbor tells you to kill your son,[18] this creates no obligation at all, even *prima facie*, for you to do so. If Satan tells you to avoid eating pork, this creates no obligation to obey. There must be something special about God, if *His* commands are to create moral obligations. What is it?

I argue that the divine command theorist has no satisfactory answer to this question. In outline:

1. If no characteristics of God ground an obligation to obey God's commands, then there is no obligation to obey God's commands.
2. The morally neutral characteristics of God do not ground an obligation to obey God's commands.
3. If the morally significant characteristics of God ground an obligation to obey his commands, then some moral facts are independent of God's commands and attitudes.
4. If either (a) there is no obligation to obey God's commands or (b) some moral facts are independent of God's commands and attitudes, then the divine command theory is false.
5. Therefore, the divine command theory is false.

Premise (1) has already been motivated. If there is nothing special about God that sets him apart from most other beings, explaining why we must obey him in particular, then, since we are not *in general* obligated to obey other beings, we are not obligated to obey God.

In premises (2) and (3), a 'morally neutral' characteristic is one that it is possible to have without having an evaluative property; a morally significant characteristic is one that one cannot have without having an evaluative property. For instance, being powerful and being the creator of the Earth are morally neutral characteristics. Being just and being cruel are morally significant characteristics, since one cannot be just without being good in some respect, nor can one be cruel without being bad in some respect.

(2) can be supported by hypothetical examples. For any morally neutral characteristic of God, it is possible to imagine an evil being—Satan, say—having that characteristic. In such a situation, intuitively, there would be no moral obligation to follow Satan's commands. For example, it might be said that we should obey God because He is our creator. But imagine that you found out that you had actually been specially created by Satan. In that case, would you be under a general obligation to follow Satan's will? It is also said that God has unlimited power over us, and can bestow eternal punishments and rewards. Imagine that Satan had unlimited power over you, and could bestow eternal punishments and rewards. In that case, no doubt it would be *prudent* to obey Satan's commands. But would it be *morally obligatory*

to do so; would you be *immoral* if you were to resist Satan's evil plans? Lastly, suppose Satan were all-knowing and all-powerful (but still thoroughly evil). Would it then be morally obligatory to follow his will? In all of these cases, the answer is surely that you would not be obligated to follow the will of Satan. Therefore, none of these properties—being our creator, having the ability to reward and punish us, being all-knowing, being all-powerful, or any combination of these—can ground an obligation of obedience on our part towards another being.

There is one crucial respect, or family of respects, in which God differs from Satan in my hypothetical scenarios. This is that Satan is evil, whereas God is purely good, just, benevolent, and so forth. It is plausible that if a *supremely good* being tells you to do something, then you are thereupon obligated to do it. But here is where premise (3) comes in. If the reason we must obey God turns on God's goodness, then some moral facts must exist prior to God's commands. By hypothesis, the capacity of God's commands to generate moral truths depends upon God's goodness; on pain of circularity, therefore, it cannot also be the case that God's goodness is generated by his commands. (It cannot be, for example, that God is good because he approves of himself, or because he commands us to worship him. Imagine Satan likewise approving of himself and commanding us to worship *him*.) God must *already* be good, so there must already be a standard of value in place—for example, that lovingness, mercy, and justice are good—prior to God's commands.

Apropos of this, recall Robert Adams' solution to the problem of God's possible command to kill children. Adams finds God's lovingness relevant to the obligation to obey Him and argues that a loving God could not order such killing. But what motivates Adams to single out *lovingness*? Is it not that he considers this trait a virtue, or in some way *good*?[19] It is hard to imagine someone who placed no value on love giving Adams' reply. Thus, it seems that the ability of a loving God's commands to create obligations depends upon the independently assumed *value* of love.

Finally, premise (4) is true because the divine command theory holds that what is morally obligatory is so in virtue of God's commanding it, and that something similar holds for all other moral properties (such as goodness and wrongness). This implies both that it is obligatory to obey God's commands, and that nothing has any moral property independently of God's commands.

The conclusion (5) follows from premises (1)–(4): God's non-moral characteristics cannot ground an obligation of obedience. God's moral characteristics can ground such an obligation only if there are moral facts independent of God's commands. So either there is no reason to obey God, or there are moral facts independent of God's commands. Either of these alternatives conflicts with the divine command theory. So that theory must be rejected.

A closely related point can be made more succinctly. Why does God command what he does? If God has no moral reasons for his commands, then they are merely arbitrary—and why should we obey arbitrary commands? But if God *has* moral reasons for his commands, then some moral truths must exist independently of his commands. Either way, the divine command theory is false.[20]

One response to this is that God's commands may escape arbitrariness by virtue of God's having *non-moral* reasons for his commands.[21] I don't think this helps, any more than the suggestion that God has *bad* reasons for his commands would help. How would God's having a reason *with no moral weight* for a command serve to render that command non-arbitrary in a morally relevant sense, that is, in such a way that we morally ought to follow it?

## *3.5  The ideal observer theory

Ideal Observer theories say that a thing is good, or an action right, if an 'ideal observer' would take some pro-attitude towards it.[22] This is similar to the divine command theory (God being the ultimate in ideal observers), but it does not require any godlike being to actually exist; instead, we are to answer moral questions by reasoning hypothetically about what the ideal observer *would* favor, if there were one. I classify this as a form of subjectivism, since it makes value depend constitutively upon a (hypothetical) observer's attitudes.[23]

This statement of the theory raises three questions. First, what sort of 'pro-attitude' is the ideal observer supposed to take? Second, what is meant by an 'ideal observer'? And third, is the good what *all* ideal observers would necessarily favor, what *an* ideal observer might favor, or what?

I won't dwell on the first question. The pro-attitude might be desire, approval, or something else. In the following, I shall speak in terms of desire, but analogous arguments can be made regardless of which pro-attitude the ideal observer theorist makes use of.

In response to the second question, here are some traits that have been attributed to the 'ideal observer':

He knows all the non-moral facts.
He imagines all relevant states of affairs perfectly vividly.
He is perfectly rational.

He is disinterested and dispassionate; that is, he lacks desires and emotions that refer to specific individuals.

He is benevolent.

He is in other respects normal (for instance, he's not crazy).[24]

Different philosophers may pick slightly different collections of traits, leading to different versions of ideal observer theory. We needn't worry about this. However, there are two important points about what the ideal observer can *not* be taken to be: The ideal observer should not be assigned any *moral* properties; for instance, he is not to be understood as a perfectly virtuous being. This would land the theory in circularity, given its aim to explain all moral properties. Also, though the ideal observer may be granted full awareness of non-moral facts, he should not be ascribed *moral* knowledge, or any traits entailing a capacity for moral knowledge (such as a faculty of ethical intuition). Again, the concern would be one of circularity; such a capacity would presuppose the existence of moral facts independent of the observer.

In response to our third question, there are two kinds of ideal observer theory. One takes the good to be that which every ideal observer would necessarily approve of.[25] The problem is that this seems to result in nothing's being good. The traits listed above (apart from benevolence) do not entail that the observer so described has any desires at all, let alone feelings of approval or disapproval. We might appeal to the 'normalcy' condition to deal with this—a being without desires would be abnormal. Perhaps there are some desires that all normal people must have. Now the problem is that the definition of the ideal observer seems to illicitly include an evaluative term: when 'normal' is used to mean 'has normal desires', it is evaluative. For example, people who think homosexuality is wrong refuse to call homosexual desires 'normal'; those who consider it permissible call those desires 'normal'. We call pedophilia 'abnormal' because it is bad. The defender of the ideal observer theory would probably want to exclude observers with sadistic desires; if this is done on the basis of such desires' 'abnormality', this would seem to be because 'abnormal' functions evaluatively. A similar point would apply to attempting to use the 'rationality' requirement to rule out apathetic ideal observers.

We might try simply stipulating what desires the ideal observer has; for instance, that he is benevolent (desires the welfare of people in general).[26] One problem with this is that, in stipulating the ideal observer's motivations, we would simply be stipulating the content of moral theory. If we say, 'Ideal observers desire $x$, $y$, and $z$', then we are in effect stipulating that $x$, $y$, and $z$ are the sole goods. This is because nothing *else* in the definition of the ideal observer entails any motivations, so the only things that *all* ideal observers would desire would be $x$, $y$, and $z$. But then we might as well take the simpler theory, 'For a thing to be good is for it to be $x$, $y$, or $z'$, and call ourselves ethical naturalists. No work is done by adding the rest of the ideal-observer apparatus.

Richard Brandt offers a better approach to our third question: he relativizes value to the individual, and says that what is good *for* a given person is what *that person* would desire, if *he* were fully rational, fully informed, and so on.[27] This enables us to start from our actual desires, and merely consider what changes would be made if we were to become fully rational. Presumably, my becoming fully rational would not require my losing all my desires, so some things will be good (relative to me) on this theory.

All of that was by way of identifying what I take to be the best version of ideal observer theory. Now for what is wrong with it.

The problems are familiar. First, the *problem of horrible desires*: Suppose I want to see lots of death and destruction for its own sake. Vividly imagining the destruction only increases my desire for it. The desire was not caused by any false beliefs of mine, nor have I been brainwashed into it, etc.; I'm just a nasty person.[28] No further non-moral information would change my mind about this. According to the Ideal Observer Theory, it seems, death and destruction is good (for me), and I should aim at it. Brandt might respond that no actual person is like that. I see no reason for assuming that, but we need not debate that. Here is a more realistic example: there is an individual who has a basic aversion to people of dark-skinned races. If given full non-moral information, but no moral arguments or intuitions, he would continue to feel this aversion. The aversion, let's suppose, is a genetically programmed hostility that some people bear for people of other races and social groups. In this situation, the ideal observer theory would apparently counsel that this person should favor racist actions and policies, perhaps even slavery for the members of the despised race.

Brandt might claim that actual racists are not like this, that racist attitudes are in fact based on false non-moral beliefs about other races. I see little reason to believe this; at least equally plausible is that racist beliefs about the personality traits and intellectual and other abilities of minority races are accepted as rationalizations for preexisting racist feelings. Regardless, the ideal observer theory is committed to holding that *if* racist attitudes are fundamental and not caused by factual errors, brainwashing, and so on, then racist policies are good (for the racists), and people with those attitudes *should* seek the unequal treatment of minorities.

Second, the *Problem of Disagreement*: On Brandt's version of the ideal observer theory, people who appear to be disagreeing about morals are not really disagreeing. This is true regardless of whether most people are similar enough that the ideally rational versions of them would desire the same things. It is true in virtue of the logical form of moral statements according to the theory: each person is talking about what *he* would desire if fully informed, etc. So '*x* is good' and '*x* is not good' do not contradict each other, if said by different people.

Third, the *Problem of Fallibility*: the ideal observer theory can explain how my actual preferences can be bad, since they may fail to match those I would have were I fully informed, etc. What it cannot accommodate is the fact that even a fully informed person may be morally fallible—correctness about all *non*-moral matters does not, conceptually, rule out moral error. If there were an ideal observer, he could intelligibly ask himself, 'Are the things I want really good?'

Fourth and finally, the *Problem of Arbitrariness*: Why does the ideal observer desire what he does? If he desires it because it is good, or for any other moral reason, then there are moral facts independent of his attitudes. But if he has no moral reason for desiring what he does, then his desires are arbitrary and have no moral import. Why would someone's desiring or approving of something *for no reason* make that thing good? This is essentially an appeal to the ethical intuition that *being desired* does not convert a morally neutral or bad object into a good one (not to be confused with the claim that *desire-satisfaction* isn't good).

## 3.6 The subjectivist fallacy

Why has anyone held a subjective theory of value? Individual subjectivists and cultural relativists commonly attempt to support their views with one or both of the following kinds of evidence: (*i*) evidence that moral beliefs vary among individuals or cultures; (*ii*) evidence that moral beliefs are influenced by emotions, peer pressure, and other non-rational causes. The argument seems to be:

1. Different people/cultures have many different sets of moral beliefs.
2. Therefore, there are many different moral truths (many different moral perspectives are equally correct).

Or:

3. People's moral beliefs are generally caused by emotions and/or their society's conventions.
4. Therefore, a moral belief is just a belief about emotions and/or conventions.

It is hard to believe that anyone needs to have the fallacies in the above pointed out to them. The first argument is invalid as it stands; for (1) to support (2), one would have to add the premise, 'Whatever people believe is true'. That premise is false, and well known to be false. The second argument is equally invalid; for (3) to support (4), one would have to add the premise, 'People's beliefs are always caused by what they are about'. That is also well known to be false. People are often wrong, and they often adopt beliefs for irrational reasons.

Arguments of this kind deserve the label 'the Subjectivist Fallacy', since they are virtually the only arguments given by subjectivists, and since they are given by nearly all subjectivists.[29] The underlying mistake is simple: it consists in confusing representations with reality. The first argument above overtly confuses *beliefs* with *truths*. The second confuses the way people form a belief with what the belief is about.

To illustrate, suppose three gamblers at the racetrack all think, for purely emotional reasons, that a different horse is going to win. It does not follow that the race will have three different outcomes, one in which each gambler is right. Nor does it follow that to say a horse is going to win the race is just to say that one has a certain emotion. Yet that is the sort of reasoning involved in the Subjectivist Fallacy.

In sum, the most commonly held forms of subjectivism are motivated by obvious confusions. Furthermore, all ethical subjectivists face at least three major problems:

i) *The Problem of Horrible Attitudes:* Subjectivists must hold that seemingly horrible actions, such as murder and torture, are morally right as long as the appropriate person or group endorses them.
ii) *The Problem of Disagreement:* Subjectivists cannot plausibly account for moral disagreement.
iii) *The Problem of Arbitrariness:* Subjectivists must hold that things are made good, or actions made obligatory, by merely arbitrary rules or attitudes.

In addition, individual subjectivists, cultural relativists, and ideal observer theorists face:

*iv) The Problem of Fallibility:* They cannot explain the intuition that the relevant person or group could have morally incorrect attitudes.

And divine command theorists face:

*v)* *The Problem of God's Existence:* It is doubtful whether God exists.
*vi)* *The Problem of Knowing God's Wishes:* Even if He exists, it is unclear what God wants.

These reasons seem more than sufficient for rejecting subjectivism. But, even if I am wrong about all of these problems, subjectivists will still face the problems raised for all reductionists in the following chapter.

# 4
# Reductionism

In the present chapter, I defend two main theses, as against the views of ethical reductionists: that at least some evaluative properties are irreducible, and that moral knowledge cannot be explained without appeal to ethical intuition.

## 4.1 What is reductionism?

Both ethical naturalism and subjectivism are forms of *reductionism* about ethics. Reductionism holds that all evaluative properties are reducible to natural properties.

What does that mean? I take 'natural properties' to include all properties (including relational properties) that can be referred to using non-evaluative terms.[1] This includes both physical properties (such as mass, shape, and electric charge) and mental properties (such as believing, feeling sad, and having a tickling sensation). Naturalists and subjectivists disagree with each other over whether certain sorts of mental properties—namely, observers' attitudes towards objects of evaluation—should be included among those to which value properties reduce; but they agree that value properties reduce to *some* sort of natural properties. To say that an evaluative property 'reduces' to some collection of natural properties is to say that one could explain the nature of the evaluative property—explain *what it is*— entirely in terms of those natural properties.

Initially, reductionism might seem paradoxical: how could wholly *non*-evaluative terms be used to explain the nature of value? To see that this is not so paradoxical, consider an analogy: some say that for an object to be red is just for it to reflect predominantly light with wavelengths in the neighborhood of 650 nanometers. Notice that this explanation is given entirely using non-color terms ('reflect', 'wavelength', etc.), so that a person with no previous awareness of color could, if the explanation is correct, come to understand the nature of redness on the basis of it. Whether or not this account of the nature of redness is correct, it is at least not *obviously* false. Similarly, perhaps it is possible to give an explanation of what goodness is which will not use any evaluative terms.[2]

A key advantage often claimed for reductionism is that it holds the promise of rendering our *knowledge* of morality intelligible. If moral properties are irreducible, non-natural properties, then it seems that the only way we might be aware of them is by 'intuition'—a faculty that contemporary philosophers have been reluctant to embrace. But the view that moral properties are reducible to natural properties holds out the hope that we might know moral facts in a manner similar to how we know (other) natural facts, such as by observation or scientific reasoning.[3]

In the remainder of this chapter, I argue both that reductionism about ethics is false, and that this alleged advantage of the theory is illusory: reductionists cannot escape the appeal to intuition as a source of moral knowledge.[4]

## 4.2 Analytic reductionism

*Analytic reductionism* holds that the meaning of any moral term can be given using non-moral terms. For example, an analytic reductionist might hold that '*x* is good' is synonymous with '*x* increases the total amount of enjoyment in the world'. Or one might hold that '*x* is good' is synonymous with '*x* is something that we desire to desire'.[5]

G. E. Moore's Open Question Argument refutes analytic reductionism.[6] Suppose '*N*' is an expression containing only non-evaluative terms that denotes some property. 'Are things that have *N* good?' is an *open question*. What this means is that a person could coherently give either answer to the question. But 'Are good things good?' is not an open question; a person could not coherently give either answer to *that* question. Therefore, the two questions are not equivalent. Therefore, 'good things' is not synonymous with 'things that have *N*'. To illustrate, consider the theory that '*x* is good' means '*x* increases the amount of enjoyment in the world'. Moore would argue:

1. 'Is it good to do what increases the amount of enjoyment in the world?' is an open question.
2. 'Is it good to do what is good?' is not an open question.

3. Therefore, the questions in (1) and (2) are not synonymous.
4. Therefore, 'increases the amount of enjoyment in the world' is not synonymous with 'is good'.

The idea behind premise (1) is that a person could coherently wonder whether increasing enjoyment is good (after all, an ascetic value system is logically consistent). But as (2) observes, one could not wonder whether doing good is good; no coherent value system denies that doing good is good.

The idea behind (3) is that since one question is open and the other is not, they are not the same question. One might also simply see immediately that the two questions are different, even without invoking the notion of 'open questions'.

Step (4) follows from (3) because the questions in (1) and (2) differ only in that one of them substitutes the predicate 'is good' for the predicate 'increases the amount of enjoyment in the world'; there-fore, the difference in meaning between the two questions must be traced to a difference in meaning between those two predicates. If the two predicates had the same meaning, as the reductionist claims, one should be able to substitute one for the other in any sentence without changing the meaning of the sentence.

Moore says that a similar argument will work against *any* analytic reductionist theory. I know of one apparent exception to this: consider an analytic ideal observer theory, which holds that '*x* is good' means something like, 'An ideally rational, knowledgeable, sensitive being would approve of *x*'. The Open Question Argument may fail against this theory, because the first premise is not clearly true.[7] That is, it is not clear that questions like 'Are the things that an ideally rational, informed, sensitive being would approve of really good?' are open questions. One may think that, provided we characterize ideal observers correctly, an ideal observer is bound to get things right.

I think that there are two ways of understanding this sort of theory, one that makes it non-reductionist and immune to the Open Question Argument, and another that makes it reductionist but vulnerable to the Open Question Argument. On the one hand, if 'ideal rationality' is taken to include the capacity for making rational evaluations, 'ideal knowledge' is taken to include moral knowledge, or 'ideal sensitivity' is taken to include sensitivity to the moral features of things, then I think 'Are the things that an ideally rational, informed, sensitive being would approve of really good?' is not an open question. But in that case, I think we have a non-reductionist theory, since the existence of other evaluative facts or features must be presupposed in defining 'good'. I am not concerned here to refute non-reductionist accounts of value.

If, on the other hand, ideal rationality only includes rationality in the making of non-moral judgments, ideal knowledge only includes non-moral knowledge, and ideal sensitivity only includes non-moral sensitivity, then I think it is an open question whether an ideally rational, knowledgeable, and sensitive being would also possess correct moral beliefs; therefore, it is an open question whether what such a being approved of would be good. Conceivably, a being might be perfectly rational, informed, and sensitive in all non-evaluative areas and yet lack any correct moral judgments. In such a case, this being might fail to approve of what is good, or even approve of things that are bad.

I believe, then, that Moore's argument succeeds against all genuinely reductionist theories of the meanings of evaluative expressions. Reductionists typically grant that *if* the Open Question Argument succeeds against such theories as the theory that 'good' means 'conducive to pleasure', then it succeeds against all analytic reductionist theories. However, they have said that Moore's argument fails even against the theory that 'good' means 'conducive to pleasure', for at least two reasons.

First, some say that Moore begs the question. Since the reductionist we're confronting holds that the good is just whatever increases enjoyment, obviously he will say that it is *not* an open question whether it is good to do what increases enjoyment. For Moore to assert otherwise just assumes that the reductionist theory is false.[8]

This response employs an overly expansive conception of 'begging the question'. It is not the case that whenever an argument deploys a premise that directly and obviously contradicts an opponent's position, the argument begs the question. Still less is it true that whenever a consistent opponent would reject at least one of an argument's premises, the argument begs the question. (The latter condition applies to every valid argument.) Consider another famous philosophical argument: Philosopher *A* claims that 'knowledge' means 'justified, true belief'. Philosopher *G* points out the following sort of example:

Suppose that Smith justifiably believes that Jones owns a Ford (he has often seen Jones driving a Ford, has seen the title to the car, and so forth). Smith correctly infers from this that the following statement is also true: 'Jones owns a Ford, or Brown is in Barcelona'. (Barcelona was selected randomly; Smith has no idea where Brown is.) But suppose that, improbably enough, Jones actually does *not* own a Ford; it was sold just a few minutes ago. But by pure coincidence, Brown happens to be in Barcelona. In this case, Smith believes [Jones owns a Ford, or Brown is in Barcelona]; he is justified in believing this (since he correctly inferred it from a justified belief); and it is true (since Brown is in Barcelona). But intuitively, Smith does not *know* [Jones owns a Ford or Brown is in Barcelona]. Thus, justified, true belief is not the same as knowledge.

The above argument is widely, and rightly, taken to conclusively refute the 'justified, true belief' account of knowledge; indeed, it is one of the few, and one of the most celebrated, examples of a conclusive refutation of a previously widely-held view in modern philosophy.[9] How weak it would be for *A* to reply:

G has merely begged the question. I say that knowledge is justified, true belief. From this, it directly and obviously follows that Smith *does* know [Jones owns a Ford or Brown is in Barcelona] in *G*'s example. For *G* to assert that Smith lacks such knowledge just assumes that my definition is wrong. So *G* has proven nothing.

*A* is correct to note that *G*'s premise directly and obviously contradicts *A*'s theory. But this does not mean that *G* begged the question; it means only that *G*'s refutation of *A* was direct and obvious. *G* succeeds while *A* fails because *G*'s premise, once stated, is intuitively obvious, while *A*'s theory is not intuitively obvious but needs to be tested by considering examples. *A* thus is not in a position to simply appeal to his theory as a justification for denying the premise that would be used to refute the theory.

Similarly, Moore succeeds against the reductionist because Moore is able to adduce premises that, once stated, are intuitively obvious to competent English speakers, whereas the reductionist's proposed analysis of 'good' is not intuitively obvious. We have a sense of when a statement is contradictory, and 'Enjoyment isn't good' does not sound contradictory. The reductionist thus is not in a position to simply appeal to his theory to justify rejecting the premises Moore would use against it. Nor should the reductionist question the general reliability of our judgments of consistency and inconsistency. For judgments of this kind are the essence of our knowledge of logic, without which none of us are in a position to advance or evaluate any arguments.

The second reply to Moore begins with the observation that even for individuals who understand a given word, it is often difficult off-hand to identify the correct definition of that word. For instance, one who knows the word 'circle' may still have difficulty coming up with the definition, 'the set of all points a given distance from a given point'. Thus, a question may often appear to someone to be open even when it is not, simply because the person does not realize what the correct analysis of his own concept is. Perhaps Moore's question, 'Is it good to do what increases the amount of enjoyment in the world?' only appears open to us because we do not at first realize what the correct analysis of 'good' is.[10]

This response rests on an uncharitable reading of Moore. Moore need not assume that the correct analysis of a given concept is always immediately obvious to anyone who has the concept. Instead, Moore can get by with only the assumption that, once a specific definition has been stated, and once competent speakers of the language have thoroughly understood and reflected carefully on that definition, their linguistic intuitions provide at least a *prima facie* guide to the definition's correctness. This assumption is much weaker and more reasonable than the assumption that the analysis of one's concepts is always immediately obvious, and it is difficult to see how anyone engaged in attempting to define words or concepts—as the analytic reductionist is—can reject it. For without it, it is hard to see how we could ever know what the definition of anything is.

The intuitions to which Moore appeals—for example, that 'Pleasure is not good' is consistent, and that 'Is pleasure good?' does not mean 'Is pleasure conducive to pleasure?'[11]—are ones that occur after competent speakers of English have thoroughly understood the definition of 'good' under discussion and have reflected carefully on it. Therefore, these intuitions provide at least a *prima facie* test of the definition's correctness. That is, in the absence of specific, independent grounds for rejecting these intuitions or holding them to be unreliable, they provide adequate reason for rejecting the reductionist's definition. Since reductionists have in fact provided no such grounds, we should reject the proposed definition.[12]

Moore's claim to refute *all* forms of analytic reductionism rests on his ability to produce similar intuitions for every proposed definition of 'good'. Consider some other potential definitions, and some premises that might be used in Moorean arguments against them:

| *Proposed Analysis* | *Moorean Premise* |
| --- | --- |
| $x$ is good = God approves of $x$. | 'God is good' does not mean 'God approves of himself'. |

| | |
|---|---|
| $x$ is right = $x$ is in accord with the prevailing social customs. | 'Is it right to obey social customs?' does not mean 'Does obeying social customs accord with social customs?' |
| $x$ is good = I approve of $x$. | 'Are the things I approve of really good?' does not mean 'Do I really approve of the things I approve of?' |
| $x$ is good = $x$ promotes life.[13] | 'Is life good?' does not mean 'Does life promote itself?' |

I cannot discuss every possible analysis of 'good' here. But the above examples (including the case of the definition involving enjoyment) suggest that Moore could indeed adduce relevant, plausible premises for his argument against any form of analytic reductionism. I am not making an inductive argument based on five cases here. Rather, I am suggesting that upon considering these five cases, one can see a pattern, a method Moore could use to generate Open Question-type arguments in further cases.

## 4.3   The is-ought gap

### 4.3.1   Hume's law: an initial statement

Closely related to Moore's refutation of analytic reductionism is another doctrine in metaethics known as that of the 'is-ought gap', or 'Hume's Law'. This is the idea that it is impossible to validly derive an evaluative conclusion from wholly non-evaluative premises—or, as it is sometimes said, one cannot deduce conclusions about what *ought* to be from premises about what *is*. The *locus classicus* of this idea is the following well-worn passage from David Hume:

> In every system of morality, which I have hitherto met with, I have always remark'd, that the author proceeds for some time in the ordinary way of reasoning, and establishes the being of a God, or makes observations concerning human affairs; when of a sudden I am surpriz'd to find, that instead of the usual copulations of propositions, *is*, and *is not*, I meet with no proposition that is not connected with an *ought*, or an *ought not*. This change is imperceptible; but is, however, of the last consequence. For as this *ought*, or *ought not*, expresses some new relation or affirmation, 'tis necessary that it shou'd be observ'd and explain'd; and at the same time that a reason should be given, for what seems

altogether inconceivable, how this new relation can be a deduction from others, which are entirely different from it.[14]

Note that Hume is not merely observing that from '*x* is the case' one cannot validly infer '*x* ought to be the case'. Rather, he is making the general point that *no* collection of facts about what is the case entail *any* claim about what ought to be. Another way of stating the principle is to say that any (non-evaluative) description of the world can consistently be combined with any value system, or even with nihilism.[15]

Consider a simple challenge to Hume's Law. Suppose I pronounce that communism is bad. You ask me why I believe this. I say: 'It caused tens of millions of deaths, widespread poverty, and a great deal of human suffering. It is reasonable to believe that it would continue to have such effects in the future. Therefore, it is a bad system of government'. Assume that my historical claim is adequately established, and assume that you accept my generalization that communism can be expected to continue to have similar effects. Is not my conclusion thereby justified? Surely it is not merely some sort of simple logical fallacy I have committed. Yet the premises of my argument are entirely non-evaluative, while the conclusion is evaluative.

According to the standard doctrine, which I endorse, the argument fails to bridge the is-ought gap because it contains certain *implicit premises* which are evaluative. Specifically, the argument implicitly assumes that life is good and that poverty and human suffering are bad—if we do not assume these things, then the conclusion that communism is bad does not follow. Now, these assumptions may be perfectly reasonable, but they are, nevertheless, evaluative premises; therefore, the argument in question is not an example of a derivation of an evaluative conclusion *from wholly non-evaluative premises*.[16] A similar point applies to all of the familiar ways in which we typically argue for evaluative conclusions; we generally argue that *x* is good by presupposing some evaluative standards. If we know that *y* is good, then we may argue that *x* is good by showing that *x* leads to *y*. If we know that people should do *A* when in circumstances of type *C*, then we may argue that *S* should do *A* by showing that *S* is in *C*.

This shows that some familiar moral arguments fail to bridge the is-ought gap. But what justifies the general conclusion that no argument can possibly do so? I think the initial justification for Hume's Law is intuitive: it simply is very difficult to see, on the face of it, how some mere description of how the world in fact is (in non-evaluative respects) could rule out some otherwise possible value system. It is equally difficult to see how a nihilist who recognized the natural properties of things but failed to value anything could be convicted of contradicting himself; it seems that nihilism would always remain a coherent position in the face of any purely natural facts. I do not say that it would be a *plausible* or *justified* position, but it would be coherent.

Another reason philosophers have given for the existence of the is-ought gap is that it is just a special case of a general principle of logic: one cannot validly deduce a conclusion that applies a predicate *P*, from premises that nowhere contain that predicate.[17] This is nothing special about evaluative predicates; it applies to any predicate whatsoever. For instance, one cannot infer a conclusion stating that something is red from premises that nowhere contain the word 'red'.

Before turning to objections to Hume's Law, it is important to understand what I take the doctrine's significance to be. I do not claim that Hume's Law refutes ethical reductionism.[18] Rather, I see Hume's Law as an important lemma in my larger argument that one cannot account for moral knowledge without appealing to something like ethical intuition. To that end, I argue: (a) that we cannot know moral truths by observation, (b) that we cannot know (non-trivial) moral truths by deducing them from non-moral truths, (c) that we cannot know (non-trivial) moral truths by conceptual analysis, and (d) that we cannot know moral truths by scientific reasoning or inference to the best explanation. This understanding of the use I make of Hume's Law has implications for how we should treat alleged exceptions to the Law: such exceptions are important only if they represent possible ways of *coming to know* moral truths on the basis of non-moral truths. Thus, if there should prove to be a valid deductive inference containing only non-evaluative premises and an evaluative conclusion, but for some reason this inference could not be the source of our knowledge of the conclusion, then it would be irrelevant to my purposes here. It would be an exception to Hume's Law as traditionally stated, but not one that damages my argument in this chapter.

### *4.3.2 Searle's challenge

John Searle asks us to consider the following sequence of statements:

1. Jones uttered the words, 'I hereby promise to pay you, Smith, five dollars'.
2. Jones promised to pay Smith five dollars.

3. Jones placed himself under (undertook) an obligation to pay Smith five dollars.
4. Jones is under an obligation to pay Smith five dollars.
5. Jones ought to pay Smith five dollars.

(1) by itself does not entail (2); in order to conclude that Jones promised to pay Smith five dollars, we must have a body of background knowledge about the conventions in Jones' society (those that determine the meanings of Jones' words, how promises are made, etc.) and the circumstances of Jones' utterance (Jones was not joking, reading lines for a play, etc.). But this additional information consists entirely of natural facts. So let us just imagine that this information is all added to the premises of the argument, and ask whether the argument then would bridge the is-ought gap.

(3) follows from (2), Searle says, because it is part of the concept of promising that a promise is the undertaking of an obligation; this is what distinguishes promising to do something from merely predicting that one will do it or expressing an intention to do it.

From (3) it follows at least that *other things being equal* (provided nothing else happens to remove the obligation), Jones is under an obligation to pay Smith five dollars.

From (4) it follows that, other things being equal (provided there is no more important, conflicting obligation), Jones ought to pay Smith five dollars. Thus, it seems that we can at least get some such conclusion as 'Other things being equal, Jones ought to pay Smith five dollars' from non-evaluative premises.[19]

What is wrong with this argument? To begin with, let us distinguish two senses of 'undertook', which I will call the strong sense and the weak sense. In the strong sense, to undertake an obligation is to successfully place oneself under an obligation, such that it logically follows that one is in fact under an obligation. In the weak sense, to undertake an obligation is, roughly, to *purport* to place oneself under an obligation and/or to agree to accept such an obligation. (The exact analysis is not important here.) A person who undertakes an obligation in the weak sense need not ever actually have an obligation. Consider an analogy: suppose you call me collect, and I agree to accept the charges, but due to a mistake, the phone company never actually charges me. My having 'accepted' the charges does not entail that I ever actually receive the charges. In a similar sense, a person might conceivably 'accept' an obligation without ever actually having the obligation. Why might this happen? Well, suppose, for example, that nihilism is true: that there are no moral properties whatsoever. Then although people frequently 'accept' and 'undertake' (in the weak sense) obligations, their undertakings would always fail to actually place them under obligations.

Of course, I believe that nihilism is false and that we do have obligations to keep our promises. But Searle has not refuted nihilism, and so he has not proven an 'ought' statement. There is no purely natural fact that the nihilist is unable to recognize. The nihilist, confronted with Searle's derivation, should grant that Jones made a promise, when this is understood as the acceptance or undertaking of an obligation in the weak sense; but he should deny that Jones undertook an obligation in the strong sense of successfully placing himself under an obligation.

Searle might argue that the weak notion of undertaking obligations does not do justice to our concept of 'promising'; if so, the nihilist should say, then no one ever really promises; at most we *purport* to promise. The conventions of our society may dictate that saying such words as 'I hereby promise to pay you five dollars' is taken as creating an obligation, but mere conventions cannot make it the case that such things as 'obligations' really exist; we cannot render nihilism false by mere fiat.[20]

## *4.3.3  Geach's challenge

Peter Geach proposes the following alleged counter-example to Hume's Law:

1.  If Evan were to promise to adopt some practice then he would adopt it. (Premise.)
2.  If Evan were to utter sentence $W$, he would be promising to adopt the practice of doing something wrong twice a day. (Premise.)
3.  Nobody should adopt the practice of doing something wrong twice a day. (Premise.)
4.  If Evan were to utter $W$, he would adopt the practice of doing something wrong twice a day. (From 1, 2.)
5.  Therefore, Evan should not utter $W$. (From 3, 4.)[21]

We imagine $W$ to be some such sentence as, 'I promise henceforth to do two wrong things each day', and we imagine Evan to be a person with a very strong commitment to promise-keeping, such that (1) is true. The above appears to be a valid inference from premises (1), (2), and (3) to conclusion (5). (5) is clearly evaluative. (1) and (2) seem to be non-evaluative. If (3) were non-evaluative, the counter-example would seem to be in good order, but in fact (3) is evaluative. Nevertheless, Geach observes that (3) is an analytic truth. By definition, no one should do what is wrong; *a fortiori*, no one should do something wrong twice a day. So at least Geach seems to have shown how to go from non-evaluative statements and/or tautologies to a non-trivial evaluative conclusion.

Geach's example has at least two flaws.[22] First, the argument is invalid. I assume that the inference from (3) and (4) to (5) is valid only if the following is a valid form of inference:

6. $S$ ought not to do $A$.
7. If $S$ did $B$, $S$ would do $A$.
8. Therefore, $S$ ought not to do $B$.

To see the problem with this, imagine the following scenario. Jon is a judge about to pass sentence on Mary, a convicted marijuana dealer. Mary's crime is minor at worst; John, however, has an intense, irrational hatred for all drug users, as a result of which he is determined to sentence Mary to either life imprisonment or death. He *could* sentence Mary to only a brief prison term, but he would not in fact do so. Now consider the following inference:

9.  John ought not to sentence Mary to life imprisonment.
10. If John were to refrain from sentencing Mary to death, then he would sentence Mary to life imprisonment.
11. Therefore, John ought not to refrain from sentencing Mary to death (that is, he ought to sentence Mary to death).

(9) is true because what John *ought* to do is to sentence Mary to a brief prison term at most. (10) is true because of what we have stipulated about John's psychology. But (11) is false. In general, this form of inference is invalid because it is possible for there to be a situation in which what one *should* do is to do $B$ and refrain from doing $A$, but what one actually *would* do after doing $B$ is to do $A$ as well. In such a situation, (6) and (7) are true and (8) is false.

The second problem with Geach's example is that the premise, 'If Evan were to promise to adopt some practice then he would adopt it', is evaluative. The relevant reading of (1) is:

$(\forall x)$(Evan promises to do $x$ $\square\rightarrow$ Evan does $x$)

('for all $x$, if Evan were to promise to do $x$, then Evan would do $x$'). This is evaluative because the following substitution instance of it is evaluative:

Evan promises to act wrongly $\square\rightarrow$ Evan acts wrongly.

That is evaluative because, once we fix the natural facts about how Evan would behave upon making such a promise, whether the whole sentence is true then depends on whether that behavior would be wrong. For example, let's suppose that, if Evan were to promise to act wrongly, he would subsequently (thinking these things to be wrong) steal a piece of candy from his five-year-old niece and order a hamburger from McDonald's. Those are the natural facts about how Evan would behave. Whether 'Evan promises to act wrongly $\Box\!\!\rightarrow$ Evan acts wrongly' is true then depends on whether stealing the candy or ordering the hamburger would in fact be *wrong*. If they would, then the quoted sentence is true; if they would not (and no other thing Evan would do would be wrong), then the quoted sentence is false. That is why 'Evan promises to act wrongly $\Box\!\!\rightarrow$ Evan acts wrongly' is evaluative. This is an application of the criterion for evaluative statements developed below in section 4.3.5.

### *4.3.4 Prior's challenge

A. N. Prior offers the following inference allegedly spanning the is-ought gap:

(A)  1. Tea-drinking is common in England.
  2. Therefore, tea-drinking is common in England, or all New Zealanders ought to be shot.[23]

The inference is perfectly valid, 'ought' appears in the conclusion, but it does not appear in the premise.

We might respond by denying that the conclusion is genuinely evaluative. But this would only open up the possibility of a different inference bridging the is-ought gap:

(A')  1'. Tea-drinking is not common in England.
  2. Tea-drinking is common in England, or all New Zealanders ought to be shot.
  3. Therefore, all New Zealanders ought to be shot.

If (2) is evaluative, then argument (A) spans the is-ought gap; if (2) is non-evaluative, then (A') spans the is-ought gap.

However, this point has little bearing on the problem of moral knowledge, as neither of these inferences provides a plausible general model of moral knowledge. Although (A) may give us knowledge of an 'evaluative conclusion' in some sense, it is not an interesting evaluative conclusion. It is not one that, for example, we might use to guide our action, nor does it entail that anything actually has any evaluative property. The conclusion of (A'), on the other hand, is an interesting evaluation—but (A') provides no model for moral knowledge since there is no obvious way in which we could know both of its premises. If (1') were true, then we could readily discover it by empirical means, but there is no apparent way in which we could simultaneously discover (2) to be true without relying on an evaluative assumption.

What would be helpful would be an argument that combined the virtues of (A) and (A'): an argument that started from something obviously empirically verifiable, like (1), and concluded with an interesting, action-guiding evaluation, like (3). But Prior's example suggests no way of constructing such an argument. Obviously, we cannot simply combine the premises of (A) and (A'): that would indeed give us a valid argument from non-evaluative premises to an evaluative conclusion. But since the premises would be inconsistent, this argument would provide no plausible model of how we come to know moral truths.

### *4.3.5 Karmo's proof

The preceding response to Prior may leave one worried: once it has been shown that the is-ought barrier is not in principle impregnable, how can we be sure that every argument penetrating that barrier will prove as useless in accounting for moral knowledge as Prior's example? Can we devise a general proof for some useful form of Hume's Law?

Toomas Karmo has provided such an argument.[24] Assume that there is both a class of *uncontroversially* evaluative statements which clearly attribute evaluative properties to things—such as 'All New Zealanders ought to be shot' and 'Pleasure is good'—and a class of uncontroversially descriptive statements which clearly attribute only non-evaluative properties—such as 'Tea-drinking is common in England'. There are also some statements whose status is initially unclear, such as 'Tea-drinking is common in England, or all New Zealanders ought to be shot' and 'Everything Alfie says is true'. The latter statements, Karmo says, may be evaluative or non-evaluative, depending on what the world is like in non-evaluative respects. For instance, if tea-drinking is in fact common in England, then 'Tea-drinking is common in England, or all New Zealanders ought to be shot' is *non*-evaluative (roughly, because its truth does not then depend on whether New Zealanders ought to be shot); otherwise, the statement is evaluative. Similarly, if Alfie has in fact made some evaluative statements and has made no false descriptive statements, then 'Everything Alfie says is true' is evaluative, since its truth then depends on whether Alfie's evaluative statements were true; other-wise, it is non-evaluative.

Following is a more precise statement of Karmo's idea. Let a 'value system' be a maximal consistent conjunction of uncontroversially evaluative statements (that is, a conjunction of uncontroversially evaluative statements that is consistent and such that no further such statements could be added to it without creating an inconsistency). Similarly, let a 'possible world' be a maximal consistent conjunction of uncontroversially descriptive statements. The 'actual world' is the possible world that is true (the correct description of the world). I assume the following principle, which I shall call the Determinacy Assumption:

Determinacy    A possible world together with a value system are consistent with at most one assignment of truth-values for all statements.

That is, if $w$ is a possible world, $v$ is a value system, and $S$ is any statement, then either ($w$ & $v$) entails $S$, or ($w$ & $v$) entails $\sim S$.[25]

Now, for statements whose status as evaluative or descriptive is initially unclear, classify them as follows: a statement $S$ is evaluative *in possible world w* if, *given w*, the truth-value of $S$ depends on which value system is correct. In other words, $S$ is evaluative in $w$ provided that there are two value systems such that one of them, combined with the uncontroversially descriptive statements in $w$, implies that $S$ is true, while the other, combined with the same descriptive statements, implies that $S$ is false. This characterization yields the result, for example, that 'Everything Alfie says is true' is evaluative in any possible world in which Alfie has made an evaluative statement and has made no false descriptive statements, but non-evaluative in any other possible world.

What we would like to see is whether there can be an argument such that

*i)*  Its premises are actually true,
*ii)*  Its premises are non-evaluative in the actual world,
*iii)* Its premises entail its conclusion,
*iv)* Its conclusion is evaluative in the actual world, and
*v)*  Its conclusion is non-trivial.

Conditions (*ii*), (*iii*), and (*iv*) are required for the argument to count as spanning the is-ought gap. Condition (*i*) is required for the argument to count as a way of gaining knowledge. Condition (*v*) is required for the argument to be interesting vis-a-vis the problem of moral knowledge—the conclusion should not be a mere tautology such as 'Right acts ought to be performed' or 'Bad things are bad' (these statements trivially follow from any set of premises). I assume that an evaluative statement is non-trivial only if there is at least one value system that rejects it.

Now assume for *reductio* that there is an argument satisfying conditions (*i*)-(*v*). Let $P_1$, $P_2$, ... be the premises of this argument, and let $C$ be its conclusion. Let $w$ be the actual world. Then we have the following:

1. $P_1$, $P_2$, ... entail $C$. (Condition (*iii*).)
2. $C$ is non-trivial and evaluative in $w$. (Conditions (*iv*) and (*v*).)
3. There exist value systems $v_1$ and $v_2$ such that ($w$ & $v_1$) entails $C$ and ($w$ & $v_2$) entails $\sim C$. (From 2.)
4. $\sim C$ entails that at least one of $\{P_1, P_2, ...\}$ is false. (From 1.)
5. ($w$ & $v_2$) entails that at least one of $\{P_1, P_2, ...\}$ is false. (From 3, 4.)
6. There is a specific premise in $\{P_1, P_2, ...\}$, call it $P_i$, such that ($w$ & $v_2$) entails $\sim P_i$. (From 5 and Determinacy.)
7. $w$ conjoined with the correct value system entails $P_i$. (From condition (*i*) and Determinacy.)
8. $P_i$ is evaluative in $w$. (From 6, 7.)

Conclusion (8) follows from (6) and (7) because, given $w$, the truth of $P_i$ turns on what the correct value system is—$P_i$ is true according to the correct value system but would be false according to $v_2$. But (8) contradicts condition (*ii*). Thus, there is no argument satisfying all of conditions (*i*)-(*v*).

I take it that Karmo's proof succeeds. However, Stephen Maitzen has objected to the argument.[26] Without going into detail, I note that Maitzen's objection turns on a criticism of Karmo's taxonomy, a criticism that depends on the assumption that nihilism—defined as the thesis that every evaluative statement is false—is logically possible. Among other things, Maitzen argues that Karmo's taxonomy is defective since it implies that the following statement is evaluative in every possible world:

B. Every evaluative statement is false, or torturing babies is wrong.

According to Karmo's taxonomy, this is evaluative in every possible world, since there is always a value system that makes the statement true (any value system that forbids baby-torture makes (B) true) and another value system that makes the statement false (any value system that endorses baby-torture will make both disjuncts of (B) false). But Maitzen says the statement should be classified as non-evaluative in at least some possible worlds, for:

1. Nihilism is logically possible. (Premise.)
2. Nihilism entails (B). (By ∨-introduction.)
3. Therefore, it is possible that nihilism and (B) both hold. (From 1, 2.)
4. In any possible world in which nihilism and (B) both hold, (B) is non-evaluative. (In such a world, every evaluative statement is false, since nihilism holds. But (B) also holds, so (B) must not be an evaluative statement.)
5. So there is at least one possible world in which (B) is non-evaluative. (From 3, 4.)

This example, Maitzen says, 'immediately falsifies Karmo's taxonomy of ethical sentences'.[27]

Maitzen is mistaken because nihilism—understood as the thesis that every 'evaluative statement' *in Karmo's sense* is false—is logically impossible. One reason for this is that nihilism itself seems to be an evaluative statement;[28] therefore, in denying all evaluative statements, it contradicts itself. Another reason is that in any possible world, both 'Torturing babies is wrong' and 'It is not the case that torturing babies is wrong' are evaluative statements in Karmo's sense. But it is logically necessary that at least one of these two statements be true. So it is logically impossible that all evaluative statements be false. Of course, nihilism in some *other* sense might be logically possible—for example, perhaps it is possible that nothing has an evaluative property. But this would not refute Karmo's argument. Similarly, it might be that Karmo's sense of 'evaluative statement' differs from established usage—certainly it differs from Maitzen's usage—but this would not show Karmo's argument to be unsound either. In general, there is no question of 'falsifying' Karmo's characterization of evaluative statements, as long as that characterization is understood—as I believe it should be—as a stipulative definition.

Given that the definition is purely stipulative, one may legitimately wonder whether Karmo's proof is relevant to what we were initially interested in—in particular, does Karmo's version of the is-ought gap help to establish that there is a problem in accounting for moral knowledge? I think it does. Karmo shows that there is no way of knowing evaluative statements by deduction from non-evaluative statements, in his sense of 'evaluative statements'. But Karmo's sense *includes* all the statements traditionally considered 'evaluative' by moral philosophers; thus, if it is difficult to know evaluative statements in Karmo's sense, it is also difficult to know evaluative statements in the traditional sense. Nor does Karmo appear to have expanded the sense of 'evaluative statement' so much that we might know some evaluative statements, for example, by observation: in Karmo's sense, an evaluative statement is one whose truth, once all the descriptive facts are fixed, still turns on which value system is correct. Barring appeals to such things as moral intuition, it remains difficult on the face of it to see how we might know such statements non-inferentially. Since Karmo has shown that we also cannot in general know such statements by deduction from non-evaluative statements, there is an interesting problem of moral knowledge.

In the next section, we consider attempts to show that we can know evaluative truths by *non*-deductive inferences from non-evaluative truths.

## 4.4  Synthetic reductionism

*Synthetic Reductionists* appear to escape the Open Question Argument.[29] They maintain that there is some true statement of the form, 'For a thing to be good is . . . ', where the ellipsis is filled in using non-evaluative terms. But they admit that as Moore showed, what fills in the ellipsis will not be *synonymous* with 'for it to be good'. Consider some analogous cases:

> For a thing to be hot is for its molecules to have high average kinetic energy.
> For a substance to be water is for it to consist of $H_2O$ molecules.
> For a thing to make a sound is for it to cause a compression wave in the surrounding medium.

Quibbles aside, all of those statements are true. But they cannot be verified solely by considering the meanings of the words 'hot', 'water', and 'sound' in English. People knew these words and used them in the same sense we presently do for centuries without knowing the facts expressed by the above statements. Very specialized observations and scientific reasoning were required to confirm those facts. Just so, says the synthetic reductionist, we will someday find (if we have not already found) a theory of what it is for something to be good, and that theory will not be known simply on the basis of the meaning of the word 'good' in English. Instead, it will be known in a way analogous to how the above statements are known to be true, by a kind of inference to the best explanation.[30]

In this section, I argue that the synthetic reductionists' account of moral knowledge fails: no theory about the nature of goodness can be known in any manner analogous to how the above theories of heat, water, and sound are known. In the end, the synthetic reductionist will have to appeal to ethical intuition, just as the intuitionists do. This deprives their position of one of its central alleged advantages.

### 4.4.1 Can moral facts be known by observation?

The analogy just drawn between ethical reductionism and various scientific theories plays a fairly serious role in motivating synthetic reductionism. But the analogy fails at a crucial point.

Suppose we are speaking to a synthetic reductionist who holds that for a thing to be good is for it to be $N$, where $N$ is some natural property, or for short:

Good = $N$.

The reductionist says this is analogous to the theories mentioned above, which I shall abbreviate as follows:

Heat = Molecular kinetic energy.
Water = $H_2O$.
Sound = Compression waves.

In each of these cases, we have two *different concepts* that *refer to the same phenomenon* (the concept 'water' is different from the concept '$H_2O$', but there is one thing in reality that both these concepts pick out). In each case, the concept on the left hand side is observational (we can apply it to a thing on the basis of observation), while the concept on the right hand side is theoretical (we apply it to a thing on the basis of inference, including an inference to a scientific theory) and is taken to *explain the nature of* the phenomenon in question. Thus, we knew that things were *hot*, initially, because we could feel heat with our hands. We know that things have *molecular kinetic energy* on the basis of complex inferences from observational data to the molecular theory of matter, and so on. The idea of molecular kinetic energy is thought to explain the underlying nature of heat. Similarly, we know that there is water on the basis of casual observation, but we know that there is $H_2O$ on the basis of complex scientific reasoning. And 'H₂O' explains the underlying nature of water.

Now, in the reductionist's analogy, which term is 'good' supposed to be analogous to: the term on the left hand side of the '=', or the term on the right? Is 'good' supposed to be like 'heat' or like 'molecular kinetic energy'? Initially, it seems that 'good' is supposed to be analogous to 'heat', because the reductionist's theory is supposed to explain the underlying nature of goodness in terms of natural properties, just as the scientific theory explains the underlying nature of heat in terms of motions of molecules. Certainly ethical reductionists do not take themselves to be explaining the underlying nature of some natural properties in terms of moral properties.

This suggests that moral concepts should be observational, just as 'heat', 'water', and 'sound' are. The reason why we believe, for example, that water = H₂O is, roughly, that (*i*) we have independent (that is, pre-theoretical), direct awareness of the presence of water, and (*ii*) the theory that this substance of which we are aware is composed of H₂O molecules helps explain many of its observable features (again, features of which we know independently of our scientific theory). If we are to take the synthetic reductionist's analogies seriously, then, we should say that we have independent, direct awareness of the presence of goodness, and that the theory that goodness is identical with *N* helps explain many of the observable features of goodness.

The problem is that in fact, moral properties are entirely unobservable.[31] Moral value does not look like anything, sound like anything, feel (to the touch) like anything, smell like anything, or taste like anything. The only plausible way to maintain that we have direct awareness of moral facts would be to appeal to either 'ethical intuition' or a 'moral sense'—which is precisely the sort of 'mysterious', 'spooky' thing the reductionist wants to avoid.

Gilbert Harman discusses an alleged example of moral observation.[32] You see a group of hoodlums pour gasoline on a cat and ignite it. You immediately think that what they are doing is wrong. According to Harman, 'you do not need to figure anything out; you can *see* that it is wrong'. But this quotation is misleading by itself; Harman does not think that the wrongness of the action somehow modifies the light rays traveling to your eyes, nor does he think that your alleged ability to see wrongness ultimately explains your moral knowledge. Rather, he thinks that you have background moral beliefs, or a moral sensibility, which cause you, upon seeing an event such as the one described, to immediately (without thinking about it) form the belief, 'That is wrong'. Since the 'seeing' of wrongness depends upon prior moral beliefs, it does not aid in the ultimate explanation of how we know moral truths.

Why does Harman consider this a case of observation at all? He seems to think that to 'observe' that *p* is just to form a belief that *p* as a fairly direct result of perception.[33] This is mistaken; a belief formed as a fairly direct result of perception need not be an *observation*. Suppose I am superstitious and whenever I see a black cat, I immediately (without thinking about it) believe that an airplane is going to crash the next day. I am now seeing a black cat. Do I thereby observe a plane crash? No. More is required for observation. For someone to observe that an object is *F*, where *F* is some property, there must be *a way that* F *things look* (or sound, smell, etc.), and the object must look (sound, smell, etc.) that way.[34] For instance, I have a pair of artificial leather shoes. Most people can perceive by touch that they are not leather, because there is a way that real leather feels, and these shoes do not feel that way. The point of interest here is that there is no such thing as *the way that wrongful actions look* or *the way that permissible actions look*. That is why you cannot literally see, with your eyes, that an action is wrong.[35]

Consider another argument for the possibility of moral observation. Michael Moore argues that since moral properties *are* natural properties (per his ethical naturalist stance), and since we may be able to perceive the relevant natural properties, we can therefore perceive moral properties. In short, Moore takes the following argument to be valid:

I can perceive *N*.
Good = *N*.
Therefore, I can perceive goodness.[36]

Before addressing this, I must make a small correction: the relevant question is not whether one can *perceive goodness*; it is whether one can *perceive that a particular thing is good*. These are two different questions, and only the latter bears on the problem of moral knowledge. To illustrate, compare this case: I can see your car (your car reflects light to my eyes, and so on) without being in a position to know that the car is yours. If I could see *that it is your car*, that would enable me to know that it is yours, but merely seeing your car doesn't give me that knowledge. So let us modify Moore's argument as follows:

I can perceive that *x* is *N*.
Good = *N*.
Therefore, I can perceive that *x* is good.

If this inference were valid, Moore would have a viable account of how we can know moral truths. But in fact, the inference is invalid. It has the same form as the following inference:

> I can perceive that $x$ is hot.
> Heat = Molecular kinetic energy.
> Therefore, I can perceive that $x$'s molecules have high average kinetic energy.

Here, I use one of the reductionists' examples against them. The first two premises may be true, but the conclusion is certainly false. For instance, one can perceive by touch that a stove is hot. But one does not, merely by feeling it, perceive that the stove is composed of fast-moving molecules (even though that is really what it is for the stove to be hot). One has to do some sophisticated theorizing to find that out. Similarly, even if Good = $N$, and even if one can perceive that $x$ is $N$, one does not therefore perceive that $x$ is good.[37]

Value facts, then, are unobservable. This is a problem for the synthetic reductionist's analogies: we were able to discover that heat = molecular kinetic energy, only because we could first identify which things were hot by observation. If we have no pre-theoretical knowledge of which things are good, then we cannot discover that Good = $N$ in any analogous way. The situation would be like the following scenario: someone tells you that there is an unobservable property called 'torfness'. You are given no initial information about the nature of torfness or which things in the world, if any, are torf. You are told only that torfness is reducible to some scientific property. Your assignment: figure out which scientific property torfness is reducible to.

It seems clear that you do not have enough information to carry out the assignment. Likewise, with no initial information about the nature of goodness or which things have it, we would have no basis for framing any hypotheses as to what natural property goodness might be reducible to. As we have just seen, observation furnishes us with no such initial information. Nor, according to the naturalists, does intuition. One might be tempted to propose that we simply rely on our common sense beliefs about good and bad. But unless we are justified in thinking these beliefs are generally true, this would be arbitrary, and we have as yet seen no account of why those beliefs are justified. Moreover, if the naturalist could give an account of our initial knowledge of the nature of value or of which things are good, he wouldn't need the story about inference to the best explanation that naturalists have been at such pains to develop (see subsections 4.4.2–4.4.4).

### 4.4.2  Can moral facts be known by inference to the best explanation?

Some reductionists have argued that we are justified in believing moral claims because they provide the best explanations for certain non-moral facts of which we have independent awareness. For instance, the best explanation for why Hitler ordered the Final Solution is that Hitler was depraved; only a depraved person would do such a thing.[38] Furthermore, since we know empirically that Hitler ordered the Final Solution, and our justification for believing he was depraved is that that explains why he ordered the Final Solution, our knowledge that he was depraved is also empirical. In short:

1. Moral claims help explain observable facts. For instance, Hitler's depravity helps explain why he ordered the Final Solution.
2. If a claim helps to explain observable facts, then we have empirical justification for believing that claim.
3. Therefore, we have empirical justification for believing some moral claims, such as that Hitler was depraved.

The conclusion in (3) is to be understood as implying that we can have *purely* empirical justification for believing some moral claims— that is, justification that does not ultimately depend, even partly, upon intuition or any other non-observational source of information.

Most of the discussion in the literature centers on premise (1). There are two main arguments for (1). I call them 'the causal argument' and 'the counterfactual argument'.

The causal argument holds that for $x$ to explain $y$ is for $x$ to be (part of) the cause of $y$. Hitler's ordering of the Final Solution was caused by certain psychological traits of his, such as extreme racism, hatred, and a lack of respect for human life. According to the ethical reductionists, these traits *constituted* Hitler's depravity. Therefore, Hitler's depravity caused his ordering of the Final Solution. (This argument employs the valid principle that if $A$ causes $C$, and $B$ is identical with $A$, then $B$ causes $C$.) Therefore, Hitler's depravity explained his order.[39]

The counterfactual argument holds that $x$ explains $y$ (at least in part) provided the following is true: if $x$ had not occurred, $y$ would not have occurred. Now, if Hitler had not been depraved, he would not have ordered the Final Solution. Since moral facts are reducible to natural facts, if Hitler had not been depraved, he would have to have had different psychological traits from those he actually had— for instance, he would have to have not hated the Jews, or have had more respect for human life, etc. And if that were the case, then he would not have ordered the Final Solution. So his depravity explains (at least in part) why he ordered the Final Solution.[40]

I agree that moral facts can be explanatory; premise (1) is true. But premise (2) is false. To see why, return to the reductionists' favorite analogy: the theory that water = $H_2O$. Imagine a scientist attempting to justify that theory by the means suggested by ethical reductionists. Suppose Lavoisier had published a paper arguing that we are justified in believing that water is composed of hydrogen and oxygen, on the grounds that the presence of such a compound explains certain observable facts. For instance, I have an observable stain on my coffee table that was caused by water. Since water = $H_2O$, we can also say that the stain was caused by $H_2O$. Therefore, $H_2O$ explains an observable fact. Therefore, we have empirical justification for believing in $H_2O$.

Here is another argument. If $H_2O$ wasn't spilled on my coffee table, there wouldn't be a water stain there now. For remember, water consists of $H_2O$, so in order for $H_2O$ not to have been on my coffee table, there would have to have been no water on my coffee table. And if that were the case, there would not be a water stain there now. Thus, the (past) presence of $H_2O$ explains a currently observable fact. So again, we are justified in believing in $H_2O$.

Thankfully, this is not how scientists reason. Here is part of why scientists believe water = $H_2O$: if you apply an electric potential to a sample of water, bubbles of hydrogen form at the cathode. Bubbles of oxygen form at the anode. The mass of water present decreases by the same amount that the mass of hydrogen and oxygen present increases.[41] Furthermore, two parts hydrogen are formed for every one part oxygen (by moles). That is just one of several relevant pieces of experimental evidence, but that will do for illustrative purposes. The moral theorist has no empirical evidence to offer that is analogous to that.

This example suggests that the causal and counterfactual arguments do *not* show how moral claims can be justified, since analogous arguments would not work for scientific claims. But exactly what is wrong with those arguments?

Begin with the causal argument. If ethical reductionism is true, then *moral properties* can cause observable effects. Nevertheless, this would not explain how we know moral claims. For us to know a moral claim on the basis of inference to the best explanation, the *moral claim* would have to explain some observable fact *that could not otherwise be explained.* For instance, we can know that Hitler was depraved by inference to the best explanation, if the claim that Hitler was depraved provides an explanation for some fact that cannot be explained without invoking moral claims. But in fact, the hypothesis of Hitler's depravity does not explain any new facts about his behavior that aren't already explained by non-moral claims about him, such as that he hated Jews, that he had a lust for power, that he lacked respect for human life, and so on. Since the truth of non-moral claims of that kind is not in dispute, the moral explanation is superfluous and provides no justification for adopting any moral theories. This is not to say, of course, that we have no justification for our moral claims about Hitler; if we were *already* justified (perhaps on the basis of moral intuition) in accepting moral theories such as that mass murderers are evil, then we can infer that Hitler was evil. The point is that neither our general moral theories nor our moral judgments about Hitler can be established solely on the basis of observation.

The same applies to the counterfactual argument. Given that racial hatred and so on constitute depravity, it is true that had Hitler not been depraved, he would not have acted as he did. But we can explain Hitler's behavior equally well without saying that racial hatred and so on constitute depravity: had Hitler lacked racial hatred, power lust, and so on—whether or not these things constitute depravity—he would not have acted as he did. So moral assumptions add no explanatory power.

To confirm this diagnosis, recall the water/$H_2O$ example. The water stain on my coffee table fails to confirm the past presence of $H_2O$, since the hypothesis that $H_2O$ was spilled on the table does not explain any *new* fact that was not already explicable merely by the hypothesis that water was spilled on the table. But the electrolysis experiment confirms that $H_2O$ is present, because the hypothesis that $H_2O$ is present explains where the hydrogen and oxygen are coming from. That is *not* explained merely by the hypothesis that *water* is present, without assuming that water is composed of hydrogen and oxygen.

### *4.4.3   Can moral claims be tested?

Perhaps moral claims are justifiable because they make empirical predictions that can be tested. For instance, the two moral claims 'Hitler was an admirable person' and 'No admirable person would kill millions of people' together entail the following prediction: 'Hitler would not kill millions of people'. This prediction is testable and, as a matter of fact, false. So we see that moral claims are testable just as scientific theories are.

In case you are tempted to object that neither moral claim *by itself* entails any testable predictions, Nicholas Sturgeon reminds us that it is also true that individual scientific claims do not, in general, entail any testable predictions by themselves; normally a scientific theory makes a testable prediction only given a large background of other scientific knowledge.[42]

Even granting the last point, it does not seem that this accounts for moral knowledge. Imagine that Lavoisier had argued analogously: Collections of claims about $H_2O$ entail testable predictions. For instance, the pair of claims 'Water = $H_2O$' and '$H_2O$ boils at 212°F' together entail the testable prediction, 'Water boils at 212°F'. Since the latter prediction is in fact true, my $H_2O$ beliefs thereby receive confirmation.

The problem is that not all predictions made by a theory create ways the theory can be usefully confirmed. If each prediction is made with the help of a separate *ad hoc* posit, then the theory's success at prediction will be unimpressive. Thus, the 'Water = $H_2O$' theory can make a series of testable predictions about the nature of water, if we add to it the *ad hoc* suppositions that $H_2O$ would be a clear, odorless liquid, that it would boil at 212°F, and so on; but the success of these predictions is evidentially nugatory. In contrast, the idea that water = $H_2O$ naturally suggests that water should be decomposable into hydrogen and oxygen in a 2:1 ratio; this prediction requires no *ad hoc* posits.

The predictions made by moral theories all appear to require *ad hoc* posits. The moral theory that killing millions of people is wrong enables us to predict that Hitler won't kill millions of people, only if we make the unmotivated assumption that Hitler is morally admirable (or at least not evil). But the possibility of deriving predictions from an *arbitrary* combination of moral statements is of no epistemological interest.

Sturgeon gives another example. The pair of claims, 'Injustice causes political instability' and 'Natural property $X$ constitutes injustice' together entail that $X$ causes instability.[43] Provided $X$ is independently detectable, this is a testable prediction. Here, Sturgeon's assumption that injustice causes instability does not seem *ad hoc*; it seems like a natural assumption about the nature of injustice. But why? Presumably because we assume (a) that people can typically identify injustice, and (b) that they object to it. Given these assumptions, when injustice is widespread in a society, it is natural to expect that the society will be politically unstable. If people had no means of moral knowledge to begin with, then there would be no reason to expect that moral properties would be correlated to their behavior in any interesting way.

The problem now is that our ability to make a prediction based on moral claims in this case depends on our assuming that people already have some way of gaining reliable moral beliefs. And what might that be? If we accepted that people have a reliable faculty of moral intuition, say, or that people can observe moral facts, or that they can deduce moral facts from non-moral facts, then we could accept this. But the synthetic reductionist rejects the first possibility, and we have rejected the latter two already. Moreover, if the reductionist could answer this question, then he wouldn't *need* the present argument—he would already have an account of moral knowledge.

In sum, if we are given all the non-moral properties of a thing, the additional hypothesis that one of those properties constitutes *goodness*, say, does not seem to naturally generate any *new* predictions about what we should observe, without a separate *ad hoc* posit for each desired prediction. Consequently, starting from a system of purely non-moral beliefs, we would not be justified in adding any moral beliefs. There is one exception: it seems natural and not *ad hoc* to expect that intelligent beings will by and large pursue the good, feel gratified when it is obtained, and so on. But this prediction depends upon the prior assumption that people have some independent means of detecting moral properties, so it is of no use in accounting for the origin of moral knowledge.

### *4.4.4  The unifying power of moral explanations

Perhaps, despite the fact that they only provide explanations for things we already have non-moral explanations for, moral claims can still be justified because they provide *better* explanations than those formulated using non-moral claims. Michael S. Moore has developed this suggestion, arguing that moral explanations can achieve a kind of unification not otherwise available.

An analogy will help. We find that a certain peg will not fit into a certain hole. On one level, we could try to explain this fact by citing the trajectories of all the atoms in the block and the chemical and other forces acting on each of them. But a more perspicuous explanation would be: 'This is a square peg, and that's a round hole'. The latter explanation is superior in its unifying power: given this explanation, we know what to expect when we try putting another square peg into another round hole (with a diameter less than the diagonal of the square). The atomic-level explanation misses this higher-level regularity: the next square peg we encounter may be made of a different substance and will certainly have a different arrangement of atoms, so on the atomic level, the same explanation will not apply to it; we will have to give a distinct explanation in each case. In contrast, the 'square peg, round hole' explanation identifies the essential feature common to all these situations.[44]

Now, suppose the property of goodness is identical with some disjunction of natural properties, that is,

Good = (F or G or H),

where 'F', 'G', and 'H' are non-evaluative terms. And suppose there is some effect, E, which occurs whenever *any* of F, G, or H is present. In that case, although the occurrence of E on a given occasion might be explained by citing the presence of F, the *better* explanation would be the one that cites the presence of goodness. For the latter explanation would achieve a kind of unification the former explanation does not—it enables one to correctly predict what will happen when another instance of goodness occurs.[45]

The crucial question here is, how would one come up with the idea that Good = (F or G or H)? Presumably, the mere fact that each of several distinct properties brings about a single effect does not justify identifying goodness with the disjunction of those properties. One might be tempted to appeal to common sense beliefs about which things are good—but that would be to revert to a mistake we have earlier criticized. Since at this point the reductionist has not yet successfully explained how people can access moral reality, he is not entitled to assume that our common sense moral beliefs are reliable. Since no advantage of the proposed moral explanation has been identified other than its unifying power, any equally simple explanation that achieves the same unifying power ought to be equally acceptable. Thus, it would apparently make just as much sense to propose that Bad = (F or G or H). Or why not invent some other, non-evaluative concept, say 'torfness', and say that Torf = (F or G or H)—why not, in other words, say that (F or G or H) is identical with a single property, but that property is not evaluative?

Synthetic reductionists concede that the *meaning* of an evaluative term is not captured by any non-evaluative expression. What the questions of the last paragraph illustrate is that the distinctive, positively evaluative meaning of 'good' plays no role in the sort of explanations the reductionist would offer us—since all that matters is that F, G, and H be brought under a single concept, a negatively evaluative concept or a non-evaluative concept would serve just as well. This stands in contrast with legitimate scientific explanations. When the hypothesis that water = $H_2O$ explains the result of the electrolysis of water, the specific meaning of '$H_2O$' ('a compound of two hydrogen atoms and one oxygen atom') plays an essential role. One cannot substitute some entirely different concept, such as 'NaCl', in the theory and still produce an equally good explanation—the hypothesis 'water = NaCl' does not explain the experimental result.

## 4.5   The argument from radical dissimilarity

One argument against ethical reductionism that has received little attention is the argument that, from our grasp of evaluative concepts, we can simply see the falsity of reductionist theories. On the face of it, for example, *wrongness* seems to be a completely different *kind* of property from, say, *weighing 5 pounds*. In brief:

1. Value properties are radically different from natural properties.[46]
2. If two things are radically different, then one is not reducible to the other.
3. So value properties are not reducible to natural properties.

If this argument sounds thin to you, it is probably because you accept one of the following two responses.

First, a reductionist might say that we cannot simply *see* the nature of a thing merely because we have a concept of it. We could not see, merely from our concept of water, that water was identical with $H_2O$. But my argument doesn't assume that we can see *everything* about the nature of those things we have concepts of; it only assumes that we can see *some* things about them, and that in the case of physical and psychological properties, we can see that they are not evaluative. To illustrate, suppose a philosopher proposes that the planet Neptune is Beethoven's Ninth Symphony. I think we can see that that is false, simply by virtue of our concept of Neptune and our concept of symphonies. Neptune is an entirely different kind of thing from Beethoven's Ninth Symphony. No further argument is needed. Indeed, if a person *couldn't* see that Neptune is not a symphony, we would say he either had no idea what Neptune was, or had no idea what a symphony was.

Second, a reductionist might say that the argument, if accepted, would also 'refute' the theory that Water = $H_2O$, for 'water' and '$H_2O$' just seem very different on their face. Similarly, the argument would seem to refute the theory that sound consists of compression waves in the air, because 'sound' and 'compression waves' seem very different.

But this is not so. On the face of it, water *doesn't seem to be* $H_2O$; but it is not the case that water *seems to not be* $H_2O$. Our pre-scientific concept of water takes it to be a clear, odorless, tasteless, etc., liquid. We cannot, on the basis of this concept, discern anything about what its micro-structure might be like. We have no experience of just seeing that there are no tiny particles composing it, and so on. Nor do we have the sense that water is a different *category* of thing from $H_2O$; on the contrary, we see that they are the same category of thing, namely, physical substances.

I would likewise deny that we have an experience of seeing that sound doesn't consist of compression waves, or that they are different categories of things. We can see that they are the same category of thing: physical events. I suggest that *if* you have the intuition that sound obviously can't be a compression wave in the air, then it is because by 'sound' you actually mean *the experience of sound*, which really is a different kind of thing from the compression waves in the air.

The point about the broad category that a thing belongs to is important, because in my view, our having, at least roughly and for the most part, correct intuitions or beliefs about the nature of $x$ is a precondition on our referring to $x$. I can talk about Plotinus without knowing much about him; about all I know is that he was a philosopher who lived a long time ago. But I could not talk about Plotinus if I had completely inaccurate beliefs (allegedly) about him; for example, if I thought 'Plotinus' referred to a cake, then I would not be talking about Plotinus (the person) at all.[47] Similarly, if 'good' seems to us to refer to something of a fundamentally different category from natural properties, then when we say 'good' we are not talking about a natural property.

## 4.6  Explaining moral beliefs

I claim to have shown, in sections 4.2 and 4.5, that evaluative properties cannot be reduced to natural properties. In sections 4.3 and 4.4, I have shown that moral knowledge is not empirical. The structure of this latter argument was as follows:

1. Moral claims are known empirically only if they are known by observation or by either deductive or scientific reasoning from observations. (Premise.)
2. Moral claims are not known by observation. (§4.4.1)
3. Moral claims are not known by deduction from non-moral premises. (§4.3)
4. Moral claims are not known by scientific reasoning from non-moral premises. (§4.4)

5. Therefore, moral claims are not known empirically. (From 1, 2, 3, 4.)

I want to make one final, general point about the prospects for reductionism in ethics. The reason why we believe that such phenomena as heat, water, and sound are reducible is that we have compelling scientific arguments for identifying these phenomena with *specific* theoretical entities. No one doubts the existence of the relevant theoretical entities, because of the systematic power of the scientific theories they belong to in explaining and predicting a host of observable phenomena. Without those theories, no one would believe reductionism about heat, water, or sound.

In ethics, we have no comparable theories in hand. Reductionists typically only *predict* that moral claims will prove to be reducible.[48] They theorize in the abstract about how it might be possible to justify moral beliefs, but without presenting a detailed argument for any specific moral belief. In fact, moral philosophers have labored for two millennia without achieving a consensus on any general moral theory. In such a situation, the reductionist's position raises two questions. The first and more obvious is why we should believe that a reduction of moral terms is possible.

The second is how the reductionist explains people's actual moral beliefs. Even if one of the proposals discussed in section 4.4 were viable, none of them corresponds to how we actually form moral beliefs. If 'good' is a theoretical term like '$H_2O$', shouldn't we expect that the concept would be developed only concurrently with the theory of which it is a part—and that identifiable arguments would have been given before that theory was accepted? Any chemist can identify uncontroversial examples of the sort of observations that molecular theory is needed to explain. Why are so many people unable to identify any of the observations that their moral beliefs are needed to explain? Many professionals in the field deny that there *are* any such observations, and even ethical reductionists will likely admit that the empirical reasoning behind moral theories is subtle and has yet to be clearly articulated. Yet moral beliefs abound in every society in the world, among the young and the old, the educated and the uneducated. Why? Rather than declaring that nearly all moral beliefs are as yet unjustified, shouldn't we look for some much simpler means of gaining moral knowledge?

# Part II
# Ethical Intuitionism

# 5
# Moral Knowledge

In the last three chapters, we have seen that moral claims are assertions about a class of irreducible, objective properties, which cannot be known on the basis of observation. How, if at all, can these claims be known? Is it rational to think any of these claims are true? In the present chapter, I explain how we can know or be justified in believing evaluative statements on the basis of ethical intuition.

## 5.1 The principle of Phenomenal Conservatism

Other things being equal, it is reasonable to assume that things are the way they appear. I call this principle 'Phenomenal Conservatism' ('phenomenal' meaning 'pertaining to appearances'). I have discussed the principle elsewhere, so here I will be relatively brief.[1]

There is a type of mental state, which I call an 'appearance', that we avow when we say such things as 'It seems to me that $p$', 'It appears that $p$', or '$p$ is obvious', where $p$ is some proposition. Appearances have propositional contents—things they represent to be the case—but they are not beliefs, as can be seen from the intelligibility of, 'The arch *seems* to be taller than it is wide, but I don't think it is'. Nevertheless, appearances normally lead us to form beliefs. 'Appearance' is a broad category that includes mental states involved in perception, memory, introspection, and intellection. Thus, we can say, 'This line seems longer than that one', 'I seem to recall reading something about that', 'It seems to me that I have a headache', and 'It seems that any two points can be joined by a single straight line'.[2] All of those statements make sense, using the same sense of 'seems'.

Appearances can be deceiving, and appearances can conflict with one another, as in the Müller-Lyer illusion:

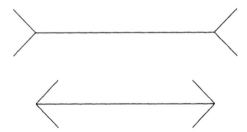

It initially seems that the top line is longer than the bottom line. But if you get out a ruler and measure them, you will find them to be of the same length. The top line will seem, when holding a ruler next to it, to be 2 inches long, and the bottom line will similarly appear to be 2 inches long. So, all things considered, it seems that the two lines are of the same length. As this example illustrates, an initial appearance can be overruled by other appearances (this does not mean the initial appearance goes away, but only that we don't *believe* it), and *only* by other appearances. Some appearances are stronger than others—as we say, some things are 'more obvious' than others—and this determines what we hold on to and what we reject in case of conflict. Presumably, it more clearly seems to you that the result of measuring the lines is accurate than that the result of eyeballing them is, so you believe the measurement result (this may have to do with background beliefs you have about the reliability of different procedures—which would themselves be based upon the way other things seem to you). Things can become complicated when many different beliefs and/or appearances are involved, but the basic principle is that we are more inclined to accept what more strongly seems to us to be true.

Appearances can be intellectual, as opposed to sensory, mnemonic, or introspective. It seems to us that the shortest path between any two points must be a straight line; that time is one-dimensional and totally ordered (for any two moments in time, one is earlier than the other); and that no object can be completely red and completely blue at the same time. I accept those things on intellectual grounds. I am not looking at all the possible pairs of points and all the possible paths connecting each pair and seeing, with my eyes, that the straight path is the shortest in each case. Instead, I am 'seeing' intellectually that it must be true—that is, when I think about it, it becomes obvious.

Logical judgments rest on intellectual appearances. We think the following inference logically valid (the premises entail the conclusion, regardless of whether the premises are true):

Socrates is a man.
All men are inconsiderate.
Therefore, Socrates is inconsiderate.

but the next one invalid:

Socrates is inconsiderate.
All men are inconsiderate.
Therefore, Socrates is a platypus.

We 'see' this, not with our eyes, but with our intellect or reason.

All judgments are based upon how things seem to the judging subject: a rational person believes only what seems to him to be true, though he need not believe *everything* that seems true.[3] The function of arguments is to change the way things seem to one's audience, by presenting other propositions (premises) that seem true and seem to support something (the conclusion) that may not initially have seemed true to the audience. An argument has force only to the extent that its premises seem true and seem to support its conclusion. Intellectual inquiry presupposes Phenomenal Conservatism, in the sense that such inquiry proceeds by assuming things are the way they appear, until evidence (itself drawn from appearances) arises to cast doubt on this. Even the arguments of a philosophical skeptic who says we aren't justified in believing anything rest upon the skeptic's own beliefs, which are based upon what seems to the skeptic to be true.

This indicates in brief why I take any denial of Phenomenal Conservatism to be self-defeating. Be that as it may, we have already laid down in chapter 1 that general philosophical skepticism is off the table in the present discussion. Since all judgment and reasoning presupposes Phenomenal Conservatism, a rejection of Phenomenal Conservatism amounts to a general philosophical skepticism. Therefore, we assume Phenomenal Conservatism to be correct.

## 5.2 Ethical intuitions

Reasoning sometimes changes how things seem to us. But there is also a way things seem to us prior to reasoning; otherwise, reasoning could not get started. The way things seem prior to reasoning we may call an 'initial appearance'. An initial, *intellectual* appearance is an 'intuition'. That is, an intuition that *p* is a state of its seeming to one that *p* that is not dependent on inference from other beliefs and that results from thinking about *p*, as opposed to perceiving, remembering, or introspecting.[4] An ethical intuition is an intuition whose content is an evaluative proposition.

Many philosophers complain either that they don't know what an intuition is or that the term 'intuition' is essentially empty and provides no account at all of how one might know something.[5] I take it that these critics have just been answered.

Some question whether intuitions exist.[6] We have seen some examples of intuitions in the previous section. Here are some examples in ethics:

Enjoyment is better than suffering.
If *A* is better than *B* and *B* is better than *C*, then *A* is better than *C*.
It is unjust to punish a person for a crime he did not commit.
Courage, benevolence, and honesty are virtues.
If a person has a right to do something, then no person has a right to forcibly prevent him from doing that thing.

Prior to entertaining arguments for or against them, each of these propositions seems true. In each case, the appearance is intellectual; you do not perceive that these things are the case with your eyes, ears, etc. And they are evaluative.[7] So the relevant mental states are ethical intuitions.

Here are some examples of ethical claims that, I take it, are *not* intuitive, even for those who believe them:

The United States should not have gone to war in Iraq in 2003.
We should privatize Social Security.
Abortion is wrong.

Though these propositions seem true to some, the relevant appearances do not count as 'intuitions' because they depend on other beliefs. For instance, the sense that the United States should not have invaded Iraq depends on such beliefs as that the war predictably caused thousands of deaths, that this is bad, that Iraq did not have weapons of mass destruction, and so on. This is not to deny that intuition has a role in one's coming to the conclusion that the U.S. should not have gone to war. It is intuition that tells us that killing people is *prima facie* wrong. Intuition is also involved in the weighing of competing values—for instance, we may have intuitions about whether it is right to kill many people in order to depose a tyrant, if the facts of the case are as we believe them to be.

Some think that intuitions are just beliefs, and thus that 'intuition' does not name a way of knowing anything,[8] for we do not want to say that merely by believing something, I know it. A more sophisticated worry is that what we think of as intuitions may be *products of* antecedently existing beliefs, perhaps via subconscious inferences. Perhaps 'Enjoyment is better than suffering' only seems true to me because I already believe it, or believe things from which it follows. There are two replies to these worries. First, the view that intuitions are or are caused by beliefs fails to explain the origin of our moral beliefs. Undoubtedly some moral beliefs are accounted for by inference from other moral beliefs. But since no moral belief can be derived from wholly non-moral premises, we must start with some moral beliefs that are not inferred from any other beliefs. Where do these starting moral beliefs come from? Do we just adopt them entirely arbitrarily? No; this is not the phenomenology of moral belief. We adopt fundamental moral beliefs because they seem right to us; we don't select them randomly.

Second, moral intuitions are not in general caused by antecedent moral beliefs, since moral intuitions often either conflict with our antecedently held moral theories, or are simply unexplained by them. Here are two famous hypothetical examples from the ethics literature:

*Example 1:* A doctor in a hospital has five patients who need organ transplants; otherwise, they will die. They all need different organs. He also has one healthy patient, in for a routine checkup, who happens to be compatible with the five. Should the doctor kill the healthy patient and distribute his organs to the other five?

*Example 2:* A runaway trolley is heading for a fork in the track. If it takes the left fork, it will collide with and kill five people; if it takes the right fork, it will collide with and kill one person. None of the people can be moved out of the way in time. There is a switch that determines which fork the trolley takes. It is presently set to send the trolley to the left. You can flip the switch, sending the trolley to the right instead. Should you flip the switch?[9]

Most people's intuitive answers are 'no' to example 1 and 'yes' to example 2. Some philosophers hold that the morally correct action is always the action with the best overall consequences. Their view implies that the answer to example 1 is *yes*. But even these philosophers, when confronted with the example, admit that their answer is counter-intuitive, that it *seems* wrong to kill the healthy patient and harvest his organs.[10] One's intuitions do not simply follow along with what one *believes* about morality. Relatedly, most people have difficulty explaining why they feel inclined to answer one way in example 1, and the opposite way in example 2; both cases introduce the possibility of sacrificing one person to save five. Philosophers have proposed various explanations of this (which remain controversial). The point is that no moral theory held *prior* to considering cases such as those above is likely to afford us an explanation for why the sacrifice should be found unacceptable in example 1 but acceptable in example 2.

The point that intuition is often independent of belief is important, since it enables intuition to provide the sort of constraint needed for adjudicating between competing moral theories. If intuition simply followed moral belief, then it could not help us decide which moral beliefs are correct. But this point is compatible with intuition's showing *some* degree of responsiveness to our beliefs, and I do not want to claim that a person's intuitions will in general remain entirely uninfluenced by the theories they adopt. Compare the observation that sensory perceptions are largely, but not entirely, independent of our background beliefs—for example, even if I believe Big Foot does not exist, if Big Foot should walk up to me, I will still see him.

Among intuitive moral propositions, some are *more* intuitive than others. Compare the above two examples to the following:

> *Example 3:* As in example 2, except that there is no one on the right fork; if the trolley goes down the right fork, it will run into a pile of sand which will safely stop it. Should you flip the switch?

Everyone answers 'yes' to this one, even those who answered 'no' to example 2. Our intuitions about example 3 are clearer and more certain than those about examples 1 and 2. This gives the belief that you should flip the switch in example 3 a higher level of justification than the corresponding beliefs about examples 1 and 2.

Upon hearing these examples, some people try to deny the intuitions I have noted by posing such problems as: 'In example 1, what if the healthy patient is the future mother of Josef Stalin?' 'In example 3, what if the five people on the left fork are suicidal people who went there to get run over and are just going to go find some other way to kill themselves?' And when considering the intuition that enjoyment is better than suffering: 'What if the enjoyment is a sadistic or perverted pleasure?' The answer to all of these queries is the same: I stipulate that those things are not the case. In all of my examples, all conditions are to be assumed normal unless otherwise specified; likewise, most moral principles have an implicit 'in normal conditions' clause. The purpose of considering such examples is not to initiate a legalistic exercise in searching for loopholes in a statement and ways of filling such loopholes. Our present aim is simply to show the existence and nature of ethical intuitions.

Not all intuitions are equal—some are more credible than others. As the above remarks suggest, one reason for this is that some intuitions are simply stronger, or more clearly seem true, than others. Another reason is that some intuitions are more widely shared than others; other things being equal, an intuition that many disagree with is more likely to be an error than is an intuition that nearly everyone shares. Another reason is that some intuitions have simpler contents than others, and are therefore less prone to error. And there are various reasons why some kinds of intuitions may be more open to bias than others. These facts point to the conclusion that intuitions should not be embraced uncritically, and that conflicting intuitions should be weighed against each other taking into account our best judgments as to their relative levels of reliability. I shall return to this point in the following chapter, when we come to the question of resolving ethical disagreements (sections 6.4 and 6.6).

## 5.3  Misunderstandings of intuitionism

The intuitive propositions we've been discussing are *prima facie* justified. That is, we are justified in believing them unless countervailing evidence should arise that is strong enough to defeat the initial presumption in their favor. Such defeating evidence would consist either of evidence directly against the proposition that intuitively seemed true, or of evidence that our initial intuition was unreliable.

We can now see that at least one objection to intuitionism rests on a misconstrual of the doctrine. Karl Popper writes:

> 'Intuitionism' is the name of a philosophical school which teaches that we have some faculty or capacity of intellectual intuition allowing us to 'see' the truth; so that what we have seen to be true must indeed be true. It is thus a theory of some authoritative source of knowledge.

He goes on to criticize intuitionism on the grounds that intuitions can be mistaken and we should remain open to revising our ethical views.[11] Presumably he thinks intuitionists deny those things, but few if any intuitionists have done so, nor is there any reason why they should.[12] The same misunderstanding may be behind the occasional charge that intuitionism is 'dogmatic'.[13] I do not wish to *rule out* (as Popper does) the possibility of some intuitions' being infallible; I simply deny that they *must* be infallible.

Tara Smith misunderstands intuitionism as the view that all moral truths are 'self-evident'. In fact, intuitionists hold *at most* that *some* moral truths are self-evident,[14] and my own form of intuitionism holds only that some moral beliefs are rendered *prima facie* justified by intuitions. Thus, no problem for intuitionism is generated by citing examples of moral principles that rest on reasoning, nor by citing moral principles that are less than 100 per cent certain. Nor does intuitionism assert 'the irrelevance of argument' in general.[15] Once we have a fund of *prima facie* justified moral beliefs to start from, there is great scope for moral reasoning to expand, refine, and even revise our moral beliefs, in exactly the manner that the contemporary literature in philosophical ethics displays.

Admittedly, critics of intuitionism have not been without excuse in the above misunderstandings.[16] H. A. Prichard, a major figure in twentieth-century intuitionism, at least invited them, and perhaps in his case they were not even misunderstandings:

> This realization of [our obligations'] self-evidence is positive knowledge, and so far, and so far only, as the term Moral Philosophy is confined to this knowledge and to the knowledge of the parallel immediacy of the apprehension of the goodness of the various virtues and of good dispositions generally, is there such a thing as Moral Philosophy.[17]

His use of the term 'self-evidence' encourages Popper's reading (though in fact he says all he means by 'self-evident' is 'non-derivative'), and the rest of the passage encourages Tara Smith's reading. But—leaving aside the interpretive question—a philosopher discussing a theory should address the strongest version of the theory, not the weakest. Granting the justification, on the basis of intuition, of common sense moral principles, there is no motivation stemming from any core assumption of intuitionism for denying that moral philosophy can construct further arguments, arriving at moral truths not immediately evident. The analogy Prichard draws with mathematics should if anything suggest to us that derivative items of ethical knowledge might far outnumber intuitive ones.

Some may think that the *foundationalism* of intuitionism requires a doctrine of infallibility: that is, the idea that we can start from some moral principles, without having to justify them by argument, implies that those moral principles must be infallible, incorrigible, or the like. I have never been able to get anyone to tell me why this would be so.[18] Why may we not hold our starting points open to revision in the event that tensions arise with other justified beliefs? Suppose I seem to see a glass of water on the table. That is enough for me to be justified in believing there is a glass of water, in the absence of any countervailing evidence. However, I may still hold this open to revision: if I reach for the 'glass' and find my hand passing through it, and if a dozen other people in the room say there is no glass there, I may decide there wasn't a glass there after all. As this example illustrates, we normally take perceptual beliefs to be *prima facie* justified, just as the principle of Phenomenal Conservatism dictates. There is no obvious obstacle to holding intuitive beliefs to be justified similarly.

## 5.4  Common epistemological objections

*Objection 1:*
    We need reasons for believing our ethical intuitions, or the faculty of intuition in general, to be reliable. Otherwise, intuitions cannot justify our moral beliefs.[19]

*Reply:*
    What happens if we apply the principle generally: 'We need positive reasons for trusting appearances'? Then we need positive reasons for trusting sense perception, memory, introspection, even reason itself. The result is global skepticism. Nothing can be accepted until we first give a positive reason for trusting that kind of belief. But we cannot give such a reason without relying on sense perception, memory, introspection, reason—or in general, on *some* source. Hence, we shall never be able to trust anything.[20] Of course, this means we also could not trust the reasoning of this paragraph.
    We have stipulated that general philosophical skepticism is not our concern. We are not interested here in discussing the view that no one can know moral truths because no one can know anything whatsoever. One might try avoiding the skeptical threat by recourse to a coherence theory of justification, according to which beliefs are justified by their relations of mutual support with each other, rather than being built up from independently-justified foundations. In my view, there are compelling objections to such a theory, but I cannot discuss them here.[21] For present purposes, let it suffice to say that if

such a theory can succeed in accounting for the justification of our other beliefs, there is no apparent reason why it could not also vindicate moral beliefs. Moral beliefs can mutually support each other as well as any other kind of belief. One might worry about how moral intuition would be worked into such a theory—but then, one might equally well worry about how perception would be worked into the coherence theory. If the coherentist can somehow accommodate the role of perception in the justification of our empirical beliefs, it is unclear why he could not accommodate intuition similarly.

But I don't think proponents of this first objection intend to endorse either coherentism or skepticism in epistemology. Rather, they believe intuition is somehow special, in a way that subjects it to a general demand for justifying grounds, a demand from which perception, memory, introspection, and reasoning are exempt. In view of the principle of Phenomenal Conservatism, it is obscure why this should be so; intuitions are just another kind of appearance, along with perceptual experiences, memory experiences, and so on. Furthermore, we saw examples in section 5.1 of non-moral intuitions that, I take it, nearly everyone would accept. If one accepts *those* intuitions, it would seem arbitrary not to accept ethical intuitions as well, at least *prima facie*.

*Objection 2:*

The problem with intuitions is that we can never *check* whether an ethical intuition is correct, without relying on intuition.[22] In contrast, empirical beliefs can often be checked by other means. If I doubt whether the table I see is real, I can test this by trying to touch it, by asking other people if they also see it, or trying to put a glass on it.

*Reply:*

There are three replies to this objection. First, the objection sounds suspiciously like Objection 1. If we take beliefs to be *prima facie* justified on the basis of appearances, then it is unclear why intuitive beliefs should be thought to require checking, in the absence of any positive grounds for doubting them. If, on the other hand, we reject this conception of *prima facie* justification, then it is unclear how one is supposed to check anything. If belief *A* has no *prima facie* justification, and belief *B* also has no *prima facie* justification, then one can not legitimately 'check on' or 'verify' *A*'s truth by appealing to *B*. Unless we are allowed to take something for granted, nothing can count as verifying anything.

Second, it is doubtful that all of our non-moral knowledge can be checked in the sense required by the objection. I believe I have mental states—beliefs, desires, feelings, and so on—because I (seem to) have introspective awareness of them. I am not sure how I would go about checking on the reliability of introspection by non-introspective means, and I do not believe I have ever done so. Nevertheless, it is quite certain that I have mental states. Likewise, it is unclear how I might go about checking on the general reliability of memory, without relying on memory; on the reliability of inductive reasoning, without relying on induction; or on the reliability of reason in general, without relying on reason.[23] Even the examples given in the statement of the objection might not count as checking an empirical belief *by other means*—if the belief that there is a table here is classified as being based on 'sense perception', then all the suggested means of verifying the belief rely on the same source. This objection, then, is in danger of devolving into general philosophical skepticism.

Third, if one takes a liberal view of what counts as checking a belief—as one must in order to allow most non-moral beliefs to be 'checked'—then it appears that intuitions *can* be checked. I can check my belief that murder is wrong by asking other people whether murder also seems wrong to them. If it is legitimate, as surely it is, to check a perceptual belief in this way, then why should this not be an equally valid check on an intuitive belief? One can also check an intuitive belief by seeing whether it coheres with other intuitive beliefs, just as one can check a perceptual belief by seeing whether it coheres with other perceptual beliefs. Thus, suppose someone reports an intuition that abortion is wrong. He may check on this by (a) seeing whether his intuition coheres with the intuitions of others, and (b) seeing whether his intuition about abortion coheres with his intuition about, say, Thomson's violinist case.[24] These sorts of tests are nontrivial—many intuitions fail them, though many others pass. It is not as though the intuitionist immediately refers every moral question to intuition, with no possibility of further discussion or reasoning.

*Objection 3:*

If we allow moral beliefs to be rested on mere appeals to intuition, then anyone can claim any moral belief to be justified. 'If Thelma could be noninferentially justified in believing that eating meat *is* wrong, then Louise could also be noninferentially justified in believing that eating meat is *not* wrong, even if neither can infer her belief from any reason.'[25]

*Reply:*

When one perceives a physical object, one is *prima facie* justified in believing some things about the object, things that can be perceptually discerned. It does not follow from this that any arbitrarily chosen claim about the physical world is justified. Likewise, I hold that when one has an ethical intuition, one is *prima facie* justified in believing the relevant evaluative proposition; it does not follow from this that any arbitrarily chosen evaluative proposition is justified.

Perhaps the point is that Louise would be justified in thinking that eating meat is not wrong, *if* she were to have a corresponding ethical intuition. Granted, this follows from my theory. It is also true that *if* someone *were* to look up at the sky and have a visual experience of redness, then they would be *prima facie* justified in believing that the sky is red. What is the problem?

Perhaps the objection relies on the assumption that many people in fact *do* have the intuition that eating meat is not wrong. This would be a problem for someone who wants to maintain that eating meat is wrong, just as it would be a problem for someone who thinks the sky is blue if many people looked up and saw different colors. If this is the objection, then it falls under the heading of the argument from disagreement, to be discussed in chapter 6.

One thing that is *not* a problem for the intuitionist is the possibility of people who indiscriminately claim to have intuitions, perhaps because they don't feel like stating the actual reasons for their beliefs. We have no general technique for forcing people to be sincere and careful. This is regrettable. But it has no bearing on the reality of intuition or its validity as a source of knowledge. Analogously, eyewitnesses can and do exaggerate, make hasty judgments, and outright lie. No one thinks this refutes the validity of sense perception as a means of knowledge. Nor do we charge the philosopher of perception with the task of stopping people from doing those things. No more, then, is it the job of the ethical intuitionist to produce a technique for forcing everyone to be circumspect and honest in their value claims.

*Objection 4:*

John Mackie calls ethical intuition 'queer' and 'utterly different from our ordinary ways of knowing everything else'. 'None of our ordinary accounts of sensory perception or introspection or the framing and confirming of explanatory hypotheses or inference or logical construction or conceptual analysis, or any combination of these' can explain ethical knowledge.[26]

*Reply:*

Given the reality of intuition in general, *ethical* intuition is not very different at all from other kinds of intuition. The only difference between ethical intuitions and non-ethical intuitions is in what they are about—and that cannot be taken as grounds for the queerness Mackie sees, unless we are to reject ethical knowledge merely for being ethical.

Doubtless Mackie would say it is intuition in general that is weird and utterly different from other means of knowing. It is conspicuously absent from his list of our 'ordinary' ways of knowing things. But it is no argument against intuitive knowledge to say that it cannot be accounted for by any of the non-intuitive means we have of knowing things.[27] One might as well argue that perception is queer, since perceptual knowledge cannot be accounted for by introspection, intuition, conceptual analysis, or reasoning. The fact is that Mackie has identified no specific feature of intuition that would render it problematic. One suspects that his reference to the 'queerness' of moral knowledge lacks cognitive meaning, serving rather to express his own aversion to such things than to describe any objective feature of it.[28]

Behind Mackie's distaste for intuition there no doubt lies some of the strong empiricist sentiment of twentieth-century philosophy. Empiricism—roughly, the idea that all 'informative' knowledge, or knowledge of the mind-independent, language-independent world, must derive from sense perception—has been fashionable for the last century, though less so, I think, in the past decade. I cannot do justice to this subject here; nevertheless, I will briefly report how things seem to me. First, it is so easy to enumerate what appear on their face to be counter-examples to the thesis of empiricism, and at the same time so difficult to find arguments for the thesis, that the underlying motivation for the doctrine can only be assumed to be a prejudice. Second, I think that in the last several years, if not earlier, the doctrine has been shown to be untenable.[29] Here, I will give two of the better-known counter-examples to empiricism.

*First example:* Nothing can be both entirely red and entirely green.[30] How do I know that? Note that the question is not how I came upon the concepts 'red' and 'green', nor how I came to understand this proposition. The question is why, having understood it, I am *justified in affirming it*, rather than denying it or withholding judgment. It seems to be justified intuitively, that is, simply because it seems obvious on reflection. How else might it be justified?

A naive empiricist might appeal to my experiences with colored objects: I have seen many colored objects, and none of them have ever been both red and green. One thing that makes this implausible as an explanation of how I know that nothing can be both red and green is the *necessity* of the judgment. Contrast the following two statements:

> Nothing is both green and red.
> Nothing is both green and a million miles long.

We have never observed a counter-example to either statement, so it would seem that the second is at least as well-supported by observation as the first. The second statement is probably true, since we have never observed a green object that is a million miles long, although there seems to be no reason why there *couldn't* be such a thing. We have a clear conception of what it would be like to observe such a thing, and it would not be senseless to look for one. But the first statement is different: we can see that there simply couldn't be a green object that is red, and it seems that no matter what our experience had been like, we would not have said that there was such an object; consequently, it would be senseless even to look for one. These points are difficult to square with the contention that both statements are justified in the same way, by the mere failure to observe a counter-example. Furthermore, suppose it turned out that all or most of your observations of colored objects have been hallucinatory (perhaps, like Neo, you learn that you are living in the Matrix). According to the present empiricist account, you would then have to suspend judgment on whether, in the real world, red objects are sometimes also green. This seems absurd.

For this sort of reason, most of those sympathetic to empiricism are more inclined to claim instead that 'Nothing can be both red and green' is somehow made true by virtue of the definitions of 'red' and 'green'. This is often thought to be an acceptable way of avoiding reliance on intuition. But it is not enough just to make this kind of claim; to make good on it, the empiricist must *produce the definitions* of 'red' and 'green' together with the actual *derivation*, from those definitions, of the statement 'Nothing can be both red and green'. No one has done this; indeed, the project seems stymied at stage one by the absence of any analytical definition of either 'red' or 'green'. It is here that some are tempted to appeal to scientific knowledge about the underlying nature of colors to construct definitions (saying, for example, 'red is the disposition to reflect such-and-such wavelengths of light'). But this approach leads to the absurd consequence that, say, 300 years ago, people were in no position to know whether it was possible for a red object to be green—indeed, did not even understand the meanings of those words—since they did not know the scientific theory of colors.

*Second example:* I know that 'Socrates is a man' and 'All men are chauvinists' together entail 'Socrates is a chauvinist'. How do I know that? One might say I know it because I know a general rule that all inferences of the form '$x$ is an $A$; all $A$'s are $B$; therefore, $x$ is $B$' are logically valid—but, in the first place, this would only push the question to how I know that rule to be valid, and in the second place, it would only introduce another inference I have to make: 'All inferences of such-and-such form are valid; this inference is of that form; therefore, this inference is valid'. So that is no help. Nor should one say that logical judgments in general are based on arguments, since the validity of the latter arguments would then have to be ascertained, leading to a problem of circularity or infinite regress.[31] Nor, finally, are logical judgments known by observation—the validity of a piece of reasoning is not seen with the eyes, heard with the ears, etc. It seems that intuition is the only remaining possibility. Moreover, upon introspecting, we notice that we do in fact have logical intuitions, and that they do in fact make us think some inferences to be valid.

This sort of example is particularly interesting, since all reasoning depends upon principles of logic. Any kind of reasoning thus depends upon intuition, including the reasoning the reader is doing at the moment, and including any reasoning that might be deployed to impugn the reliability of intuition.

One possible response to this argument is that we need not have *a priori* knowledge of truths of logic, such as that a given inference is valid; instead, it would be enough for us to have an innate *disposition* to *make* valid inferences. While this response may undermine the claim that all reasoning depends upon intuitions, it does not obviate the need for intuition at some stage, for the simple reason that we do in fact know the principles of logic, and this knowledge must still be accounted for. I take it that one cannot, without some undesirable form of circularity, argue that a certain inference form is valid using an argument of that very form; hence, the point remains that knowledge of the rules of inference cannot in general be inferential.

As with the previous example, some would argue that the rules of logic are made true 'by definition' or by some sort of conventions. The idea that the truth of the laws of logic is convention-dependent would seem to suggest that we could have made conventions or stipulations in such a way that (without changing the meanings of any of the following words), the following inference would have been *invalid*:

> Socrates is a man.
> All men are mortal.
> Therefore, Socrates is mortal.

and the following would have been *valid*:

> Socrates is a man.
> Therefore, Socrates is immortal.

For Socrates' sake, I think we should shift to conventions of that kind.

We *could*, of course, change the use of the *word* 'valid' by convention. But that is irrelevant; we could similarly change the use of the word 'teeth' by convention, but no one takes this to show that the fact that sharks have teeth is in any relevant sense conventional. (If you are ever pursued by a shark, I do not advise you to pin your hopes on a timely change in linguistic conventions.) *Any* true statement could be converted to a false one by a suitable change in the meanings of the words it contains. The question is whether the *fact* that the statement expresses is dependent on a convention—that is, whether, once the meaning of the statement is fixed, convention plays some *further* role in determining whether what is said is true. The test of that is whether we could render the statement false by a change in some convention, without changing what the statement means.[32] For example, consider:

A. People in the United States drive on the right-hand side of the road.

Statement (A) is made true by convention in a substantive sense: there is a convention beyond those determining the meanings of the words in (A) that goes into making (A) true, namely, our convention of driving on the right side of the road. If we eliminated this convention, (A) would be rendered false, with no change in its meaning. Now contrast:

B. The syllogism, 'Socrates is a man; all men are chauvinists; therefore, Socrates is a chauvinist', is valid.

Statement (B) is obviously not convention-dependent in that way.

The meanings of the words in (B) depend on conventions, as is the case with all statements. But no other conventions are relevant to the truth of (B). We cannot render (B) false by changing any conventions, without changing the meaning of (B). The same is true of all logical principles. The laws of logic are thus examples of non-conventional, objective facts that are known independently of experience.

That will have to do for an overview of some of the difficulties for empiricism. Others have dealt with this issue more thoroughly and conclusively. But this should suffice to make clear why Mackie is not entitled to take empiricism for granted as a premise from which to attack intuitionism.

## 5.5   The implausibility of nihilism: a Moorean argument

Nihilism holds that nothing is good, bad, right, or wrong. I have said enough to show why we are *prima facie* justified in rejecting this. A nihilist might accept this point but maintain that there are nevertheless strong arguments for nihilism that overcome the initial presumption against it.[33] In the last section we saw some objections a nihilist might raise against realism, and we will see others in later chapters. What I argue in this section is that the presumption against nihilism is very strong, so that the arguments for nihilism would have to be extremely powerful to justify the nihilist's position.

So far, I have focused on the qualitative point that many moral beliefs have *prima facie* justification. But justification comes in degrees: my justification for thinking that China exists is stronger than my justification for thinking that the theory of evolution is true, which is stronger than my justification for thinking that tomorrow will be sunny. What determines the *degree* to which an intuitive belief is *prima facie* justified? If one accepts Phenomenal Conservatism, the natural view to take is that the more obvious something seems, the stronger is its *prima facie* justification. Very clear and firm intuitions should take precedence over weak or wavering intuitions.

Now consider in outline one of the arguments for nihilism:

1. Moral good and bad, if they exist, would be intrinsically motivating—that is, things that any rational being would necessarily be motivated to pursue (in the case of good) or avoid (in the case of bad).
2. It is impossible for anything to be intrinsically motivating in that sense.
3. Therefore, good and bad do not exist.[34]

More needs to be said to properly assess each of those premises, but I won't say it now. Right now I just want to use this argument to illustrate a general epistemological point. Given the nihilist conclusion in (3), one could validly infer such further conclusions as:

4. It is not the case that a nuclear war would be bad.
5. It is never the case that enjoyment is better than excruciating pain.

And so on.

Now, just as someone who accepted (1) and (2) might be moved by the above reasoning to accept (4) and (5), a realist might argue against (1) and (2) as follows:

1'. A nuclear war would be bad.
2'. Enjoyment is sometimes (if not always) better than excruciating pain.
3'. Therefore, good and bad *do* exist.
4'. Therefore, either
   a. Good and bad need not be intrinsically motivating, or
   b. It is possible for something to be intrinsically motivating.

Some would charge this realist argument with 'begging the question' against nihilism, since premises (1') and (2') are precisely what the nihilist denies in his conclusion. But this embodies a naive conception of the burdens of dialectic, granting a presumption to whichever argument happens to be stated first. For if the realist argument had been stated first, then we could presumably say that the nihilist argument 'begs the question' against the realist since its premises (1) and (2) (conjointly) are precisely what the realist denies in *his* conclusion. The relationship between the two arguments is symmetric: each argument takes as premises the denial of the other argument's conclusion.[35] How, then, should we decide between them?

The strength of an argument depends upon how well justified the premises are and how well they support the conclusion. Both of the above arguments support their conclusions equally well—both are deductively valid. So of the two arguments, the better is the one whose premises are more initially plausible. Now which seems more obvious: 'Enjoyment is better than excruciating pain' or 'It is impossible for anything to be intrinsically motivating'? To me, the former seems far more obvious. And I do not think my judgment on this point is idiosyncratic. Therefore, it would be irrational to reject the former proposition on the basis of the latter.[36]

To justify his position, the nihilist would have to produce premises more plausible than any moral judgment—more plausible than 'Murder is wrong', more plausible than 'Pain is worse than pleasure', and so on. But some moral judgments are about as plausible as anything is. So the nihilist's prospects look very bleak from the outset.

Finally, a comment on philosophical method. The nihilist argument above, as well as the empiricist argument discussed earlier (section 5.4, Objection 4), evince a kind of rationalistic methodology common in philosophy. The method is roughly this: begin by laying down as obvious some abstract principle of the form, 'No *A* can be *B*'. (For example, 'No substantive knowledge can be *a priori*'; 'No objective property can be intrinsically motivating'; 'No unverifiable statement can be meaningful'.) Then use the general principle as a *constraint* in the interpretation of cases: if there should arise cases of *A*'s that for all the world *look like B*'s, argue that they cannot really be *B*'s because that conflicts with the principle, and seek some other interpretation of the cases. One of the great ironies of philosophy is that this rationalistic methodology is commonly employed by *empiricists*. One might have expected them to adopt the opposite approach: start by looking at cases, and only form generalizations that conform to the way all of the cases appear; stand ready to revise any generalizations upon discovery of counter-examples; treat the *cases* as a constraint on the *generalizations*.

My method is something between those two: begin with whatever seems true, both about cases and about general rules. If conflicts arise, resolve them in favor of whichever proposition appears most obvious. Roughly speaking, we want to adopt the coherent belief system that is closest to the appearances, where fidelity to appearances is a matter of how many apparently-true propositions are maintained, with these propositions weighted by their initial degree of plausibility. We can call this the method of reflective equilibrium.[37,38] The method of reflective equilibrium leads us to endorse some moral judgments. It is highly unlikely that it could ever lead us to endorse nihilism, as the latter requires a rejection of our entire body of moral beliefs. Indeed, it would be hard to devise a theory *less* faithful to the appearances.

## 5.6  Direct realism and the subjective inversion

I turn to another epistemological objection to intuitionism, which will help clarify intuition's role in producing knowledge. Consider a pair of statements of the form,

1. *S* has an intuition that *p*.
2. *p*.

where *S* is some person and *p* is some proposition. The intuitionist claims that (1) plays some role in the justification of (2) (at least for *S*). But how? Not only does (1) fail to logically imply (2), but they typically do not even belong to the same subject matter. Suppose *p* is the proposition that the shortest path between two points is a straight line. Then (2) is a geometrical statement; it says something about the structure of space. (1) is not a geometrical but a psychological statement; it says only that someone has a certain mental state. What *relevance* could (1) possibly bear to (2)?

Things would be alright if we could argue that, notwithstanding their logical independence, (1) renders (2) *more probable*. But how would the occurrence of some mere subjective mental state render probable a proposition about the external world? The obvious suggestion is that it would do so if we had reason to believe the mental state was a *sign* of the external fact—in other words, that in general, when *S* has an intuition that *p*, *p* is usually true. In order to ascertain that, it seems that we would need to observe a number of cases in which a person had an intuition, compare these intuitions with the facts, and see whether there is generally a correlation. The problem in this process is the stage of comparing the intuitions with the facts. If, as intuitionists seem to think, we have no access to the relevant facts without using intuition, then no such comparison can be made. Therefore, it is impossible to tell whether an intuition that *p* is a sign of *p*'s truth or not.

This, my opponent would argue, exhausts the ways in which (1) might be relevant to the justification of (2). The point of worrying about the 'justification' of beliefs is that we want our beliefs to be by and large true; a justified belief is a belief formed in such a way as to render it at least probable that it is true.[39] (1) does not guarantee the truth of (2), nor have we any reason for believing that it increases the probability that (2) is true. So it apparently has nothing to do with the justification of (2).

Perhaps those who resist intuitionism have something like this in mind;[40] perhaps this is what really underlies the fallacious objections of section 5.4. Those who make this argument would object to the reliance on intuitions across the board, and not merely to ethical intuitions.

Before discussing *what* is wrong with this argument, I want to make two preliminary points to show *that* it is wrong. The first is that the argument is merely the adaptation to intuition of a classic argument for global skepticism.[41] Consider the statements,

3. I have a sensory experience of $x$.[42]
4. $x$ exists.

where $x$ is some kind of physical thing. (3) does not entail (4); (3) is a mere psychological report, while (4) is a claim about the physical world. Nor can we verify that (3) renders (4) probable. To do so, we would have to compare sensory experience with physical reality on a number of occasions to establish that the one is usually correlated with the other in a particular way. We cannot perform such a comparison, since we have no way of accessing physical reality without relying on sensory experience. Thus, it seems that (3) has no bearing on the justification of (4).

Similarly, consider the statements,

5. I have a memory experience of $e$.
6. $e$ happened.

where $e$ is some putative past event. We can argue that (5) plays no role in justifying (6). (5) is about a present mental state, while (6) is about an entirely distinct (alleged) past event. And we cannot confirm that memories are reliable signs of past events, since we have no means independent of memory of accessing the past.

I think similar arguments apply to all possible kinds of (alleged) knowledge, but I will leave it at those two examples. These two arguments are exactly analogous to the skeptical argument about intuition. Since I assume we wish to endorse neither skepticism about the physical world nor skepticism about the past, we must look for the mistake in the argument.

The second point designed to show that the argument must be wrong is its self-refuting character. Intuitions are not some exotic, theoretical entities invented by a few philosophers. They do not merely play some minor, recherché role, such that we could excise them and our intellectual life would go on pretty much the way it does now. Nor is there some alternative, intuition-independent methodology being implemented by some other group of philosophers. Intuitions are nothing but *initial intellectual appearances*. That is, they are the way things seem, intellectually, prior to argument. They comprise such things as (i) the 'plausibility' of the starting premises of philosophical arguments, (ii) our 'seeing' the logical connection between the premises and the conclusion of an argument, (iii) the general plausibility judgments that run throughout intellectual discourse and reasoning, whether explicitly stated or not. In the skeptical argument with which I opened this section, how is it that we know:

That (1) ('*S* has an intuition that *p*') does not entail (2) ('*p*');
That psychological statements do not entail geometrical ones;
That (1) renders (2) probable only if (1) is a sign of (2);
That (1) is a sign of (2) only if intuitions in general are correlated with the facts;
That we can't verify that intuitions are correlated with the facts unless we have non-intuitive knowledge of the facts;
That (1) plays a role in justifying (2) only if (1) either entails (2) or renders (2) probable?

Of course, attempting to give arguments for these things would simply lead me to ask how we know the premises of those arguments. When you read the skeptical argument as I initially presented it—if the argument sounded reasonable to you—you were 'intuiting' all those things. Intuitions are not something that only a few philosophers, the intuitionists, use; other philosophers merely refrain from *calling* their intuitions 'intuitions'. Accordingly, the idea that there are two ways of proceeding in intellectual discourse—appealing to intuitions, and 'showing one's claims to be true'—is pure confusion. All I can do by way of 'showing something to be true' in an article or book is to write down a series of sentences. The sentences count as showing something only if, when you read them, they seem true (at least some of them) and they seem to support my conclusion.[43] Appealing to intuitions is thus an integral part of showing things to be true, not an alternative to showing things to be true.

The preceding remarks are intended to motivate the search for a flaw in the skeptical argument and to make us receptive to proposed diagnoses. They don't explain what that flaw is. In my view, the flaw consists in a basic misunderstanding of the structure of a foundationalist theory of knowledge. Intuitionism does not hold that from 'I have an intuition that *p*' one may infer '*p*'; nor does the principle of Phenomenal Conservatism hold that 'It seems to me that *p*' is a reason for '*p*'. Those would be claims about *inferential* justification.[44] Phenomenal Conservatism and my version of intuitionism are forms of *foundationalism*: they hold that we are justified in some beliefs without the need for supporting evidence. The role of conditions (1), (3), and (5) in the theory of justification is that of conditions under which certain beliefs—respectively, those expressed by (2), (4), and (6)—*require no evidence*, rather than that of evidence supporting those beliefs.[45] The logical point that (1), (3), and (5) do not provide convincing arguments for (2), (4), and (6) is thus irrelevant to the theory.

Skeptics disagree; global skeptics will deny that there is any condition that enables a belief to be justified in the absence of reasons for it. But I am not writing now to convince global skeptics. I am writing for non-skeptics, to *diagnose* skepticism. The skeptic, I suggest, has a theory about the relationship between consciousness and its objects, according to which what we are immediately aware of must always be an internal, mental state. On this view, when we perceive, we are aware, first and foremost, of sensory experiences; when we remember, we are aware of memory images; when we contemplate abstract matters, we are aware of concepts and intuitions. The function of sensory experiences, memory experiences, and intuitions is thus merely that of pieces of *evidence* from which we attempt to *infer* conclusions about extra-mental reality. The failure of this inference, in turn, is a victory for skepticism.

If we grant the skeptic's starting point, I think the rest of his reasoning is cogent. But that starting point is neither natural nor supported by any good arguments. A more natural view is that we are first of all aware of *things*—that is, external things. Then we reflect on our awareness of those things, whereupon we notice (or perhaps infer) that such awareness involves our having internal states that somehow represent external things. These internal states should not be allowed to supplant the real objects in our philosophy; their central function is that of vehicles of the awareness of external things. The 'subjective inversion' of the skeptic turns cognitive states that were posited to explain our awareness of the world into a veil that blocks our view of the world, and it makes consciousness essentially introverted, contemplating only itself. In contrast, the more natural, 'direct realist' view is that the primary function of sensory experience is to partly *constitute* our awareness of external things, rather than to be an intermediary *object* of awareness. A related idea in the philosophy of perception called 'the transparency of experience' holds that the way we determine the properties of our sensory experiences is by looking at the *objects* we're perceiving; when we try to look at our experiences, we just 'see through' them to the objects they represent.[46]

That is a rough, summary statement of direct realism in the philosophy of perception. What does it have to do with moral philosophy? The intuitionist, I contend, should be a direct realist about ethics. He should not say that intuitions function as a kind of *evidence* from which we do or should infer moral conclusions. He should say that for some moral truths, we need no evidence, since we are directly aware of them, and that awareness takes the form of intuitions; that is, intuitions just (partly) *constitute* our awareness of moral facts.[47] Intuitions are not the objects of our awareness when we do moral philosophy; they are just the vehicles of our awareness, which we 'see through' to the moral reality.

This does not imply that intuition is infallible. Some intuitions may be mistaken, in which case *they* do not constitute direct awareness of moral facts. But this does not prevent the remaining intuitions, those that are true, from constituting direct awareness of moral facts. (Compare: hallucinations do not constitute awareness of physical objects, but this does not prevent normal perception from constituting such awareness.)

The thesis of the transparency of perception, like the parallel thesis of the transparency of intuition, is a phenomenological one: in perception, we find ourselves presented with physical phenomena of various kinds; we do not find ourselves presented with *mental states*. Even if the presentation should be false (as in a hallucination), we would still not be aware of a mental state; we would then merely fail to be aware of anything real, though it seemed as though we were. Likewise, in ethical intuition, as a point of phenomenological fact, we find ourselves presented with moral properties and relationships, not with mental states. This blocks the attempt to construe experiences and intuitions as evidence from which we draw inferences (fallaciously, as it would turn out) about the world.

## *5.7   The isolation of the moral realm

I conclude with a final epistemological objection to intuitionism. Even if moral properties are real, it does not seem that they could *affect* anything. They do not produce physical effects, so they do not affect our brain processes, so they probably do not affect our *mental* processes either.[48] Here is an argument for that: The basic evaluative truths that we intuit are necessary truths, such as 'Enjoyment is intrinsically good'.[49] These facts are atemporal; that is, there is no *change* in the realm of fundamental moral truths. A particular event might become or cease to be good by, for example, becoming or ceasing to be pleasurable; but the abstract fact that *enjoyment is good* cannot cease to obtain. But this means that nothing ever *happens*—there are no *events*—in the purely moral realm. And that implies that the moral realm is causally inert.

Some philosophers maintain that knowledge of a thing requires some kind of interaction with it.[50] For instance, I can have knowledge of the white cat on the sofa because the cat's presence produces an effect on me (it causes me to have a white-cat-representing sensory experience). But moral facts have no effect on me; therefore, I do not know any moral facts.

A closely related argument premises that I know *p* only if, if *p* were not true, I would not believe that it was.[51] But if the moral facts were different from how they actually are, or if there were no moral facts, I would have all the same moral beliefs that I presently have, since the moral facts do not cause my beliefs. Therefore, I do not know the moral facts.

It is easy enough to respond by rejecting the accounts of knowledge assumed in the preceding two paragraphs. There are serious objections to both of them—not least of which is the very fact that they cannot accommodate *a priori* knowledge—and there are several alternative analyses of 'knowledge' available.[52]

But I don't say there is no problem here. There is a more general condition on knowledge that everyone in epistemology accepts: I know *p* only if it is not a mere accident (not a matter of chance) that I am right about whether *p*. The challenge for the moral realist, then, is to explain how it would be anything more than chance if my moral beliefs were true, given that I do not interact with moral properties.

Consider one abortive answer: It is not accidental that my moral beliefs are true, because the moral facts, in general, are necessary; they could not have been otherwise. For instance, there is no possible world in which enjoyment is not intrinsically good. Therefore, it is no accident that I am right when I affirm that enjoyment is good.

To see why this answer is wrong, imagine someone who makes a miscalculation while multiplying 57 by 69, but then makes a second error that just happens to cancel out the first one, so that he comes to the correct answer (3933) anyway. In this case, the thing he believes is necessarily true: there is no possible world in which 57 × 69 does not equal 3933. But it is still accidental that his belief is true. Why? Because making one or two errors in a calculation cannot normally be expected to result in one's coming to the correct conclusion. When we ask why it is non-accidental that a belief is true, what we mean is: how does the way that the belief was formed make it predictable that it would be true?

Now, this problem is not specific to moral knowledge. It is a general problem about *a priori* knowledge. Paul Benacerraf originally raised it as a problem about mathematics: since we have no interaction with the number 2—we do not bump into it on the street, and so on—how can we have knowledge of it? I might plead that it is not the moral philosopher's job to answer this. Whether or not there is moral knowledge, there is *a priori* knowledge of other kinds, so there must be some solution to Benacerraf's problem. Whatever the explanation for *a priori* knowledge in general is, there is no reason to think it would not work equally well for moral knowledge.

I think this would be a fair response. Nevertheless, if I rested with this, some readers would be disappointed and would want to know my view of *a priori* knowledge. Since this is a book neither of epistemology nor of metaphysics, I will give only a brief outline. My view of *a priori* knowledge has four main elements.

*First:* Universals exist necessarily. 'Universals' are abstract things (features, relationships, types) that two or more particular things or groups can have in common. For instance, *yellow* is a universal. It is something that lemons, the sun, and school buses, among other things, all have in common. Yellow is 'abstract' in the sense that it is not a particular object with a particular location; you will not bump into yellow, just sitting there by itself, on the street. Nevertheless, yellow certainly exists. Here is an argument for that:

1. The following statement is true:

   (Y) Yellow is a color.

2. The truth of (Y) requires that yellow exist.
3. Therefore, yellow exists.[53]

Comment: Suppose I say, 'The King of Colorado is fluffy'. Since there is no king of Colorado, some would say the sentence is false; others would say it is neither true nor false. But no one thinks it would be *true*. Similarly, suppose I say, 'God is loving'. This sentence obviously could not be true unless 'God' refers to something—that is, unless God exists. Sentence (Y) is of the same form, so it can be true only if 'yellow' refers to something—that is, only if yellow exists.

Some philosophers (the 'nominalists') say that the only thing multiple particulars have in common is that we apply the same *word* or *idea* to them.[54] Here is an argument against that:

4. Yellow is a color, and lemons have it.
5. No word or idea is a color, nor do lemons 'have' words or ideas.
6. Therefore, yellow is not a word or an idea.

Yellowness is something lemons, the sun, and so on have in common; so what they have in common is not (merely) a word or idea. Some philosophers will say I have oversimplified this issue. I say I have simplified but not oversimplified; the existence of universals is a trivial truth.

*Second:* In having concepts, we grasp (understand) universals.[55] To have the concept of yellow is to understand (at least partly) what yellow is. Grasping comes in degrees: one may grasp something better or worse. An *adequate* grasp of a universal is a concept that is:

i) *Consistent.* For instance, the concept of a round square is inconsistent; accordingly, it does not count as an adequate grasp of a universal. Subtler inconsistencies exist, such as that perhaps involved in the concept of the largest prime number.
ii) *Clear,* as opposed to confused. For instance, someone who has read a little about chaos theory may think that 'chaos' is like 'randomness'. He may, that is, fail to distinguish these two concepts. In that case, his concept of chaos is confused and is not an adequate grasp of the nature of chaos.
iii) *Determinate,* as opposed to vague or unsettled. Imagine someone arguing about abortion. You tell him about the RU-486 pill and ask whether it counts as abortion. He doesn't know. In this case, his concept of abortion is indeterminate; the criteria for applying the concept are unsettled in his mind.

The above characteristics come in degrees; we say a person's understanding is adequate if his concept has these traits to a high degree.[56]

*Third:* Having an adequate grasp of a universal puts one in a position to see that it has certain properties and/or relationships to other universals that you adequately grasp. If you know what yellow is (you adequately grasp yellowness), then you can intuit that yellow is a color. If you know what the numbers two and three are (you adequately grasp two and three), then you can intuit that two is less than three. Anyone who could not see these things would have to have failed to understand the relevant universals. This is not because these things are 'analytic', or true by virtue of the definitions of the relevant concepts, since in my view hardly any concepts are definable (in the philosophers' sense[57]); it is because understanding the nature of a universal inherently tends to cause one to apprehend certain basic facts about it. Of course, not every intuition is essential to understanding the relevant concepts, but a person who has any grasp of a universal will necessarily have at least some correct intuitions about it.

The grounds for the second and third claims above are introspective: introspection reveals that we sometimes understand concepts, and that we sometimes have the experience of seeing something to be true, because of that understanding.

*Fourth:* All *a priori* knowledge is, or derives from, knowledge of the properties and relations of universals. For instance, we know *a priori* that all spinsters are unmarried. This derives from our knowledge that *spinsterhood* contains or implies *unmarriedness*. We know *a priori* that purple is a color: this is knowledge of a property of purple. And we know *a priori* that pleasure is good: this is knowledge of a property of pleasure.

Now, to come back to Benacerraf's problem: the question is, given the way *a priori* beliefs are (at least sometimes) formed, why is it more than accidental that they are true? To begin with, I propose that having a clear, consistent, and determinate concept is *sufficient* for one's grasping a universal or universals. There is no possibility of one's failing to refer to anything (universals are plentiful in this sense, and their existence is necessary).[58] Notice, however, that the defining characteristics of an adequate grasp are *intrinsic*—consistency, clarity, and determinacy belong to the nature of a concept in itself, as opposed to depending on relationships between the concept and something else. So the intrinsic characteristics of a concept sometimes are sufficient for its constituting an adequate understanding of the nature of a universal. Furthermore, adequately grasping a universal cannot cause false intuitions about it.[59] Therefore, in some cases—namely, when one's intuitions are caused (only) by clear, consistent, and determinate understanding—the internal process by which one forms beliefs guarantees their truth.

Some will say that 'guarantees' is too strong; all I need say is 'renders highly probable'. But I think the 'guarantee' claim is correct. Notice that the claim is not that all intuitions are true. Nor is the claim that all intuitions of a person who adequately grasps the relevant concepts are true. As we shall see in chapter 6, there are many ways we can go wrong. The claim is that *adequately grasping a concept* cannot itself cause a mistake. In other words, if a person has a false intuition, this false intuition must be caused by something else—by misunderstanding, bias, confusion, or the like. It is consistent with this that there be many false intuitions. This would not undermine my claim to solve Benacerraf's problem. The problem was to explain how the way in which some *a priori* beliefs are formed makes it predictable that they would be true. Beliefs that are formed by processes involving bias, confusion, etc., are formed in a different way from beliefs that are caused by adequate understanding without such bias, confusion, and so on. The unreliability of the former sort of beliefs is therefore no bar to the latter sort of beliefs' counting as knowledge.

The above is not a theory of the *justification* of *a priori* beliefs. My view is *not* that one justifies *a priori* beliefs by going through the reflections I just have. Rather, my theory of justification was given in sections 5.1–5.2. The above was addressed to a distinct problem, the problem of why, even if true and justified, our moral beliefs would not be merely *accidentally* true.[60]

# 6
# Disagreement and Error

I claim to have refuted, in the last four chapters, four of the five theories in metaethics: non-cognitivism, subjectivism, naturalism, and nihilism. As is usual in philosophy, the 'refutations' are provisional: those theories have been shown to face grave problems that justify rejecting them as long as any plausible alternative exists. Ethical intuitionism is the remaining alternative. But the received view in the field has long been that intuitionism is a hopelessly naive idea that can be dismissed in a few sentences. 'I propose to ignore this theory', writes Brandt of a related thesis; but most authors simply ignore it with no prior announcement. Ethics textbooks now contain one-paragraph 'refutations' of the doctrine, if they discuss it at all. All of this evidences the esteem in which intuitionism is held these days.[1] So, the naive onlooker might conclude, contemporary philosophers must know some obvious and decisive objections to the theory. What are they?

Most experts take the existence of moral disagreement and error as the main reason for rejecting intuitionism. There are three versions of the argument. One is that the occurrence of disagreement entails that morality is not objective. Another is that intuitionists cannot plausibly *explain* disagreement or error. The last is that intuitionists have no method of *resolving* disagreements.

Before elaborating these arguments, let us review the phenomenon their proponents have in mind.

## 6.1 The prevalence of moral disagreement

There are three main kinds of moral disagreement:

First, disagreements among cultures. Members of a tribe in New Guinea used to eat the brains of dead kinswomen, as part of their mourning ceremonies. Aztec priests used to perform human sacrifices, cutting out the still-beating hearts of victims to feed them to the sun god. Many societies, including our own before the last century, have routinely practiced slavery. All of these practices horrify modern Western observers, yet other societies have found them acceptable, or even obligatory.[2]

Second, popular disagreements within our society. Some believe that abortion is murder and is therefore among the worst crimes one can commit; others believe it is not wrong at all. Some believe that justice demands capital punishment for heinous criminals; others consider capital punishment uncivilized and unjust. Some think that affirmative action is needed to make reparations for past injustices; others think it adds to the injustice.

Third, theoretical disagreements of philosophers. Some philosophers think the right action is always the one with the best consequences; others say that the ends don't justify the means, and that some kinds of action are wrong even if they produce the best consequences. Some philosophers maintain that the sole good in life is pleasure; others think there are many goods. Some philosophers hold that we ought to value others' interests just as much as our own; others say we are beholden to none but ourselves.

These are a few of the many examples that could be given. They paint a picture of strong, fundamental disagreements as the norm in moral matters. But this is misleading for two reasons. First, many of these disagreements are not *fundamentally* moral disagreements, but instead turn on differences in the (non-moral) circumstances people find themselves in, or believe themselves to be in. To borrow one of James Rachels' examples, it initially seems that the Eskimos, in their acceptance of infanticide, have very different values from us. But their acceptance of infanticide is explained by the harsh conditions under which they live, in which food is in short supply. In these conditions, families may be unable to provide for all infants, and attempting to do so may threaten the survival of others. Thus, in their circumstances, infanticide makes sense; it need not indicate a lesser respect for life on the part of Eskimos, nor fundamentally different values from ours.[3] To take another example, the practice of human sacrifice had roots in religious beliefs. Primitive peoples thought the gods demanded sacrifice. The Aztecs believed the sun would literally stop shining if human sacrifices were not performed; furthermore, they believed the souls of sacrificial victims went to the best afterlife, so the priests were actually doing them a favor. Our society rejects human sacrifice because we reject those beliefs, not because we have fundamentally different values.

Many moral disputes within our society have non-moral roots. Pro-life and pro-choice activists may differ over such questions as whether fetuses are sentient, whether they have souls, and whether God forbids abortion. Disagreements about affirmative action may involve disagreements about the causes of economic inequalities among races. I do not say this accounts for all moral disagreements, but it reduces the prevalence and importance of the disagreements that can be regarded as fundamentally moral.

A second reason why the examples of disagreement are misleading is that they are deliberately selected from a much greater number of moral issues about which there is generally agreement. The cases of abortion, capital punishment, and affirmative action have not been randomly selected from all moral issues; they are selected for attention because they are among the most notorious subjects of controversy. The proponent of the argument from disagreement does not draw our attention to *paradigmatic* instances of murder—say, killing a store owner during an armed robbery so that one cannot later be identified. Nor does he raise the issue of the wrongness of indiscriminate lying, stealing, and breaking of promises. Those things are closer to the core of our moral code, but they do not attract attention or become subjects of public discussion. Public discourse naturally focuses instead on areas of disagreement. This gives us an exaggerated impression of the importance of such disagreement.

The disagreements of philosophers too are somewhat exaggerated. Philosophers agree on paradigm cases of wrongful actions—killing people for fun, torture, typical cases of theft. Moral philosophers argue with one another largely by appealing to hypothetical cases about which we generally have the same intuitions. Indeed, if we did not agree on most cases, we could have no interesting discussion—we might not even understand one another's words, since if your conception of the good bears no resemblance to mine, then I will not understand your words as referring to goodness at all, nor can I credit you with any rational arguments on the subject. What philosophers disagree about is what *account* is to be given of the paradigm cases. For example, they may differ over whether murder is wrong because it violates a right to life, or because it decreases the total amount of value in the world.

None of this is to deny the existence of important disagreements about values. It is only to say that these disagreements are less prevalent than is sometimes thought, and that they take place against a backdrop of substantial moral agreement.

## 6.2 The idiot's veto

The first version of the argument from disagreement claims that the existence of disagreement about morality is incompatible with morality's being 'objective'.[4] I shall not dwell on this argument long, since few philosophers would be guilty of advancing it. The argument's premise is that a claim is 'objectively' true only if everyone agrees or would agree with it (perhaps after hearing the arguments for it).

This premise introduces what I call an 'idiot's veto'. The Idiot's Veto is the principle that one can bar any (would-be) fact from the realm of objectivity merely by failing to apprehend it. In effect, the premise grants individuals with limited cognitive abilities or stubbornly skeptical dispositions a *veto power* over any would-be objective truth. Thus, suppose a physics teacher encounters a student who refuses to accept the Second Law of Thermodynamics (such individuals are the source of the perennial efforts to design 'perpetual motion machines'). According to the Idiot's Veto, this would rule out the objectivity of the Second Law of Thermodynamics.

No interesting sense of 'objective' makes that true. Take the definition according to which objectivity is a matter of independence from observers. On this interpretation, the Idiot's Veto claims that for a thing to exist independently of observers, everyone must agree that it exists. This is a *non sequitur*. The definition of objectivity says nothing about agreement.

A second conception takes an 'objective' truth to be one that has been or can be *proven*. On this interpretation, the Idiot's Veto maintains that if at least one person would not agree with $x$, then $x$ has not been proven. But on any ordinary understanding of 'proof', it is possible for a person to not accept the conclusion of a proof—whether through lack of understanding, mistake, bias, or what have you—and their failure to believe that conclusion does not invalidate the proof. A proof is, roughly, an argument with no flaws; someone's mere failure to accept the conclusion of an argument does not constitute a flaw in the argument.

Of course, one could simply *stipulate* that 'objective' mean 'would be agreed to by everyone'. But this would deprive the argument of any philosophical interest. Not only would this be a misleading use of the term, but it would be a use according to which there may well be no proposition whatever that is 'objective'. The interest of the debate about moral objectivity comes from the anti-realists' view that ethics differs in some crucial way from other, more 'objective' fields such as physics and mathematics. The Idiot's Veto identifies no such difference. It implies that the Second Law of Thermodynamics is not objective, as we have seen. It implies that the Theory of Evolution is not objectively true, since Creationists reject it. And it implies that the very existence of the material world is not objective, since Bishop Berkeley rejected it.

To give this version of the Argument from Disagreement any plausibility, we must qualify its premise. Perhaps the premise should be that if some *fully rational, fully informed* person would not agree with a claim, then the claim lacks objectivity.[5] But rational and informed people still make mistakes. One who makes a miscalculation, or who misunderstands or fails to understand a concept, is not thereby irrational, misinformed, or uninformed. Presumably, someone's making an error about $x$ does not refute $x$'s objectivity in any interesting sense, so the premise needs to be qualified again. We may also add a qualification concerning bias, since failure to agree with $x$ due to bias should not impugn $x$'s objectivity. Our new version of the premise (no longer an Idiot's Veto) is this: If some fully rational, informed, and unbiased person, who correctly and fully understands $x$ and makes no mistakes, would not agree with $x$, then $x$ is not objectively true.

Perhaps the premise in this latest version is correct. But now the problem is that of showing that there are any moral disagreements of the relevant kind. While we can readily observe disagreements about moral issues, few if any humans are completely rational, informed, or unbiased. And how shall we establish that both parties to a disagreement correctly and fully understand the issue and have made no mistakes? There are many ways in which humans can make mistakes, most of which are common in moral matters, as we see in the next section.

## 6.3   Can intuitionists explain disagreement?

The second version of the Argument from Disagreement asserts that the evidence of moral disagreement strongly favors anti-realism over intuitionism, because anti-realists are better able to explain disagreement than intuitionists are. Anti-realists understand inter-cultural disagreements as being due to differing forms of life, together with the absence of any facts determining the 'correct' form of life. They understand interpersonal disagreements as arising from differing personal preferences, together with the absence of any facts determining the 'correct' preferences. The intuitionist, in contrast, must say people are subject to widespread error, but he has no account of why this would be so. In short:

1. There is widespread disagreement about values.
2. If intuitionism were true, there (probably) would not be widespread disagreement about values.
3. Therefore (probably), intuitionism is false.[6]

### 6.3.1 The caricature

How is intuitionism supposed to preclude the possibility of widespread error? Here is one popular answer; I call it 'the Caricature':

*Caricature*   Intuitionists hold: (i) All moral questions can be resolved by *direct* appeal to intuition. There is no place for reasoning or any other process of investigation in moral philosophy. (ii) Intuition is infallible. And (iii) everyone knows these things. It follows that everyone can immediately obtain an answer to any moral question by simply consulting his intuition. These answers must all agree, since intuition is infallible. And since everyone knows these facts, no one will ever form a moral belief by any other means. So everyone will agree.[7]

If the history of philosophy has seen a less charitable misreading of a major philosophical position, I do not know what it is. I know of no one who has ever held the views there attributed to intuitionism. Intuitionists have repeatedly denied the claim of infallibility in particular.[8] Nowell-Smith supports the attribution with the following quotation from the eighteenth-century intuitionist Samuel Clarke:

These things are so notoriously plain and self-evident, that nothing but the extremist stupidity of mind, corruption of manners or perversity of spirit can possibly make any man entertain the least doubt concerning them.[9]

Nowell-Smith produces this quotation while discussing the intuitionist's alleged inability to accommodate moral disagreement; he neglects to inform his readers what 'these things' refers to in the passage, leaving them perhaps to infer that it refers to all moral truths. In fact, Clarke is referring to a specific series of moral principles that he has listed, principles such as the following:

> [I]n Men's dealing and conversing one with another, 'tis undeniably more Fit . . . that all Men should endeavour to promote universal good and welfare of All, than that Men should be continually contriving the ruin and destruction of All.[10]

While there are important moral matters that people disagree over, the above principle is not among them. The only of Clarke's examples that are at all controversial are those concerning obligations of and to God, where the source of controversy is metaphysical, rather than ethical. Thus, the quoted passage does not justify attributing to Clarke the view that we are infallible about all moral matters—to say nothing of other intuitionists.

In any event, if anyone has held the absurdly strong and simplistic views described in the Caricature, I do not.

### 6.3.2   The prevalence of non-moral disagreement

Perhaps I have been unkind to the argument from disagreement. A more subtle version holds, not that intuitionism rules out any moral disagreement, but that intuitionism *renders improbable* disagreements *of the kind and number* that we find in moral philosophy. Disagreements in moral philosophy are very widespread, are often apparently unresolvable, and sometimes concern fundamental questions of the sort that we would expect intuition to speak to. It is this specific pattern of disagreement that the intuitionist allegedly cannot explain. Though they reject infallibility, presumably intuitionists at least believe that intuition is generally reliable at producing correct beliefs; otherwise, it could hardly account for moral knowledge. But the observed pattern of moral disagreement impugns the reliability of moral intuition and moral reasoning, since if we had available a reliable method of identifying moral truths, there should be relatively few disagreements, and disagreements should frequently be resolved by application of that method.[11]

I disagree. I don't think the availability of moral knowledge is incompatible with frequent and persistent moral disagreements. This subsection brings out the first part of my case for this: the prevalence of non-moral disagreements with the same problematic features as moral disagreements. Consider some examples:

1. Who shot JFK? Forty years after the assassination, many remain *convinced* that there was a conspiracy, possibly involving Cubans,

the mafia, or the CIA. Others are equally certain that a lone gunman, Lee Harvey Oswald, was responsible.

2. What is the best football team in America?
3. How should quantum mechanics be interpreted? Einstein and Bohr debated whether the formalism of quantum mechanics was complete, without issue. To this day, there remain multiple interpretations of quantum mechanics, each with their own advocates.
4. What are the actual practices of other cultures? Anthropologists for decades took there to have been many cultures in which cannibalism was common. In 1979, William Arens argued that this was a myth, that in fact no culture ever practiced widespread cannibalism. Anthropologists disagreed sharply in their assessments of Arens' work. Similarly, a heated debate arose when in 1983 Derek Freeman purported to show that Margaret Mead's famous account of life in Samoa was entirely inaccurate. Both controversies aroused strong emotions and continue to this day.[12]
5. What are the economic effects of government social programs? Some think they have been essential in ameliorating the great poverty and suffering that would otherwise be the lot of the lower classes in a capitalist country. Others think those same programs actually *harm* the poor.[13]
6. What religion, if any, is correct? We've had millennia to think about it, and we haven't even agreed on whether there is a God, let alone what He wants.
7. Are there paranormal phenomena? I suspect most readers will answer no. But a quarter of Americans believe in astrology, half believe in ESP, and a quarter believe they have had a telepathic experience.[14]
8. What causes illness? The same cultures that have very different moral beliefs from ours also accept very different answers to this question. Many think illnesses can be caused magically by others' ill will. Western society accepted for centuries that diseases were caused by imbalances of the body's four humors.

Many more examples could be given. The disagreements in examples 1–7 have the following features:

*i)* They are widespread among people who have an opinion about the issues; it isn't just a few people going against a consensus.
*ii)* They are apparently unresolvable. Anyone who thinks they can resolve who shot JFK by 'just going in and looking at the facts' is invited to try. You may well figure out 'the answer' (by your

lights), but only the uninitiated will imagine they have a chance of convincing the other side(s).

*iii)* They concern objective, non-evaluative facts. Indeed, such questions as who shot JFK and whether a particular culture practiced cannibalism are *paradigms* of objective questions.

In the case of example 8, there was an agreed upon answer in our society for several centuries, but this answer was completely wrong.

I have listed a number of examples to illustrate the scope of human disagreement. People disagree about historical events, about apparently straightforward matters of empirical fact, about things allegedly established by science, about the interpretation of accepted theories, and about many philosophical matters, among other things. Even when we agree, that is no guarantee of our being right, as example 8 shows. I have, admittedly, given a partial view of our intellectual life: I have intentionally selected notable cases of strong and persistent disagreements. But then, the anti-realist has done likewise for the moral realm in calling forth such examples as abortion and capital punishment.

Persistent non-moral disagreements are common. Yet virtually no one takes this to refute the possibility of knowledge in such fields as history, anthropology, and economics. I suspect few would draw even the slightly skeptical conclusion that we cannot gain knowledge concerning the specific issues about which we disagree (even if we haven't yet done so). How, then, is moral disagreement supposed to refute the possibility of moral knowledge?

Perhaps there is something especially problematic about disagreements in areas where knowledge depends on *intuitions*, as opposed to areas where knowledge depends on other means, such as observation and scientific reasoning. If there is, I have no idea what it is. Intuitionists need not and do not maintain that knowledge based on intuition is *superior* to empirical knowledge; they need not take reasoning based on moral intuitions to be more reliable than science, for example. Opponents of intuitionism are simply applying an epistemological double standard: If scientific and other empirical reasoning fails to produce agreement in many cases, yet this does not invalidate it as a source of knowledge, then why should intuition's similar failure to produce agreement invalidate *it* as a source of knowledge?

Perhaps the problem is that in the case of moral philosophy, we have many disputes all within the same subject matter, whereas the non-moral disputes are isolated instances distributed across many different subjects. But this is not so. There are numerous disputes on the subject of religion, even its non-moral claims; all branches of philosophy; sports, particularly the merits of various players and teams and what people 'should' do (in a non-moral sense) at various points in a game; the relative abilities of specific individuals one may know (for example, is Sally smarter than me?); and everything bearing on politics, again including non-moral questions. Yet none of these are areas in which objective facts don't exist, nor in which we lack cognitive faculties capable of apprehending facts of that kind.

### 6.3.3  A menagerie of error

What is surprising about disagreement, such that it calls for special explanation? Beliefs, we think, aim at the truth. If people *attain* the truth, then they will agree with each other. So widespread disagreement entails widespread error, even though we are ostensibly trying to avoid error. Why don't we just stop using the unreliable belief-forming methods that lead us into disagreements? Why don't we just sit down, taking our logic and critical thinking textbooks in hand, and figure out who is making the bad arguments?

The preceding questions rest on naive assumptions. While beliefs in some sense aim at the truth, people's beliefs may gratify many other passions besides the rational hankering after the truth. Nor do the canons of logic and critical thinking algorithmically determine what is and isn't a bad argument. People seldom satisfy ideal conditions for reasoning, and even the best of cognitive conditions do not render humans infallible. The causes of our beliefs can be highly complex and largely hidden from us. We often cannot articulate some of the reasons for our beliefs. The intuitionist can no more produce an algorithm for computing the correct moral theory than we can produce a general algorithm for computing correct empirical theories.

Critics have charged that the intuitionist has available no account of moral error other than 'blindness', stupidity, or deliberate mendacity.[15] To better assess this charge, let us review some of the sources of error in general:

1. *Bias:* People who are biased are moved by emotions and desires, other than the desire to have true beliefs and avoid false ones, to view some claims favorably and others unfavorably. In other words, there are some things we *want* to believe, and others we want not to believe. Often, we want to believe what is in our interests to believe, or to convince others of; what we would like to be true; what would be in the interests of the social group with which we identify to believe; and what coheres with the self-

image we want to maintain. These are just some of the possible biases we may suffer from.[16]

2. *Miscalculation:* While performing a calculation, I forget to carry a '1', resulting in an incorrect answer. If no one points it out to me, I may never realize my error. I may fully understand the mathematical principles involved in the problem; be rational, unbiased, and intelligent; and yet still make a mistake.

3. *Confusion:* This involves failure to distinguish two superficially similar things. For example, the student who thinks that because we cannot talk about anything without using language, we cannot talk about the language-independent world, is committing a confusion.

4. *Misunderstanding and lack of understanding:* Concepts and theories can be misunderstood. A student who thinks that chaos theory makes room for free will suffers from a lack of understanding of the concept of chaos and perhaps of free will. The philosopher who finds intuitionism absurd because it makes no room for moral debate suffers from a misunderstanding of the theory.

5. *Oversight:* People may fail to notice relevant considerations, including some of the implications of their statements. Someone asks me whether I think two solid objects can overlap in space. I answer 'No', based on my immediate impression—overlooking such examples as my hand and my body, or a statue and the mass of clay of which it is composed. Relatedly, people may exercise *selective attention*, that is, they may attend to only some of the relevant features of a situation, whether because of bias or simply because the situation is too complex to take everything in at once.

6. *Hasty judgments:* People often make a judgment based on an initial appearance, when longer, more careful thought would have resulted in a different judgment.

7. *False or incomplete information:* Sometimes people do not know all the facts that are relevant to making a judgment, and sometimes they make mistaken assumptions. For instance, two people arguing about gun control may have received radically different information, one by consulting NRA literature, the other by consulting literature from Handgun Control, Inc. Some of their information may be false, while neither has complete information.

8. *Unarticulated assumptions:* Imagine two people arguing about whether abortion should be legal. One assumes that they are arguing about whether abortion should *ever* be allowed, while the other assumes they are arguing about whether it should *always* be

allowed. Or perhaps neither of them really knows which of these questions, if either, they intend to discuss.

9. *Stubbornness:* People may simply refuse to reconsider old beliefs, even when new, relevant evidence appears.

10. *Fallacies:* These are illusions of reason—forms of reasoning that may superficially appear cogent but in fact are not; for example, equivocation, affirming the consequent, argument ad hominem. Especially important is misplaced trust in authority: people may believe a thing because others—parents, religious leaders, reporters, or other members of their society—have asserted it. But those others may not have known what they were talking about.

11. *Forgetfulness:* People may forget or simply not notice their own reasons for holding a belief, and they may forget other relevant evidence. In this case, they are in a poor position to recognize when the belief has been undermined.

12. *Intrinsic difficulty of issues:* Some issues, such as those that are particularly abstract or complex, are more difficult to grasp clearly and make judgments about than others.

13. *Inarticulate evidence:* Sometimes we have grounds for belief that we cannot articulate. Suppose a friend has been accused of embezzling money from her company. Because I know her well, I know she would not do such a thing. But I could not *prove* this to a third party. This sort of inarticulate evidence can cause disagreement.

14. *Mental defects:* Last and perhaps least, a few people lack cognitive capacities that most others have, or have cognitive capacities whose functioning is seriously distorted, as in the case of schizophrenics, autists, and psychopaths. Though a paranoid schizophrenic may otherwise appear a competent reasoner, you will have no luck reasoning him out of his delusions.

These sources of error are not all independent of each other; some overlap and some influence others.

I cannot claim completeness for my menagerie of error; perhaps there are further sources of error I have overlooked. Given the multitude of ways human beings can go wrong, why do anti-realists think that moral disagreement must be explained by a shortage of objective facts? All of the above sources of error and disagreement operate in non-moral matters whose objectivity is undisputed; there is no obvious reason why they should not also operate in moral matters.

### 6.3.4   Disagreement is predictable

Proponents of the argument from disagreement, all too eager in their rejections of intuitionism, have neglected to justify the crucial second premise of their argument—

2. If intuitionism were true, there would not be widespread disagreement about values.

As we have seen, there are many ways human beings can go wrong, and there are many persistent disagreements about objective, in principle knowable facts. In light of this, we have no obvious grounds for predicting that there would not be widespread disputes about values.

But now I want to say something stronger: I think that we *have* obvious grounds for predicting that there *would* be widespread disputes about values, even if intuitionism were true. This requires looking at the kinds of cases in which disagreement and error are common, in general. There are at least four kinds of cases to consider.

*First:* Disagreement and error are common where there are strong and frequent biases. Bias is particularly important, since it increases the frequency and seriousness of most other kinds of errors, such as oversight, misunderstanding, forgetfulness, and so on. It probably plays a major role in the disagreements listed in section 6.3.2. Here are some common sources of bias, all of which may affect moral questions:

*Self-interest:* It would be in my interests, for example, to believe that the things I want to do are morally acceptable, and that the things I want others to do are obligatory. It would be even more clearly in my interests to convince others of these things.

*Wishful thinking:* I would like it to be true that the world is just; that the way things actually are, is good; that I and my social group are especially praiseworthy; that our practices are justified.

*Group interests:* It would be in the interests of my social group to believe that we are superior to other groups, that the things we want to do are justified, and so forth.

*Self-image:* Sometimes the self-images we want to construct affect what beliefs we adopt. If I wish to portray myself as compassionate and forgiving, I may want to reject capital punishment; but if

I prefer to portray myself as tough and uncompromising, then I may want to embrace capital punishment.

*Second:* Disagreement and error are common in areas where people defer to their cultures' traditions. Cultural traditions are a notoriously unreliable source of information. The cultures with the surprising moral beliefs, which are supposed to make us doubt the reality of moral facts, also have a host of surprising non-moral beliefs—about such things as the causes of disease, the structure of the cosmos, human history, and the workings of the physical world—that we know, scientifically, to be false.

*Third:* Disagreement and error are common in areas where people defer to religion, another unreliable source of information. In section 3.4, I mentioned some false moral beliefs supported by the Bible. Here are some false factual beliefs also apparently supported by the Bible:

Rabbits chew cud. (*Deuteronomy* 14:6-7)
Some insects are four-legged. (*Leviticus* 11:20-22)
The Earth is flat. (*Matthew* 4:8)
$\pi = 3$. (*1 Kings* 7:23)
The Earth is stationary and rests on a foundation. (*Psalms* 104:5)
The Earth is about 6000 years old. (Allegedly supported by various parts of the Bible.[17])

*Fourth:* Disagreement is common in all areas of philosophy. For centuries, philosophers have disagreed about such things as God, free will, universals, *a priori* knowledge, and the nature of the mind, to name a few. The level of disagreement in ethics is no greater than that found in metaphysics, epistemology, philosophy of mind, or philosophy of language.[18]

On all four counts, we should expect moral issues to be especially prone to disagreement. My response to the major premise of the argument from disagreement, then, is this: even if there were objective moral truths and we had available ways of knowing them, widespread, strong, and persistent disagreements could still be expected. No anti-realist assumption is required to predict the phenomenon.

## 6.4 Can intuitionists resolve disagreements?

The final version of the Argument from Disagreement goes something like this:

1. Intuitionism provides no way of resolving moral disagreements.
2. If a metaethical theory provides no way of resolving moral disagreements, then it is false.
3. Therefore, intuitionism is false.

Typically, only premise (1) is stated explicitly. Premise (2) is also needed, but its justification remains obscure.

### 6.4.1   Hypothetical disagreements

How should we interpret (1)—which disagreements is the intuitionist to be castigated for his inability to resolve? For some critics, the complaint seems to be that the intuitionist has no way to resolve certain *hypothetical* disagreements. Thus, Nowell-Smith stipulates a case in which someone disagrees with us about a moral issue and will not accept any premise we might use to support our view. In such a case, he says, there is no way to resolve the dispute through reasoning.[19] While he is undoubtedly right about this, this hardly points up a flaw in intuitionism. *No one* can provide a way of rationally resolving *any* kind of dispute if we stipulate that each party refuses to accept any premises that the other party might use. How is this supposed to be a problem?

### 6.4.2   Controversial moral questions

Perhaps the complaint is that there are some *actual* disagreements that the intuitionist can give us no way to resolve, such as the disputes over abortion, capital punishment, and affirmative action. While this is plausible, it is at least as plausible to think that no one *else* can provide a way of resolving such disputes either. Why should we think that a metaethical theory can only be true if it provides a way of resolving all disputes? Perhaps this is supposed to be an adequacy condition only for *realist* theories, but even then it remains unmotivated. Suppose I have just given a philosophical theory according to which there are objective facts about physical objects, and all our knowledge of such facts derives from perception. Would the following be a fair objection: 'You haven't provided a way of settling who shot JFK. Therefore, your theory is wrong'?

### 6.4.3   Foundational moral controversies

Perhaps the complaint is that some disagreements about *foundational* moral claims—moral claims that do not depend on other beliefs—cannot be resolved. The dispute about JFK concerns beliefs that depend on reasoning, not foundational beliefs, so it is not analogous.

If this is the argument, we should first note that foundational moral disputes are relatively rare; the disputes about abortion and affirmative action are not instances, since our beliefs about those issues depend on further beliefs. For example, most who think abortion is wrong think so because they believe that fetuses are people, that it is generally wrong to kill persons, and that abortion kills fetuses. Moreover, the literature is replete with examples of rational moral arguments concerning abortion and other notorious matters of controversy, showing that we need not throw up our hands when confronted with such disputes.[20] Although Ayer claims that foundational moral disagreements are 'notorious', he provides no examples. The most plausible examples are things that for the most part, only philosophers argue about, such as whether we ought to weigh other people's interests equally with our own, or whether the action with the best consequences is always right.

Second, as long as our foundationalism is of a moderate form, it is not impossible to reason about intuitive moral principles. We may hold even intuitive moral principles open to revision in the light of further evidence. The examples given in the previous paragraph are principles we have intuitions about, but moral philosophers have hardly given up reasoning about them. I shall return to this point in the following section.[21]

Third, while the inability to resolve disputes is a serious *practical* problem, it is simply unclear how it is supposed to constitute *evidence* that the theory of intuitionism is *false*.

Fourth, it is unclear why reasoning is not subjected to the same demands as other means of cognition. There are many apparently unresolvable disputes about beliefs that depend on reasoning, but that does not convince us that reasoning is not a legitimate means of cognition. So why would apparently unresolvable disputes about beliefs that depend on intuition convince us that intuition is not a legitimate means of cognition? Perhaps the argument presupposes that we *have* straightforward ways of determining, in all cases, whether a piece of reasoning is cogent. But of course that is false. There is no generally accepted, comprehensive, and useful set of rules for what counts as evidence for what. That is what such examples as the JFK dispute illustrate: no one can establish, in a way that all intelligent parties would agree with, whether the available evidence supports a conspiracy theory.

Finally, imagine a dispute about a non-intuitive, foundational claim. Two witnesses at a trial give different versions of events, both claiming to have *seen* what they report. This sort of case is not unusual. Both witnesses may give every known sign of sincerely believing what they say.[22] Is it the job of a philosophical theory of perception to provide a way to resolve that dispute? If I cannot do so, is my theory of perception—say, my claim that the physical world is objective, or my claim that perception is a legitimate source of knowledge—thereby refuted? If not, then how would the failure to resolve some moral disputes refute either the existence of objective values, or the claim that ethical intuition is a legitimate means of cognition?

### 6.4.4  Disputes in general

Some charge that intuitionists have no way to resolve *any* disputes, or at least not any disputes about intuitions.[23] Faced with disagreement, intuitionists must immediately break out the clubs and start hitting people over the head.[24] Unlike the others, this charge would identify a serious flaw in intuitionism, since in fact some disputes *are* resolvable. But the charge is false.

Faced with a disagreement, an intuitionist may, among other things, attempt to determine whether one of the common causes of error discussed in section 6.3.3 is operative, and to remedy the situation if it is. He may investigate such questions as whether one party is biased; whether there are misunderstandings or confusions about some of the concepts or views involved in the debate; whether one party has made a hasty judgment or oversight; whether either party has false or incomplete information; and so on. Any of these problems could adversely affect one's intuitive judgments. In addition, some intuitions may turn out to depend (causally) on further beliefs in ways one was not initially aware of. This can sometimes be brought out by considering further hypothetical scenarios ('Would you still say *x* was wrong if *p* were the case?'), and these further beliefs can then be examined.

The problem of bias is the most troubling one. Although bias is pervasive in intellectual life, accusations of bias rarely advance discussion. They are more likely to lead to each side's searching for arguments to show that the other side is more biased, and these arguments are likely to be assessed with at least as much bias as the original moral issue. For this reason, there may be little we can do about the biases of others. But we can try to counter our own biases. Merely identifying a bias goes a great distance towards counteracting it. When approaching a moral issue, we should think about whether we are subject to the sorts of biases previously discussed. Along these lines, we should ask whether we hold the moral beliefs that we do because of our culture or religion, and if so, we should be suspicious of those beliefs. A belief's being endorsed by our culture or religion is not evidence that it is false, but it is evidence that our belief is *unreliable*, that we would likely hold the belief whether it was true or not.

An example from Peter Singer illustrates the point. After defending the permissibility of abortion, Singer confronts the charge that his arguments cannot distinguish between fetuses and newborn infants and thus imply that infanticide is also permissible in many cases (roughly, because newborn infants have no more sophisticated mental capacities than fetuses). He responds, in part, by informing the reader that many societies have considered infanticide acceptable and even obligatory in certain cases. Plato, Aristotle, and Seneca all recommended the killing of deformed infants. What is Singer's point here? Is he making an appeal to authority, to defend infanticide? No; his point is that our horror at the thought of killing infants is probably more a product of our particular culture (particularly, he thinks, of Christianity) than of the objective facts about infants. He also suggests that a good part of the cause of our belief is the cuteness of infants, which is morally irrelevant.[25]

I make no attempt to resolve the disputes about abortion and infanticide. My aim is simply to illustrate the importance of looking beyond one's culture. Singer is correct to urge that the culture-specific nature of beliefs about infanticide diminishes their authority.

Reducing bias is only part of a reasonable strategy for ameliorating moral disagreement. Moral arguments must also play a major role in the effort to resolve disputes, even disputes about intuitive principles. Philosophers may reason with one another about a moral principle by, for example, considering how well it coheres with other moral principles; looking for previously unnoticed consequences of the principle; considering how it applies to specific situations about which we have intuitions; drawing analogies between the principle and other principles that we accept or reject; and looking for plausible general constraints on moral theories (for instance: 'A moral theory should make it understandable how people can be motivated by the good' or, 'A moral theory should imply that when $A$ is better than $B$ and $B$ is better than $C$, $A$ is better than $C$').[26] Philosophers have far from given up on resolving moral issues, though we recognize that the project is a long-term one.[27] Intuitionists will naturally embrace all or nearly all of the current methods of normative ethics. In light of this, the majority of ethicists cannot reject intuitionism on the grounds that it fails to license a reasonable approach to disputed moral questions.

Why might intuitionism be thought to preclude reasoning about intuitions? It might be thought that *foundationalists* cannot allow reasoning about foundational beliefs. But this is a misunderstanding.

A foundational belief is defined as one that *does not need* a reason in order to be justified to some degree; it is not defined as a belief that *cannot have* a reason. Moreover, most foundationalists embrace the notion of *prima facie* justification discussed in section 5.1 above. My principle of Phenomenal Conservatism is a case in point: it holds only that appearances are rationally presumed true, until evidence of their falsity or unreliability appears. Intuitionists should allow that intuitive justification for a moral belief can be defeated, either because of tensions with other moral beliefs (one's own or others'), or because of empirical evidence of its unreliability (for example, evidence of bias). So intuitionists seem to have at least as good prospects for resolving disputes as anyone in moral philosophy.

You might feel some justified skepticism about the prospects for resolving disagreements by the means I have suggested. Few people, whatever they may say, will conscientiously work to root out their own biases. Most will continue to unreflectively defer to their culture and religion. Even moral philosophers will likely continue, for the most part, to rationalize their favored theories. For at least this reason, moral disagreement is here to stay. This reveals a grievous flaw in human nature. But it reveals no flaw in ethical intuitionism.

## 6.5 The self-refutation problem

The argument from disagreement is double-edged: it can be turned against the views of its proponents as easily as it can be turned against intuitionism. To begin with, notice that proponents of other metaethical positions take their own views to be objectively true. In asserting their theories about the nature of moral claims, they are not purporting merely to express or describe their emotions, for example; they are purporting to state a fact that we have adequate grounds for believing (if there are no moral facts, it is a [non-moral] fact that there are no moral facts). But if the argument from disagreement is sound, then it refutes itself, since many people do not agree with the argument from disagreement. The argument would likewise refute any metaethical position, due to the nature of disagreement in metaethics. Recall the three versions of the argument from disagreement:

a) *The Idiot's Veto:* If someone's disagreeing with a claim, in general, prevents that claim from being objectively true, then the disagreements in metaethics prevent any metaethical view from being objectively true. Similarly, some people reject the argument from disagreement, so it cannot be objectively correct.

b) *The problem of explaining disagreement:* The disagreement over metaethical theories is at least as widespread and persistent as that over ethical theories. Should we explain this by denying the existence of any correct metaethical theory? Similarly, there is no general agreement on whether the argument from disagreement is correct; does this suggest that there is no fact about whether it is correct?

If ethical disagreements are problematic for the intuitionist because they suggest that intuition is unreliable, then disagreements in metaethics are equally problematic for *any* metaethicist because they suggest that philosophical reflection and reasoning— or whatever methods metaethicists have been using—are unreliable. Many of the central ideas and arguments in the field have been around for decades, and philosophers have yet to agree on their soundness.

c) *The problem of resolving disagreement:* Similarly, if the intuitionist lacks an effective method for resolving ethical disputes, we all lack an effective method for resolving metaethical disputes. Again, the methods actually employed by philosophers have so far proved no more successful in resolving metaethical issues than they have in resolving ethical issues.

One reason for this is that the choice of a philosophical theory generally depends on broad judgments of overall plausibility made in the light of numerous inconclusive arguments, the relationship of the theory to other philosophical theories, and the various 'theoretical advantages' and disadvantages of competing views.[28] I see no alternative to this approach, but it means that most major philosophical disputes are unlikely to be resolved in the foreseeable future.

How should we react to the phenomenon of disagreement in philosophy? One might justifiably conclude that philosophical knowledge is very difficult to attain and that very little of it has been attained. One might thus be moved to take a hesitant and modest attitude towards one's philosophical beliefs. What one should not say—not just because it would be self-defeating, but because it is evidently false—is that we lack the cognitive faculties required for approaching philosophical questions. However difficult they may be and however prone we may be to error, we are not simply *closed off* to philosophical questions (in the sense in which my cat is)—we understand them and can make rational arguments about them. Intuitionism's opponents do not deny this; if they did, they would not engage in philosophical discourse. Similarly, a modest attitude towards controversial moral beliefs is supported by the phenomenon of moral disagreement; what is not warranted is a denial that moral questions have answers or that we have the cognitive faculties for approaching them.

## 6.6 Disagreement as an argument for realism

The argument from disagreement is typically advanced by anti-realists. But for the reasons we have seen, the phenomenon of disagreement provides no significant evidence for their view. In fact, I shall now argue that disagreement is more of a problem for *anti*-realists than it is for realists.

### 6.6.1 Can anti-realists explain disagreement?

To start with, how can anti-realists explain why we argue with others about moral issues, asserting them to be mistaken, and so on? We have already seen the difficulties for subjectivists (chapter 3): According to individualist subjectivism, you can't disagree with someone's moral claim unless you think he's falsely reporting his own feelings. According to cultural relativism, you can't disagree with someone's moral claim unless you think he's wrong about what his society's customs are. It is hard to see why there should be wide-spread, unresolvable disputes about what our emotions or conventions are. On a non-cognitivist view, there aren't even any propositions to disagree about. People *can* have 'conflicting attitudes'[29]—but this would not explain why, for example, one would try to *reason with* opponents of euthanasia or tell them they are *mistaken*. One does not normally argue with people or tell them they are 'mistaken' merely because they have different feelings from one's own.

Consider three replies to this. *First:* Perhaps we argue about moral issues because we mistakenly *think* moral realism is true. This reply works for nihilists. It does not work for subjectivists or non-cognitivists. Our belief in objective values only explains our arguing about moral questions if we take moral terms to refer to those objective value properties. But the subjectivist or non-cognitivist thinks moral language does not refer to any alleged objective properties but only expresses or reports subjective mental states. This leaves them with the bizarre idea that almost everyone is fundamentally wrong about the meanings of common words in our language and that, although we believe in objective value properties, we don't have any words for them.

*Second:* Perhaps our arguments about moral issues do not concern *fundamental* value judgments; what we're arguing about is really only the non-moral facts that moral judgments depend upon. For instance, perhaps those who disagree about whether euthanasia is permissible really just disagree about the effects that allowing euthanasia would have. But this reply surrenders the fundamental premise of the argument from disagreement—namely, that there are widespread, fundamental moral disputes.

*Third:* Perhaps we argue about moral issues in an effort to change others' non-cognitive attitudes, not to change their beliefs. But we don't try to change others' attitudes by merely emoting at them; when we argue with others about morality, we say and think that they are *mistaken*, and we purport to give them intellectual reasons for changing their minds. This could make sense on an anti-realist view only if we think others are mistaken about some non-moral facts that their moral attitudes depend upon. In that case, argumentation could hope to change others' attitudes by correcting their mistaken factual assumptions. But again, this requires that moral disagreements fundamentally derive from mistakes about non-moral matters, contrary to the assumption of the argument from disagreement.

Non-cognitivists and subjectivists are, therefore, in no position to press the intuitionist's alleged inability to explain moral disagreement; moreover, to the extent that we are convinced that some moral disagreements really are fundamental, we have reason to reject non-cognitivism and subjectivism.

The situation for nihilists is more complex. They can explain moral disagreement by appealing to our widespread, mistaken belief in realism—but only if they can explain why people would make such an error. On the face of it, the simplest explanation for why nearly everyone thinks moral realism is true, is that it *is* true. Nihilists have proposed alternate explanations,[30] but it would take us too far afield to discuss them; for now, then, let us allow that nihilists may be able to account for moral disagreement.

### 6.6.2 Can anti-realists resolve disagreements?

The most that anti-realists might claim is that intuitionists have no way to resolve *fundamental* moral disagreements—that is, moral disagreements that do not depend upon factual errors or errors in reasoning. Allegedly, intuitionists can only exhort interlocutors to concentrate harder on the moral issue, and perhaps hit them over the head. But what does the anti-realist have to offer? For anti-realists, there are no objective value facts, so when it comes to fundamental value disputes, there is nothing *cognitive* that we can do; all we can do is, perhaps, to cajole, threaten, or agree to disagree. (Nihilists just say that *everyone* is wrong.) How is this supposed to be superior to ethical intuitionism, even on the least sophisticated interpretation of intuitionism?

It is at this point that anti-realists will express optimism about how much people really have in common and about how many moral disputes will turn out to depend on errors of fact and reasoning.[31] But the grounds for thinking people to have fundamentally different sensibilities seem at least as strong as those for thinking people to have fundamentally different intuitions.

Most anti-realists would want to embrace the methods of contemporary ethics, just as most contemporary ethicists embrace anti-realism. Is this consistent? Current practice in moral philosophy includes:

a) *Ubiquitous appeal to intuitions* (with or without using the *word* 'intuition'). Every moral argument employs one or more intuitions. Take Peter Singer's well-known argument for a strong obligation to assist the poor: he relies on the 'plausible principle' that if we can prevent something bad without sacrificing anything of comparable significance, we ought to do so. Not content with this, he appeals to a hypothetical example in which he passes by a child drowning in a shallow pond. Singer appeals to our moral intuition (what else can it be called?) that he is obligated to help the child.[32] As this case shows, intuitions both about general principles and about particular cases are used.

How can an anti-realist accommodate this? The nihilist can have no truck with any of this, since he thinks the relevant moral statements are all false—unless, perhaps, he proposes to *reform* our moral language, so that we come to use it as the non-cognitivists or subjectivists think we do.

For the non-cognitivist, moral discourse only expresses our attitudes. For the subjectivist, it reports our attitudes. Either way, it would seem that the only cognitive task for a moral philosopher is to study our feelings, desires, and other attitudes. Perhaps it will be said that the arguments based on moral intuitions are simply in the service of that aim—Singer is just drawing to our attention that we in fact approve of acts of preventing-bad-things-without-sacrificing-things-of-comparable-significance, including such acts as removing drowning children from shallow ponds. Perhaps it is not *intuitions* that his argument relies on, but moral *emotions*.

This would be fine, were it not for the second feature of contemporary discourse in moral philosophy:

b) *Criticisms of biases.* Sometimes it is argued that certain moral intuitions or beliefs are unreliable, since they are just due to our culture, our religion, or plain selfishness. Recall, for example, Singer's argument that our intuitions about infanticide are unreliable since they are just due to cultural programming.[33] Elsewhere, he has suggested that our belief in the superiority of the human species is due to selfishness and to religious teachings that reflect our self-interest.[34]

This makes sense to a moral realist: if a moral belief is due to biases of a kind that in general frequently cause false beliefs, then that belief likely fails to correspond to the moral facts. But what should an anti-realist say? The notion of 'bias' presupposes realism—a bias is a desire, emotion, or other psychological state that tends to distort our perceptions, to lead us away from the truth. That presupposes that there is a truth independent of our perceptions. For a cultural relativist, Singer's argument concerning infanticide is worse than a *non sequitur*: his premise that our beliefs about infanticide are caused by cultural indoctrination would *prove those beliefs correct*, rather than undermining them as Singer assumes. Even for a subjectivist or non-cognitivist, our culture is just one more source of our moral emotions; on what grounds could moral reactions caused by it be considered 'incorrect'?[35] The same applies to the supposed bias due to self-interest: if self-interest colors our moral emotions, all that shows is that self-interest partly determines what is morally right or good.

Perhaps the anti-realist would say that once we realize what causes some of our moral emotions, we will lose those emotions. Perhaps when we realize that our horror at infanticide is culturally programmed, we will stop feeling it. Or perhaps not. If moral emotions were caused by putative perceptions of moral facts, or if there were some outside standard of 'appropriateness' of moral emotions, perhaps then we would lose our moral emotions on discovering their parochial source. But once we renounce the idea that there is any moral truth independent of our feelings, why should the unsurprising discovery that some of our moral emotions are caused by cultural conditioning undermine those feelings?

A third aspect of our moral discourse is closely related to the second:

c) *Criticisms of moral intuitions based on other intuitions.* Peter Singer, again, has suggested that 'our intuitive judgments [about particular cases] are based on things that are obviously of no moral significance at all'. For example, he thinks our intuitions are biased towards those who are physically closest to us (so that we think we have stronger obligations to people in our neighborhood, say, than to those on other continents). How does Singer know that physical proximity is not morally relevant? The answer seems to be that that is 'obvious' or 'self-evident'—in short, it is an intuition.[36]

The intuitionist can understand this: intuitions are a fallible form of access to moral truth. We can correct errant intuitions by appeal to firmer and more reliable ones. But what should an anti-realist say?

A 'morally relevant' property is one that affects whether a thing is good, bad, right, or wrong. On the subjectivist or non-cognitivist view of morality, this can only mean a property that affects (a certain subset of) our attitudes. So if physical proximity really affects our moral attitudes as Singer says, then that just proves that physical proximity *is* morally relevant.

Perhaps it would be argued that what is moral is determined, not by our current attitudes, but by the attitudes we *would* have if we were to become fully informed and rational (removing all inconsistencies and factual errors from our minds, and so on; see above, section 3.5). It is plausible *on a realist view* that a fully rational person would not have the bias towards those physically close to him that Singer describes, since he would recognize it *as a bias*. But there appears nothing *inconsistent* in our having this attitude, nor does it depend on a factual error, nor does Singer attempt to argue that it does. So why should a rational anti-realist lose the attitude? The fact that Singer's argument is regarded as forceful by ethicists, rather than an obvious *non sequitur*, suggests that moral philosophers illicitly employ an intuitionist methodology while purporting to reject intuitionism.

Now here are some things that do not normally appear in the ethics literature:

d) *Mere appeals to common practices.* Critics of the notion of animal rights do not, for example, argue that since eating meat is the custom around here, it is right. Nor do animal rights supporters take the widespread maltreatment of animals to refute their own moral views.

e) *Mere appeals to the author's or audience's emotions and desires.* Abortion opponents do not, for example, say that abortion is wrong because they or their audience has sympathetic feelings about cute little fetuses. Abortion defenders do not argue that abortion is not murder because abortion doesn't make them feel the way murder does.

f) *Naked rhetoric.* Philosophers do not attempt to 'convince' their audience of their moral views by simply using emotionally charged language, telling tear-jerking stories, or directing demands at the audience.

If some form of subjectivism, relativism, or non-cognitivism is true, why shouldn't the above be the common practice?

Subjectivists and non-cognitivists would advise us to be more subtle than merely to make direct appeals to current attitudes in all cases; they would say that we need to do some reasoning to make sure our attitudes are consistent and rest on no factual errors. Perhaps that is what moral reasoning is about. This suggestion, however, bears little resemblance to actual moral reasoning, nor is it likely to succeed in resolving many disputes. Recall the suggestion discussed in section 3.3 that the practice of slavery was criticizable from within our culture because it was inconsistent with our custom of respect for persons in general: why shouldn't the slavery-advocate simply reply, 'No, we don't have a custom of respect for *all* persons. We have a custom of respect for *white* persons'? One may be tempted to object that this rests on an arbitrary distinction—but if what is morally arbitrary or significant is just determined by customs, then skin color *is* morally significant, in many cultures. Compare the idea, perhaps supported by Singer, that our failure to aid the Third World poor is inconsistent with our general sympathy for other people: why shouldn't one simply reply, 'No, I don't have a feeling of sympathy for *all* other people. I have a feeling of sympathy for *nearby* people, who belong to my social group'? Those replies would make sense if we were subjectivists or non-cognitivists—they should *at least* have an important place in the debate—but in fact no one makes replies of that kind.

I grant that there are cases in which we act inconsistently with our customs—a few people occasionally slurping directly from the bowl does not refute the claim that our custom is to eat soup with a spoon; those few people are just violating the custom. Similarly, people's occasionally maltreating blacks would not refute the claim that we have a custom of respect for persons in general. But if the members of a society *intentionally* and *routinely* maltreat members of a certain race, then we don't say that they have two customs: a custom of respect for all persons, plus a custom of disrespect for one race. We say they have a custom of respect for members of certain races and not others. A similar point applies to individual attitudes as applies to customs.

The anti-realist does, in fact, have available methods of resolving moral disagreements. The anti-realist should be employing methods (d), (e), and/or (f). The intuitionist should be employing (a), (b), and (c). Almost no one would find the anti-realist's approach more attractive than the intuitionist's.

This concludes our treatment of the most popular objection to intuitionism. The widespread confidence that ethical disagreement provides an immediate refutation of intuitionism appears to rest on little more than caricatures of the theory, epistemological double standards, and disregard of the phenomena of disagreement and error outside of normative ethics. Intuitionists do not hold moral error to be impossible, ethics is far from the only area where we find persistent disagreements, and intuitionists can take moral errors to be caused by the same kinds of factors as cause mistakes in other areas. Nor are intuitionists at a loss for ways of trying to reduce moral disagreement; they can endorse the very argumentative strategies currently employed by moral philosophers, including strategies designed to identify which intuitions are most likely to be in error. Intuitionists cannot promise a swift resolution of most moral controversies, but nor can anyone else. Finally, the arguments against intuitionism based on disagreement could be made with at least equal force against other metaethical theories, yet only against intuitionism have they been considered persuasive. This suggests that the argument from disagreement has seemed plausible only because philosophers had already rejected intuitionism for other reasons.

# 7
# Practical Reasons

Many anti-realists have charged that if moral realism were true, there would be *no reason* for acting morally. In this chapter, I argue instead that only the intuitionist has a plausible account of our reasons for being moral.

## 7.1 The Humean argument against realism

What reasons do we have for behaving morally? There are at least two interpretations of this question, because there are two senses of 'reason': there are motivating reasons and normative reasons.

*Motivating reasons* (or 'motives') are the sort of things that explain why people do what they do. One's having a motivating reason for doing *A* does not entail that one will do *A*; it means only that one has at least *some* tendency or temptation to do *A*, given the opportunity. For example, my hunger, combined with my belief that the sandwich before me is food, constitutes a motive for me to eat the sandwich.

*Normative reasons* are the sort of things that explain why people *should* do certain things, from the standpoint of reason.[1] A normative reason for performing an action is a consideration in favor of the action, though not necessarily a decisive consideration. Like motivating reasons, normative reasons can conflict. What it is rational to do is what one has the *most* normative reason to do. For example, the fact that I need food, together with the fact that the sandwich before me is food, constitutes a normative reason for me to eat the sandwich.

We typically have normative reasons and motivating reasons for the same things. In the above example, I have both a motivating and a normative reason for eating the sandwich. But often the *strength* of our motives fails to match the strength of our normative reasons. Suppose I have a choice between a nutritious veggie sandwich and a delicious ice cream sandwich. I may have *better reasons*, all things considered, for eating the veggie sandwich, but I may find, alas, that I have *more motivation* to eat the ice cream. The anticipated gustatory pleasure of the ice cream is *some* justification for choosing it (insofar as pleasure is a good), but this justification may be rationally outweighed by long-term health considerations. These long-term health considerations produce in me *some* tendency to choose the veggies, but this tendency may be outweighed, motivationally, by the desire for sugary pleasure, and I may thus make the irrational choice.

The following three principles about reasons for action are widely accepted in philosophy; the first two are standard assumptions in economics as well:

i) *The Humean Conception of Reasons* (hereafter, 'the Humean Conception'): All reasons for action derive from pre-existing desires. In particular,

   a) You have a motivating reason to do *A* if and only if there is something you desire for its own sake that you believe *A* would or might accomplish. The strength of your reason to do *A* is proportional to the strength of that desire.

   b) You have a normative reason to do *A* if and only if there is something you desire for its own sake that you have reason to believe *A* would or might accomplish.[2]

ii) *The Belief/Desire Gap*: Beliefs don't entail desires: it is possible to believe any given objective fact obtains, while lacking any given desire.

iii) *The Magnetism of Values*:

   a) If one accepts a moral value, one necessarily has a motivating reason for action. For instance, if you take stealing to be wrong, then you must have at least some motivation to avoid stealing.

   b) Moral facts, if there are any, necessarily provide normative reasons for action. If stealing is wrong, or at least if one has reason to believe it to be wrong, then one has a normative reason to avoid stealing.

These principles are commonly thought to refute moral realism. How so? There are two versions of the argument:[3]

*First Version:*
1. Motives for action require desires. (The Humean Conception.)
2. No belief about an objective fact entails the presence of any desire. (The Belief/Desire Gap.)
3. Therefore, no belief about an objective fact, by itself, entails the presence of any motive for action. (From 1, 2.)
4. Moral attitudes (the attitudes expressed by moral claims) entail the presence of motives for action. (The Magnetism of Values.)
5. Therefore, moral attitudes are not beliefs about objective facts. (From 3, 4.)

*Second Version:*
6. Normative reasons for action require desires. (The Humean Conception.)
7. No objective fact entails the presence of a desire. (Because objective facts are facts in the external world, apart from our desires and attitudes.)
8. No objective fact, by itself, entails the presence of any normative reason for action. (From 6, 7.)
9. Moral facts, if there are any, entail the presence of normative reasons for action. (The Magnetism of Values.)
10. Therefore, there are no objective moral facts. (From 8, 9.)

In brief, moral claims state reasons for action. Reasons for action, of either kind, require the existence of desires. But no objective fact, or belief about an objective fact, can by itself entail the existence of any desires. Therefore, moral claims do not merely report objective facts; they must contain some subjective or non-cognitive element.

There are three ways for a moral realist to respond: reject the Humean Conception, reject the Belief/Desire Gap, or reject the Magnetism of Values. Each way has been taken by at least some philosophers.[4] I shall criticize the Humean Conception and propose an alternative conception of reasons.

## 7.2 The connection between motivating and normative reasons

A natural response to the first version of the Humean argument is to question (4). If I take stealing to be wrong, then perhaps it follows that I *ought* to be, or that I *think* I ought to be, motivated to avoid stealing. But it does not obviously follow that I *am* in fact motivated to avoid stealing. I might be an immoral person, even by my own lights—that is, I might fail to be motivated by what I take to be morally correct. For similar reasons, we might doubt (6) in the second version. If I have a *normative* reason to help Jimmy with his homework, perhaps it follows that I *should* desire to help Jimmy, or that I would desire to do so *were I fully rational*, but it does not obviously follow that I *in fact* have some desire that would be satisfied by helping Jimmy. There is reason to suspect that the argument trades on an equivocation: the Humean thesis—that reasons for action require desires—is plausible only if we take 'reasons' to mean 'motivating reasons'. But the Magnetism of Values premise—that moral claims state reasons for action—is plausible only if we take 'reasons' to mean 'normative reasons'. That is, it is plausible that our being *motivated* to do something requires our having a desire appropriately related to the action, but not that our having a *normative* reason to do something requires such a desire; and it is plausible that our justifiedly taking something to be good must give us a *normative* reason to pursue it, but not that it must actually motivate us to pursue it. But the argument requires both the Humean Conception and the Magnetism of Values to be true for the same sense of 'reason'.

That is not my ultimate response to the argument, however. I raise this point to show why a proponent of the Humean argument should want to defend some strong connection between motivating and normative reasons, roughly to the effect that the two kinds of reasons always go together. Fortunately for them, they can do so by means of at least two plausible arguments.

First, an argument from the *'ought* implies *can'* principle: To say that you *should* do A implies that you *can* do A of your own free will.[5] This implies that you can freely choose to do A, which in turn implies that you can be motivated to do A; a person cannot freely choose to do something while having no motivation at all for doing it. Now, to say that you have a normative reason for doing A implies that you should do A (provided there are no countervailing considerations). It follows that you are capable of being motivated to do A (provided there are no countervailing considerations). But if you had no *motive* that would appear to you to be served by doing A, then, since you also have no choice about what motives you have, you would be *incapable* of being motivated to do A. Therefore, the claim that you have a normative reason for doing A implies that you have some available motivation for doing A.[6] In short:

1. If S has a normative reason for doing A, then S should do A, provided there are no countervailing reasons.

2. If *S* should do *A*, then *S* can freely do *A*.
3. If *S* can freely do *A*, then *S* can be motivated to do *A*.
4. Therefore, if *S* has a normative reason for doing *A*, then *S* can be motivated to do *A*, provided there are no countervailing reasons. (From 1, 2, 3.)
5. If *S* has no available motivating reason to do *A*, then *S* can not be motivated to do *A*, even if there are no countervailing reasons against *A*.
6. Therefore, if *S* has a normative reason for doing *A*, then *S* has an available motivating reason for doing *A*. (From 4, 5.)

To illustrate, suppose someone tells me that I have a normative reason to donate $500 to Oxfam. Suppose, however, that I am so lacking in concern for my fellow human beings that I have no desire to help the poor, nor any other desire that would be satisfied by donating this money. Suppose that after thorough and correct deliberation, I realize these facts. Furthermore, I cannot help any of this; I cannot help the fact that I don't care about the poor, nor the fact that I know that donating $500 to Oxfam satisfies none of my desires. In this situation, I cannot be motivated to donate the money. Therefore, I simply cannot donate the money of my own free will. And therefore, it is false to say that I *should* donate the money. Conversely, for it to be *true* that I should donate the money, one of the above assumptions would have to be false; I would have to have some desire that I thought donating the money might satisfy.

That is an argument a Humean might make, to draw the connection between motivating and normative reasons, and thereby to bolster the contention that '*S* should do *A*' implies that *S* has some sort of desire.

A second argument for this connection I call the Argument from Interpretation. Our normal way of interpreting other people's behavior (including their statements) relies on an assumption of rationality: when you are trying to figure out what another person believes, desires, and so on, you look at his behavior and attribute to him the beliefs, desires, and so on that would make that behavior make the most sense. For example, if someone eats a lot of chocolate, I infer that she likes chocolate and thus is undertaking the correct means of satisfying her preferences. If I instead assumed that she was irrational, I might hypothesize that she *hates* chocolate and that is why she eats it. A similar point applies to attributing beliefs to others: I assume my chocolate-eating friend believes that she is eating chocolate, because that is what it would make sense for her to believe, given her actual circumstances. If I took her to be irrational,

I might instead hypothesize that she thinks she is swimming the English Channel, and she likes swimming the Channel, so that is why she eats the chocolate. The hypotheses that assume irrationality might 'explain' the same behavior, but we rightly regard them as *prima facie* ridiculous. The point is that we need to assume others are at least generally rational in order to select an appropriate account of their behavior from among the indefinitely many possible accounts.

Something like this principle is widely accepted under the name of 'the Principle of Charity'.[7] The principle is not that all actions or beliefs are rational, but only that we should interpret others to be by and large rational, if possible. Sometimes, people's statements and behavior provide evidence that they are irrational in certain respects. The Principle of Charity does not deny this, but it holds that rationality is a default assumption, and that we should not attribute more irrationality than necessary. The point is not merely one about how we in fact interpret others, but about what is the *correct* way of interpreting others. Notice also that the principle is not an empirical one: it is not that we have, by observing people for a long time, *discovered* that they are by and large rational. Rather, the assumption of general rationality is one that we bring to our observations, as a constraint on their interpretation. We do not directly observe others' beliefs and desires, so we would have no way of finding out whether people were by and large rational, without first having some way of inferring their mental states from their behavior. That sort of inference is just what 'interpretation' is. Since the assumption of rationality is required for interpreting behavior, the assumption of rationality cannot be tested by observing people's behavior. At most, what could be discovered empirically is that people exhibit behavior which is *capable* of a rational interpretation, but we cannot determine empirically that interpretations of people as rational are *pro tanto* better than competing interpretations of people as irrational.

The Principle of Charity is almost universally accepted. But what is its basis? It seems that the principle could be correct only if we were justified in believing, in general, that people are by and large rational. But for the reasons just discussed, this belief cannot be justified by observation. So it must be *a priori*. How can that be? Here is a natural answer: because it is a necessary truth that whenever one has a normative reason for action, one has a motivating reason for action. Suppose the contrary: suppose, that is, that one can have a normative reason to do *A* but no motive for doing *A*. If this is possible, then it seems that it would also be possible for a person to lack motives, *in general*, for doing the things he had normative reasons for doing. Such a person would be generally irrational. But if it is possible for a person to be generally irrational, then how could we know *a priori* that people are in fact by and large rational?

The preceding argument may be weakest at its first stage, where I construed the Principle of Charity to imply that we should interpret people as being by and large rational. Perhaps instead we need only interpret people as being rational *in certain respects*, which leaves open the possibility that we might discover other broad, systematic respects in which people are not rational. However, I shall not pursue this line. I find it plausible that normative reasons have the kind of 'magnetism' the Humean argument posits. The idea is not that all beings are moved by all normative reasons. The idea is that if a being can and does *recognize* a normative reason, then the being must have at least some tendency to be moved by that reason. But there may be many beings who fail to recognize many normative reasons.

So far, I have sought to state the Humean case as strongly as possible: it seems that evaluative claims imply the existence of normative reasons for action; this, in turn, implies or strongly suggests the existence of motivating reasons for action; and that implies the existence of desires that are appropriately related to the actions in question. But no objective fact can imply the existence of a desire; therefore, evaluative claims are not objective, factual claims. Where I challenge this argument is in its assumption that all motivation stems from desire.

## 7.3 A rationalist conception of motivation

There are at least four kinds of motivations we are subject to:

i) *Appetites:* Appetites include such things as hunger, thirst, and lust. They are simple, often instinctive desires, whose satisfaction is normally attended by physical (that is, sensory[8]) pleasure, and/or whose frustration is attended by physical pain or discomfort.

ii) *Emotions:* Emotional desires, such as those occasioned by anger, fear, and love, differ from appetites in that their satisfaction or frustration is normally associated with a different (emotional) kind of enjoyment or suffering, rather than sensory pleasure or pain. In addition, emotional desires require a more sophisticated kind of cognition than appetites. To be angry at someone involves perceiving something he has done as being bad in a certain way; to fear something involves perceiving it as dangerous; to love someone involves perceiving his existence and one's relationship to him as valuable; and so on. No such sophisticated perceptions are required for the appetites. Correspondingly, emotions can have much more sophisticated objects; one may be angry about a fact that requires quite abstract concepts to be aware of—say, the fact that a student plagiarized an assignment. Our emotions commonly have longer-term effects as well—said anger may result in one's giving the student a low grade, months later. Appetites have simpler objects and shorter-term effects.

iii) *Prudence:* Prudence is the motivation to pursue (or avoid) a thing because one recognizes it as furthering (or setting back) one's own interests. Prudence differs from, and often opposes, appetitive and emotional desires. To return to an earlier example, my appetite for ice cream may conflict with my prudential motive to maintain good health. Likewise, my anger at someone may tempt me to hit him, while prudence bids me to restrain myself.

iv) *Impartial Reasons:* Sometimes we are motivated to act in particular ways by our recognition of what is good, fair, honest, and so on. These reasons are impartial, in the sense that they don't appeal to our own interests or to our personal preferences. This sort of motive may conflict with any of the first three; for instance, a man may desire to cheat on his wife, but believe that this would be unfaithful (and hence bad). Or a judge may consider taking a bribe, which would promote his own interests, but believe that this would be dishonest (and hence bad).

These seem to be the main kinds of motives. There are several interesting questions about them. First, what is the object of an appetitive desire—that is, when one has an appetite, what is it that one wants? One traditional view is that it is physical pleasure or the avoidance of physical pain, and this has led some thinkers to the generalization that *all* desire boils down to the desire for pleasure and the absence of pain.[9] This, however, is a mistake. One may of course desire pleasure, but this is not what typical appetites consist in, even though pleasure normally attends the satisfaction of those appetites. When you are hungry, what you want is food. You may *also* want gustatory pleasure, but *that* desire is not what your hunger consists in; hunger consists in the desire for food. To illustrate, suppose you are hungry. Some mad scientists stimulate your brain so that you have an incredibly realistic hallucination of eating a salmon filet, and so that at the same time you stop feeling hungry. In this case, I would say that your desire (the hunger) *went away* without being *satisfied*— you did not get what you wanted, although you may have been tricked into thinking you did. Our desires are typically focused on *the world*, not on our minds.[10]

Similarly, what are the objects of emotional desires? If one is tempted to view typical appetites as desires for physical pleasure, one might be similarly tempted to treat emotional desires as desires for emotional satisfaction. Thus, one might view a man's love for his children as giving rise chiefly to a desire for the emotional satisfaction of seeing them well off. But in fact, what love gives rise to is the desire that loved ones *be* better off. That is why, for example, taking steps to ensure that one's children are provided for after one's death is a manifestation of love.

To illustrate, imagine that you are offered a chance to sell your children into slavery for $10,000. The children will be miserable for the rest of their lives. However, as part of the deal, you will receive a hypnosis session that will cause you to forget that the children were sold into slavery and will, furthermore, induce in you a permanent delusion that the children are extremely happy and successful. You will thereby enjoy the satisfaction of *thinking* your children to be well off. Assuming that you love your children very much, would you take the deal? If you answered 'no', then your chief desire is not for emotional satisfaction.[11]

Where does the desire for pleasure fit into my taxonomy of motivations? I think that it fits under prudence, in the admittedly broad sense in which I have defined 'prudence'. The desire to secure pleasures for oneself is a desire to promote one's interests in a certain way. We may also just have an appetite for pleasure.

This brings us to another simplistic but common psychological theory: the theory that all actions are motivated by concern for self-interest. This theory falls to much the same objection as the previous one. We are moved by a variety of different desires—desires for food, sex, power, wealth, love, fame, and so on—most of which are for things logically independent of the advancement of our interests. No recherché or even particularly noble examples are required to refute psychological egoism. Consider a desire, prompted by anger, to hit someone: one need not take such an action to be in any way in one's interests in order to feel the desire, and one may well take it to be very much against one's interests.[12]

These remarks undermine two particular Humean theories of reasons: the view that all actions are motivated by the desire to secure pleasure and avoid pain, and the view that all actions are motivated by the desire to promote one's own interests. But they leave intact the more general Humean framework, according to which all actions are motivated by desires of *some* kind.

Where does morality fit into the taxonomy? I take moral principles to be a species of impartial reasons. Thus, considerations of what is good, fair, honest, and so on are both moral reasons and impartial reasons for action. There may be other impartial reasons that are not moral (perhaps the fact that a certain procedure is the most efficient way of producing pencils is an impartial reason, but not a moral reason, for one to cause the pencil factory to make pencils in that way), but I won't discuss them here.

We always have an impartial reason for doing what we know to be morally correct. But this is not to say that that reason is the only, or even the primary reason we have for acting morally. We also have many non-moral reasons for being moral. Consider, for example, a person who does what he believes is right, not merely because it is right, but because he believes God will punish wrongdoers; or a person who refrains from stealing, not merely because he recognizes theft as wrong, but because stealing makes him feel bad. These would be, respectively, prudential and emotional motives for doing what is right.

How does the notion of 'desire' map onto my taxonomy of motives? In ordinary language, appetites and emotional motives are commonly called 'desires', while prudential and impartial motives are not. Imagine a student who knows she has an exam tomorrow morning, for which she has not studied. A friend invites her to a party. The dialogue might go like this:

Friend:    Hey, you wanna go to a party tonight?
Student:   I really want to go, but I should study tonight.
Friend:    So you're saying you'd rather study than party?
Student:   Of course I don't *want* to study; I'd much rather be party-
           ing. But I really need to study.

The natural interpretation is that the student has described her motivations correctly: she has an emotional desire to party, no desire to study, but recognizes—that is, believes—that it would be very much in her interests to study (she 'needs' to). The latter, prudential motivation may overrule her desire.

Or imagine a judge who has been offered a bribe to acquit a criminal. The dialogue might go like this:

Judge:     I won't take your bribe.
Criminal:  What's the matter, don't you want $100,000?
Judge:     Of course I want $100,000. But acquitting you would be
           wrong.
Criminal:  So you're saying that you want to send me to prison more
           than you want to have $100,000? You must really hate
           me.

Judge:      It doesn't matter how I feel about you. You committed a crime, and criminals should be punished, and it's my job to see to it.

Criminal:   Look, I bet my money could buy you a lot more enjoyment than whatever satisfaction you'd get from seeing me punished.

Judge:      You just don't get it.

The natural interpretation is that the judge recognizes that taking the bribe would best promote his own interests, satisfy his desires, and increase his enjoyment, but he believes it would be wrong. His moral belief overrules his personal interests.

What would the Humean say? That in the first example, the student *wants* to get a good grade on the test, more than she wants to go partying, and that in the second example, the judge *wants* the criminal to be punished more than he wants the $100,000. Is this true? Not in any non-trivial sense. 'Desire', in English, seems often to refer to appetites and emotions, as the above examples illustrate. In that sense, the Humean's claim is false. The student may well feel more desire to go partying than to get a good grade on the test, but still recognize that it would be more in her interests to study. The judge may feel more desire to take the $100,000 than to punish the criminal, but recognize that justice requires him to punish the criminal. Introspectively, there is simply no evidence for the Humean claim.

In another sense, however, a 'desire' is simply any motivation, of whatever kind.[13] In this sense, it is trivial that in my examples, the student desires to study and the judge desires to refuse the bribe. On this interpretation, the core Humean thesis that motives for action require desires amounts to no more than the following tautology, with which even the staunchest rationalist will agree: Motives for action require motives for action. But surely no interesting conclusion can be inferred from this. In particular, on the present conception of desire, it can no longer be assumed that beliefs are not desires; if a belief motivates action, then it would *ipso facto* be a 'desire' in the present sense. And we should simply have to distinguish two kinds of 'desires': the kind that are constituted by beliefs, and the kind that are constituted by appetites or emotions.

I take it that the Humean does not want to trivialize his thesis in this way; most Humeans will say that we have some independent conception of 'desire', as an introspectively identifiable type of mental state, on which it is not an open question whether a desire can be a belief.[14] But on introspecting, the only such mental states I can find that might be called 'desires' are the appetites and emotions. And it is not debatable whether I always act on my currently strongest appetites and emotions—I know that, thankfully, I do not.

## 7.4    Why believe the Humean conception?

### 7.4.1    The intuitive appeal of the Humean conception

Why have so many philosophers embraced the Humean Conception of Reasons? Most seem simply to consider it intuitively obvious—it is just obvious that reasons for action require goals, and it is just obvious that only our desires, and not mere beliefs about the world outside of us, can provide us with goals.[15] Let us first discuss this appeal to intuition, and then turn to some arguments for the Humean Conception.

I am at least as willing as the next person to consider intuitions. But I remain unpersuaded by the widespread intuition supporting the Humean Conception. This intuition is a *general* one; that is, its content is a universal generalization ('All reasons have such-and-such form' or 'No belief can be inherently motivating'). I think that intuitions of this kind can often be easily undermined by particular examples of things that defy the generalization. For example, consider the principle, 'Two solid objects cannot occupy the same space at the same time'. On its face, this seems obviously true. But now consider this case: you have a lump of clay, which we can call 'Lumpy'. You proceed to mold the clay in such a way as to form a statue. Call the statue 'Venus'. It seems that Lumpy still exists; it has simply been molded into a different shape. Furthermore, Lumpy and Venus now occupy the same space. Both are solid objects. And they are distinct objects, since Lumpy existed before Venus did. Therefore, we have two solid objects occupying the same space at the same time. Isn't this a deep philosophical paradox?

No, it isn't. We should respond to the puzzle by saying: 'Okay, if you're going to count cases like *that*, then two solid objects can occupy the same space at the same time. When I said this was impossible, I had in mind pairs of objects like: my hand and this table. If I had been thinking of "pairs of objects" like the statue and the mass of clay it is composed of, I would never have said that two solid objects couldn't occupy the same space, because obviously *those* things can'. Thus, I think that the general intuition we began with— even though it was quite a firm and widely-shared intuition—has no probative force against the judgment that Lumpy and Venus are in the same place, or that they are two solid objects. The reason is that the general intuition depended on our having certain kinds of cases, and not others, in mind in the first place.

I am not claiming that this is true of *all* general intuitions, but it is true of many of them. And in particular, I think it is true of the intuition supporting the Humean Conception. When someone puts forward the general principle, 'Beliefs cannot by themselves be motivating', I think that we can only judge the plausibility of that generalization by running through different kinds of beliefs in our minds. To be sure, the principle seems plausible when we think about *most* beliefs—for instance, the belief that my house is on fire, the belief that the weasels are mammals, the belief that 13 is prime, and so on. In fact, it seems plausible when you consider any belief about any purely natural, external fact. But now consider another class of beliefs: beliefs about *value*. For instance, the belief that stealing is *morally wrong*, the belief that happiness is *good*, and so on. If you're counting *this* sort of belief, then the principle does not seem at all obvious; indeed, it seems very *im*plausible. I think the principle that only desires can motivate seems obvious only when we are ignoring certain cases—just as the principle that two solid objects can't occupy the same space only seems obvious when we are ignoring certain cases.

Consider why it seems plausible that a belief about a natural fact cannot be inherently motivating. One reason is that it is unclear what would determine *which* course of action the natural fact is supposed to favor. Thus, suppose you see someone sitting in a train station. You inform him that the train for New Brunswick is about to leave. Can this fact, by itself, motivate him to act in some way—for instance, to get up and board the train? One reason for denying that it can is that there doesn't seem to be any particular course of action that uniquely bears any special relation to the fact. Granted, the fact that the train is about to leave implies that getting up and boarding the train is required *in order to get to New Brunswick on that train*. On the other hand, refraining from getting up and boarding the train is required *in order to keep out of New Brunswick*. The mere fact that the train is about to leave does not tell us whether getting to New Brunswick is good or bad, so it doesn't pick out any particular course of action as the one to take.

But evaluative facts are obviously different. They *do* tell us what is good or bad, and there is no puzzle about which course of action an evaluative judgment supports. The judgment that one should keep promises obviously bears a special relationship to promise-keeping that it does not bear to other kinds of actions.

Now consider Hume's main argument against the Rationalist

Conception: Hume says that the function of reason is only to determine what is true and false. But actions cannot be true or false. Therefore, actions cannot be evaluated by reason, and therefore they cannot be rational or irrational.[16]

That is an awful argument. Consider a parallel argument: Reason can only judge truth and falsity. Numbers cannot be true or false. Therefore, reason cannot make any judgments about numbers—for instance, reason cannot tell us that seven is prime. Presumably Hume would say that this is a misapplication of his principle. Presumably, he would say that although numbers themselves cannot be true or false, *propositions about them*, including the proposition that seven is prime, *can* be true or false; and that is why the judgment that seven is prime can fall under the purview of reason. But if that's right, then a parallel response applies to Hume's argument: of course actions themselves cannot be true or false, but *propositions about them*, including the proposition that some particular action is right, can be; and that is why the judgment that an action is right can fall under the purview of reason.

## *7.4.2 Smith's argument

Michael Smith provides an argument similar in spirit to Hume's, but stronger. Smith's argument begins with a technical notion, that of 'direction of fit'. Here is a story to illustrate that notion. There are two men in a supermarket. One has a shopping list and is going through the supermarket collecting items from the list. The other is a detective who is tracking the movements of the first man. The detective makes a list of the things the shopper buys. By the time the shopper gets to the checkout stand, both men have identical lists in their hands. Furthermore, both of them want the items on their list to match what the shopper has in his cart. But there is a difference: the shopper is supposed to make the *world* match his *list*; the detective is supposed to make his *list* match the *world*. Thus, if the detective should notice that his list says 'Twinkies' but the shopper has no Twinkies in the cart, he can fix the problem by simply crossing out the word 'Twinkies'. But if the *shopper* should notice that his list says 'Twinkies' but he has no Twinkies in the cart, he cannot fix the problem by crossing out 'Twinkies'; rather, he has to go back and put some Twinkies in the cart. We might express this difference by saying that the shopper's list has world-to-list direction of fit; the detective's list has list-to-world direction of fit.[17]

Now, there is something analogous to be said about the difference between beliefs and desires: Beliefs, we might say, have 'mind-to-world direction of fit', meaning that beliefs aim to match reality. If your belief fails to correspond to reality (that is, it is false), then the belief is thereby defective and should be changed. Desires, in contrast, have 'world-to-mind direction of fit', meaning that we aim to make reality match our desires. If a desire fails to correspond to reality (that is, it is unsatisfied), the desire is not thereby defective; rather, one has reason to try to change *the world*.[18]

With this background, we can state Smith's argument against the Rationalist Conception of motivating reasons:

1. Having a motivating reason requires having a goal.
2. Having a goal is being in a state with world-to-mind direction of fit.
3. Beliefs have mind-to-world direction of fit, not world-to-mind.
4. Therefore, beliefs cannot be motivating reasons.[19]

(4) conflicts with the rationalist conception, since rationalists say that a moral belief can constitute a motivating reason.

Where might a rationalist challenge this argument? I think the crucial premise is (2).[20] First, let us clarify (2) by replacing the metaphorical expression 'world-to-mind direction of fit' with its literal meaning. I take it that the literal meaning of (2) is roughly this:

> Having a goal is being in a state such that, if one notices that the world does not match that state, then one will have a tendency to try to change the world to remove the discrepancy.[21]

But this remains ambiguous. What does it mean for a mental state to 'match' or 'fit' the world? This might mean either that the *content* of the mental state is realized, or that the *goal* that the mental state represents is realized. This gives rise to the following two readings of (2):

$2_C$. Having a goal is being in a state such that, if one notices that the *content* of that state is not realized, then one will have a tendency to try to change the world to bring about the content of that state.

$2_G$. Having a goal is being in a state such that, if one notices that the *goal* represented by that state is not realized, then one will have a tendency to try to change the world to bring about that goal.

To illustrate the distinction, suppose I have the goal of increasing my happiness. According to the Rationalist Conception, my having this goal might consist simply in my believing that my happiness is good.[22] Now, the *content* of this belief—the thing I believe to be the case—is: *my happiness is good*. But the *goal* that the mental state represents is simply *my happiness*. This is just part of the rationalist view—the rationalist view is that one's goal is the thing that one believes to be good. Thus, $(2_C)$ implies: if I notice that happiness is not in fact good, then I will have a tendency to try to bring it about that happiness is good. $(2_G)$, on the other hand, implies that, if I notice that I am not in fact happy, then I will try to bring it about that I am happy.

Obviously, if (2) means $(2_C)$, then the rationalist should reject the premise. If I somehow discover that happiness is not good, I will not try to bring it about that happiness is good (how could I do that? I cannot change the facts of ethics). On the other hand, if (2) means $(2_G)$, we should accept it, but then we should reject premise (3). For, to avoid equivocation, (3) will now have to be read:

$3_G$.  If one notices that the goal represented by a belief is not realized, then one will have a tendency to modify one's mind, *not* to try to change the world to bring about the goal.

This is false. If I notice that my happiness (the goal represented by my 'my happiness is good' belief) is not realized, then I *will* have a tendency to try to change the world to bring about that goal, that is, to bring it about that I am happy.

Why does Smith not notice the ambiguity in (2)? Perhaps because, on *his* view of motivation, there is no such ambiguity. On the Humean view, when one has a goal, the content of one's mental state is the same thing as the goal that it represents. For instance, when I want to take over the world, the content of the desire is 'that I take over the world', and the goal it represents is also *that I take over the world*. So, on the Humean view, there is no distinction to be drawn between $(2_C)$ and $(2_G)$. But there *is* a distinction on the rationalist view. When one has a moral belief, if the goal that is represented is $G$, then the content of the belief is not $G$, but rather '$G$ is good'.

Note that I am not, in this section, trying to refute the Humean Conception. I am only trying to show that Smith does not succeed in refuting the Rationalist Conception. For Smith to succeed, he cannot assume the Humean Conception to start with. Thus, he cannot assume that $(2_C)$ and $(2_G)$ are equivalent. So he must tell us which of those he means. If we are taking the Rationalist Conception seriously, there is no reason why we would accept both (2) and (3) of Smith's argument: depending on how the notion of a mental state's 'matching' reality is read, we will either find (2) obviously implausible (if it is read as [$2_C$]) or find (3) obviously implausible (if it is read as [$3_G$]). Smith therefore fails to provide a non-question-begging argument against the Rationalist.

So far, I have criticized the motivations for the Humean Conception. In the next two sections, I propose to demonstrate its deep implausibility.

## 7.5  Extending the Humean conception?

David Hume himself held a very simple version of the Humean Conception. In his view, it is impossible for any action or desire to be irrational; only beliefs can be evaluated by reason:

> Actions may be laudable or blameable, but they cannot be reasonable or unreasonable.[23]

> 'Tis not contrary to reason to prefer the destruction of the whole world to the scratching of my finger. 'Tis not contrary to reason for me to chuse my total ruin, to prevent the least uneasiness of an Indian or person wholly unknown to me. 'Tis as little contrary to reason to prefer even my own acknowledg'd lesser good to my greater.[24]

This is absurd. Even modern-day Humeans do not follow Hume this far. Examples of irrational actions are easy to come by; indeed, the strikingness that has made the second quotation above famous stems precisely from the fact that the three examples Hume gives of things 'not contrary to reason' would normally be considered *paradigms* of irrationality. The only justification Hume offers for his counter-intuitive assessments of those examples consists in a deduction from the Humean Conception of reasons. But why should we accept that conception? If a proposed theory of practical rationality is unable to account for seemingly central examples of practical irrationality—and especially if it is so anemic as to be incapable of drawing *any* distinction at all between rational and irrational behavior—then it is difficult to see why we should take that theory seriously.

Fortunately, modern-day Humeans are eager to assure us, the Humean conception entails no such results. Of course there are such things as reasonable and unreasonable decisions, and what it is rational to do is not simply determined by whatever happens to be the agent's strongest desire at the time of the choice. Rather, there is a process of rational deliberation, whose outcome determines what is the rational course of action.[25] This view is still broadly Humean, because the process of rational deliberation is not taken to generate any new goals independently of the subject's desires. Hereafter, I shall refer to any view that accepts roughly the Humean Conception while adding some constraints on rational action that go beyond 'choose whatever you most want now', the 'Neo-Humean view'. I shall consider five conditions on normative reasons that have been proposed by Neo-Humeans:

i) *The Foresight Constraint:* What normative reasons we have, as well as their strength, is determined not only by our current desires, but also by the desires we know we will have in the future.[26] It is thus irrational to perform an action to satisfy a current desire, if one knows that more and stronger desires will consequently be frustrated in the future. This is why the student in the example from section 7.3 would be irrational to spend the night partying.

ii) *The Imagination Constraint:* What we have normative reason to do is partly determined by what we *would* desire, if we were to imagine relevant situations vividly and accurately.[27] For instance, suppose that, were I to vividly imagine the plight of the starving Africans, I would desire to help them by sending money to Oxfam; then I presently have a normative reason to help them.

iii) *The Consistency Constraint:* If one has an inconsistent set of desires—that is, desires that logically could not all be satisfied— then one has a normative reason to change one's desires to render them consistent. For instance, if I find that I want to shoot up heroin every day, but I also want to not be an habitual drug user, then I have reason to attempt to eradicate one of those desires.

iv) *The Coherence Constraint:* We have a normative reason to modify our desires in such a way as to yield a more coherent set of desires, just as we have reason to modify our beliefs in such a way as to yield a more coherent belief system, where coherence is a matter of how systematic and unified a collection of desires/beliefs is, the degree to which some desires/beliefs can explain others, and the like. It is thus rational to adopt new desires that would help explain and systematize our existing desires, and to relinquish desires that don't fit well with the rest of our desires.[28] For example, suppose you desire the well-being of human beings except for members of one specific race, and you have no explanation for your discounting of that race. Then you could achieve a more coherent overall set of desires by giving up your racial prejudice and moving to a desire for the welfare of all human beings.

v) *The Deliberation Constraint:* We have a normative reason, before acting, to engage in rational deliberation about what will best satisfy our desires, and we have a normative reason for doing the things that such deliberation *would* find to be most suited to satisfying our desires. A person thus acts irrationally if he does what appears to him best suited to satisfying his desires, when further deliberation would have shown some other course of action to be better.

The Neo-Humean view, I shall argue, is unstable. Once we adopt a broadly Humean conception of reasons, none of these rationality constraints can be defended. A Humean is thus left with the view, either that there is no such thing as rational or irrational action, or that it is rational merely to do whatever one most wants to do at the moment.

### 7.5.1 The Foresight Constraint

Suppose that you presently have no desire that $A$ occur but instead desire that $A$ not occur; however, you know that at some future time, your psychological set will change in such a way that you will come to desire $A$ (but not as a result of any change in beliefs). Do you *now* have a reason—either motivating or normative—to take steps to bring about $A$? A Humean should answer 'no'. Only an individual's desires at the time of decision can help explain his actions; a desire that you will have in the future but *do not now have* cannot motivate any present actions, any more than can a desire that you used to have but no longer have. If we accept the arguments of section 7.2 for a strong connection between motivating and normative reasons, this suggests that such a future desire also gives you no *normative* reasons, any more than a merely past desire does. Compare an argument of Bernard Williams': Williams contends that in order for something to be a normative reason for $S$ to do $A$, it must be something that *could* be $S$'s actual reason for doing $A$; but only something that includes one or more of $S$'s desires could possibly be $S$'s reason for doing anything; therefore, normative reasons must involve desires.[29] To this we might add that only something including one or more of $S$'s *present* desires could possibly be $S$'s reason for doing anything now; therefore, the same argument leads to the conclusion that normative reasons must involve present desires.

The story of Odysseus and the Sirens illustrates this point: Odysseus plans to sail past the Sirens, whose songs have lured many sailors to their deaths. He now strongly desires that the same *not* happen to him. But Odysseus knows that once he hears the Sirens' song, he will be overcome by a desire to sail towards them, come what may. This desire, let us suppose, will be so strong that he will consider death a price worth paying to be closer to the Sirens. But, to repeat, he *now* desires that he *not* go to the Sirens. His solution: he has himself tied to the mast while sailing past the Sirens. Is Odysseus rational in doing this? Does the desire that he will have when he hears the Sirens' song provide him with a normative reason now for taking steps to ensure that he will be able to join the Sirens? I take it that the answers are clearly 'yes' and 'no'. This fits with what I have said the Humean should say.

Here is another illustration of the same point. Sunflower is presently a socialist college student. To her dismay, she has observed that many former socialists have 'sold out' as they became older, changing their values to conform to those of their society. Suppose Sunflower justifiedly believes that when she gets older, her own personality and values will also change in a way that will lead her, without acquiring any false non-evaluative beliefs, to endorse capitalism. But, to repeat, she presently opposes capitalism and supports socialism. Does Sunflower now have a reason to work towards the maintenance of the capitalist order? I take it that the correct answer, and the answer the Humean will embrace, is 'no'.

Next, suppose that you presently have a desire of a certain strength for $A$ to occur, but you know that at some future time, your desire will be stronger or weaker than it presently is. *How much* reason do you now have for trying to bring about $A$? It is obvious that how strongly I am motivated to do something must be determined by how strong my desires are now, not how strong they were or will be at some other time. And given the arguments of section 7.2, this suggests that the same is true of our normative reasons. Moreover, this answer seems to be required by what we have already said: once we accept that *what* we now have reason to do is determined by what we presently desire, we should surely also say that *how much* reason we now have for doing a thing is determined by the present strength of our desires.

But now we have surrendered the Foresight Constraint entirely. Only present desires are relevant either to what reasons we have or to how strong those reasons are. Future desires are irrelevant. Or rather, future desires can only be relevant in the way that any other fact about the world can be relevant. If I happen to have a current desire that my future desires be satisfied, then the fact that in the future I will desire $x$ is relevant to my action—but only in the way that, if I happen to desire that Zbigniew Brzezinski's desires be satisfied, then the fact that Zbigniew Brzezinski desires $x$ is relevant to my action. In both cases, it is my present desire that provides the motivation for my action, and in both cases, I could have lacked that desire and still been perfectly rational. Just as Humeans say there is no rational reason why I must want someone else's desires to be satisfied, so they should say there is no rational reason why I must want my own future desires to be satisfied.[30]

Thus, there is no apparent reason why the student in my earlier example would be irrational to spend the night partying. If she chooses to do so, it will be because her desire to party was, at the time she made the choice, stronger than her desire to pass the class, graduate, and so on (how else could her action even be understood?). Though she knew that *later* her desire to pass the class would be much stronger, this is irrelevant. Even if the student had a desire that her future desires be satisfied, this would not render her action irrational; the fact that she chose to party would merely show that, at the time she made the choice, her desire to party was stronger.

### 7.5.2 The Imagination Constraint

The Imagination Constraint holds that our reasons for action are partly a function of desires that we do not have but would have if we were to vividly and accurately imagine certain situations. Vivid imagination might alter our desires by causing us to notice features of a situation that we would otherwise overlook, or by enabling us to better grasp a situation that we otherwise would not understand; we might then have new conative reactions to the situation. In these and other ways, vivid imagination might cause us to experience different emotions or appetites—for example, by awakening a sense of sympathy in us (we are not here concerned with purely cognitive effects of imagination).

It is not clear, however, why a desire that I *don't have* but would have if I were to go through some imaginative exercise should be thought relevant to my actual practical reasons. Such a merely potential desire cannot serve as a motivating reason; only actual desires can move me to act. Given the connection between motivating and normative reasons, it seems that it cannot serve as a normative reason either. Granted, vividly imagining a situation may change my emotional state and so change my desires, but what makes the new set of desires any better, or 'more rational', than the old set? Perhaps if correcting some errors in my reasoning would alter my desires, there would be an intelligible sense in which the new desires would be more rational—they would be more a product of the correct use of reason. But this is not the sort of change we are discussing here.

Consider an example: suppose my doctor has told me that I need surgery to remove my appendix. I have just arrived at the hospital on the day my surgery is scheduled for. I know that, because of my squeamish disposition, if I were to imagine the surgical procedure in vivid detail, I would be so horrified at the images of the surgeon cutting me open and so on, that I would experience an overpowering urge to flee the hospital. However, I do not presently have such an urge, and I presently desire that I go through with the surgery. What is it rational for me to do? It seems clear that I should go through with the surgery, and just refrain from vividly imagining it. In this case, the desire that I would have were I to vividly imagine the surgery provides no reason for action on my part.

But now return to the example of Oxfam and the starving Africans. Suppose I presently do not want to give money to Oxfam, because I would get much more enjoyment from spending the money on a new stereo. But I also know that if I were to vividly imagine the situation in Africa, I would feel so bad about it that I would wind up sending a lot of money to Oxfam, instead of enjoying the new stereo. On a Humean conception of reasons, why should I not just conclude, 'Well, then I better *not* vividly imagine the situation in Africa', and proceed with my stereo-purchasing plans?

### 7.5.3 The Consistency and Coherence Constraints

At least the Humean can defend a rational requirement of consistency and coherence for our desires, in the same way that reason requires consistent and coherent beliefs, can't he?

No, he can't. First, let us review the basic difference between beliefs and desires. Recall that Michael Smith, the very philosopher who wants to defend a coherence requirement for desires, characterizes the difference between beliefs and desires in terms of 'direction of fit'. Beliefs have 'mind-to-world direction of fit', meaning that they aim to match reality. Desires have 'world-to-mind direction of fit', meaning that we aim to make reality match our desires.

Second, let us review what is bad about inconsistency in beliefs. An inconsistent belief is one that cannot be true. Since beliefs have mind-to-world direction of fit, this marks out such beliefs as inherently defective; there is always a reason for giving up such beliefs. If a (small) set of beliefs is inconsistent, one should change one's beliefs to eliminate the inconsistency, for the same reason, namely, to attain a more accurate belief system.[31] But this line of thinking does not apply to desires. If a desire is inconsistent, then it cannot be satisfied. But since desires have world-to-mind direction of fit, a desire's unsatisfiability does *not* mark it out as defective. Since, that is, we try (or have reason to try) to make reality conform to our desires *rather than* to make our desires conform to reality, the fact that a desire does not, or even can not match reality is not a reason for changing the desire. Nor, therefore, does the impossibility of satisfying all the members of a *set* of desires render that set of desires defective.

To illustrate, suppose that I both *believe* God exists and *want* God to exist. But an atheist gives me an argument proving that God cannot exist.[32] At this point, my belief is shown to have been seriously defective (that is, wrong), and if I am rational, I must stop having that belief. But my *desire* is not thereby shown to have been 'wrong' in any sense, nor am I irrational if I continue to wish there were a God, nor is there anything defective about a value system according to which it would be good if there were a God.

We should distinguish this point from some superficially similar but false claims. As I have said, the unsatisfiability of a *desire* constitutes no defect in the desire. However, I do not deny that the impossibility of carrying out an *intention*, realizing a *hope*, or succeeding in an *attempt* constitutes a rational reason for giving up the intention, hope, or attempt. Why? Because intentions, hopes, and attempts all involve more than just desires. An intention to do *A* involves a *belief* that one will do *A* (contrast 'I intend to win this race' with 'I want to win this race'). A hope that *p* involves a belief that *p* is possible. And an attempt, besides perhaps involving the same sort of belief as an intention, normally requires, as part of its practical justification, the belief that the attempt will or might help to further some goal; but unsuccessful attempts generally do not further one's goals. This is why intentions, hopes, and attempts are open to criticism in terms of the impossibility of their objects, whereas desires are not.

Still, one might well feel that at least some desires are irrational because their objects are impossible. For instance, it seems that I would be irrational to want 2 to be equal to 3, or to desire that it both rain and not rain at the same time. I think that if these desires are irrational, it is not merely because they cannot be satisfied; perhaps they are irrational because it is unintelligible how their objects could be *good*, or because one cannot coherently conceive of their supposed objects, making it impossible for a fully rational being to entertain those desires. But in any event, these cases scarcely concern us, since such unintelligible desires are extremely rare, if they exist at all. The issue in this section is whether the Humean can provide enough constraints to give us a plausible account of rational action. The ability to criticize these unintelligible desires would still leave the Humean with a very limited conception of normative reasons, taking us very little distance towards a robust notion of practical rationality.

I should address one argument for the claim that we have a normative reason to eliminate inconsistent desires: We want it to be the case that our desires, overall, are well-satisfied, for the more of our desires are satisfied, the happier we will be, and we want to be happy. If we have inconsistent desires, we know they won't be satisfied. Therefore, we have a good reason to try to change our desires to ones that are consistent. This is a straightforward piece of means-end reasoning: we should eliminate inconsistent desires, because doing so will help achieve an end we desire. Notice that if this argument were correct, it would apply not only to desires that cannot be satisfied, but also to desires that are *unlikely* to be satisfied or that are *difficult* to satisfy. It would show that we have a normative reason to convert to a set of easily satisfiable desires, such as the desire that squares have four sides, that rocks be made of atoms, and so on. Since world hunger is unlikely to be eliminated in the foreseeable future, we have a reason to eradicate, if possible, the desire that people not starve. Of course, we might find it difficult or impossible to eradicate that desire, but then the same might be true of any other desire. For the Humean, there is no principled difference between inconsistent desires and hard-to-satisfy desires on this score.

These last results are quite implausible; we do not think of the desire for an end to world hunger as to any extent irrational, and we do not think that a being who desired only the unavoidable would thereby be more rational than we.[33] There is a straightforward, non-Humean explanation for this: since many avoidable states of affairs are good, we see desires for them as *appropriate*. We likewise see indifference towards bad states of affairs as inappropriate. Thus, we think that the nature of world hunger is such that it calls out for some negative emotional reaction, and that a person who lacked any such reaction would thereby be morally deficient.

A Humean might attempt to accommodate this idea by treating it as a matter of further desires that we have—in particular, desires that we keep our present desires. But if this works, then the same might hold of an agent with inconsistent desires: he too may desire that he keep his present desires. Again, the Humean has no theoretical rationale for treating inconsistent desires differently from merely hard-to-satisfy desires.

Once we see this, Michael Smith's idea that we should seek a coherent set of desires loses all plausibility. The reason why epistemologists consider a coherent set of *beliefs* desirable is that such a set is more likely to be by and large true.[34] But since it is not the job of desires to conform to reality, one cannot sustain the parallel argument that a systematic and unified set of desires is to be preferred on the grounds that it is more likely to be by and large satisfied. The point that desires have world-to-mind direction of fit frustrates the parallel that Smith wants to draw.

### 7.5.4 The Deliberation Constraint

I have just attacked some of the main tenets of the Neo-Humean account of practical rationality. What remains is perhaps the most central and putatively impregnable tenet of the view: that we at least have a normative reason for figuring out what would satisfy our current desires, and adhering to the results of such reasoning. But I shall argue that even this cannot serve as a constraint enabling some behavior to be rationally criticized.

If we accept that only current, actual desires can feature in reasons (either motivating or normative) for action, then it is plausible that we should say the same about beliefs: only a person's current, actual beliefs—not beliefs he will have at some future time, and not beliefs he would have in some counterfactual situation—can figure in the reasons for action he presently has. The arguments seem to be the same: a belief that one *does not now have* cannot have any influence on one's current behavior. Furthermore, given this, it seems that such a (non-)belief cannot feature in any normative reasons that one presently has.

To illustrate, suppose you are considering whether to enter a new career as a trapeze artist in the circus, or to stick with your job as a professor. You have plenty of time to decide. After thinking about it for five minutes, it appears to you that becoming a trapeze artist would best satisfy your desires, and you decide to do that. But suppose that, if you had only deliberated a little longer and a little more carefully, you *would have* rationally and correctly come to the conclusion that remaining a professor would better satisfy your desires. Can you be rationally criticized, on a Humean view, for joining the circus? Let us divide this into two questions:

First, *given* your beliefs and desires at the time of the decision, can you be rationally criticized for joining the circus? No. You decided to join the circus because you had a certain set of desires, and you thought that decision would best satisfy them. If this were not so—if you had expected the other option to better satisfy your desires—then there would simply be no explanation, given a Humean conception of motivation, of how you could wind up choosing the circus. The very explicability of your action guarantees its rationality in terms of your beliefs and desires at the time. The only way for a Humean to rationally criticize your action, then, is to level some criticism at your beliefs at the time of the decision.

Second, then, can you be rationally criticized for believing as you did? The Humean wants to say 'yes'. Consider two forms the criticism might take: (a) You might be criticized for something over which you had no control—for instance, for not being smarter, or not having some information that you had no reasonable way of obtaining. But this hardly seems acceptable. The sort of criticism we are interested in in the first place is an indictment of the practical rationality of your decision to become a trapeze artist—that is, a criticism to the effect that you rationally *ought* to have done otherwise than you did. A criticism of something that you had no control over, whether or not that thing led up to your action, hardly seems relevant to showing that you ought to have acted differently than you did. (b) You might be criticized for something over which you *had* control— for instance, for not spending more time deliberating or expending more effort to be careful. But this criticism will fail for the reasons given in the preceding paragraph. Your act, say, of spending a certain amount of time deliberating will itself have to be assessed as rational *given* the beliefs and desires you had at the time you performed this action, if the action is explicable at all. If you had thought that deliberating longer would best serve your ends, then (given the Humean account of motivation) you would have done so. If you did not think that deliberating longer would best serve your ends, then it was rational, given that, for you not to deliberate longer. Thus, the Humean can criticize you for not deliberating longer only if he can criticize you for some *further* belief(s). A regress looms, in which at each stage the Humean's attempted criticism of you demands some further belief for which you are criticizable. In sum, for any person, *S*, and any occurrence or state of affairs, *x*:

1. If *S* does not control *x*, then *S* cannot be rationally criticized for *x*.
2. If *S* controls *x*, then *S* can be rationally criticized for *x*, on Humean grounds, only if there is something *else* that *S* can be rationally criticized for.
3. Therefore, *S* can be rationally criticized for something, on Humean grounds, only if there is an infinite series of things *S* can be rationally criticized for.
4. There never is such an infinite series.
5. So no person can be rationally criticized, on Humean grounds, for anything.

Premise (1) is true because a person cannot be held unreasonable for failing to do something he could not do. (2) is true because, on the Humean view, an action or choice always makes sense *given* the agent's beliefs and desires; it can only be irrational if one of those beliefs or desires is irrational. Step (3) follows (assuming we disallow circular reasoning in criticisms of actions), because the 'something else' mentioned in (2) must (by (1)) be another thing over which *S* has control. But for *S* to be criticized for this second thing, there will have to be a *third* thing over which *S* has control and for which *S* can be rationally criticized . . . and so on. I take (4) as an intuitively obvious premise. (5) follows from (3) and (4).

One might object that either (1) or (2) is false, because a person can be rationally criticized for certain beliefs (say, beliefs for which there is no evidence), without there being anything else he is criticizable for. But what sort of criticism is it that can be leveled at beliefs? One sort of criticism of a belief would be that the belief is not true, or not likely to be true.[35] Another sort would be a practical criticism: that one *ought not* to have adopted the belief, that one had good normative reasons not to adopt it. But the first kind of criticism appears irrelevant for our purposes. If a person has done everything that it made sense for him to do given his beliefs, *and* he could not have done anything to get better beliefs, then I do not see how any criticism of his beliefs could show that he nevertheless *ought*, rationally, to have *acted* differently. Now consider the second kind of criticism. One might hold (though most philosophers doubt this) that we can control our beliefs, and we have normative practical reasons for adopting epistemically rational beliefs.[36] But this would return us to the above-mentioned regress: your act of adopting an epistemically irrational belief would itself be subject to the Humean account of practical rationality, in which case any criticism of this act would require that there be something *else* for which you are criticizable.

### 7.5.5  Coda: the need for evaluative facts

I have argued that none of the proposed rationality constraints can be motivated within a broadly Humean conception. Furthermore, in each case we can adduce clear examples, both of rational actions or desires that violate the constraint, and of irrational ones. Therefore, some extra structure not contained in the Humean Conception is needed in a theory of practical rationality, to accommodate paradigmatic examples of rational and irrational action. That extra structure, I contend, is provided by *evaluative facts*.

Consider again the Foresight Constraint. Odysseus is rational in violating the constraint when he attaches no weight to his future desire to sail closer to the Sirens. But the partying student is irrational in violating the constraint, if she fails to attach proper weight to her future desire to pass her exam. To a Humean, this is paradoxical: sometimes we take future desires to be relevant to what is rational, and other times we do not. If basic desires cannot be evaluated, then it seems that we should either let in all basic future desires, or exclude all basic future desires from our reasons for action. From a common sense standpoint, the solution to the puzzle is obvious: Odysseus rationally judges his future desire to be an *inappropriate* one, a desire for what is in reality bad. But the partying student rationally judges, or ought to judge, her future desires to be *appropriate* ones, desires for what is in reality good. That is why it is rational for Odysseus to intentionally frustrate his future desire, but irrational for the student to do likewise. Now, the Humean might wish to argue that Odysseus' anticipated desire would be misguided on the basis of some *other* Neo-Humean rationality constraint. But this move is unavailable if my arguments in regard to the other proposed constraints have succeeded.

Second, consider the Imagination Constraint. In the surgery case, I rationally violate this constraint by attaching no weight to the desire I would form were I to vividly imagine my upcoming surgery. But in the Oxfam case, it seems that I irrationally violate the constraint when I attach no weight to the desire I would form were I to vividly imagine the plight of the starving Africans. Again, this is a puzzle for Humeans, but the common sense explanation is straightforward: the counterfactual desire in the surgery case would be a misguided desire, a desire for what is bad. The counterfactual desire in the Oxfam case would be a fitting desire, a desire for what is good. That is why we think it rational to merely evade the former would-be desire by refraining from thinking too much about the surgery, but we do not think it rational to evade the latter desire by refraining from thinking too much about world hunger.

Third, consider the Consistency Constraint. On the assumption that God cannot exist, my desire for God to exist would rationally violate this, or a closely related constraint. On the other hand, a desire for two to equal three would seem to irrationally violate the constraint. Why? Because even if we suppose the existence of God to be impossible, we can still understand how the existence of a perfect being would be good. But we cannot understand how two's equaling three would be good.

Finally, recall Michael Smith's Coherence Constraint. If my aesthetic preferences are eclectic, I am not thereby irrational to any extent. On the other hand, it seems that the racist who has concern for all humans except the members of a specific race *is* thereby irrational. Evaluative facts once again aid in explaining this: my aesthetic tastes need not reflect any moral facts. If I like one piece of music but dislike another, very similar one, I need not hold the view that the one piece has an objective evaluative (or even aesthetic) property that the other lacks. But one's regard for people's welfare, we think, ought to reflect, at least in part, the *worth* of human beings. Since we can find no morally relevant distinction between one race and another, we think that people of all races have equal worth as human beings. A lack of regard for members of one race therefore evinces a blindness to that worth. Cases in which the coherence constraint seems appropriate can be understood as cases in which we think there are evaluative facts that constrain appropriate desires.

In assessing the promise of this approach, I commend two questions to the reader. First, are the practical rationality assessments I have made about the preceding examples plausible? Second, is it plausible that our tendency to accept those assessments is explained by our acceptance of evaluative judgments about the appropriateness of desires, of the sort I have suggested? If so, then the standard, Humean view of the relation between desires and evaluations gets things backwards. The Humean view is that it is rational to act in accordance with our evaluative judgments only because doing so helps satisfy our desires. I maintain that it is rational to act in accordance with our desires only when we would be justified in judging the satisfaction of those desires to be good. Evaluative judgments give normative force to desires, not the other way around.

This conclusion clearly points us towards ethical intuitionism. For if there are facts that provide normative reasons for action, it seems that they must fall into one of three categories: (a) facts about our psychology; (b) facts about the external, natural world; or (c) some species of non-natural, objective facts. My criticisms of the Humean Conception show that (a) is insufficient to account for all our normative reasons, given that the only psychological facts that are plausibly taken to supply reasons for action are facts about desires. Furthermore, it is generally agreed that facts of type (b) do not by themselves provide reasons for action (see section 7.4). So only (c) is left: some of our reasons for action consist of non-natural, objective facts, such as the facts that certain things are *good* or *bad*. But only intuitionists can embrace this answer, for only intuitionists are metaethical dualists (see section 1.4): it is only the intuitionists who believe that there *are* any facts of kind (c). Whatever their differences, the partisans of the other four metaethical views all agree that the only facts that exist are facts about our psychology and about the natural world.

T. M. Scanlon seems to provide an alternative to the intuitionist's non-natural facts. He maintains that we can speak of evaluative judgments being true or false without positing a realm of evaluative facts independent of us. All that is necessary is that there should be standards for correct ways of arriving at evaluative judgments. Evaluative judgments that are arrived at in ways that accord with the standards are true; those arrived at in ways that conflict with the standards are false. Of course, an evaluative claim is not made true by its conformity to any arbitrary standard; it must correspond to *correct* standards of evaluative judgment. As Scanlon recognizes, the judgment that a standard for forming evaluative judgments is correct is itself an evaluative judgment of the kind that the standard applies to.[37]

It seems that some sort of circularity is involved in Scanlon's account, and indeed I think this prevents his view from constituting a real alternative to intuitionism. Consider some evaluative judgment:

A. Compassion is good.

Suppose that what makes (A) true is the fact that judgment (A) can be arrived at in a way that conforms to the correct standards for arriving at evaluative judgments. I shall abbreviate this fact as follows:

B. Judgment (A) conforms to the right standards.

Now, the judgment expressed by (B) is also evaluative. What makes *it* true? To be consistent, we should say:

C. Judgment (B) conforms to the right standards.

This is also evaluative, and we can ask the same question about it, and so on ad infinitum. Scanlon's view thus entails that the truth conditions for any evaluative statement are infinitely complex.[38] This strikes me as unbelievable. Furthermore, at no point in the infinite series of conditions is the evaluative element removed; thus, the account does not show that one can accommodate evaluative truths by appealing solely to natural facts.

## 7.6  The authority of morality

### 7.6.1  The authority of morality: a rationalist view

Some of our reasons for action derive from desires, specifically, from appetites and emotions. Others—the prudential and impartial reasons—derive from cognitions of facts: the fact that an action best serves my interests in the long run constitutes a prudential reason for me to take that course of action; the fact that an action would promote the good constitutes an impartial, moral reason for me to take that course of action.

What should one do when reasons of different kinds conflict? This seems like a reasonable and important question, but what does it mean? If 'What should one do?' means 'What is one morally required to do?', then the answer is trivial: obviously, one is morally required to act on one's moral reasons, if any. When we ask the question, intending it to be non-trivial, I think our conception is this: there are different sorts of reasons we have for action, including emotional reasons, prudential reasons, and moral reasons. These are not 'reasons' in different *senses* of the word, but merely different reasons we might have, in some generic sense of 'reason'. These reasons thus can be weighed against each other. So the question arises, when we weigh up all the various reasons we have, what do we have *the most* reason, overall, to do? For instance, do we always have the most reason to be moral, or is it sometimes more reasonable to be immoral? My own view is that prudence trumps desires, and morality trumps prudence. Thus, it is always most rational to act morally. This feature of morality is what I call 'the authority of morality'. The term suggests an analogy to legal authority: for instance, in the American political system, the Constitution takes precedence over statutes, which in turn take precedence over regulations; the Constitution has ultimate authority. This is a normative, not a descriptive claim: it is not that, as a matter of fact, no statutes will ever be enforced that contravene the Constitution, but that such statutes are illegitimate; it is legally required that such statutes not be made or enforced. Analogously, morality takes precedence over prudence, which takes precedence over desires. This does not mean that, as a matter of fact, no immoral actions will ever be intentionally undertaken. It just means that such actions are irrational; one always has sufficient reason against performing such actions.

Why does prudence take precedence over desires? Because a prudential judgment, if formed correctly, *already takes into account* one's present desires. This judgment is not itself a desire, but it is made in the light of a consideration of what one presently desires and how strong those desires are. If one's prudential judgment is that one should act in such a way as *not* to satisfy some present desire, then one has already evaluated some other end as more important than the satisfaction of that desire. To then proceed to weigh the present desire against that judgment would be an unwarranted double-counting of the desire. Notice the asymmetry here: prudential judgments involve evaluations of desires; desires do not involve evaluations of prudential judgments.

I have not here given a general justification of the demands of prudence—I have not tried to explain why a rational person must assign some weight to his future well-being. I simply assume that. Rather, I have explained why, given one's capacity for prudential judgments, one should not conceive of prudential considerations as being *weighed against* emotions or appetites.

Now why does morality take precedence over self-interest? The answer, I suggest, is structurally the same: because moral judgment, if formed correctly, already takes self-interest into account. This depends on a substantive ethical thesis: that morality is not insensitive to agents' own interests. We are morally entitled to pursue our own interests, within certain limits. For instance, if you pass an accident victim in need of medical attention, you are obligated to call an ambulance, given that the cost to yourself is trivial. But if you witness a mugging, you are not obligated to help the victim by fighting the mugger off, since doing so would put yourself in grave danger.

Thus, if one judges that one is morally required to act against one's own interests on some occasion, that means that one has already weighed one's particular interest in the circumstances against whatever other considerations are at stake, and found one's own interest to be outweighed by those other considerations. To then proceed to weigh one's self-interest against that moral judgment would be an unwarranted double-counting of one's interest. Again, notice the asymmetry: moral judgments involve evaluations of desires and self-interested concerns; desires and prudential judgments do not involve evaluations of moral concerns.

I have not here given a general justification for morality, nor have I refuted ethical egoism. I have merely explained why, given that one has the capacity for moral judgment, one should not conceive of one's moral judgments as being *weighed against* one's selfish motives.

The point here is not that moral considerations are a larger category of which prudential considerations are a subset, nor that prudential considerations are a larger category of which desires are a subset. Desires are not prudential beliefs; they are different in kind. The point is that prudential beliefs include intellectual judgments of the appropriateness and importance of desires. Similarly, prudential beliefs are not moral beliefs.[39] The point is just that moral beliefs include intellectual judgments of the appropriateness and importance of self-interested motives. This is what, I claim, gives prudence authority over desire, and gives morality authority over prudence.

### 7.6.2   The arbitrariness of morality on the Humean view

A Humean can give no similar account of the authority of prudence or morality. We have already seen, in the previous section, the inadequacy of the Humean account of prudence: the Humean must portray prudential reasoning as being, at most, reasoning about how to satisfy a particular present desire, the desire that one's future desires be satisfied. But there is no reason, within the Humean conception, why one must have such a desire, and even if one has it, there is no reason why it should be given any special weight relative to other present desires. The Humean thus has no account of the intuitive notion of the rational authority of prudence.

Likewise, the Humean has no account of the authority of morality, nor any plausible account of why we should attach to morality anything like the importance that we do. A Humean must portray morality as stemming ultimately from some species of desire, such as a desire for the well-being of others. Hume himself posited 'natural sympathy' for other human beings as the source of morality.[40] All of moral theorizing and moral reasoning is therefore held to be concerned merely with how to satisfy the desires stemming from this particular psychological tendency. But sympathy is just one source of emotion among others; there is no reason for attaching any special weight to the desires it occasions, as opposed to those caused by other emotions. Thus, it would make just as much sense for us to devote a special field of enquiry, complete with complex systems of principles and so on, to figuring out how to satisfy the desires caused by *envy*, *lust*, or *hate*, as it does to devote such a field to sympathy. If my hostile emotions should conflict with my natural sympathy, there is no Humean reason why the latter should generally take precedence. Moral judgments appear to correspond to nothing but an arbitrarily selected subset of our emotions and desires.

How might a Humean try to avoid this consequence? One way might be to portray morality as resulting, not from some particular emotion or subset of emotions, but from a combination of *all* our desires. But if this were so, then we should consider all emotions to give rise to moral reasons, and we should assign moral weight to all desires in proportion to their strength. This is not the case. We do not consider love and hate as providing equally good moral reasons. We do not, for example, think that a sufficiently strong hatred provides a justification for murder; in most circumstances we would take that emotion to provide no reason for action, or even to render actions prompted by it *worse*.

Another approach for a Humean might be to portray morality as stemming from second-order desires, such as the desire to acquire or lose some other desire. This might make sense of the notion that moral considerations include evaluations of other motives. But this approach faces the same sort of problem as the previous one. Suppose we meet someone who not only hates women, but wants to continue to hate them. We would not characterize his second-order desire as a moral motive, any more than the first-order desire is. Furthermore, for a Humean, one's behavior is always determined by what one *presently wants*, not what one wants to want, what one will want in the future, or anything else. Therefore, relegating moral judgments to judgments about what satisfies second-order desires would prevent them from directly influencing actions. That would be a mistake; moral judgments evaluate actions and outcomes in the world, and it is thus that they can directly conflict with, and perhaps take precedence over, desires and prudential judgments.

### 7.6.3 The problem of weakness of will

Weakness of the will—the phenomenon in which an individual succumbs to a temptation to act against his own better judgment—is a common experience. It comes in two varieties. In the first, a person acts on some desire, against his own acknowledged best interests. An example is the student who decides to spend the night partying instead of studying, despite her belief that studying would best promote her long-term interests. In the second variety, a person acts on some desire or prudential belief, against his own moral values. An example would be an official who accepts a bribe, despite his awareness that doing so is wrong.

When told of the phenomenon, some people insist that it is impossible for anyone not to do what he thinks best.[41] I assume this view is wrong. Weakness of will is a commonly observed phenomenon. It is the business of theory to accommodate observed facts, not vice versa.

The salient features of the phenomenon include the following:

*i)* The agent judges some action, *A*, to be the best.
*ii)* The agent feels 'tempted' to do some other action, *B*.
*iii)* We say (and, when the agent is us, feel) that the agent's will is 'weak' in some sense; that if the agent were stronger, he would do *A*. Relatedly, it is 'difficult' to do *A* but 'easy' to do *B*.
*iv)* The agent typically feels guilt or remorse upon doing *B*.
*v)* We judge that the agent is to some degree irrational in doing *B*.
*vi)* Although the agent may say such things as 'I couldn't resist', the agent acts voluntarily. He does not, for instance, suddenly lose

control of his muscles and wind up doing *B* in the manner of a muscle spasm. He does not try to do *A* but 'miss' and do *B* by accident. His psyche is not taken over by an alternate personality. No outside force interferes with his decision-making process. Apart from the feeling of conflict between his different motives, the agent's action comes about in exactly the way that intentional actions normally do. He may even engage in conscious planning in order to carry out act *B*, as in the case of the cigarette smoker who, though ostensibly 'trying to quit', deliberately goes to the store to buy a pack of cigarettes.

I have stated the last point with some elaboration because victims of weakness of will have a tendency to make excuses, claiming that they 'can't help' their behavior, that they are 'addicted' (to cigarettes, fatty foods, etc.), and so on. A philosophical grasp of the phenomenon requires resisting that tendency. There is no reason, apart from our desires to avoid incurring blame and to avoid hurting others' feelings by blaming them, to deny that victims of weakness of will can control their behavior. Other than their paradigmatic blameworthiness, weak-willed actions exhibit every feature typical of voluntary, intentional actions.

Now notice the asymmetries implicit in the above features: one is tempted to do *B*; one is not *tempted* to do *A*. Doing *A* is hard; doing *B* is easy. *A* accords with one's 'better judgment'; *B* does not. All of this implies that the reasons for doing *A* are superior to those for doing *B*, but the agent most *wants* to do *B*. A Humean can make no sense of this. For the Humean, when two motives conflict, the only question is, which desire is stronger? If *A* satisfies a stronger desire than *B* does, then the agent will do *A*. If, on the other hand, *B* answers to the stronger desire, then the agent should, rationally, choose to do *B*. In what sense would the agent then be 'weak'? In what sense would he be 'giving in' to a temptation? Why would the agent feel guilt or remorse? And what sense can be made of the idea of one alternative's being 'harder' to choose than the other? Of course, on a Humean view, one might say it is 'difficult' to perform the action for which one has the weaker motives—more precisely, it is impossible.[42] But this is not the relevant sense of 'difficult', since strong-willed actions are not impossible.

Our ordinary conception of the phenomenon implies that, in cases of weakness of the will, the conflicting motives differ *in kind*. Suppose, for instance, that I am trying to decide between ordering the salmon and ordering the fettuccine for dinner. Suppose the only consideration I have in mind is that of taste. And suppose I determine that the salmon will taste better. There is no scope for 'weakness of will' here. If I order the salmon, that will not be 'weak'. If I somehow order the fettuccine, that would merely be some bizarre psychological malfunction, not an exercise of strength of will. For a Humean, all motivation is fundamentally of a piece—it is all a matter of present desires of various strengths. Therefore, all cases of conflicting motives are relevantly like the salmon-fettuccine conflict.

The rationalist conception, however, introduces fundamentally different kinds of motivation: our *desires* may conflict with our *judgments* about what to do. That is the essence of weakness of will. And the doctrines of the authority of prudence and of morality explain the asymmetries pertaining to 'weakness', guilt, and irrationality.

The 'problem of weakness of will' is generally taken to be that of explaining how weakness of will is possible. Before answering that, let us first ask: why *wouldn't* it be possible? I contend that the Humean Conception of practical reasons implies that weakness of will is impossible, whereas the Rationalist Conception has no such implication. In a case of weakness of will, the agent acts of his own free will, but he knows that he has sufficient normative reasons for doing something else instead. There are two features of the Humean Conception that rule out such cases. First, as we saw in section 7.5, the Humean account implies that the factors that determine the *normative strength* of reasons are the same as those that determine the *motivating force* of reasons. It would thus be impossible for what an agent is motivated to do to come apart from what it is rational for him to do, as it does in cases of weakness of will.

Second, on the Humean account, all motivations can be compared along a single dimension, where that dimension is the only thing relevant to their capacity to induce action. On the Humean view, it is the strength of the relevant desire that determines its capacity to induce action, and all desires can be compared in terms of their strength.[43] The Humean account of motivation therefore strongly suggests a doctrine of *determinism*, that is, that in any given situation (taking into account the agent's motivations), there is only one thing a given agent can do. And this seems, at least on its face, to conflict with the observation that weak-willed actions are freely chosen.[44] More specifically, it seems that when one describes a scenario in which a person experiences conflicting motivations, and is tempted to act against his better judgment, *either decision is possible*; whichever course of action the agent chooses, it seems that there could have been a situation in which a person had the same reasons available but chose the other course of action.

A Humean might try to explain this by proposing that in such cases, the agent has exactly *equally strong* motivations for each course of action. But if strength of desire varies continuously, then the probability of two distinct desires happening to have exactly the same strength is zero;[45] therefore, it would not seem reasonable to believe that this is the explanation of weakness of will. And again, the 'exact tie' theory would not explain the various asymmetries implied in the notion of weakness of will, such as the fact that one course of action and not the other is said to accord with one's better judgment, to be rational, to be difficult, and so on.

The Rationalist Conception of reasons does not face the problems that the Humean Conception faces, since the rationalist conception rejects both of the problematic tenets of the Humean view. First, it rejects the idea that the normative strength of reasons is determined by the same factors that determine motivating force. The normative strength of a reason for action is determined, rather, by the objective values—by, for example, how much goodness a given action would produce (or how much one believes it would produce). There is no suggestion on this theory that there must be some psychological dimension of motivating force that this always corresponds to. Second, it rejects the idea that all motivations can be compared along a single dimension of 'strength'. Rather, while *desires* can be compared in terms of strength, our normative *judgments* are a qualitatively different kind of motivation. Judgments have no psychological dimension that can be weighed against the strength of a desire. There is, of course, such a thing as the 'strength' of a belief (that is, the believer's level of certainty), and there is the degree of objective value that one believes some goal to have—but neither of these things is commensurable with the strength of desires. The rationalist conception, consequently, fails to support a deterministic picture of human decision-making. The psychological incommensurability of desires and normative beliefs may explain why, in cases of weakness of will, we think that either decision is possible.

Now I want to clarify two things about this explanation. First, I do not claim that the rationalist conception of practical reasons entails the existence of weakness of will. It is theoretically possible to combine the rationalist conception of reasons with a view in which, in cases of conflicts between different kinds of motives, people always do what they perceive to be morally required—or one in which they always do what they expect to best satisfy their desires. The rationalist conception does not *entail* either indeterminism or the existence of free will, nor does it, by itself, explain 'how free will works'. I have no account to offer of how free will works. What I am arguing is that the rationalist conception is superior to the Humean conception in that the rationalist conception does not imply that weakness of will is *impossible*, as the Humean conception does.

Second, it is important to understand why, in allowing for cases of weakness of will in the way I have suggested, I am not going back on the thesis of section 7.2. I still maintain that an agent's recognition of normative reasons necessarily produces at least some motivation to act in accordance with those reasons. Recall that there were two central arguments in section 7.2. The first turned on the thought that it must always be *possible* for an agent to do what he rationally ought to do. The second turned on the idea that we are justified *a priori* in interpreting other people, if possible, as being by and large rational. These arguments do not demand a deterministic account of human choice, nor do they imply that the strength of a normative reason must be matched by the strength of the agent's motive in any sense.

### 7.6.4  How anti-realism undermines morality

We are now in a position to see how belief in anti-realism undermines morality. It undermines both our moral beliefs and our motivation for behaving morally. This fact does not show that anti-realism is false. But it shows that, if anti-realism is false, it is also pernicious.

Some of my anti-realist colleagues seem to find this thesis surprising and hard to accept. Before addressing what they say, it may put things in perspective to observe that it is not only I and other realists who believe this; even some prominent anti-realists have in effect admitted that their work undermines morality, though they don't put it quite that way. Just before attacking the notion of objective value, J. L. Mackie concedes that 'ordinary moral judgments include a claim to objectivity, an assumption that there are objective values in just the sense in which I am concerned to deny this'.[46] It follows that his own book serves to undermine ordinary moral beliefs. Mackie may believe he can put something better in their place,[47] but this is quite dubious for the reasons discussed in this section. But it is when anti-realists come to explaining why other people believe in objective morality that they most clearly reveal how their own theories, if accepted, would undermine moral motivation. Consider these explanations provided, respectively, by the anti-realist philosophers J. L. Mackie and Michael Ruse:

> We need morality to regulate interpersonal relations, to control some of the ways in which people behave towards one another,

often in opposition to contrary inclinations. We therefore want our moral judgments to be authoritative for other agents as well as for ourselves: objective validity would give them the authority required.[48]

The point about morality . . . is that it is an adaptation to get us to go beyond regular wishes, desires and fears, and to interact socially with people. How does it get us to do this? By filling us full of thoughts about obligations and duties, and so forth. . . . [W]e are then moved to action, precisely because we think morality is something laid upon us. . . . If morality did not have this air of externality or objectivity, it would not be morality and (from a biological perspective) would fail to do what it is intended to do.[49]

It follows that anti-realists, in attacking its objectivity, are working to undermine these important functions of morality.

The point is also clear, I take it, from what I have said above. The only reason anti-realists can offer as to why we should behave morally is that doing so will allegedly help satisfy some pre-existing desire of ours, such as a desire to help other people. If we find that we do not have this desire, or if we find that some other desire happens to be stronger at the moment, then, on the Humean account, it would be irrational to be moral. In any case, the appeal to *moral requirements* would have no special force, relative to any other appeal to desire. Furthermore, if I am right in some of my central claims in this book, both about the meanings of moral claims and about how they motivate us to act, then anti-realism undermines moral motivation in a very direct way: it attacks the beliefs that constitute our reasons for acting morally.

Many anti-realists would resist this conclusion. They would say that moral motivation comes entirely from emotions, so what is needed to bolster morality is simply to train people (applying non-cognitive influences) to have stronger sympathetic, social feelings; and an anti-realist can do this just as well as a realist can. I say that emotions are not enough. People often just do not have the emotions the Humean moralist wants them to have, and they may have no Humean reason (that is, no reason provided by their current desires) for doing anything to change that situation—they may, for example, have no Humean reason for submitting themselves to moral instruction or exhortation.

Consider two illustrations. First, suppose I have just read Peter Singer's argument to show that we have a moral obligation to help the poor.[50] According to Singer, each of us is obligated to donate great portions of our income to charities fighting world poverty. Suppose that I find Singer's argument convincing, considered from within the moral standpoint. But then I reflect that if I were to actually do what is 'morally required' according to the argument, I would miss out on a lot of things I presently enjoy—such as going out to eat, going to the movies, and other luxuries. I really like those things. So I'd rather not have to give away my money. So I might think to ask myself: sure, donating to charity is 'morally required', but do I really have to be moral? I turn to the field of metaethics, where I find most experts proclaiming that there are no objective moral requirements. I reflect that this 'moral requirement' Singer proposes is just a matter of social conventions (as the cultural relativists say), or is just something that I have a particular sort of emotion about (as the non-cognitivists and individual subjectivists say), or is just a delusion (as the nihilists say). Believing one of these things, why would I obey the moral require-ment? Why would I get out my checkbook and start donating that money, knowing that my own interests will be severely set back in doing so? The only reason Singer can offer me is that by acting morally, I will help satisfy some desire of mine, and perhaps make myself happier.[51] This is pathetically inadequate in light of the kind of sacrifice Singer is calling for. Sure, I have some feelings about the Third World poor—I'm sorry that they're starving, and I feel some satisfaction when I send money to help them. But by no stretch of the imagination are these feelings anywhere close to being strong enough to get me to give away, say, $30,000 a year. Introspectively, the amount of enjoyment that I derive from sending money to Oxfam is not obviously greater—indeed, it seems much *less*—than the enjoyment I derive, say, from reading a good novel.[52] And the novel only costs about $8. So why would I give away thousands of dollars to charity? Granted, my desires are not merely for enjoyment, but the point remains: my desire to help the poor is just not as strong as many of the desires that it competes with. Once I 'realize' that the only reason for obeying moral requirements would be to help me satisfy my personal preferences, I will surely feel entitled to make the judgment that, overall, I'd prefer not to be moral—and to act accordingly. The moral philosopher's telling me that I just don't realize the strength of my sympathetic feelings for other people, and so on, will strike me as about as credible as someone who doesn't know me telling me that I would rather have been a fireman than a professor.

Second, suppose Jon, a married man, is considering whether to cheat on his wife. He comes to his best friend, Sam, for advice, and the following dialogue ensues:

Jon:  [After explaining the situation:] So, do you think I should cheat on Kate?

Sam:  Kate would be crushed if she knew you were even considering this.

Jon:  Don't worry, she won't find out. [Jon discusses how he's going to make sure Kate doesn't know.]

Sam:  Don't you think it's wrong to cheat on your wife?

Jon:  Oh, that. That's just an arbitrary convention people made up. I know that a lot of people *don't like* marital infidelity, but why should I listen to them?

Sam:  Don't you feel just a little bit guilty for thinking about betraying Kate, after all you've been through together?

Jon:  Well, I was feeling guilty for a while. But then I realized that it was stupid to feel guilty. I mean, who says people have to be faithful to their wives? That's just some arbitrary rule someone made up. If I don't want to be faithful, why should I? I admit that I may experience some irrational guilt anyway, but I think it'll still be worth it for all the fun I'm going to have.

Jon has learned the lessons from his philosophy classes well. He may not have followed all the subtleties and complications of the various versions of anti-realism, but he got the gist: we *make up* moral requirements, prompted by some arbitrarily selected subset of our emotions and desires. Our moral sense 'has no authority over those who dissent from its recommendations or even over us if we are inclined to change our minds'.[53]

I don't think my two examples are unusual. Nor do I see any fundamental flaw in either Jon's or my reasoning in the above examples, apart from the mistake of failing to recognize objective values.

We often hear complaints about the decay of morality in modern society. I do not know whether these complaints are just; I have no statistics on the frequency of immoral acts in different times. But the widespread acceptance of anti-realism in our culture cannot be good for morality. There must surely be people who disregard many of the demands of morality, once they decide that morality is unreal. Of course, ethical intuitionism cannot guarantee moral behavior, any more than it can guarantee correct moral beliefs. No mere philosophical theory can stop people from indulging in weakness of the will.

But at least the theory does not positively encourage such lapses by clothing them in the mantle of practical rationality.

## 7.7   Why be moral?

Why should we behave morally? The ethical intuitionist's answer is as follows. Our intuitions render us *prima facie* justified in adopting certain moral beliefs. Provided these moral beliefs survive any challenges from potential defeaters, they are justified *tout court.* These beliefs in themselves constitute reasons for action, in virtue of their evaluative content. There is no further question to answer as to why one should be motivated by correct evaluations; it is simply the nature of *evaluation* that it answers questions about what to do. To accept an evaluative judgment *is* to judge something as a reason for action—to accept the judgment that stealing is wrong, for example, is to accept another person's ownership of *x* as a normative reason not to take *x* without his permission.[54]

Some philosophers, with whom I have much sympathy, hold that 'Why should I be moral?' is a nonsense question.[55] Consider three interpretations of the question:

*i*)   'Why should I do what I am morally required to do?' This seems to mean, 'Why should I do what I should do?', which is a nonsense question.

*ii*)   'Why should I do the things that are generally considered, and that perhaps I myself have hitherto considered, moral?' Here, the answer would seem to be, 'Because those moral beliefs are by and large true'.[56] If it is asked why one should accept those beliefs, the answer is that we are justified in believing the contents our ethical intuitions, in the absence of defeaters, as discussed in chapter 5.

*iii*)   'Why is it *rational* to be moral?' This interpretation offers the best hope of making sense of the question. If this is what it means, the answer is that moral judgments are themselves products of reason; they are intellectual evaluations of actions, states of affairs, and so on. Furthermore, they are evaluations of a kind that take into account all the relevant reasons, including prudential reasons and one's current desires, as discussed in section 7.6.1. Thus, what we judge moral is what reason evaluates as choiceworthy.

Some readers may be unsatisfied by my answers, for either of two reasons. On the one hand, some may think that, despite my answer to question (*iii*), there remains a question as to why one should be rational. Others may think that, despite what I have said about it, question (*i*) *seems* like a real question. Of course, it sounds better if one replaces 'what I should do' with 'what is morally right' and if one deletes 'should I', thus: 'Why do what is morally right?' I agree that on its face, this *sounds* like a meaningful question. I now want to give a reason for thinking that this appearance is illusory, and that neither 'Why be rational?' nor 'Why do what is morally right?' is a legitimate question.

In order for these questions to be 'meaningful' and 'serious' in the intended sense, there must first of all be something that, in the present context, would count as a satisfactory answer to a question of the form, 'Why do *x*?' This answer would presumably say something which is true of *x* but is not true of other actions that should not be performed. Let that 'something' be *F*. Suppose, in other words, that 'Because *x* is *F*' is a satisfactory answer to the general philosophical question, 'Why do *x*?' I am not assuming that 'Why be moral?' or 'Why be rational?' *has* a satisfactory answer; I do not assume that moral actions or rational actions have *F*. I assume only that there is *something* that could be said about these actions that, *if true*, would count as answering those questions. This seems like a reasonable requirement to impose on questions that we are to take seriously.

Yet even if there were such a property *F*, some philosophers might still say, 'Yes, but why do the *F* things?' Their question would certainly be grammatically well-formed; moreover, it would probably *sound*, to many at least, as if it were a meaningful question. But by the nature of the case, it could not be a legitimate question; by hypothesis, *F* is the property that *answers* 'why do so-and-so' questions. Once it has been said that an action is *F*, therefore, there cannot be any further question as to why one should do it. Conversely, if some such further question needs to be answered, then 'Because *x* is *F*' would not have been a sufficient answer to the question of why one should do *x*.

We may predict, therefore, that there should be some question or questions of the form, 'Why do the things that have feature *F*?' that superficially sound legitimate but are not. These would be questions where the feature cited *already* inherently constitutes (or entails the existence of) a reason for action. What would be the most plausible candidates for such questions? It seems that the most obvious candidates for *F* are 'moral' and 'rational' (more than one feature may play the role of *F*)—if *anything* would count as inherently entailing the existence of an adequate reason to do *x*, it would be that *x* is right, or that *x* is rational.[57]

The only other obvious candidate for *F* is the property of satisfying one's desires. But might I not ask, 'Why should I satisfy my desires?' To this, a Humean would respond that the question is illegitimate, because my desiring something already constitutes a reason for me to pursue it. But isn't it just as clear that something's being good already constitutes a reason for me to pursue it? If anything, this seems *more* clear. For suppose I have some desires that I myself judge to be desires for the bad. For instance, I feel a sudden, inexplicable urge to jump off a building. Is it really obvious that I then have a reason to jump off the building—that is, something that would make my jumping off the building *prima facie* rational?[58] Is it obvious, on the other hand, that I have a reason *not* to jump off the building? Of course, I might have both a reason for and a reason against. The point is that it is more obvious that I have a reason not to jump in virtue of knowing that jumping off the building would be bad, than it is that I have a reason to jump in virtue of feeling a desire to jump.

I conclude that such questions as 'Why be moral?' and 'Why be rational?' are among the clearest candidates for illegitimate 'why' questions. They are like the pseudo-question, 'Why is 10 pounds heavier than 5 pounds?'

# 8
# Further Objections

In the last three chapters, I have addressed three of the most prominent objections to intuitionism, those concerned with intuitionism's ability to account for moral knowledge, its ability to explain and resolve moral disagreement, and its ability to account for moral motivation. In this chapter, I address miscellaneous further objections.

## 8.1 The argument from weirdness

I begin with J. L. Mackie's famous contention that objective moral properties would be 'queer'.[1] This objection is voiced in conversation more often than it is put in writing. Philosophers often dismiss moral realism, intuitionism, and many other views as too 'weird', 'spooky', or 'mysterious' for them.[2] This may well be the main source of resistance to intuitionism. No matter how forcefully I make the rest of the arguments in this book, intuitionism will never be accepted as long as philosophers find it 'weird'.

Mackie had a few specific things to say about *how* moral properties would be queer that I will not discuss in this section, as they are dealt with elsewhere.[3] Here, my focus is his general contention that moral properties would be properties 'of a very strange sort, utterly different from anything else in the universe'.[4]

Anti-realists may be right in pegging objective values as strange. But how would this be a reason for denying their existence? Perhaps the argument is:

1. Objective values would be weird.
2. If something would be weird, then it (probably) does not exist.
3. Therefore, objective values (probably) do not exist.

What does it mean for something to be 'weird'? This might seem a frivolous question, were it not for the enormous influence that the sense of 'weirdness' has on what positions are respected and seriously investigated in philosophy. Consider four interpretations of the notion:

*First:* Perhaps to say a kind of thing is weird is to say that it is *counter-intuitive* that things of that kind exist. But Mackie does not accept intuition as a justification for believing (or disbelieving) anything, so this is an unlikely interpretation. And if Mackie *did* accept the validity of intuition, then we could simply appeal to the various intuitions cited in this book to show that objective values exist. Since Mackie thinks a claim to objectivity is embedded in all ordinary moral thinking and discourse,[5] the case that objectivism is counter-intuitive would be a tough one to make.

*Second:* Perhaps to say *x* is weird is to say that *x* is very dissimilar from all or most other things that exist. In this case, premise (2) becomes: 'If something is very dissimilar from other things that exist, then it (probably) does not exist'. Why should we accept this? Consider this partial list of what exists:

| | |
|---|---|
| time | mental states |
| space | physical states |
| numbers | aesthetic properties |
| propositions | fields (e.g., the gravitational field) |
| substances | the past |
| properties | dispositional properties |
| relationships | moral properties |

One could say of any item on that list that it is utterly different from everything else that exists. At least it seems that way, and yet all those things seem clearly to exist. This isn't just the trivial point that everything is different from everything else; the point here is that the above things are each *very* different, different in kind, from everything else. So, on the face of it, this version of the argument from weirdness goes nowhere.

*Third:* Perhaps anti-realism about weirdness is correct. Perhaps 'weirdness' is the property of causing some sort of reaction in human observers, such as surprise, wonder, or disbelief; perhaps '*x* is weird' expresses a non-cognitive reaction towards *x*; or perhaps there simply is no such thing as weirdness. If *moral* anti-realism is true, then I think anti-realism about *weirdness* is almost certainly true. But then it is very unclear how calling something weird could count as giving evidence against its existence.

*Fourth:* Perhaps to say something is weird is to say we do not clearly understand its nature. This would be a version of the third interpretation, and the same objection applies: it is unclear how our failure to clearly understand something is evidence against its existence. Nor do I see reason, in any case, for thinking we do not understand moral properties reasonably well.

On this score, the anti-realist might point to intuitionists' failure to explain the nature of moral properties. But intuitionists have said many things about the nature of moral properties—that goodness is an objective property; that it depends on but is not reducible to the natural properties of a thing; that it comes in degrees; that awareness of it intrinsically provides us with reasons for action; that it is the opposite of badness; that things which have it are appropriate objects of such attitudes as approval and admiration; that it is a property that such things as happiness, knowledge, benevolence, and honesty have in common.

Still, the anti-realist might point to intuitionists' failure to *define* moral concepts. But this is no reason for denying that we understand moral concepts, nor for denying that they refer to anything. We often understand a concept well enough to know that it applies to some things, without being able to define it. I cannot define 'table', and I don't believe I have ever met anyone who could.[6] But I still know there are tables. For a more interesting example, analytic philosophers have tried for 40 years to define 'knowledge', but no definition has been generally accepted, and in my view, every definition proposed is subject to decisive counter-examples. But no one thinks this proves that we don't understand 'knows' or that it doesn't apply to anything. Indeed, my own view is that no correct, non-stipulative definition of *any* philosophically interesting concept has ever been produced. Obviously, I cannot show that here, but I can report that I know of no such definition that has been *generally accepted* in any branch of philosophy. The intuitionists' inability to define 'good', therefore, hardly shows goodness to be queer in a way that justifies denying its existence.

## *8.2  Troubles with supervenience

### *8.2.1  Mackie's objection

All or nearly all realists agree that moral properties depend on non-moral properties. For example, if Pol Pot is evil, there must be something else *about* him that *makes* him evil—say, his disregard for human life, his tyrannical personality, and so on. And whatever this property or collection of properties is, any other person who had it would also thereby be evil. We express this idea by saying that moral properties 'supervene on' non-moral properties.[7]

J. L. Mackie finds this dependence of moral properties on non-moral properties mysterious:

> What is the connection between the natural fact that an action is a piece of deliberate cruelty—say, causing pain just for fun—and the moral fact that it is wrong? It cannot be an entailment, a logical or semantic necessity. Yet it is not merely that the two features occur together. The wrongness must somehow be 'consequential' or 'supervenient'; it is wrong because it is a piece of deliberate cruelty. But just what *in the world* is signified by this 'because'?[8]

He goes on to worry that our awareness of this relationship would require a mysterious 'intuition'. Apart from that, the above quotation is the entire exposition of the objection.

*Pace* Mackie, I do not believe that the above passage articulates any objection to moral realism at all. I see nothing there that provides a reason for denying that a property can depend on other properties. Mackie has identified nothing problematic about this relation; all he says about it is that it is not logical or semantic entailment. The rest of the passage's content seems to consist of a tone of incredulity.

Perhaps Mackie's idea is that this dependence relation is queer, just as moral properties are, or that intuitionists' failure to define it is a reason for denying that it exists. If so, my replies in section 8.1 apply.

However, I do not deny that there are philosophical puzzles concerning supervenience; we shall see some in the following subsections.

## *8.2.2   Objections to the notion of *prima facie* rightness

Some intuitionists, myself included, believe that our intuitions tell us, not that certain kinds of action are always right, but that certain kinds of action are *prima facie right*. A *prima facie* right type of action is a type of action that *tends* to be right, or is morally right *other things being equal*.[9] The reason for introducing this notion is that all or most of the generalizations we can think of about what is right or wrong have exceptions. For instance, it is generally wrong to burn cats. But if the cat had a deadly, contagious disease, and the microbes could only be killed by burning, then it would be alright to burn a cat. Furthermore, it proves exceedingly difficult to state all the conditions under which cat-burning would be permissible. So some intuitionists say that we can merely see that causing suffering is *prima facie* wrong—it is wrong as long as no special exculpatory or justificatory circumstances exist.

Peter Strawson objects that this idea conflicts with the original idea that the moral properties of a thing follow from its non-moral properties. If $B$ follows from $A$, then $B$ must be present whenever $A$ is, not merely 'tend to be' present when $A$ is, or be present *most* of the time when $A$ is. Furthermore, to say a type of action 'tends to be wrong' is just to say that *most* actions of that kind are wrong. But a statement of the form 'Most $A$'s are $B$' cannot be a necessary truth. Yet intuitionists claim the basic moral truths to be necessary.[10]

This objection has a few false premises. Intuitionists think that the moral status of an action follows from the *total set* of its non-moral properties, not from any one *prima facie* right-making or wrong-making feature. Nor does 'Cat-burning is *prima facie* wrong' mean 'Most cat-burnings are wrong'. It means that an act's being a case of cat-burning counts against that action; it is logically compatible with this that *most* of the time there *do* exist exculpatory circumstances. (Imagine that most of the world's cats had a deadly disease, etc.)[11]

To see that this conception of *prima facie* rightness is perfectly coherent, compare an example from classical physics. Newton tells us that a body will accelerate in the direction of the net force acting on it. He also gives us a law of gravity governing *one* of the forces that acts on bodies. It is physically necessary that a massive body experience a gravitational pull—something that has a tendency to accelerate it—towards any other massive body. If there are no other forces, then the body will accelerate in that direction. But there may be other forces, such as electric or magnetic ones, that overcome that pull.

*Prima facie* rightness and wrongness are analogous to 'forces' that pull an action towards rightness or wrongness.[12] Just as, in classical physics, the acceleration of any body is determined by the physical configuration of the system it belongs to, so the rightness or wrongness of actions is determined by their non-moral features (including relational features). Just as it is physically necessary that a given configuration generates a certain amount of gravitational force, it is (metaphysically) necessary that a given non-moral property generates a certain degree of *prima facie* wrongness. Just as the law of gravity does not mean that *most* objects are falling (perhaps most are being supported by counter-balancing forces), the principle of the *prima facie* wrongness of cat-burning does not mean that most cat-burnings are wrong.

Admittedly, this analogy is misleading in at least two ways. First, in the case of classical physics, there is a simple mathematical law for the composition of forces (that is, how to compute 'total force' when given the individual forces): the parallelogram law. I do not mean to suggest that the law for the composition of *prima facie* rightnesses and wrongnesses (the principle that takes you from the various right-making and wrong-making features of an action to its overall degree of rightness or wrongness) is similar in form to the parallelogram law for the composition of forces, nor indeed that it has any simple mathematical formulation. The only point here is that there is nothing incoherent in the general framework of *prima facie* duties.

Second, in classical physics, a force can be outweighed by a greater force, but it cannot be removed when the conditions specified in the relevant force law obtain. For instance, gravitational force can be *counterbalanced*, but there is no way to *remove* the gravitational force a body experiences, as long as the body is in the vicinity of another massive body. In contrast, moral considerations may be not only counterbalanced, but also removed. For example, assume that it is *prima facie* right to make people happy. But now suppose that some particular act would produce happiness for a sadist by allowing him the pleasure of watching other people suffer. In this case, the point is not merely that the value of the sadist's pleasure is *outweighed* by the suffering of his victims; rather, the sadistic nature of the enjoyment to be produced deprives it of *any* moral value. The sadist's pleasure is not a reason *at all* in favor of the proposed action.[13]

Now, one might think that this creates a problem for the very notion of *prima facie* rightness. Suppose that a *prima facie* right type of action is understood to be a type of action such that an act's being of that type counts as a reason in its favor. The sort of example we have just discussed shows that it is difficult to find any type of action such that an act's being of that type is *always* a reason in its favor—

there can always, it seems, be further circumstances that neutralize any would-be reason in favor of an action.[14]

There are at least two ways we might respond to this. On the one hand, we might say that this sort of example only shows that one has misidentified what is *prima facie* right: it is not the production of happiness that is *prima facie* right, we might say, but the production of *innocent* pleasures. Alternately, we might simply liberalize the notion of *prima facie* rightness: we might say that when a type of action is *prima facie* right, then we have a reason to perform acts of that type *other things being equal*, or *in normal conditions*; this is compatible with the possibility of special circumstances that would neutralize this reason. Of course, we have not hereby produced a satisfactory moral theory—to do that, we would have to say much more, about such matters as which things are *prima facie* right and which sorts of considerations neutralize which sorts of reasons. All I am aiming at here is to defend intuitionism against the charge that it has available no coherent notion of how moral properties are related to natural properties.[15]

Consider a second analogy. No one doubts that there are objective facts about what is a good move in chess—not morally good, but good from the standpoint of winning and not losing the game. Whether a move is good supervenes on the arrangement of pieces on the board (perhaps together with the capacities of the players). There are rules that help one choose good moves: try to develop your pieces early, try to control the center of the board, rooks are more valuable than knights, and so on. All these rules are defeasible; some possible positions call for violating them. Nevertheless, these principles can be seen, rationally, to be correct. A person with no experience playing chess but who knew the rules and objective of the game could see that these things make sense.[16] Furthermore, they are necessary truths. (It is contingent what the rules of the game are, but *given* these rules, it is necessary, in a manner similar to mathematical truths, that these rules represent generally good strategies.[17])

This analogy refutes Strawson's contention that it cannot be necessary that some class of things *tend* to have some property. And it demonstrates the coherence of the intuitionist's conception of the relationship between evaluative and natural facts. It does not show that conception to be *correct*—perhaps morality is not like chess—but it shows the conception to be coherent, by showing that there actually exists a realm in which the facts and our reasoning about them exemplify the structure the intuitionist attributes to moral facts and moral reasoning.

### *8.2.3   Blackburn's objection

Let *A* be some act which is morally wrong. Let *N* be the complete set of natural properties of *A*.[18] According to Blackburn, proposition (2) below is analytically true, but (1) is not:

1. If *A* has *N*, it is wrong.
2. If *A* has *N* and is wrong, then every action that has *N* is wrong.

In other words, you can coherently hold (without thereby proving that you don't understand the concept of wrongness), '*A* has *N* but isn't wrong'. But you cannot coherently hold, '*A* has *N* and is wrong, but other things with exactly the same natural properties are not wrong'. Blackburn thinks that the realist cannot explain this. If wrongness is some extra property of *A*, which does not follow from *A*'s natural properties, then why shouldn't it be possible for there to be one object that has wrongness, and another object with the same natural properties but without wrongness?[19]

That (1) is not analytic follows from my earlier argument against analytic naturalism (section 4.2), so I will grant that. (2) follows from the principle of the supervenience of moral properties. But it is not at all obvious, as Blackburn assumes, that (2) is analytic, rather than a synthetic, necessary truth. For (2) to be analytic, there must be a way of substituting synonymous expressions into (2) that results in a truth of logic. Blackburn makes no attempt to demonstrate this, nor can I see any way of doing so. Still, let us grant for the sake of argument that (2) is analytic.

What does Blackburn think is the correct, anti-realist explanation for the analyticity of (2)? He thinks that if someone were to reject supervenience, 'it would betray the whole purpose for which we moralize, which is to choose, commend, rank, approve, or forbid things on the basis of their natural properties'.[20] This is a very thin explanation. If we deleted 'on the basis of their natural properties' from that sentence, Blackburn would have no explanation at all. Why must we approve (etc.) things *on the basis of their natural properties*? Why, on an anti-realist view, would it be inappropriate to value things on whim, praising one action but, for no reason, condemning another, indistinguishable action? Blackburn just proposes as a brute fact that such attitudes would not count as moral.

Why, then, may not the moral realist propose the following brute fact: the concept of moral properties includes that they depend on natural properties? Even if this were all the realist had to say, his account would be no less explanatory than Blackburn's.

But the realist has available another explanation. Let us introduce the term 'good-making' as a predicate that can be applied, not to particular objects or events, but to *features* of objects or events. Good-making features are those that tend to make the thing that has them good (this is obviously related to the notion of *prima facie* rightness discussed above). For example, we can say, 'Pleasurableness is good-making'. Analogously, we can say, 'Being-an-act-of-cruelty is wrong-making'. Now here is a hypothesis: (a) Our most fundamental moral intuitions are about facts of the form '$F$ is good-making', '$G$ is wrong-making', and so on. When a person says that intuitively, killing is wrong, he is really reporting the intuition that being-a-killing is wrong-making. (b) To say a thing is good is to say something like: its good-making features predominate over its bad-making features, or that its *total set* of natural features is good-making.[21] This seems a plausible hypothesis, consistent with introspective evidence. If it is true, then it is analytic that if a thing is good, every qualitatively indistinguishable thing is also good. Analytically, the only way for a thing to be good is for its total set of natural properties to be good-making. It follows that any other object that has that total set of properties has a good-making total set of properties, and therefore is good. This gives Blackburn what he asked for: an explanation of why the supervenience of moral properties is analytic that does not imply that individual moral standards are analytic. The realist now fares better in solving Blackburn's puzzle than Blackburn himself does.

### *8.2.4  Jackson's objection

Frank Jackson argues that the supervenience of the moral on the non-moral is difficult to reconcile with the irreducibility of the moral. Assume that goodness supervenes on natural properties. There may be many possible ways for a thing to be good—many natural properties, that is, that would make a thing good. Let these natural properties be $N_1$, $N_2$, and so on. For each of them, it is necessary that anything that has them is good (that is the principle of supervenience). Since we are stipulating that $\{N_1, N_2, \ldots\}$ is a *complete* list of the possible ways for a thing to be good, it is also necessary that anything that is good has at least one of these properties. Therefore, there are two predicates, 'good' and '$N_1$ or $N_2$ or . . .', that apply to exactly the same things in every possible situation.[22] If these predicates refer to the same property, this is unproblematic. But the intuitionist holds that there are two different properties here, a natural property and a non-natural one, and that 'good' refers to the non-natural one. Jackson's objection here is subtle: what a word refers to is normally determined by its usage—what sorts of things we apply it to, including which hypothetical situations we would apply it in. But 'good' and '$N_1$ or $N_2$ or . . .' have the same usage in that sense. So, even if there were two properties there, what would make it the case that our word 'good' referred to the non-natural property, rather than the natural one? Furthermore, even if there was something that made the word refer to the non-natural property, how would children learning the language learn that 'good' was supposed to refer to the non-natural property instead of the natural one?[23]

I think that the answer to this is fairly straightforward for a full-blooded intuitionist. What a word refers to is determined not solely by what we apply it to, but also at least partly by speakers' *intentions*. When we think about certain kinds of events (say), we see intuitively that they have this further, evaluative property in addition to their natural properties, and we intend our word 'good' to refer to that property. We intend to refer to the supervenient property, not the subvenient one; to the property the recognition of which inherently constitutes a reason for action; to the simple property that explains what $N_1$, $N_2$, and so on have in common. Furthermore, when children first learn the language, they take 'good' to refer to goodness rather than to ($N_1$ or $N_2$ or . . .), because we assume by default that an unfamiliar word refers to the most simple, unified (as opposed to disjunctive) property consistent with its usage.

Jackson's objection really depends on a further assumption: 'Our minds do not house detectors of the nonnatural properties Mooreans believe in'. Given *this* assumption, Jackson correctly infers that 'the story about the acquisition of ethical language must be one about latching onto patterns in the naturalistic'.[24] Given that, it is indeed puzzling how 'good' could come to refer to anything other than some pattern of natural properties. But Jackson's assumption obviously begs the question against intuitionism, nor does he give any *argument* against the existence of ethical intuition. His argument would thus have force only against someone who posited irreducible value properties but refused to countenance either intuition or any similar faculty for knowing them.

### *8.2.5   An analogy: the supervenience of logical properties

The logical properties of an argument supervene on the meanings and arrangement of the symbols it contains. This is in some respects analogous to the supervenience of value properties on non-evaluative properties. Just as it is impossible for two actions to differ in respect of rightness without differing in some natural property, so it is impossible for two arguments to differ in respect of validity without differing in the meaning or arrangement of their symbols. Just as an action's ethical properties are *determined by* its natural properties, an argument's logical properties are determined by the meanings and arrangement of its symbols (especially the logical symbols). And just as (many philosophers believe) there is nevertheless no general algorithm for determining what is morally right, there is no general algorithm for computing what is logically necessary. For the last claim, I rely on Gödel's Theorem, assuming that we wish to count the truths of arithmetic as logically necessary.[25] (If you do not view truths of arithmetic as logically necessary, then substitute some notion of mathematical necessity here, and change the analogy to one of the supervenience of mathematical necessity on meanings.) This shows that these aspects of the doctrine of the supervenience of the ethical are perfectly coherent.

One disanalogy between ethics and deductive logic concerns the notion of *prima facie* rightness. There is no parallel notion of '*prima facie* validity'; the rules of deductive logic tell us that inferences of certain kinds are always valid, not that they tend to be valid. We can, however, find an analogy to *prima facie* rightness if we look to *non*-demonstrative reasoning.[26] It is possible that *A* non-demonstratively supports *B* but that, if certain further information, *C*, were added to one's background beliefs, *A* would no longer support *B*. We might then say that *A* is '*prima facie*' evidence for *B*, or is evidence for *B* in normal conditions. For example, relative to a normal background belief system, Jim's attesting that he owns a motorcycle is good evidence that he owns a motorcycle. But if one also knows that Jim is a pathological liar who has been falsely posing as a motorcycle gang member for years, then Jim's testimony is no longer good evidence that he owns a motorcycle. It thus seems that non-deductive logic is analogous in the relevant respects to ethics. Yet no one suggests that these features of non-deductive logic—the fact that its relations of evidential support are supervenient and that they are defeasible—support anti-realism about evidential support.

## 8.3   How can we understand 'good'?

How do we initially learn the meaning of the word 'good'?[27] There seem to be two ways of explaining the meaning of a word to someone. The first is to give a definition. But intuitionists deny that 'good' can be defined, so that is out. The second way is to specify some things the word applies to. For instance, one points to a number of dogs, saying 'dog', and the child gets the idea that the word refers to things of that type. One cannot point to goodness, since goodness is not perceivable by the senses, but perhaps one may tell a child some examples of things that are good, whereupon he gets the idea that 'good' refers to what those things have in common. The problem is that people disagree substantially about what is good, so how can it be established that they all mean the same thing by 'good'?

The suggestions of the previous paragraph about how words are learned are oversimplified. Hardly any of the vast vocabulary of an ordinary person is acquired through anyone's expressly *teaching* him the words, either by defining them or by giving him lists of examples. Nearly every word is learned by one's hearing it used in conversations in which no explicit effort to explain the word is made.

In any case, there is substantial agreement on what things are good, on an everyday level. Nearly everyone calls happiness, health, friendship, knowledge, and long life 'good'. Furthermore, people tend to pursue the things they call 'good', try to get other people to pursue them, and say things implying that the 'goodness' of a thing is a reason to pursue it. Children can learn that 'good' refers to goodness because that interpretation makes sense of most of the things that are said using the word, and no other, comparably simple interpretation comes close to doing that.

A related objection is that 'good' cannot refer to any one property, since so many utterly different things are called 'good'—people, actions, states of affairs, facts, events. This is a mistake—extremely dissimilar things may still have some abstract feature in common. Compare the fact that numbers can apply to physical objects, ideas, propositions, actions, and so on—'three' means the same thing in 'I have three pairs of shoes' and 'There are three main reasons for buying a PC'. Likewise for logical properties or relationships, such as identity and set membership, or metaphysical 'properties' such as existence or determinateness. Likewise, there is no obstacle to goodness' applying to widely disparate things.

## 8.4   Is intuitionism too subjective?

Some have accused intuitionism of devolving into a form of subjectivism. Some complain that intuitionists do not provide much of a *method* for arriving at moral conclusions, or that they provide no method for distinguishing correct from incorrect intuitions.[28] The latter charge has been discussed previously (section 6.4). As to the absence of method, compare the 'method' by which we arrive at many physical-object beliefs: we perceive things, and then we believe things are the way we perceive them to be. This is a very simple 'method', but that does not impugn the objectivity of perceptual knowledge; no more, then, does the comparably simple intuitionist 'method' of coming by moral knowledge impugn the latter's objectivity.

Another version of the complaint is that intuitionism makes the truth of a moral theory depend upon its comporting with our intuitions and is therefore a form of subjectivism.[29] This is simply a misunderstanding of the theory. Intuition is our *means of cognizing* moral truths. It does not create moral truth, any more than perception creates truths about the physical world.

Still, it might be thought that intuitionism advocates a troublingly subjective epistemology, insofar as intuitions—mere internal mental states—are made the ultimate source of justification for all claims in some allegedly objective field. This objection, too, may rest on a misunderstanding: intuitionism as I understand it does not advocate appealing to intuitions as *evidence* from which to *infer* normative conclusions (see above, section 5.6). It does, however, hold that whether a moral belief is justified depends upon the believer's mental states, including his intuitions. A consequence of this is that justification is observer-relative: one person may be justified in believing what another is unjustified in believing. This, however, far from being an objectionable form of 'subjectivism', is true of all kinds of beliefs.[30] The justification for perceptual beliefs depends upon one's perceptual experiences. The justification for beliefs about the past depends upon one's memories. Inferential justification depends upon one's other beliefs. The fact that the justification for moral beliefs depends upon the believer's mental states is thus unsurprising and no cause for alarm.

## 8.5 Do my arguments prove too much?

Assume that my arguments against moral anti-realism succeed. Would arguments of the same kind demonstrate realism about beauty? Perhaps. Some philosophers accept aesthetic realism in any case; moreover, 'beauty' may itself be an evaluative term—'beautiful' may imply 'good'—so this result would not be terribly surprising. Here is a more troubling question: Would such arguments also demonstrate realism about *sexiness, funniness,* and *coolness* (as in, '*The Matrix* is a cool movie')? Realism about such properties is considerably less attractive than realism about value.[31]

To start with, consider non-cognitivism. Since sentences like 'I believe that Steven is funny' and 'If Steven is funny, then the audience will laugh' make sense and are sometimes appropriately asserted, it seems that non-cognitivism about funniness faces more or less the same problems as non-cognitivism about value. The linguistic arguments will probably work in exactly the same way, with about equal plausibility, in the case of *any* sentences that take the grammatical form of assertions, for any such sentences will probably be able to be embedded in larger sentences, just as evaluative claims can be. No intuitions specifically about the nature of funniness are required to make this argument.

The argument against 'nihilism' about funniness also seems analogous to the argument against value nihilism: the argument would consist in the display of some paradigmatically funny things, things that almost everyone would laugh at. Some searching might be required, since senses of humor vary, but let's assume we find such a paradigm.[32] Suppose it is this joke:

> An engineer, a scientist, a mathematician, and a philosopher are off in Ireland together, when they see a black sheep alone in a field. The engineer says, 'Hey, it looks like the sheep around here are black'. The scientist looks at him skeptically and replies, 'Well, at least *some* of them are'. Then the mathematician gives them another skeptical look and says, 'Well, at least *one* of them is'. Finally, the philosopher turns to them and says, 'Well, at least *on one side*'.

Pretend that upon hearing that, everyone laughs uproariously (including you). I invite you to agree that it was funny. How absurd it would be for the nihilist to claim, because of some dubious philosophical theory, that the joke wasn't funny!

Still, we might well feel humor nihilism to be less problematic than value nihilism. Giving up funniness assertions would involve a minor change to our belief systems. We won't have to stop laughing at things, since laughter is not a belief, nor is it caused or 'justified' by beliefs about funniness.

I would rather not deny that the above joke is funny. It seems funny to me. Perhaps our best bet is a subjectivist theory of funniness. Let's review the problems with value subjectivism from chapter 3 and see whether they apply to humor subjectivism:

i) *The Problem of Horrible Attitudes:* Imagine someone whose sense of humor diverges radically from ours (but not in a way that might be *morally* offensive, such as laughing at another's suffering). He goes outside and sees an ordinary stick, whereupon he breaks into hysterical laughter. The subjectivist says: 'For him, the stick is funny'. This does not seem obviously wrong, in the way that 'For Ted Bundy, murder is permissible' is obviously wrong.

On the other hand, some would likely describe this person as follows: 'He laughs at things that aren't funny'. Perhaps in this context, 'is funny' means approximately, 'would tend to make typical people laugh'. This implies that, if most of us are disposed to laugh at sticks, then sticks are funny. Again, this does not seem unacceptable in the way that 'If most of us approve of slavery, then slavery is good' is.

ii) *The Problem of Disagreement*: After hearing the same joke, one person says, 'That was funny', and another says, 'That was not funny'. The subjectivist says they are not disagreeing: one of them just means the joke was funny to him, while the other says it wasn't funny to *him*. This is not implausible. The sentence 'The joke is funny to me' makes sense, and the first person may well be willing to agree that that was what he meant. He is very unlikely to insist that the second person is *wrong*, nor to present arguments to show that the joke was funny, unless perhaps to say that most people would laugh at it. In contrast, the sentence, 'Abortion is wrong to me' does not make sense and cannot be substituted for 'Abortion is wrong'. If someone says 'Abortion is not wrong', pro-lifers will say he is mistaken and will give arguments to show that abortion is wrong. Their arguments will not appeal to the claim that most people disapprove of abortion.

iii) *The Problem of Arbitrariness*: We argued that value subjectivism makes the attitudes or commands of the relevant person or group arbitrary. Such questions as 'Why should we obey arbitrary rules?' and 'How would someone's approving of *x for no reason* make *x* good?' then seem appropriate. Humor subjectivism, likewise, makes our laughter arbitrary—not in the sense that it cannot be causally explained, but in the sense that it cannot be *justified*. But this is not disturbing at all, in the way that arbitrariness in ethics would be. The question 'Why should we laugh at that joke?' does not naturally arise, and 'How would our being disposed to laugh at *x* for no reason make *x* funny?' seems uncompelling—we do not generally expect people to have *reasons* (that is, justifications) for laughter, in the sense that we might have reasons for our actions.

iv) *The Problem of Fallibility*: Fallibilism about humor likewise seems uncompelling. Suppose someone says, 'I find that joke funny, but I could be mistaken'. I find it hard to understand this—unless the speaker is referring to what most people would laugh at, or something of the sort. (Imagine someone who runs a comedy club trying to decide whom to hire for the evening's entertainment. He finds Sally funny, but later decides he was mistaken about her funniness when the audience merely groans.)

It seems, then, that humor subjectivism is far more defensible than moral subjectivism.

One further point. Many examples of 'obviously subjective' properties may have evaluative components, and this will stymie any attempt to give them purely subjectivist analyses. 'If baby-killing impressed a lot of people, then baby-killing would be cool' is false because baby-killing is *bad*, and 'cool' implies 'good' (whatever else it implies). Similarly, in some cases, a person may argue that something is 'not funny' on moral grounds—for instance, that it is inappropriate to laugh at a thing because doing so would offend others or express a bad attitude. Perhaps 'funny' implies 'not bad to laugh at'. 'Sexy' may similarly imply 'not bad (or abnormal) to feel sexual attraction towards'. If this is so, then of course these concepts will resist purely subjectivist treatments, but that would not pose a challenge to the arguments of this book.

## 8.6   Evolution and ethics

### 8.6.1   The evolutionary objection to realism

Sociobiologists (or 'evolutionary psychologists', in the current lingo) have offered explanations for moral behavior and moral beliefs, in terms of the theory of evolution. Since evolution generally leads us to expect selfishness, the main problem has been taken to be that of explaining why we often help others at some cost to ourselves. Proffered partial explanations include:

*Kin selection:* We help members of our own families, often at great expense to ourselves, because family members share many of the same genes. Helping one's family is thus an indirect way of increasing the reproduction of one's genes.

*Reciprocal altruism:* We help others because doing so tends to make them want to help us in return. Harming others or breaking agreements with them tends to make them angry and make them want to harm us.

*Reputation effects:* We behave nicely because doing so improves our general reputation in our community, causing others to regard us as good trading partners, and so on. One who breaks agreements or attacks people is likely to be widely shunned.[33]

Sociobiologists do not say that we go through the above kinds of reasoning before deciding what to do, but rather that these arguments explain why our feelings of wanting to be nice to each other have reproductive value.

Some say that evolutionary theory's ability to explain our moral beliefs undermines moral realism, particularly ethical intuitionism. There are three arguments for this.[34]

*First:* Since sociobiology provides adequate explanations for our moral beliefs, and these explanations do not appeal to objective values, there is no *need* to posit objective values. They do not help us explain anything, and our overall theory is simpler without them. Nor need we posit a special cognitive faculty of moral intuition, when we could explain moral beliefs by appeal to emotions, which in turn are explained evolutionarily.

*Second:* Even if there are objective values, the evolutionary explanation of our moral beliefs gives us no reason to expect that our intuitions would tend to correspond to the moral truth. This stands in contrast to other cognitive faculties. An organism with poor vision will fare worse in terms of survival and reproduction than an organism with accurate vision. A person who mistakes tigers for peach trees will have diminished survival prospects. But we have no account of how reproductive fitness would be enhanced by correct *moral* beliefs.

*Third:* Not only do we lack an account of why we should tend to have correct moral beliefs, but the sociobiological account of moral beliefs provides positive grounds for expecting our moral beliefs *not* to be reliable, assuming there is an objective moral truth. This is because evolution would tend to give us strong biases in favor of ourselves, our kin, and members of our own social group. Evolution would mold our moral attitudes towards its own purposes, to ensure behavior that increases reproductive fitness, regardless of what is actually morally right.

The first argument suggests that there are no objective values. The latter two suggest that, even if there are, we have no way of knowing about them.

### 8.6.2 The realist's burden

It is important to remember that intuitionists do not say that we have a 'special moral sense', that is, a separate faculty dedicated solely to cognizing moral truths. Intuition is a function of *reason*. Moral intuition differs from mathematical intuition in the way that perceptions of cars differ from perceptions of trees—that is, merely in having different objects. There is thus no special explanation required for how 'the faculty of moral intuition' evolved.

Consider an analogous case: why do we have the ability to see stars? After all, our evolutionary ancestors presumably would have done just as well if they only saw things on Earth. Of course, this is a silly question. We can see the stars because we have vision, which is useful for seeing things on Earth, and once you have vision, you wind up seeing whatever is there sending light in your direction, whether it is a useful thing to see or not. Likewise, once you have intelligence, you wind up apprehending the sorts of things that can be known by reason, whether they are useful to know or not. Thus, humans are capable of learning to play chess at an incredibly sophisticated level, despite that the environment of Australopithecus contained no chess boards. If some evaluative truths can be known through reason, we would likely know them whether they were useful to know or not.[35]

Note that moral theory does not need to be positively validated by the theory of evolution, any more than any other branch of knowledge does. In order to know that 2+2=4, we do not have to first consult the sociobiologists and see whether evolution predicts that humans would have correct mathematical beliefs.[36] In order to know that there is a computer before me, I do not have to first see whether evolution predicts that humans would have correct physical-object beliefs. This is fortunate, since if this *were* a requirement, we could gain no knowledge of the physical world before we knew the theory of evolution, in which case we would have no way of verifying that theory to begin with. We have seen that some moral beliefs can reasonably be taken as foundational, just as some mathematical and perceptual beliefs can. The initial justification for beliefs about moral facts does not derive from their fitting into a sociobiological explanation, nor from the ability of moral facts to explain natural facts.

The anti-realist thus should not argue against realism on the ground that sociobiology *fails to predict* that we would have moral knowledge. That argument would be no more plausible than the argument that we should reject arithmetic because sociobiology fails to predict that we would have knowledge of it. But the anti-realist *may* argue that sociobiology predicts that we would *not* have moral knowledge. Here, the assumption would not be that morality needs outside validation, but only that it can be undermined by its tension with other justified beliefs. Therefore, in my following replies, I need only argue that the theory of evolution does not determinately predict absence of moral knowledge.

### 8.6.3 How good are evolutionary accounts of ethics?

Evolutionary explanations of ethics are unimpressive—certainly not impressive enough that their existence justifies making a radical revision of our belief system and rejecting all moral beliefs.

What would be an 'impressive' set of explanations? First, it would be one that promised specific explanations for all the major ethical intuitions, including the ones that are the *most* plausible examples of rational principles. It should explain intuitions about such things as the supervenience of value, universalizability, the asymmetry and transitivity of 'better than', rights, and the Categorical Imperative. It should promise us explanations for the *details* of our intuitions about particular situations, such as the seemingly divergent intuitions in the trolley car problem and the organ-harvesting example.[37] With few exceptions, evolutionary explanations of ethics purport to explain moral behavior only in the vaguest outlines, taking morality to consist of little more specific than the imperative, 'Cooperate'. The only relatively specific moral beliefs that sociobiologists have so far explained are the ones that initially seem the most tailor-made for evolutionary explanation and the worst candidates for rational moral beliefs—for example, moral beliefs about incest, special obligations to family, and reproductive practices.[38]

Second, it would be a set of explanations that implied unique, or at least fairly specific predictions about the content of morality. That is, it should be evident that the explanatory framework being used could *not* accommodate a vast range of different moral beliefs and behaviors, but requires moral beliefs to take fairly specific forms—so that the hypothesis that moral beliefs are evolved adaptations would have been falsified if we had had very different moral intuitions from those we actually have. For instance, we would like an explanatory framework that could explain why the Golden Rule would be accepted but could *not* accommodate widespread acceptance of egoism (given that egoism is contrary to our moral intuitions).

Why impose this requirement? Michael Ruse is arguing that the availability of evolutionary explanations of ethics is compelling evidence against moral realism. But if evolutionary explanations of ethics would most likely have been available *whether or not* realism was true—say, because one can think of an evolutionary explanation for virtually anything—then the fact that they are available is not significant evidence against realism.

Many have complained that sociobiology is 'unfalsifiable'.[39] My claim is weaker: I am not criticizing sociobiology *in general*, nor am I claiming that the idea of an evolutionary explanation for ethical beliefs could not be falsified by any evidence. My claim is that there is such a wide range of conceivable ethical beliefs that could be given an evolutionary explanation, that the fact that our actual ethical beliefs are susceptible to one (if they are) does not tell us much. If we had had a widespread intuition that ethical egoism was true (the right action is always the action that best serves one's own interests), wouldn't sociobiologists have laid claim to a rather straightforward explanation for this? But our actual moral intuitions (on this one dimension of egoism vs. altruism) are nearly the opposite. If sociobiologists can explain this too, then the range of moral beliefs they could in principle accommodate is very wide. To give a more extreme example of the flexibility of the paradigm, some sociobiologists have even claimed homosexuality to be an adaptation.[40] If even homosexuality can be fit into the sociobiological paradigm, it is unsurprising that some moral beliefs can be.

### 8.6.4 An evolutionary account of moral perception

On my account, the correct explanation for why we have ethical intuition will refer to whatever is the explanation for why we have reason and intelligence in general. However, I now want to set that point aside and suggest that there is an additional evolutionary explanation available for why people should have correct ethical beliefs. This explanation requires four assumptions:

a) A moral system fairly takes account of everyone's interests. This is not all there is to morality, but it is one (perhaps analytically) necessary aspect of morality. A system of rules that ignored interests, or that took account of some interests while arbitrarily excluding others, would not be a moral system. There are different possible ways of fairly taking account of interests, of course—for instance, consequentialist ways and rights-based ways. I won't try to analyze 'fair' here, but it is to be understood as a contrast to 'biased'.

b) Peaceful cooperation provides benefits to all that generally outweigh any benefits that could be gained by exploitation of others. Conflict with others causes harms that generally outweigh any benefits that might be non-cooperatively extracted. Suppose you have $100 that I want. I decide to go to your house and take it, whereupon a fight ensues. Since I am stronger, I win the fight and get the $100. However, I suffer a broken arm in the process, a harm much worse than the loss of $100. You are even worse off than I am (with two broken arms, say), but this is irrelevant; my goal was to benefit myself, not to hurt you, so I have failed.

c) Peaceful cooperation requires an agreed-upon set of rules. If I am operating under rules that assign ownership of that $100 to me, while you are operating under rules that assign ownership of the same $100 to you, then a conflict is likely to ensue. If the two of us are trying to cooperate in some endeavor, but we have very different understandings of what each of us is required to do, then our cooperation is likely to break down.

d) Agreement on a set of social rules is unlikely unless those rules fairly take into account everyone's interests. If I am operating under rules that are biased in my favor, then I am unlikely to find anyone who agrees with them. To achieve peaceful cooperation with others, I need to accept rules that fairly take into account both my and their interests.

This doesn't yet get us to the correct set of moral rules. My suggestion, however, is that people with a capacity for moral intuition would enjoy the advantage of agreeing with each other on a set of rules that permits social cooperation, since it fairly takes account of everyone's interests. This is not the only way that such coordination might be achieved, but it is one way. People lacking accurate moral intuition might see no reason to accept a set of social rules, or might be inclined to accept a set of rules skewed in their own favor. Even if they accepted sets of rules that fairly took account of everyone's interests, it is likely that they would still not agree, since there are many possible such sets of rules. Since there is only one truth, those with accurate moral perception avoid this problem.[41]

My claims for this explanation are modest. Perhaps it is roughly correct; perhaps not. In any case, it shows that it is possible for accurate moral perception to have survival value.

I do not deny that sociobiology can teach us something about ethics. As noted, evolution may have endowed us with biases that affect our moral judgments. Sociobiology can help us identify these biases, and so correct for them, thereby improving our moral cognition.

## 8.7 Is intuitionism too revisionary?

Given that current moral beliefs and practices can be expected to correspond strongly with our moral intuitions, it is natural to assume that intuitionism leads to very conservative ethical views. But this need not be so. Consider the analogous case of our knowledge of the external world. Science tells us that the sun is 1.3 million times larger than the Earth, that invisible force fields fill all of space, and that ordinary material objects are composed of tiny, colorless particles in rapid motion, with great spaces between them. These conclusions are surprising and quite far from the way things appear to casual observation. Yet scientists do not possess some new cognitive faculty that common folk are deprived of; science is based, solely or primarily, on observation.

Similarly, moral reasoning might lead to surprising and revisionary conclusions, despite that this reasoning must ultimately be based on intuition. An intuitionist will accept intuitions as a source of *prima facie* justification, but he should not accept intuitions *uncritically*, any more than a scientist accepts apparent observations uncritically. As we saw in chapter 6, there are many ways our intuitions and beliefs can go wrong, and the wise intuitionist will be on guard against these sources of error.

From the intuitionist perspective, there is good reason to believe that a revisionary moral theory is in fact called for. Many commonly held moral beliefs look more like products of self-interest, cultural indoctrination, or the imperatives of natural selection than like products of careful, rational reflection.[42] For example, the widespread belief that polygamy is wrong apparently derives from our particular culture.[43] Most cultures have practiced polygamy without considering it wrong at all, and few who hold the belief that polygamy is wrong can offer any plausible reasons for that judgment; nor is the wrongness of polygamy the sort of thing we would expect to simply be a fundamental evaluative truth, incapable of further explanation. Likewise, few are prepared to give any rational account of the alleged wrongness of incest; most of us, it seems, just *feel* that it is wrong.[44] Some have speculated that this has an evolutionary explanation, relating to the increased risk of birth defects resulting from incest.[45] And the widespread belief that, while killing human beings for food is one of the most heinous wrongs imaginable, killing members of any other species for food is not even slightly wrong, seems more easily explained by self-interest, culture, and/or natural selection than by rational insight. Again, the belief hardly seems like an axiomatic evaluative truth, yet most who hold it are unable to advance any credible reasons for it.[46] Anti-realists take all this as evidence against moral realism;[47] intuitionists, however, will simply take it as reason to reject the particular moral beliefs in question.

It would take us too far afield to discuss the merits of these and other common moral beliefs here. But suppose it turns out that reflection by the most careful and thorough of intuitionists leads them to deny a great many, perhaps the majority of commonly held moral beliefs. We might then worry that intuitionism is *too* revisionary. The rough idea I have in mind here is this: The meanings of (all or most of) the words in our language, including 'wrong' and 'permissible', are determined by how they are typically used by those who speak the language. For this reason, it cannot be the case that a word is *normally* misused; a sufficiently common 'misuse' of a term simply generates a new meaning for the term. By the same token, a person who uses a word radically differently (in the sense of applying it to a very different class of things) from how it is ordinarily used may be accused of simply misunderstanding the word. Thus, imagine someone who denies that such animals as German shepherds, poodles, and Scotch terriers are dogs; instead, he says, they are *chairs*. This person would rightly be accused, on these grounds alone, of misunderstanding the word 'chair'. This is not to deny that people who understand the term 'chair' can sometimes mistake non-chair items for chairs. But a person cannot understand the English word 'chair' and yet consistently take it to apply to a very different kind of object from that to which most English speakers apply it. One might say: it cannot turn out that German shepherds are chairs, because that is just not what we mean by 'chair'.

Similarly, I imagine an anti-realist arguing as follows:

1.  If intuitionism is true, then wrongness exists and is an objective property that we are aware of by rational intuition. (Premise.)
2.  There is no objective property that we are aware of by rational intuition, that most of the things people typically call 'wrong' have in common. (Premise.)
3.  Therefore, if intuitionism is true, then wrongness exists, but most of the things people typically call 'wrong' do not have it. (From 1, 2.)
4.  It cannot be the case that wrongness exists but that most of the things people typically call 'wrong' do not have it. (Premise.)
5.  Therefore, intuitionism is false. (From 3, 4.)

Premise (1) simply restates (part of) the theory of ethical intuitionism. Premise (2) is supported by the fact that people—on the basis of emotions and other non-rational causes—commonly judge actions to be 'wrong' that do not appear to have any relevant objective feature in common. Premise (4) is supported by the general conception of language just discussed, according to which the meaning of a word is normally determined by its use.[48]

How should an intuitionist respond? The first problem is that the argument for premise (4) elides an important distinction between two senses in which a word might be 'misused'. In the first and more proper sense, a word is misused when it is used to mean something that it does not mean according to the conventions of the language. For example, in the sentence, 'In saying that he would not raise taxes on the middle class, the President inferred that he might raise taxes on other groups', the word 'inferred' is incorrectly used to mean 'implied'. In the second sense, a word might be said to be 'misused' when, roughly, it is applied to something that does not have the property the word refers to. For example, in the sentence, 'Elizabeth Proctor is a witch', the word 'witch' is incorrectly applied to Proctor, who is not in fact a witch. It is not, however, misused in the first sense—it is not used to mean something that the word does not normally mean. Now, it is true, for the reason stated above (that usage determines words' meanings), that a word cannot be generally misused *in the first sense*. But as the example of the word 'witch' shows, a word *can* be generally misused in the second sense; indeed, the word 'witch' has been misused in *this* sense *every* time it has been applied to anyone—for as I assume, there are no witches. Similarly, then, it is conceivable that the word 'wrong' is commonly 'misused' in the sense of being applied to things that do not have the property of wrongness—though not, of course, in the sense of being used to mean something that it does not normally mean. Thus, premise (4) seems to be false; at any rate, it is not supported by the mere fact that word meanings are generally determined by usage.

Still, I do not think that the charge that intuitionism is too revisionary is entirely without plausibility. While the objection we have been discussing fails to show that it is conceptually incoherent to attribute massive moral error to people, it may nevertheless be true that the meaning of 'wrong' in English is such as to preclude the possibility of the kind of error I have hypothesized. Perhaps most people's understanding of the word is so closely tied to such supposed paradigms of wrongness as incest, polygamy, and cleaning the toilet with the national flag[49] that it is analytically true that, if wrongness exists at all, then those actions have it. Perhaps, at the same time, most people's understanding of 'wrong' is sufficiently loosely tied to the notion of reasons for action that the fact (if this is a fact) that there exist sufficient all-things-considered reasons for not eating non-human animals does *not* suffice to establish that such eating is wrong. I say 'perhaps' because, while I do not believe these things are the case, I am not sure that they aren't. And so I want to address the question of how an intuitionist should react if these things *are* the case and if, at the same time, reflection reveals no relevant objective property that incest, polygamy, and cleaning the toilet with the flag have in common.

Briefly, I think an intuitionist could, without rendering his position uninteresting, accept the charge of using some words, such as 'morally right' and 'morally wrong', in non-standard senses. I intend my use of the word 'wrong' to refer, roughly speaking, to the property about which (most of) the following are true: it is objective; it is not a physical property; only intentional actions can have it; murder, theft, the breaking of promises, and other actions that harm others or violate others' rights typically have it; when an action has it, there are sufficient all-things-considered reasons against performing that action; guilt and remorse are typical and appropriate reactions to the awareness that an action of one's own had it; blame is a typical and appropriate response to the awareness that an action of someone else's had it; an action has it only if the agent could have refrained from performing that action; an action cannot have it if the action is permissible, praiseworthy, or obligatory. When I say that polygamy is not wrong, I mean that polygamy has no feature of which all or most of those things are true.

The most important of the conditions is that wrong actions are actions that there are sufficient, objective reasons not to perform. The core of my intuitionism is the claim that we can sometimes see, intuitively, objective reasons for action, reasons that do not depend on any contingent desires or other psychological responses of ours. If it turns out, as might be the case, that a sufficiently large number of English speakers do not use the word 'wrong' even roughly this way—perhaps because they do not understand '$x$ is wrong' to imply that there are sufficient reasons not to do $x$, or because they understand merely subjective reasons as counting towards an action's wrongness—then I would perhaps agree to a change of terminology. Perhaps, instead of 'ethical intuitionism', I should call the theory I have been defending 'evaluative intuitionism' or 'intuitionism about practical reasons'.

# 9
# Conclusion

In the last eight chapters, I have made the case for ethical intuition-ism by rebutting the alternative theories and then responding to all the major objections to intuitionism. In essence, I have argued:

1. There are five broad views about the nature of morality: non-cognitivism, subjectivism, naturalism, nihilism, and intuitionism.
2. Non-cognitivism, subjectivism, naturalism, and nihilism all face grave difficulties.
3. Intuitionism faces no serious problems.
4. Therefore, intuitionism is probably the correct view.

But the arguments establishing points (2) and (3) have been long and complex. In this chapter, I provide a brief review of the most important arguments for these theses. I then discuss why intuition-ism has been unpopular, and why the issue is important. I conclude with some remarks about how I became an intuitionist.

## 9.1 The failures of alternative theories of metaethics

The four alternative theories of metaethics are competing views about the nature of values and value judgments. For ease of exposition, I shall give examples of what they would say about certain evaluative statements; in each case, it is to be understood that the theory says analogous things about all other evaluative statements.

### 9.1.1 Non-cognitivism

Ethical non-cognitivists say that '*x* is wrong' does not assert anything that can be true or false. Instead, it just expresses an emotion or issues an imperative. It is thus comparable to 'Boo on *x*!' or 'Don't do *x*!'

There is no linguistic evidence to support this. Every objective test that anyone has come up with for distinguishing assertions from imperatives or expressions of emotion gives the result that '*x* is wrong' is an assertion. Thus, consider the sentences (and pseudo-sentences) in the following table:

| *Normal Sentence* | *Non-Cognitivist Interpretations* | |
|---|---|---|
| Abortion is wrong. | Boo on abortion. | Don't have an abortion. |
| It is false that abortion is wrong. | It is false that boo on abortion. | It is false that don't have an abortion. |
| Abortion may be wrong. | Maybe boo on abortion. | Maybe don't have an abortion. |
| Jon believes abortion is wrong. | Jon believes boo on abortion. | Jon believes don't have an abortion. |
| I hope abortion isn't wrong. | I hope not boo on abortion. | I hope not don't have an abortion. |
| Is abortion wrong? | Boo on abortion? | Don't have an abortion? |
| If abortion is wrong, then don't do it. | If boo on abortion, then don't do it. | If don't have an abortion, then don't do it. |
| The wrongness of abortion bothers me. | The boo-ness of abortion bothers me. | The don't-have-one-ness of abortion bothers me. |

All the sentences in the first column make perfect sense and are good English. The second and third columns give attempted non-cognitivist interpretations of them. The only ones that even remotely appear to work are those in the first row. For any more complex sentence involving 'wrong', the non-cognitivist interpretation degenerates into nonsense. Not only are the expressions in the second and third columns grammatically malformed, but they fail to suggest any intelligible meanings. I have no idea, for example, what it would mean to call an emotion 'false', nor what it would mean to believe an imperative. Furthermore, for any uncontroversial case of a non-cognitive sentence—such as 'Hurray for the Broncos!' or 'Please pass the salt'—no such problems arise; we do not call them false, say we believe them, and so on.

There is little psychological evidence to support non-cognitivism either. The non-cognitivist can point to the fact that emotions often accompany and even cause our moral judgments. But this is equally true of many non-moral, factual judgments, such as people's beliefs about their own intelligence, their beliefs about who 'really won' the 2000 U.S. Presidential election, and so on. Furthermore, the strength of our emotions bears little relationship to our moral beliefs. You can know that Nero's execution of Agrippina was far more wrong than your roommate's eating of your ice cream, but still feel more outrage at the latter than at the former. You may indeed feel nothing at all about Agrippina's fate.

Introspectively, we are aware of making moral *judgments*, which have the characteristics judgments normally do. One can distinguish, for example, the degree of confidence of one's belief from the degree of wrongness one believes an action to have. One might tentatively believe that abortion is very wrong, or firmly believe that abortion is slightly wrong, and these would be different states of mind. But if a moral 'judgment' were just an emotion or desire, no such distinction could exist; there would only be the strength of the emotion or desire one felt about abortion.

We treat the things we call 'moral judgments' in exactly the way we treat judgments, rather than the way we treat typical emotions or desires. We may exercise care in making moral judgments, wonder whether we are right, argue and weigh evidence about them, do research, and so on. We may consider arguments directed at whether our judgments are biased and whether they cohere with other plausible judgments. We do none of these things for typical emotions or desires.

All of the reasonably direct and objective evidence is against non-cognitivism—moral claims and judgments act in every discernible way just like assertions and beliefs. The only thing the non-cognitivist has going for him is the supposed implausibility of other views.

### 9.1.2  Subjectivism

Ethical subjectivists say that '*x* is right' is a statement about someone's attitude towards *x*. Here are three common versions of subjectivism:

*Individual Subjectivism:* x is right = I (the speaker) approve of x.
*Cultural Relativism:* x is right = Society approves of x.
*Divine Command Theory:* x is right = God approves of x.

These theories face a host of problems. First, each implies that if the specified individual or group were to change their attitudes, then seemingly horrible things would suddenly become moral. Thus, each theory entails a statement of the following form:

If (I/society/God) were to approve of torturing and killing children for the fun of it, then it would be right to torture and kill children for the fun of it.

But this is not correct.

Second, individual subjectivism implies, absurdly, that I am morally infallible: that in general, if I approve of something then, automatically, it is morally correct. Cultural relativism similarly implies that society is morally infallible.

Third, these theories make moral disagreement difficult to understand. On the individual subjectivist view, *A* could disagree with *B*'s statement, 'x is wrong', only if *A* doubted that *B* was truthfully reporting *B*'s attitudes. On the cultural relativist view, the disagreement could only occur if the parties disagreed about what the attitudes of most of society were, and it would be impossible for anyone to criticize the prevailing social norms. On the divine command theory, moral disagreements would have to be disagreements about God's commands, and atheists and agnostics thus could not have moral views.[1]

Fourth, these theories all imply that a merely arbitrary attitude or decision can render an action obligatory. All of them imply that there are no evaluative facts independent of the attitudes of the specified individual or group. Therefore, the specified individual or group can not approve of the things they approve of *because* they are right, good, or have any other positive characteristic. Thus, these attitudes of approval would have to be arbitrary. But how would someone's *arbitrarily* approving of x make it right to do x?

Fifth, the divine command theory faces the additional problems of how we can know either that God exists, or what He wants if He does.

On top of this, there are no good arguments for subjectivism. The main arguments seem to consist in pointing out either that people have many conflicting moral beliefs or that many people form moral beliefs in irrational ways. It is obscure how either of these things could support subjectivism. The arguments make about as much sense as arguing that if three gamblers all believe, for emotional reasons, that different horses are going to win a race, then the race won't have any outcome in reality, or it will have different outcomes 'relative' to different people.

### 9.1.3 Naturalism

Ethical Naturalists hold two beliefs:

i) Moral properties are *reducible*: for instance, it is possible to explain what wrongness is without using any evaluative expressions. There are two variants of this idea:
   a) *Analytic* reductionists say that some expression containing no evaluative terms is *synonymous* with 'wrong'.
   b) *Synthetic* reductionists say that some expression containing no evaluative terms explains *what it is* to be wrong, even though it does not have the same meaning as 'wrong'.

ii) Moral truths can be known, ultimately, on the basis of observation.

Analytic reductionism was refuted by G. E. Moore. If two expressions have the same meaning, then it should be possible to substitute one expression for the other in any sentence, without changing the meaning of the sentence. Moore noticed that for any non-evaluative expression, it was possible to formulate a meaningful statement or question containing the word 'good' in which, intuitively, one *cannot* substitute the non-evaluative expression for 'good'. Thus, consider the three reductionist theories mentioned below:

| Reductionist Definition | Moorean Question | Reductionist Interpretation |
| --- | --- | --- |
| $x$ is good = $x$ promotes pleasure. | Is pleasure good? | Does pleasure promote pleasure? |
| $x$ is right = $x$ accords with social customs. | Is it right to obey social customs? | Does obeying social customs accord with social customs? |
| $x$ is good = $x$ promotes life. | Is life good? | Does life promote itself? |

In the first column are three examples of analytic reductionist theses. In the second column are questions that it makes sense to ask, in ordinary moral discourse. The Moorean point is that the questions in the third column obviously do not mean the same as those in the second column. But they should mean the same, if the reductionist theories were correct. So the reductionist theories are not correct accounts of the meanings of 'good' or 'right'.

Synthetic reductionists grant this point. They say that moral properties are reducible in a way analogous to how *water*, for example, is reducible: water is $H_2O$; however, the word 'water' is not *synonymous* with the word '$H_2O$'. This can be shown by a Moorean argument: the question, 'What is the chemical formula of water?' does not mean the same as, 'What is the chemical formula of $H_2O$?'; therefore, 'water' does not mean the same as '$H_2O$'. Nevertheless, $H_2O$ is what water is.

This form of reductionism faces two main problems. The first is that evaluative properties seem, on their face, to be radically different in kind from natural properties. Being good, for instance, is obviously a different kind of thing from being round, weighing 200 pounds, or being positively charged. This can be seen on the basis of one's grasp of the concepts of the relevant properties, just as one can see, solely on the basis of one's understanding of the concept of a symphony and the concept of a planet, that the planet Neptune is not Beethoven's Ninth Symphony.

The second problem is that synthetic reductionists cannot explain moral knowledge. We do not know about wrongness in the way we know about water—we cannot observe with the five senses that an act is wrong. Nor, according to the synthetic reductionists, can we know that an act is wrong by intuition. Nor can one deduce evaluative propositions from non-evaluative premises.

Contemporary naturalists commonly argue that we can know moral truths because some moral truths provide the best explanations for certain non-moral facts of which we have independent knowledge. For instance, Adolf Hitler's evilness supposedly provides the best explanation for why he ordered the Final Solution. But in order for this to work as an account of our moral knowledge, the naturalist would have to show that the hypothesis that Hitler was evil enables us to explain facts that *could not otherwise be explained*, and to do so without relying on any *ad hoc* assumptions about the causal powers of evil or the like. Thus, one would have to argue that Hitler's actions could not be explained as well by appealing merely to psychological facts non-morally described, such as the fact that he had an intense hatred for Jews, a lust for power, and so on. Naturalists have failed to make this case.

Another way of seeing the futility of the naturalist's project is to imagine a perverse individual with exactly opposite values to your own. This person could construct 'explanations' for observed phenomena exactly parallel to any that you could construct, but using 'bad' wherever you use 'good', and so on. Thus, if you say that Hitler's actions during World War II were explained by his evilness, the perverse individual could say that Hitler's actions were explained by his goodness. If you say that slavery was abolished because it was unjust (and people generally tend to oppose injustice), the perverse individual could say that slavery was abolished because it was just (and people generally tend to oppose justice). No doubt we would accuse this perverse person of holding corrupt values, but this could not be proven merely by citing the ability to explain observed facts, since he could offer explanations corresponding to every explanation we offered. His explanations, of course, would be counter-intuitive, but the ethical naturalist does not recognize intuition as a legitimate source of knowledge. Consequently, the naturalist would have no way of showing any given moral belief to be more justified than its exact opposite.

### 9.1.4 Nihilism

Nihilists believe that all positive evaluative claims are false. They believe this because they think that (a) evaluative claims are claims about an alleged realm of non-natural, objective moral properties, but (b) there really are no such properties. Abortion, the nihilist would say, cannot be wrong, because in order for it to be wrong there would have to be such things as objective values.

This view has such implications as the following: murder is not wrong; the most excruciating pain is not worse than the greatest ecstasy; the Holocaust was not bad; and so on. It is difficult to know how to respond to such a view, because it is difficult to think of any propositions more absurd than some of those that its proponents explicitly embrace.

In order to support their view, nihilists must bring forward powerful arguments. These arguments would have to start from premises that we are strongly convinced of—in particular, these premises would have to be more plausible than the claim that murder is wrong, that the Holocaust was bad, and so on. It is difficult to see how the nihilist could do this.

The actual arguments brought forth by nihilists have been disappointing. They depend upon the supposed implausibility of the notion of objective morality. But the notion of objective morality is not implausible, and the arguments against it have been rebutted in earlier chapters.

## 9.2 The intuitionist view

We have established so far:

1. Evaluative statements assert propositions, which can be true or false. (Non-cognitivism is false.)
2. They are not always false. (Nihilism is false.)
3. The truth of an evaluative statement is not subjective or relative. (Subjectivism is false.)
4. Evaluative facts cannot be reduced to non-evaluative facts, nor can they be known solely on the basis of observation. (Naturalism is false.)

From these points, it follows that:

5. Some evaluative statements are true. (From 1, 2.)
6. Some evaluative statements are objectively true. (From 3, 5.)
7. There are irreducible, objective, evaluative facts, which cannot be known on the basis of observation. (From 4, 6.)[2]

(7) is close to a definition of ethical intuitionism. It lacks only a positive statement of how evaluative facts are known, to which we now turn.

### 9.2.1 Intuition and moral knowledge

Some basic principles about good, bad, right, and wrong are self-evident, such as the following:

> Suffering is bad.
> If $A$ is better than $B$ and $B$ is better than $C$, then $A$ is better than $C$.
> If an action is wrong, then any qualitatively indistinguishable action (in identical circumstances) is also wrong.
> No person is blameworthy for an action they did not perform.

These principles are self-evident in the same sense that the following are:

> Nothing is both red and green.
> If $A$ is next to $B$, then $B$ is next to $A$.
> Yellow is a color.
> Everything is identical with itself.

'Socrates is a man' and 'All men are inconsiderate' together entail 'Socrates is inconsiderate'.
Time is one-dimensional.
Seven is more than two.

We are justified in believing these propositions for the same reason that we are justified in believing observations of the external world: namely, because they seem to be the case and we have no serious grounds for doubting them. The principle of *Phenomenal Conservatism* states: if it seems to one that *p*, then one has at least *prima facie* justification for believing that *p*. This principle is presupposed in all normal judgment and reasoning, since the judgments one makes are determined by what seems to oneself to be the case. What arguments a person accepts is also a matter of what arguments seem to him to be valid and to have true premises. Even skeptics who say that we know nothing say this only because it seems to them to be the case (or seems to follow from things that seem to them to be the case).

We form justified beliefs about the physical world on the basis of sensory appearances (also called 'perceptual experiences'). Similarly, we form justified beliefs about certain abstract truths, including the self-evident principles mentioned above, on the basis of *intellectual* appearances ('intuitions'). Intuitions are mental states in which something appears to be the case upon intellectual reflection (as opposed to perception, memory, or introspection), prior to argument.

When we perceive physical objects, we do not first apprehend perceptual experiences and then *infer* that there are physical objects corresponding to them. Instead, we are first aware of physical objects, directly. Our perceptual experiences are merely the form that that awareness takes; they (partly) *constitute* our awareness of the physical world. Similarly, when we know moral truths intuitively, we do not first apprehend intuitions and then *infer* that there are moral facts corresponding to them. Instead, we are directly aware of moral facts. Our intuitions are merely the form that that awareness takes; they (partly) constitute our awareness of moral truths.

Moral intuitions can be affected by bias, just as nearly all beliefs can. However, moral intuitions are not moral *beliefs*, nor are they simply caused by our moral beliefs. This is shown by the fact that, when confronted with cases we have never previously considered, we often have moral intuitions that conflict with our moral theories. Thus, even utilitarians experience the intuition that it would be wrong to kill a healthy person to distribute his organs to five other people who need transplants, although utilitarians do not *believe* this intuition. In some cases, we have difficulty even coming up with a theory that accommodates our intuitions.

### 9.2.2 Moral motivation

Why should we be moral? According to the most popular theory of practical reasons, the only *good reason*, as well as the only *motivation*, anyone can have for doing anything at all is that it would satisfy their desires. This is the Humean theory of reasons.

The Humean theory is too simplistic. There are at least two different kinds of motivation one can have: one can be motivated by desires, and one can be motivated by certain kinds of beliefs. The Humean is correct to note that *most* kinds of belief cannot by themselves motivate action. For example, my belief that I am out of cookies cannot by itself move me to buy more cookies at the store, since the belief that I am out of cookies does not by itself tell me whether having cookies is desirable or not. But there are some kinds of beliefs that are different, including prudential beliefs (beliefs about what is in one's interests) and moral beliefs. These beliefs *do*, by their very nature, tell us what is desirable and what is not. The belief that I am out of cookies may be unable to motivate action, but the belief that I am out of cookies *and* it would be *good* to have some cookies, can do so.

These evaluative beliefs render certain actions *prima facie* rational. The belief that *x* is in one's long-term interests provides one with a good reason for doing *x*. Furthermore, this reason takes precedence over any desires one may have to the contrary, in the sense that even if one *wants* more strongly to do something else, it would still be rational to do *x*. This is because the prudential belief (if formed rationally) already takes into account one's evaluation of the relative importance of one's present desires; thus, one's present desires cannot weigh against it. Similarly, the belief that *x* is morally required provides one with a good reason for doing *x*. This reason takes precedence not only over desires but also over prudential beliefs. This is because the moral belief (if formed rationally) already takes into account one's evaluation of the relative importance of one's desires and interests; thus, one's desires and interests cannot weigh against it.

But while prudential and moral beliefs have this kind of rational authority, people do not always act rationally: there are cases of weakness of the will, in which a person acts on some present desire rather than on his judgment of what is really in his interests, or of what is morally right. Weakness of will and strength of will are both possible, because the weight of rational motives for action is not commensurable with the strength of desires—this is because a rational motive is a belief, and it does not make sense to ask whether a belief is 'stronger' or 'weaker' than a desire. This view at least leaves room for free will, something the Humean theory appears unable to do.

The Humean theory of reasons is inferior in a number of ways to the account just sketched. First, the Humean theory offers us no understanding of the phenomenon of weakness of will. On the Humean view, when two motives conflict, since all motives come from desire, the only question is: which desire is stronger? The stronger desire will always be acted upon. Furthermore, since all good reasons for action come from desire, it will be *rational* to act on the stronger desire. There is nothing in this story that resembles 'weakness', that explains how agents might act irrationally, or that explains the appropriateness of remorse or blame reactions.

Second, the Humean cannot explain what is interesting or particularly important about morality. On the Humean view, the most that could be said for morality is that its rules will often help us satisfy certain desires, such as our desires for the well-being of others. But we have many other desires that may conflict with moral motivation, such as the desires caused by envy, anger, and hatred; and from a Humean point of view, there is no reason why the former desires should be somehow privileged over the latter. Morality thus merely serves some arbitrarily selected subclass of our desires, which we have no more reason to take an interest in than in any other desires we happen to have. The rationalist, anti-Humean view avoids this problem by appealing to objective evaluative facts—the fact that actions prompted by envy and hatred are generally bad, for example.

Third, the Humean conception of reasons cannot accommodate paradigmatic examples of rational and irrational actions, declaring instead that *no* action can ever be irrational. For example, the Humean is forced to say that the following are examples of equally rational actions:

*Odysseus:* Odysseus knows that when he approaches the Sirens, he will feel an intense desire to join them, but he *now* desires that he not join them. Odysseus gives no weight to his future desire, and instead has himself tied to the mast so that he will be unable in the future to act on that desire.

*The Partying Student:* A student decides to spend the night partying, knowing that this will result in her failing an important test the next day. Though she knows that tomorrow she will wish she had spent the night studying, she gives little or no weight to this future desire, and instead acts on her immediate desire to party.

For a Humean, the reasons for action one *now* has must be determined by the desires one now has. The only reason one would care about one's future desires would be if one had a *present* desire that one's future desires be satisfied—but there is no reason why one must have such a present desire. The Humean is right about Odysseus' case: we can all agree that Odysseus is rational in acting to satisfy his present desire, rather than his future desire to be with the Sirens. But the Humean is just as clearly wrong about the Partying Student case: this is a paradigm case of irrational behavior. The rationalist has a ready explanation: Odysseus' future desire to be with the Sirens will be an irrational desire, because it will be a desire for what is clearly bad; the student's future desire to pass the test, however, will be a perfectly rational desire. Thus, it is rational for Odysseus to discount his future desire, but irrational for the student to do likewise. A Humean cannot accept this natural explanation, since Humeans deny that ultimate desires can be evaluated by reason.

Fourth, a Humean cannot even account for why we should care about making our moral judgments coherent. The usual reason for wanting coherent beliefs is that coherent beliefs are more likely to be true. But for a Humean, moral principles—to the extent that we have any reason to pay attention to them—must reflect our desires and feelings, rather than our beliefs. Desires differ fundamentally from beliefs in that, whereas we aim to make our beliefs conform to reality, we do not aim to make our desires conform to reality; instead, we aim to make *reality* conform to our *desires*. Thus, whereas I would be irrational to continue to hold a belief that has been shown to be unlikely to be true, I would not be to any extent irrational to have a desire that has been shown to be unlikely to be satisfied. For this reason, one cannot argue that we should seek to have coherent desires on the grounds that such desires are more likely to match reality. With no requirement of coherence on desires, we would be left also with no requirement of coherence on moral principles.

Despite its popularity, the Humean theory fails abysmally as an account of practical rationality: it misclassifies paradigm cases of irrational actions as rational; it collapses 'rational action' into whatever an agent actually chooses; and it cannot account for weakness of will, free will, or the importance of morality. The only justification typically offered for the Humean theory is an appeal to intuition—it just seems that only desires can motivate. But this intuition depends on our considering only certain kinds of cases. When we consider *evaluative* beliefs, it is not at all intuitively obvious that such beliefs cannot motivate.

## 9.3  Select objections to intuitionism

A variety of objections have been raised to ethical intuitionism. Following are the four most common.

### 9.3.1  'Intuition cannot be proven to be reliable'

Some say that we cannot know moral truths by means of intuition unless we can first verify that intuition in general is reliable. Those who make this objection would not be satisfied by the use of intuitions to support other intuitions—showing, in other words, that one has an internally coherent system of intuitions. Nor would they be satisfied by a showing that one's intuitions cohere with those of other people. Rather, the objectors seek a verification of the reliability of intuition that does not itself rely on anyone's intuition at any point.

No such verification can be produced. But this is not a problem, for at least two reasons. First, because no such verification exists for sense perception, memory, introspection, or reason in general, either. No one can prove that sense perception is generally reliable, using only non-perceptual evidence. No one can prove that memory is generally reliable, using only information gathered at the present instant in time. No one can prove reason to be reliable, without using reason. But we do not declare all of these forms of cognition illegitimate. To do so would land us in the pit of universal skepticism. It appears, then, that the present objection relies on an epistemological double-standard: the objector imposes demands on intuition that would not be placed on any other fundamental source of knowledge.

Second, the demand was never justified in the first place. Why should any process of cognition demand a second cognitive process directed at the first one? Why not instead hold, in accordance with the principle of Phenomenal Conservatism, that our cognitive faculties are presumed innocent until proven guilty? This avoids dogmatism by leaving us open to the possibility of revising our initial beliefs if new evidence should appear defeating them, but it also avoids the extreme skepticism that would never allow us any starting points at all for our belief systems.

The demand for verification of reliability would seem appropriate *if* we conceived intuition (and perception, memory, and so on) as giving us immediate awareness of mental states, from which we try to infer conclusions about the real world. Such an inference would require the prior assumption of a correlation between such mental states and states of the real world, an assumption which would require justification. But as I have urged above, this would be a misunderstanding of the role of intuition; we should conceive of intuitions, like perceptual experiences and memory experiences, as merely vehicles of the awareness of facts that exist independent of them.

### 9.3.2 'Intuitionists cannot explain disagreement'

Some claim that intuitionism makes it impossible to understand how moral error and moral disagreement can occur. Those who press this objection often seem to have in mind an infallibilistic caricature of intuitionism that probably does not correspond to any actual intuitionist's views. Indeed, it is hard enough to find philosophers who claim infallibility about anything, let alone ethics.

Those who avoid unfairly caricaturing intuitionism argue simply that there is *more* error and disagreement than one would expect if intuitionism were true. There are at least four reasons why they are mistaken. First, they typically exaggerate the amount of disagreement and error that exists. While there is widespread disagreement about such issues as abortion, affirmative action, and capital punishment, there are no serious disputes about the desirability of such things as murder, rape, and armed robbery. The former sort of issues receive much more attention than the latter, simply because we don't normally discuss what everyone already knows. This leads to an exaggerated view of the prevalence of controversy.

Second, human error and disagreement are common with respect to many objective, factual questions. People sharply disagree about such things as who shot JFK, whether a particular basketball player is better than another, whether a particular individual is smarter than another, whether there is a God, and virtually every major issue in philosophy. Furthermore, throughout history, almost everyone who has held any views at all about them has held radically erroneous views about such things as: the causes of health and disease, the structure of the cosmos, the origin of the human species, the existence of disembodied spirits, the composition of the physical world, and the workings of the economy, to name a few. But no one concludes either that these matters are all 'subjective' or that human beings lack any legitimate cognitive faculties capable of knowing about them.

Third, in general, even when we have available a valid means of cognition, human beings are subject to a great variety of causes of error. These include bias, oversight, miscalculation, confusion, false or incomplete information, and logical fallacies, among others. It is a naive philosopher indeed who thinks that intellectual processes nearly always run smoothly and cleanly, with no defects or non-rational influences. There is no obvious reason why the problems that lead to errors and disagreements about so many other things would not occur when people think about values. Here, as with the previous objection, an epistemological double-standard is being applied: almost no one takes the validity of other means of cognition, such as empirical reasoning, to be refuted by the existence of widespread errors and disagreements, nor by our susceptibility to mistakes and non-rational influences of various kinds. Only intuition is taken to be impugned by such facts. Of course, the facts *do* warrant our being *cautious* in our ethical claims, just as we should be cautious in our claims about the other matters of controversy mentioned above.

Fourth, if we consider what sorts of issues people generally disagree about the most and make the most errors about, it is easily predictable that moral matters would be among them. For people tend to disagree and make errors the most about (a) issues they are strongly biased about, including but not limited to those in which their own interests are at stake, (b) issues on which their beliefs are largely based on cultural indoctrination, (c) issues on which their beliefs are largely based on religion, and (d) philosophical issues in general. This is true regardless of whether the issues in question are evaluative. Since moral issues fall into all four of these categories, it is to be expected that disagreement and error would be common with respect to moral issues. Thus, there is nothing surprising in the phenomenon of moral disagreement that calls for an anti-realist interpretation.

### 9.3.3　'Intuitionists cannot resolve disagreements'

Some object that intuitionism gives us no reasonable method for resolving moral disagreements. The most initially plausible form of the objection claims that there are many differences of intuitions, and that intuitionists have no method for adjudicating between contrary intuitions.

This objection fails for several reasons. First, some ethical intuitions may cohere better or worse with the *rest* of our intuitions. Thus, moral philosophers commonly argue for positions on controversial moral issues by appealing to our intuitions about (allegedly) analogous cases. They also often appeal to intuitions about what sorts of factors may be morally relevant. These are just two of the ways in which other intuitions may be brought to bear on controversial ones.

Second, we can use our knowledge of the factors that tend to affect the reliability of people's beliefs to determine which intuitions are most likely to be correct. We may have reason to believe that certain moral intuitions are unduly influenced by bias, indoctrina-tion, religion, and so on. This is true, for example, of many moral attitudes pertaining to sexuality and reproduction.

Third, even if some moral disputes turn out to be unresolvable, it is obscure how this is supposed to refute intuitionism. There are many disputes, about both moral and non-moral matters, that appear for all practical purposes unresolvable. Why should we assume that, on the correct theory, all moral disputes would be resolvable? Once again, the objection to intuitionism rests on a double standard: for no other fundamental knowledge source do we demand an algorithm for resolving all disputes.

Fourth, the objection rests on another double standard: no other metaethical theory is typically subjected to the demand to provide a method of resolving all moral disputes—and no other metaethical theory can do so. Neither the non-cognitivists, nor the subjectivists, nor the naturalists have produced a method of securing agreement on the morality of abortion, capital punishment, and the like.

Finally, all versions of the 'disagreement' objection appear to be self-refuting. Those who give the objection claim that their objection itself, together with the metaethical conclusion that it supports, is objectively correct. Yet many intelligent people continue to disagree with the argument from disagreement, and with each metaethical theory. How can anti-realists or naturalists explain this disagreement? And how can they resolve it? The prospects for resolving this disagreement seem no better than the prospects for resolving the disagreement about the morality of abortion.

### 9.3.4 'Intuitionism is weird'

Many consider ethical intuitionism too 'weird' or 'mysterious' to be embraced. There are two parts to this criticism: (a) irreducible moral facts are a weird kind of fact; (b) intuition is a weird way of knowing.

It is unclear what this criticism amounts to. Is there an objective property of 'weirdness'? If there are no objective values, then it is doubtful that there is objective weirdness either. But if there is not, then it is hard to see how the alleged weirdness of intuitionism would count as evidence against it. If, for example, '*x* is weird' just expresses a subjective reaction towards *x*, then it provides no argument against the reality of *x*.

If there is objective weirdness, what does it consist in? Consider three interpretations. First, perhaps 'weird' means 'very different from most other things'. Moral facts are very different from other kinds of facts, and intuition is very different from other kinds of awareness. But how would this tend to show that either moral facts or moral intuition doesn't exist? We live in a diverse world: there are *many* things we know of that are very different from each other.

Second, perhaps 'weird' means 'counter-intuitive'. But the existence of moral facts is not counter-intuitive. Ordinary moral discourse, in which we all engage on a daily basis, is committed to the existence of moral facts. And as my arguments against subjectivism show, and as is commonly accepted even among anti-realists, we ordinarily think of these facts as objective. It would be difficult to argue that it is the intuitionist who is taking a counter-intuitive position.

Third, perhaps 'weird' means 'poorly understood'. But again, we lack any clear reason for thinking that things which are weird in that sense do not exist. Nor is there any obvious reason for thinking that either moral properties or moral intuition is less well understood than many other things whose existence we accept, such as consciousness, numbers, dispositional properties, possibilities, time, space, fields, aesthetic properties, and propositions.

The argument from weirdness, then, is as obscure as it is influential. It is highly obscure what weirdness is, or how the charge of weirdness provides an objection to a theory. Intuitionism may well be a 'weird' position in some sense, but if it is, this does not appear to provide any evidence against its truth.

## 9.4   The revolt against values: how intuitionism lost favor

That concludes my official, philosophical case for ethical intuitionism. I am now going to indulge in psychological and sociological speculation about the resistance to ethical intuitionism. This speculation will not provide evidence for intuitionism; however, it may have some logical relevance, since it will suggest that most of those who have rejected intuitionism have formed their beliefs in an unreliable way.

### 9.4.1   Was intuitionism rationally refuted?

Ethical intuitionism was popular among English-speaking philosophers in the early twentieth century. By mid-century, it had suffered a dramatic loss of favor, continuing to the present day. Why? One account, congenial to the anti-realists, goes like this: 'Intuitionism was the first view of ethics that occurred to people, at the dawn of analytic philosophy, because it is the simplest, most naive view. Intuitionism is similar to Plato's view of ethics, which, not coincidentally, arose at the dawn of Western philosophy. As people reflected more, they quickly noticed the various fatal flaws in the system and rationally rejected it in favor of more sophisticated and defensible theories'.

I suspect that is how many contemporary philosophers see that bit of intellectual history. But I think that is utter fantasy. In my view, the broad movements in the history of philosophy look much more like shifts in temperament and intellectual fashions than like rational movements away from unworkable theories towards more objectively defensible ones. I cannot support that judgment in a general way here, since it would call for a discussion of several major philosophical issues and episodes in the history of philosophy. But I can provide some support for the contention as it applies to ethical intuitionism and its fall from philosophical favor. Intuitionism was not rejected because it was found to be unworkable. It was rejected first, then the rejection was rationalized by a handful of paper-thin objections, including those discussed in the previous section. That this was what really happened is evidenced by two salient facts.

First, there is the fact that most of the prominent objections to intuitionism rest upon epistemological double-standards, making demands of intuition and intuitionism that would not be imposed on any other basic means of cognition, or on any other metaethical theory. This sort of reasoning is characteristic of rationalizations. And one of the main objections seems to rest on nothing more than a subjective sense of 'weirdness', which is difficult to distinguish from a mere bias.

Second, there is the fact that most, if not all of the objections to intuitionism are subject to rather simple and natural replies, requiring no significant modifications to the theory; yet the critics of intuitionism have devoted virtually no energy to considering such replies. In contrast, the more fashionable metaethical theories have been the subject of numerous elaborate, technical modifications and variations over a period of decades, designed to show how they can escape from the seemingly devastating objections that lie very close to the surface. In short, metaethicists over the past fifty years never gave ethical intuitionism anything like the serious consideration they devoted to other theories.

Of course, I deny that intuitionism was ever *refuted*, since I think the theory is true and that I have shown it to be true in the preceding pages of this book. But even if you think I am wrong about this, you should still agree that I have made a case for intuitionism that is about as reasonable, at least, as the case that has been made for some of the other theories in metaethics. But in the ethics literature over the past fifty years, intuitionism has been taken far less seriously and given far less attention than any of the other four metaethical theories. So, whether or not intuitionism is actually true, it seems clear that the opposition to it has been out of proportion to any objective assessment of the weight of the arguments. Some other explanation for intuitionism's fall from favor is required.

I believe that intuitionism was rejected because it does not fit with the *spirit* of the modern age. There are at least three important tendencies of modern, Western culture that are relevant here: cynicism, political correctness, and scientism.

### 9.4.2  Cynicism

In the twentieth century, everything once held in high esteem—human nature, science, truth, objective knowledge, art, philosophy, religion, morality—had to be *debunked*. Psychologists sought to show that Man, once considered 'the rational animal', was fundamentally irrational. Freudians found us filled with lust and socially destructive impulses; Marxists found human history dominated by greed and exploitation; sociobiologists found all aspects of human life dominated by 'selfish' drives to reproduce. All three groups found human beings massively self-deceived and considered such supposedly spiritual pursuits as art, religion, and philosophy to be covers for something shallower and far less noble than they appear. Many have remarked on how tiny and insignificant humanity is, how foolish we once were to think ourselves the center of the universe, and how ignorant and helpless we are. Many philosophers, who had once seen their discipline as a rational pursuit of fundamental truths about the nature of reality and our place in it, now denied that philosophy could tell us anything of such truths, if such truths even existed. One influential school of thought declared that philosophers could do no more than discuss how people use words, and that metaphysics, theology, and ethics were all 'meaningless'. Other philosophers declared that there is no such thing as truth, that we can never know it, that we are fundamentally irrational, and/or that objectivity is impossible. American intellectuals attacked what were once their country's most revered forebears—such as Christopher Columbus, Thomas Jefferson, and George Washington—as hypocrites, bigots, and exploiters; they attacked the Declaration of Independence and the Constitution similarly. And Western intellectuals attacked Christianity more than any other religion. Modern thinkers have sought to tear down their own society's heros, its religion, its philosophy, its economic and political system—in short, its values.

I do not plan to explain all the intellectual developments

mentioned in the preceding paragraph; I rely on the reader's familiarity with contemporary intellectual culture to recognize most of what I have just mentioned. Nor do I plan to discuss their intellectual merits—in some cases, the attitudes may have been justified, while in others they were not. My point here is that, whatever else may be said about them, all those cultural developments have at least one thing in common: cynicism. Western culture of the past fifty years must be among the most cynical cultures in world history. And that thoroughgoing cynicism has made the widespread acceptance of ethical intuitionism impossible in our culture, whatever the intellectual merits of the theory. A culture that insists that humans are fundamentally selfish and ignoble will never accept my account of moral motivation. A culture that declares the notions of truth, knowledge, and objectivity delusory will never accept my account of moral knowledge. And a culture that seeks to tear down all values will never accept moral realism. Subjectivism, non-cognitivism, and nihilism have been popular, in short, because they offer the modern mind the perverse pleasure of debunking morality.

### 9.4.3  Political correctness

Political correctness has two, closely-related aspects: First, the imperative to avoid giving offense, even to the most sensitive individuals. Thus, we call garbage men 'sanitation engineers'. We call stupid people 'mentally challenged'. ('Retarded' was originally a euphemism for 'stupid', but it has since come to seem even more derogatory than 'stupid'; hence the need for a new euphemism.) What was once the vice of drunkenness has become the 'disease' of alcoholism. It is particularly *groups*, rather than individuals, that one must be wary of offending.

Second, political correctness entails an extreme egalitarianism. To be politically correct, one must avoid saying that anyone is better than anyone else in any significant way. This is a corollary to the first rule: to deny equality might give offense to those who are judged worse.

Moral realists seem to violate both of these strictures. If there are real moral requirements, then presumably not everyone is satisfying them: sometimes, people do wrong. Some people might even have to be judged *evil*, if they perpetrate sufficiently serious wrongs. In any case, if there are virtues and vices, then some people will surely turn out to have more virtues and fewer vices than others: won't we then have to call these people 'morally better' than the others? But to say such a thing would surely offend those judged to be worse. Indeed, there are few more reliable ways of offending a person than calling him immoral.

Furthermore, if there are objective facts of any kind, then some *beliefs*—those that correspond to the facts—are presumably better than others. But again, to say this would surely give offense to those who hold the 'inferior' (that is, false) beliefs. In view of this and the preceding point, it might turn out that some cultures are morally worse than others—for they might have false moral beliefs and engage in immoral practices. If we judge, for example, that men and women really have equal rights, would we not be forced to conclude that Islamic culture is bad in a very significant respect—it embraces false moral beliefs and treats women wrongly? To say such a thing would surely offend Muslims. But how could we avoid saying such things, if we believed in objective values? It seems that, to be politically correct, we must be anti-realists.

My purpose here is not to discuss Muslim culture, the nature of evil, alcoholism, and so on. My purpose is to explain the ascendance of moral anti-realism in modern times: the popularity of anti-realism, I believe, is in large part due to the perception that moral realism would force us into uncomfortable positions that would cause offense to certain groups.

### 9.4.4  Scientism

To explain what scientism is, I can hardly do better than to quote Peter van Inwagen:

> Scientism, as I use the word, is a sort of exaggerated respect for science—that is, for the physical and biological sciences—and a corresponding disparagement of all other areas of human intellectual endeavour. It hardly need be pointed out that scientism is the primary ideology of our age. It hardly need be pointed out that the illusions scientism engenders are so pervasive and so insidious that it is practically impossible to get anyone who is subject to them to consider the possibility that they might be illusions.[3]

Modern science is an excellent thing: it has given us unprecedented understanding of the world and unprecedented ability to modify the world to satisfy our needs and desires. This does not mean that such non-scientific endeavors as art, literature, and philosophy have become less worthwhile, or that such 'softer' sciences as psychology and sociology are not important fields of knowledge. But the victims of scientism feel otherwise. Victims of scientism choose beliefs that express their attitude of exaggerated respect for natural science. Consequently, they prefer to believe that the hard sciences are the only important and genuine fields of knowledge, and that the things studied in the hard sciences are the only things that exist. As a rough analogy, compare the probable motivation for the medieval doctrine that all things depend upon God for their existence and would instantly pop out of existence were God to stop willing them to exist. Medieval philosophers said this, along with many other implausible things, for the purpose of further glorifying God and augmenting His importance in their philosophy. Similarly, victims of scientism, with few restrictions, adopt whatever philosophical beliefs they feel most glorify science.

For a victim of scientism, ethical intuitionism is obviously unacceptable, for two reasons. First, ethics is not part of hard science. Neither physics, nor chemistry, nor biology studies such things as 'rightness'. Neither the theory of the big bang, nor quantum mechanics, nor the theory of evolution can explain why murder is wrong. The most that science might do is to explain the *causes* of human moral *attitudes*. Therefore, surely, the attitudes are all that there is. If moral facts were to exist in addition, then there would be something not studied by scientists.

Second, intuition is, putatively, not part of the scientific method. I think this is actually quite false—I think intuition is essential to science[4]—but it is widely believed to be true. The victims of scientism believe that science is purely empirical knowledge. If there were such a thing as intuition, then some knowledge would be different from scientific knowledge; therefore, surely there is no such thing as intuition. The only form of moral realism that victims of scientism find worthy of consideration is ethical naturalism, and that is because the ethical naturalists try to assimilate moral knowledge to scientific knowledge. Only if it can be shown to be 'like science' can ethics be legitimate.

### 9.4.5 How intuitionism became 'implausible'

The strong, widespread opposition to ethical intuitionism, then, is the result of the confluence of at least three powerful and pervasive cultural trends. Most modern intellectuals have fallen prey to cynicism, political correctness, scientism, or some combination of these attitudes, and none of these attitudes fit well with intuitionism. My contention is that this led to intuitionism's fall from favor. But we must not understand this process in a simplistic way.

First, we should not think that those who rejected intuitionism generally did so by explicitly entertaining the reasoning I have described above; we should not think that the victims of scientism, for example, explicitly entertained the practical syllogism, 'I wish to believe only that which most glorifies science; ethical intuitionism fails to glorify science; therefore, I shall reject intuitionism'. The influence of such attitudes as scientism, cynicism, and political correctness is more subtle and insidious: these attitudes operate as *biases*, rather than explicit premises. They contaminate our judgments as to what seems 'plausible' on its face, which theories are most worth spending time investigating, which objections are 'important' and 'interesting', and so on. Thus, rather than reasoning from the premise 'Only that which glorifies science is true', victims of scientism are simply influenced to feel theories which amplify the importance of science to be 'more plausible' than those that do not. Victims of political correctness simply find theories which imply that some people are better than others 'implausible'. And so on. That is why many who hear about ethical intuitionism just consider it implausible on its face, for reasons they cannot articulate.

Of course, there could be other explanations: perhaps they find intuitionism implausible because intuitionism is, in fact, radically mistaken. But I have spent this book arguing that that is not so. Furthermore, if that were so, we would expect intuitionism to have also seemed implausible to people in many other cultures and at many different times. Instead, even anti-realists seem to admit that core tenets of intuitionism—particularly moral realism—have been assumed throughout most of the history of Western philosophy and are presupposed in ordinary moral discourse.[5] This suggests that anyone who considers moral realism *counter-intuitive* has anomalous intuitions that call for some special explanation. It seems more likely that the relatively recent shift in metaethical intuitions away from moral realism is due to the sort of peculiar cultural trends I have been discussing, than that the metaethical intuitions of almost all the rest of humanity throughout history have been severely skewed and that only now are we seeing things objectively.

Next, we should not suppose that the causes I have mentioned are the only ones responsible for the rejection of intuitionism, nor should we assume that the same causes have operated in all people who rejected it. It is quite possible that cynicism, political correctness, and scientism could ultimately explain the popularity of anti-realism, even if most anti-realists were not themselves victims of cynicism, political correctness, or scientism. To see why this is so, notice three points: (a) That a *minority* may still constitute a *plurality*; thus, if 40 per cent of people hold theory *A*, this may be enough (provided more than two alternatives exist) for *A* to be the most widely-held theory.

(b) That people's beliefs are strongly influenced by other people; there is a strong drive towards conformity. Odd as it may seem, it is probably true that *most* people in our society endorse anti-realism only because other people do. (Such people probably endorse anti-realism at a rather shallow level, and they may also hold attitudes incompatible with anti-realism.) (c) That some people have a much greater intellectual influence than others—for instance, a professor, journalist, or artist probably influences others' philosophical beliefs more than an electrician would. Those who most influence others' philosophical ideas may be referred to as 'intellectuals'. Putting these three points together, we can see that, for moral anti-realism to have come to dominate our culture, it might have been sufficient that a sizeable minority of the intellectuals, who themselves are a small minority of society, should have succumbed to cynicism, political correctness, or scientism. The rest of society may have come to adopt anti-realism as a result of the influence of others.

I would not wish to be understood as claiming that reasons and evidence play no role in philosophical theorizing. But even if an individual accepts only those positions for which he can find plausible arguments, and accepts them on the basis of those arguments, non-rational biases may still play a decisive role in determining his belief system. To see why this is so, notice (a) that such biases may determine which positions one *looks for* arguments to support, (b) that there very often are plausible arguments for each of multiple competing theories, particularly in philosophy, and (c) that non-rational biases may affect how plausible one finds an argument. In view of points (b) and (c), a skilled philosopher who sets out looking for ways to defend a particular philosophical position will generally find some arguments that he will consider plausible (naturally, there are some limitations to this); thus, the decisive move is the one made right at the beginning, when one decides which theory to sympathetically investigate. And *that* move is typically more a result of bias than of arguments.

It goes without saying that, if I am right, anti-realist metaethical beliefs have generally been formed in an unreliable manner, through processes that are unlikely to lead to the truth. The fact that anti-realism enables one to express one's attitudes, feelings, or personality is no indication of its truth. The fact that moral realism causes some people to feel offended or hurts people's feelings constitutes no evidence against it. The fact that science is good and science does not study value is no evidence against the reality of value.

I do not expect my book to change all of this. Those who feel cynical, those who wish to glorify science, and those who feel offended by the idea of some cultures being more right than others will, for the most part, continue to reject moral realism. If they are philosophers, they will devise clever ways of trying to work around my arguments in this book. If they are not philosophers, they will ignore the arguments. Only a few will seriously consider changing their views. That, unfortunately, is the way of philosophy.

## 9.5 The importance of intuitionism

I would not have written this book if I did not think the truth of intuitionism mattered. It is important in two ways. First, it is theoretically important. Intuitionists posit a realm of facts—evaluative facts—different in kind from the facts recognized by all other views, and a way of knowing—intuition—different in kind from those recognized by all other views. The dispute between intuitionists and everyone else is thus a fundamental ontological and epistemological one. It is crucial to our general understanding of the world and our place in it.

Second, it is practically—morally—important. Anti-realist theories about value undermine our moral beliefs, our moral motivation, and even our sense of the meaning of life. They undermine our moral beliefs, because—as many anti-realists themselves admit—our ordinary, common sense moral beliefs are beliefs about a putative realm of objective value properties. When we say something is morally wrong, we do not merely mean that it goes against our preferences or customs, nor do we intend our remark to be heard as a mere expression of a non-cognitive emotional reaction. Most people will rightly take anti-realist arguments as implying that all we are *entitled* to say is something about our preferences or customs, or something expressing a non-cognitive attitude, which means that our moral beliefs are unjustified.

Anti-realist theories undermine our moral motivation, because they tell us that we have no good reasons for acting morally *unless* doing so will satisfy our desires. In truth, acting morally often is not, and does not appear to us to be, the best way to satisfy our desires. Most people who become convinced of the Humean account of reasons will thus draw the conclusion that they often have no good reason to be moral. (They will not instead assume that they have good reason to be moral and thence conclude that contrary to appearances, it must be that moral behavior really does satisfy their desires.) Furthermore, on the Humean theory of motivation, no person could possibly be motivated by anything other than desires; even if you were a moral realist and mistakenly thought that certain moral principles were objectively true and provided good reasons for action, the Humean would say, you *still* could not be motivated to act merely by those beliefs. I have argued that the Humean theory of motivation is false, and philosophers' endorsement of the theory cannot make it become true; however, telling people that they necessarily behave in a certain way has a tendency to make them behave *more* in that way than they otherwise would, provided they believe what you tell them. For instance, falsely telling people that everyone is completely selfish will tend to cause them—if they believe you—to start behaving more selfishly than they otherwise would. And falsely telling people that no one can be motivated by objective moral principles will tend to cause them—if they believe you—to try less hard to behave in accordance with objective moral principles. People have enough trouble with weakness of will and the temptations to rationalize selfish behavior, without philosophers telling them that disinterested moral concern is impossible and proclaiming all of morality a 'myth', as the title of one recent book has it.[6]

This last point assumes the truth of my account of moral motivation. If the Humean account of motivation is correct, then people already act solely in accordance with their desires; telling them the Humean theory cannot make them do so *more*. Indeed, none of what I have said in this section is evidence for intuitionism, nor is any of it my reason for endorsing intuitionism. It is only reason, given the truth of intuitionism, to think that truth is important.

Lastly, moral anti-realism undermines our sense of meaning in life, and this brings me to one of the reasons why I find anti-realism unbelievable. I think anti-realism really boils down to the view that *nothing matters*. Now, most anti-realists would deny this. They would proceed to devise interpretations of the sentence 'nothing matters' such that it means something that their theory is not committed to. They will say that 'nothing matters' expresses a non-cognitive emotional attitude that they do not in fact have; or that 'nothing matters' means that our society has no conventions for approving or disapproving of anything; or that it means that they themselves don't have any moral emotions; etc. All of this rings hollow to me. Despite what I know they would say, I think the anti-realist view is nevertheless that, in reality, nothing matters. Life has no meaning, because 'meaning' is one of those 'spooky', non-natural properties that anti-realists do not believe in. The anti-realists would perhaps say that life may still be said to have meaning, because we can *assign* it some significance, simply by taking the appropriate non-cognitive attitude towards it. But this too rings hollow to me. One cannot honestly just 'assign' value to things while consciously regarding that assignment as merely arbitrary, and maintaining that from the objective standpoint, those things are without value. Moral values, like all beliefs, are jealous things: they contain an inherent claim to *correctness*. If I believe that *p*, I am believing that *p* is *true*; I cannot consistently recognize the negation of *p* as an equally acceptable, or equally true, belief. Likewise, if I sincerely believe *x* is good, I regard my value judgment as correct; I cannot coherently recognize an equally (or more) correct perspective which assigns no value to *x*.

Admittedly, it is possible—as subjectivists and non-cognitivists have done—to devise interpretations of evaluative discourse such that one could deny objective value and yet still say things are 'really good' or 'really bad'. But as I have argued in previous chapters, these interpretations are simply false. When I say '*p* is true', I do not merely mean 'I believe *p*'—and this, *contra* the truth-relativists, is something about which there is no serious question. Analogously, when I say '*x* is good', I do not merely mean 'I value *x*', or anything similar. In short, I think that among anti-realists, it is only the nihilists who are entirely forthright.

## 9.6 How I became a spooky, unscientific intuitionist

I have been a moral realist for as long as I can remember. I think the reason is roughly this: it seems to me that certain things, such as pain and suffering to take the clearest example, are bad. I don't think I'm just making that up, and I don't think that is just an arbitrary personal preference of mine. If I put my finger in a flame, I have a certain experience, and I can directly see something about *it* (about the experience) that is bad.[7] Furthermore, if it is bad when I experience pain, it seems that it must also be bad when someone else experiences pain. Therefore, I should not inflict such pain on others, any more than they should inflict it on me.[8] So there is at least one example of a rational moral principle.

But I was not always an *intuitionist*: when I first learned of the theory, in the form espoused by W. D. Ross, I thought that it rendered ethics unacceptably arbitrary. Ross had given a list of several different '*prima facie* duties' that we have, such as the duty to keep promises, the duty to avoid causing harm, the duty to show gratitude for benefits given to us, and so on. Ross had no account of why these things were all duties, other than that it just seemed so to most people; nor had he any account of how to resolve conflicts between *prima facie* duties in particular cases, other than to just use one's best judgment.[9] It seemed to me that this rendered most moral judgments doubly arbitrary: there was arbitrariness both in the general principles of duty themselves, and in their application to particular circumstances.

I am not sure, now, why I thought these things. If someone had asked me, 'Do you think that every belief requires an infinite series of arguments in order to be justified?' I would surely have said no. So what was 'arbitrary' about Ross' ethical views could not have been the mere fact that he advanced some claims without argument. I think I would have been satisfied, or at least less inclined to make the 'arbitrariness' objection, if Ross had stated a single ethical principle from which all other ethical principles could be logically derived—as, for example, the utilitarians do. No one makes the charge of arbitrariness against utilitarians. But this makes little sense—if a single foundational ethical principle may be non-arbitrary, why not two? Or six? Or a hundred?

At any rate, it was not the above considerations that brought me around to Ross' point of view. Instead, the turning point came when I noticed that there were *many* things I knew that I could never prove in any scientific, intersubjectively accessible way. And these were not some sort of mystical revelations, but perfectly mundane things that there was no serious doubt at all that I knew. A friend might call me on the phone and, after perhaps one second of speech, I would know who it was. She would not have to state her name or any other self-identifying information. If someone asked me how I knew who it was, I could say nothing more informative than, 'Well, it sounds like Sue'. Of course, there must be some combination of characteristics of the voice pattern that enable me to recognize it. Perhaps cognitive psychologists could figure it out. But *I* certainly couldn't tell you. Nevertheless, there is no serious doubt at all that I know Sue's voice.

Other examples of unprovable knowledge are easy to come by. Talking to a friend, I notice that he is upset about something; I couldn't tell you how I know. I couldn't give you a satisfactory definition of 'table', but I know that the object in front of me is one, and the object I'm drinking out of is not. Modern philosophers have tended to see science and mathematics as the paradigms of knowledge, and cases of unprovable knowledge as peripheral exceptions to the rule. But this, I realized, was severely skewed: unprovable knowledge is the *norm*. This is to say nothing against scientific or mathematical knowledge, but they are the exceptions—an ordinary person may live an entire life and never do one mathematical proof or scientific experiment. But each of us constantly comes to know the sorts of things in my examples above.

So Ross' reliance on exercises of intellectual judgment in individual cases, in the absence of any identifiable algorithm, does not render his view of moral knowledge strange, in comparison with most human cognition. When we consider certain situations, such as the Trolley Car problem or the Organ Harvesting example,[10] we find that we can judge certain actions to be right or wrong, even though we lack any systematic theory capable of computing the right answer in all cases. This does not render our judgments 'arbitrary', any more than my belief that I am talking to Sue on the telephone is arbitrary. It would take an absurdly skeptical disposition to declare that since I cannot specify a set of voice pattern properties by which one could identify Sue's voice, I don't know whom I am talking to.

A second important turning point occurred when I attended a lecture by Donald Davidson at Berkeley explaining his 'anomalous monism'.[11] Davidson's lecture concerned the relationship between mental states and brain states, but an analogous view might be taken of the relationship between moral properties and natural properties. It was Davidson's view that mental states supervene on brain states— it is impossible to have a change in one's mental state without some change in the brain—but that, nevertheless, it is not possible to pick out all the mental states of a given kind using only concepts from brain physiology. For instance, the mental state of *believing that mosquitos have small teeth* might be capable of being realized by many different brain states, which might have nothing interesting in common when described solely in brain-physiology terms. Davidson explained at length that there was no conceptual difficulty in this. For me, what was important was that the obvious fact that moral properties *depend on* natural properties does not entail that one can identify some natural property, or even a finite disjunction of natural properties, that all morally right actions have in common. So there was nothing metaphysically absurd in Ross' picture of multiple duties that have no natural feature in common—that have nothing in common other than their being duties.

With that, my main source of resistance to intuitionism—the 'arbitrariness' objection—was defused, and I was free to accept that in the moral realm, things are, after all, essentially the way they appear. I have moral intuitions, just as nearly everyone else does. They seem to be cognitions of moral truths. It seems that such things as murder, torture, and theft are really wrong—and not just because I personally don't like them. I lay no claim to infallibility, either for myself or for the human community; it is logically possible that I and the rest of humanity are radically deceived (it is also 'possible' in the same sense that we are all brains in vats). But shouldn't we *first* see whether it can be maintained that everything is more or less the way it seems, before jumping to schizoid theories about radical delusions and errors? A plausible theory of morality cannot simply *ignore* our moral intuitions. Wouldn't it be simplest to say that the reason why we have the intuition that pain is bad is because pain is, in fact, bad, and our intuition is our awareness of that fact?

# Notes

## Chapter 1  Introduction

1  A few stipulations about my use of 'evaluative statement': First, I use the term broadly, so that it includes both deontic and axiological statements. Second, 'evaluative statement' is to refer to the sorts of phrases most people would think of as evaluative statements, such as 'Pleasure is good' and 'Barney is evil', regardless of whether (as the non-cognitivists dispute) those things express genuine propositions. Third, I shall also count those phrases as 'evaluative statements' when they appear embedded in larger sentences; thus, in 'If pleasure is good, then heroin is good', I call the phrase 'pleasure is good' an evaluative statement, even though it is not, strictly speaking, functioning as a statement there. Fourth, I include as 'evaluative' statements that apply thick evaluative predicates, such as 'just' or 'vicious', whose meaning includes an evaluation in addition to a descriptive claim.
2  Haidt, Koller, and Diaz (1993) have discussed the putative wrongness of eating the family dog after it has been hit by a car.
3  This is using 'awareness' in its relational sense, that in which one speaks of awareness *of* something. See my (2001, pp. 51-7) for more on the concept of awareness.
4  Compare Hume's ([1739] 1992, p. 469) remark that the viciousness of an action 'lies in yourself, not in the object'. See Fumerton (1990, pp. 35-8) for a similar definition.
5  Where 'F' is any predicate. This definition is meant to capture how the word is usually used in debates over the 'objectivity' of value, though not everyone uses the word this way. Hare (1999, p. 11) says an objective moral principle would be one 'that no rational person who knew the facts could disagree with', and Adams (1981, p. 91) says an objective fact is one that does not depend upon whether any human being thinks it obtains. Hare's definition seems to me too narrow (some physical facts might turn out to be 'subjective' on his view), while Adams' seems too broad (it seems to make everything 'objective').

   Admittedly, my definition does not tell the whole story. We are more likely to call 'Jon Stewart is funny' *subjective* than 'Jon Stewart is well-liked', even though both sentences describe people's attitudes towards Jon Stewart. Perhaps the difference is that only the former sentence superficially *appears* to attribute a non-relational property to Stewart; since 'liked' is the past participle of 'like', the latter sentence *explicitly* refers to an attitude towards Stewart.

6  Here and throughout, I distinguish between 'purported reference' and 'successful reference' (or just 'reference'). A predicate 'F' purportedly refers to a kind of property if statements of the form '*a* is F' mean that, or would standardly be used to assert that, *a* has a property of that kind. 'F' (successfully) refers to a kind of property if it purportedly refers to a property of that kind and in fact there is a unique property of that kind that satisfies the meaning of the predicate.

7  We'll see exceptions to this in chapter 2 when we come to discuss Hare's and Blackburn's views. But the present characterization of non-cognitivism will do for now.

8  That is, evaluative statements that imply that something has an evaluative property. A nihilist may accept the truth of such apparently evaluative statements as 'It is not the case that burning cats is wrong' and 'Burning cats is wrong, or it is not.'

9  There is also the possibility that one of these views holds for *some* evaluative statements, while another holds for others. And on a subjectivist view, there will undoubtedly be some false moral utterances (such as, 'Eating babies is obligatory'), so that one could say nihilism is true of these.

10  In this discussion, 'the world' means the world apart from our language and concepts; similarly, 'non-evaluative facts' means non-evaluative facts other than those about language and concepts. Hence, disputes about 'the world' and 'the non-evaluative facts' are contradistinguished from semantic disputes.

11  Lewis (1986, p. 133).

12  By 'skepticism', I mean the view that we have no justified beliefs about the external world, or perhaps about anything at all. See my (2001) for an extended treatment of this view.

## Chapter 2  Non-Cognitivism

1  This is not the only view of the function of 'good' consistent with cognitivism. Cognitivists with nominalist sympathies might reject the account, thinking that *no* word refers to a property. Even cognitivists who accept that some terms denote properties might deny that 'good' does so, following Armstrong's (1978b) sparse view of properties. Either sort of cognitivist would maintain nevertheless that 'Pleasure is good' is assertive in the same way that 'The sky is red' is.

2  Ayer (1952, chapter 6).

3  See Hare (1952) for a classic statement of prescriptivism, although Hare claims that moral statements *can* be true or false. See the discussion below, section 2.4.

4  Hare (1952).

5  Stevenson (1963, pp. 16, 64–5) attributes to moral statements the

functions both of expressing the speaker's attitudes and of influencing the audience's attitudes.

6 Gibbard (1990, chapter 4) posits a *sui generis*, non-cognitive mental state of 'norm acceptance', which is neither a kind of belief nor a kind of emotion.

7 But see below, section 2.7; Timmons might disagree with this characterization.

8 Ayer (1952, p. 106–8).

9 As Blackburn concedes, 'Nobody denies that the surface phenomena of language—the fact that we use moral predicates, and apply truth or falsity to the judgments we make when we use them—pose a problem for projectivism. This is why they tempt people into realism.' (1984, p. 196)

10 Points (a)-(e) are discussed in Glassen (1959). Jackson, Oppy, and Smith (2004) argue that the sort of syntactic criteria employed in the present section are insufficient for showing a sentence to be truth-apt, essentially because the sentence must also have a sufficiently rich pattern of usage and must be used for expressing beliefs. I do not claim here that any combination of points (a)-(g) alone *entails* that ethical statements are cognitive. Rather, I claim that (a)-(g) render non-cognitivist accounts (such as emotivism and prescriptivism) of the meanings of evaluative statements highly implausible, and that a cognitivist account is the only remaining *plausible* alternative. It is not, for example, plausible that ethical statements lack a sufficiently rich pattern of usage to be truth-apt, or that they express neither beliefs nor non-cognitive attitudes.

11 Possible exceptions are the so-called 'performatives' (Austin 1975, pp. 4–6), such as 'I hereby sentence you to death by electrocution' (said by a judge in a courtroom), but note that these utterances nevertheless express propositions, though they serve to *make* those propositions true rather than assert that they are true (Searle 1979, p. 16).

12 The problem is elaborated in Geach (1965), who derives it from a point in Frege. Searle (1969, pp. 136–41) provides an especially clear statement.

13 I focus on what can appear as the *antecedent* of a conditional. Non-cognitive clauses *may* appear as consequents, as in, 'If you see Barney, hit him'. (Compare Brighouse [1990, pp. 230–1].) This is because one may issue a conditional command, a command that takes effect conditional on some fact obtaining. One cannot, however, have a fact that is in a similar way conditional on a command, which is why an imperative cannot appear in the antecedent.

14 Compare Geach (1965, pp. 463–4).

15 The following theorem of probability underwrites this: If $P(e|h) > P(e|\sim h)$, then $P(h|\sim e) < P(h)$. Plug in 'non-cognitivism' for $h$ and 'We find the sentences listed in (4) odd, malformed, or confused' for $e$.

16 Hare (1963, pp. 21, 27–8; 1999, pp. 24–5).

17 This is a simplification of Hare's view of prescriptive meaning, since I have not mentioned the universalizability or consistency constraints on imperatives. But this is not important to my present concern.

18   To ensure relevance to Hare's view, assume that the presence of weapons of mass destruction is thought to be part of the *supervenience base* for the rightness of invasion. Naturally, the whole supervenience base, if George has remotely plausible ethical views, would have to be a much more complex state of affairs; this only serves to render Hare's thesis that George is describing the supervenience base even less plausible.

19   But see below for Hare's other theory of moral truth (the endorsement theory), which would enable Jean-Pierre to call George's statement 'false'.

20   Hare (1999, p. 25).

21   Hare (1999, p. 18); emphasis Hare's.

22   The last example is from Geach, who refutes the endorsement theory of truth in the same breath as the non-cognitivist theory of ethics (1965, pp. 457, 462–5).

23   Compare above, pp. 22–3. Note also that such a subjectivist theory of truth would be singularly implausible, implying among other things that 'Whatever I endorse is automatically true' is a tautology, rather than being the expression of egotistical dogmatism that it appears to be. See also the arguments against ethical subjectivism in chapter 3.

24   Hare (1999, p. 18); emphasis Hare's.

25   Gibbard (1990, pp. 94–9). Gibbard actually formulates his theory as a theory of *rationality*. A complete set of norms would be one that delivers a verdict (rationally required, rationally optional, or irrational) on every possible action, belief, feeling, or other object of rational evaluation. Technically, in Gibbard's view, the norms do not directly specify whether an action is morally right or wrong; they specify whether it is rational to have certain moral emotions towards an action. However, this distinction is not relevant to the question of whether Gibbard can escape the Frege-Geach problem, and I shall continue to speak as though the norms directly specify what is morally right or wrong.

26   Lewis (1986, pp. 40–50). There are objections to this view of meaning, notably the problem of logically equivalent statements that have different meanings, such as '2+2=4' and 'All spinsters are unmarried'. Though the latter problem may well refute the possible-worlds account of meaning, I will suppose for the sake of argument that the account is acceptable. Here I only want to discuss problems with Gibbard's view that have something special to do with morality.

27   I read the conditional here materially, so $(p \rightarrow q) \equiv \sim(p \,\&\, \sim q)$. If one takes a stronger reading of the conditional, I think the problems for Gibbard are even greater, but it will suffice in this section to show that Gibbard cannot interpret even a material conditional of this kind.

28   Blackburn (1998, p. 71). Hare (1970, pp. 16–19) gave a similar analysis, holding that the meaning of the 'if-then' connective is exhausted by its logical properties. Blackburn's proposal is more initially satisfactory, since Blackburn tells us *what mental state is expressed* by a conditional containing an evaluative component. In my view, Dreier's (1996, pp.

42–3) example involving the speech act of 'accosting' demonstrates the inadequacy of Hare's proposal.

29  Van Roojen (1996, pp. 333–4) makes a similar point, about disjunctions.

30  Blackburn (1998, p. 71); second emphasis added.

31  Blackburn (1984, pp. 191–6).

32  This and the following quotation about wondering are from Blackburn (1998, p. 70).

33  Berkeley ([1710] 1965, sections 33–40).

34  Timmons (1999, chapter 4). See especially pp. 143, 153, 129, 138, and 149–50. Timmons (pp. 143–4) repudiates the label 'non-cognitivist', but this is a merely verbal point; he clearly belongs with the others discussed in this chapter.

35  Timmons (p. 116) takes over this convention from Putnam. Though Timmons speaks in terms of *mind-independent* facts, it would be more accurate to speak in terms of facts that are independent of their being represented.

36  Compare Hare's endorsement theory of truth, discussed in section 2.4.

37  Dreier (2002, p. 165) has pointed this out.

38  Timmons (1999, pp. 71, 167).

39  Or, to anticipate possible responses on Timmons' part, consider 'Some *fundamental* values of mine might be mistaken' and 'My moral outlook might be mistaken in ways that I would not recognize even after thorough reflection'. Both of these are clearly intelligible.

40  Timmons (1999, p. 116).

41  I propose this as a sufficient but not a necessary condition on mind-independence. Suppose that it is wrong to burn your next door neighbor in effigy in your front yard, because this would hurt his feelings. It is plausible that if your next door neighbor had entirely different attitudes towards the action—say, he strongly desired to be burned in effigy and would consider it an honor—then the action would no longer be wrong. This example, I take it, fails to show that wrongness is mind-dependent in the intended sense, showing that condition (a) in the text is not *necessary* for mind-independence. But as long as there is at least one case of a wrong action that would be wrong even if we had entirely different attitudes about it in relevant respects, wrongness is mind-independent. See section 1.2 above for a more complete characterization of objectivity, which I take to be essentially equivalent to mind-independence.

42  Timmons (1999, pp. 145–6). On pp. 149–50, he disavows relativism.

43  The quotation is from Dreier (2002, p. 166), who presses the present point that Timmons' descriptions of his view threaten to collapse into moral realism.

44  Wright, though a minimalist about truth, lists 'to be true is to correspond to the facts' as a platitude partly definitive of 'true' (1992, p. 34). Timmons (1999, p. 153) agrees.

45  Thomson (1971); Marquis (1989); Tooley (1972).

## Chapter 3   Subjectivism

1   Really, the '=' sign is meant to stand for whatever philosophers mean when we talk about something's being 'reducible to' something. It cannot stand for synonymy or the definability relation, since that would leave the synthetic reductionists out of account. It cannot stand for identity, since identity is symmetric, whereas reducibility is supposed to be asymmetric—the things on the left hand side are being reduced to the things on the right hand side, but the things on the right are not being reduced to the things on the left. The '. . . explains what it is . . .' locution in the text is my gloss on this puzzling relation.

2   On (b), see Westermark (1960, pp. 114–16); Hume ([1739] 1992, p. 469); and Hobbes ([1651] 1996, p. 39), though Hobbes substitutes desire for approval. On (c), see Benedict (1934, p. 73); Harman (1977, p. 94); and Sumner (1907, pp. 29, 58–9, 418). On (d), see Quinn (2002) and Adams (1981; 1999).

3   The problems for subjectivism and relativism involving Nazis, disagreement, and fallibility are well-known and are commonly presented in college philosophy courses and textbooks. See James Rachels (2003, pp. 21–3, 35–6) for a particularly well-known and clear example. The problem involving disagreement is sometimes credited to G. E. Moore (1947, pp. 62–4), although it goes back at least to Thomas Reid ([1788] 1986, pp. 367–8), who deploys it to great effect against Hume.

4   By this, I mean that my moral attitudes track the moral truth infallibly, not that my *beliefs about* my moral attitudes are always correct. Conceivably, I could be mistaken about what I approve of, though I should think even this sort of error would be difficult to come by.

5   Goldhagen (1996) argues that antisemitism, even to the point of endorsing the murder of Jews, was a central element of German culture at the time, leading hundreds of thousands of ordinary Germans to participate in the Holocaust willingly. Goldhagen's thesis is controversial among historians (see the papers in Shandley 1998), but we may suppose for the sake of argument that his version of the history is correct. The relevant philosophical point is that the truth of Goldhagen's view would not render German participation in the holocaust less evil; if anything, quite the reverse.

6   G. E. Moore (1947, pp. 68–9).

7   I assume that the 'if-then' here is something stronger than the material conditional. Even if 'if-then' in English sometimes or always means the material conditional, theory (c) clearly licenses asserting something stronger than a material conditional here, something along the lines that society's approval of abortion would be enough to make it right.

8   Analogous points apply to proponents of theory (b). The name 'rigidifying move' indicates that the subjectivist proposes to treat evaluative terms as rigid designators (see Kripke 1972, p. 48). Vallentyne (1996, p. 105–9) discusses the rigidifying move as a way of avoiding

problems such as the objection from Nazis; however, Vallentyne takes this move to convert the theory into a form of objectivism.

9  This is, of course, the reason why I phrased my third objection to relativism using indicative conditionals in the first place.

10  This response derives from Harman (1977, pp. 94–5).

11  This is a paraphrase of Ivan Karamozov's views in *The Brothers Karamozov*.

12  See Adams (1981); Quinn (2002); Alston (1990); but note that Adams' theory of the good (1999, chapter 1), taking goodness to consist in resemblance to God, is not strictly a form of the divine command theory as I define the latter, since Adams does not take *goodness* to depend constitutively on God's (or anyone's) commands or attitudes. See Carson (2000, pp. 239–56) for a variant involving divine preferences, rather than commands.

13  As Quinn (2002, p. 673) proposes. An alternative would be to attempt, through historical research, to determine when errors first appeared in the accepted versions of the Bible. But I doubt that the approach of attributing Biblical errancy to human error would yield the desired results, such as allowing us to condemn slavery, unless we supposed that some of the original receivers of alleged revelation themselves made errors about God's will.

14  Quinn (2002, p. 676).

15  These points appear in Layman (1991, pp. 38–9).

16  Adams (1981, pp. 86–8). This is a slight simplification; Adams says that God's lovingness is not explicitly asserted as part of the meaning of a moral statement but is instead *presupposed* by moral statements. But this distinction does not affect my reply.

17  Here I am thinking of the Divine Command theory as a form of analytic reductionism, as I believe most who see a necessary connection between ethics and God have. See chapter 4 for more on the distinction between analytic and synthetic reductionism.

18  As God reportedly told Abraham (*Genesis* 22:2). The context of the story makes clear that Abraham is to be praised for his willingness to follow this command. Quinn (2002, p. 678) concurs on the rightness of sacrificing Isaac in such a situation.

19  Adams (1999, p. 281) confirms this, affirming that 'the goodness of God' is 'important in accrediting God's commands for their role in constituting obligation'.

20  This is sometimes called 'the Euthyphro Problem' because of its similarity to the problem raised in the *Euthyphro* (Plato 1996, pp. 14–15).

21  Carson (2000, pp. 245–6) gives this reply, but phrased in terms of preferences rather than commands.

22  See Firth (1952) and Brandt (1979; 1996). Brandt (1979, pp. 225–8) distinguishes his view from the 'ideal observer theory'; this reflects a merely terminological difference between myself and Brandt.

23  Firth (1952, pp. 322–4) disagrees with this classification, on the ground

that his theory makes value independent of any *actual* being's attitudes; but this is a merely terminological dispute.

24 This list is a composite of Firth (1952, pp. 333–45) and Brandt (1979, p. 14–15).

25 Firth (1952, p. 320).

26 Brandt (1979, pp. 227–8) discusses but does not endorse this proposal.

27 Brandt (1996, pp. 12, 60, 113).

28 Brandt (1996, pp. 51–8) lists several ways a desire can be irrational. I see no reason why my imagined sadistic desire must be irrational in any of those ways. In any event, I will argue in chapter 7 that Brandt is wrong about what makes desires irrational.

29 I except professional philosophers, such as Harman, who are generally too sophisticated to commit the Subjectivist Fallacy overtly. But it is the only kind of argument offered by Benedict (1934), Sumner (1907), and legions of undergraduates.

## Chapter 4   Reductionism

1 G. E. Moore (1960, p. 40) and Michael Smith (1994, p. 17) characterize natural phenomena as those that belong to the subject matter of natural science and/or psychology. But this seems backwards: presumably it is the naturalness of a phenomenon that makes the study of it count as 'natural science', rather than the other way around. Elsewhere, Moore defines 'natural' phenomena as those that exist *in time* (pp. 40–1), but it is unclear why Moore thought that goodness was outside time while physical properties were in time. In any case, I do not believe that either of these characterizations captures the essence of the dispute between reductionists and intuitionists in metaethics.

2 I intend this characterization of the reductionist's view to include the possibility that there exists only a very complex and disjunctive—perhaps even infinitely complex—account of the nature of goodness. I also intend to include the view that goodness should be defined in terms of some other evaluative notion (such as 'reason'), provided that it is held that the fundamental evaluative concept or concepts are reducible to non-evaluative ones. Note that, for example, Scanlon's buck-passing account of value does *not* count as a form of ethical reductionism on my characterization, since he does not take the normative notion of 'reasons' to be reducible (1998, pp. 57–8, 95–100).

3 Self-proclaimed naturalists such as Railton (1986, pp. 171–2), Michael Moore (1992, pp. 2498), and Sturgeon (1985, p. 51) have made the possibility of empirical moral knowledge a central tenet of their metaethical views.

4 The arguments of sections 4.2 and 4.4 below are paraphrased from my (2000a).

5 G. E. Moore (1960, pp. 17–19, 15–16) discusses both of these forms of

naturalism, attributing the former to Jeremy Bentham (see Bentham [1781] 1996, p. 13).

6  Moore (1960, pp. 5–21).

7  This point derives from James Rachels (in conversation). See above, section 3.5, for further exposition and criticism of ideal observer theories.

8  Frankena (1973, pp. 99–100); Harman (1977, pp. 19–20).

9  The argument is from Gettier (1963). To my knowledge, Weatherson (2003) is the only philosopher who argues that the justified-true-belief analysis may yet be correct. Moreover, probably no philosopher has maintained that Gettier's argument fails due to question-begging.

10  Frankena (1973, p. 99); Darwall, Gibbard, and Railton (1992, p. 115).

11  The point here is that, while the hedonistic analysis of 'good' might seem plausible when stated in the abstract, we can identify specific applications of that analysis in the light of which the analysis becomes implausible—much as Gettier was able to identify a specific application of the justified-true-belief analysis of knowledge in the light of which that analysis became much less plausible. Thus, it might seem credible that the goodness of friendship consists in its conduciveness to pleasure; but it is not credible that the goodness of pleasure consists in its conduciveness to pleasure. Of course, the analogy with Gettier should not be pushed too far—the Moorean argument does not, like Gettier's, involve finding a case in which the analysans applies to something while the analysandum does not.

12  There is a tricky question that I cannot fully address here, namely, why open question arguments cannot be used to refute all definitions. For instance, it seems that 'Is a bachelor the same as an unmarried man?' is not synonymous with 'Is a bachelor the same as a bachelor?' Why does this not prove that 'bachelor' does not mean 'unmarried man'? I think that the answer has to do with the fact that some sentences obliquely refer to expressions, even though they do not employ the most obvious markers of mentioning expressions, such as enclosing the relevant expressions in quotation marks. I think that 'Is a bachelor the same as an unmarried man?' does something like *mentioning* (either instead of or in addition to using) the expressions 'bachelor' and 'unmarried man', and that blocks the substitution of 'bachelor' for 'unmarried man'. But I do not think that 'Is it good to do what increases the amount of enjoyment in the world?' mentions the expression 'good' or 'what increases the amount of enjoyment in the world'. In any event, the Open Question Argument must be formulated in terms of sentences that do not mention (but only use) the relevant evaluative expression and the phrase in the proposed naturalistic definition.

13  This proposal is from Rand (1964, p. 17).

14  Hume ([1739] 1992, p. 469).

15  I assume that the negation of any evaluative claim is an evaluative claim, and that every evaluative claim is a part of some value system. Here and elsewhere, I consider only evaluative claims and value systems that are

consistent and non-tautological. Here, nihilism is the view that nothing is good, bad, right, or wrong (this differs from the usage in section 4.3.5).

16  As Stuart Rachels has pointed out (personal communication), one might, rather than positing one or more evaluative suppressed premises, construe the argument as relying on an evaluative rule of inference, along the lines of, 'From the premise that *x* causes great suffering, infer that *x* is *pro tanto* bad'. Perhaps this is a valid rule. Even so, I take it that we would still face the problem of how we are in a position to judge that rule to be valid. I take the issue of import here to be one of how we know moral truths, and it seems that inference rules of the kind in question do not put us in a position to know moral truths unless we are in some sense in a position to justifiably judge them to be valid. On this last point, see BonJour (2005, pp. 102, 116); Fumerton (forthcoming, chapter 3).

17  Pigden (1991, p. 424) states the principle more generally and precisely: '[N]o non-logical expression can occur non-vacuously in the conclusion of a valid inference unless it appears in the premises', where an expression is said to occur 'vacuously' if it can be replaced uniformly with any other expression of the same grammatical type without affecting the validity of the inference. Pigden (1989, pp. 136–7) offers a proof of the principle so stated.

18  Pigden (1991, pp. 424–5) has shown that Hume's Law is consistent with reductionism.

19  Searle (1964, pp. 44–8).

20  Perhaps Searle would challenge this; he represents the existence of obligations as 'institutional facts' created in part by social rules that determine what counts as placing oneself under an obligation, just as the rules of baseball determine, for example, what counts as a 'home run' (1964, pp. 54–8). I think the arguments against cultural relativism in section 3.3 above render this position implausible. Zaibert (2003, p. 77) argues, however, that Searle did not intend to discuss *moral* obligations at all.

21  From Geach (1977) (with slight simplification).

22  See Borowski (1980) and Hurka (1980) for further criticisms of Geach, though I find only Hurka's compelling.

23  Prior (1976, pp. 90–1). It is in response to these examples that Pigden introduces the qualification to Hume's Law mentioned in note 17.

24  Karmo (1988). I have slightly modified Karmo's argument below for ease of exposition, and I have added the Determinacy Assumption, which I think Karmo needs.

25  I elide the distinction between the law of excluded middle and the principle of bivalence, a distinction that is not important here. The Determinacy Assumption could be challenged by means of general objections to the law of excluded middle, such as those deriving from the problems of vagueness or of empty names; however, such challenges are not relevant in the metaethical context. If one likes, one could stipulate that *S* should contain no vague expressions, empty names, or other

phenomena not peculiar to ethical sentences that might create exceptions to the law of excluded middle. Though some deny in general that evaluative statements can be true or false, this is irrelevant here, as ethical reductionists accept the truth-aptness of evaluative statements, and it is to them that the present chapter is addressed.

My statement of the Determinacy principle includes the phrase 'at most one', rather than 'exactly one', because a possible world may be inconsistent with a value system. For instance, a value system that holds that all *F*'s are good and all *G*'s are bad is inconsistent with a possible world according to which some *F*'s are *G*'s, even though the value system and the possible world are each internally consistent.

26  Maitzen (1998).

27  Maitzen (1998, p. 356).

28  Maitzen himself (1998, p. 358) recognizes this fact, though he does not draw the correct conclusion that nihilism is impossible.

29  But see Horgan and Timmons (1992) for a new and, to my mind, persuasive version of the Open Question Argument that applies to synthetic reductionism.

30  For defenses of this view, see Railton (1986), Sturgeon (1985), Boyd (1988), and Michael Moore (1992).

31  Stuart Rachels (2003, p. 19) suggests that one may observe an instance of pain in oneself to be bad. While this is plausible, I believe Rachels' sense of 'observe' is different from mine in this section: I mean that evaluative facts cannot be observed by the five senses, that is, that they cannot be seen, heard, tasted, touched, or smelled. I suspect that Rachels' 'observation' is what I would call an intuition.

McGrath (2004) has also apparently disputed my thesis here; she proposes that we sometimes know moral truths by perception. But again, I am not sure that what she has in mind is perception in my sense, rather than intuition. See especially her illustrative example on pp. 224–5.

32  Harman (1977, pp. 4–5).

33  Harman (1977, p. 5): '[P]erception involves forming a belief as a fairly direct result of observing something. . . . If we say that observation has occurred whenever an opinion is a direct result of perception, we must allow that there is moral observation. . . .'

34  Two qualifications: a) There may be several distinctive ways *F* things look. b) It is also sufficient that there be a way that *non-F* things look, and that the observed object fail to look that way.

This is only one necessary condition on observation. For more on the nature of observation, see my (2001, pp. 57–65, 93).

35  A second objection to Harman's implicit account of observation is that observation does not require belief. Suppose I see a pink rat, but I mistakenly think I am hallucinating. Then I *observe* a pink rat but do not *believe* there is a pink rat. See my (2001, p. 93).

36  Moore (1992, p. 2517).

37  In technical language, the point is that Michael Moore's argument is

fallacious because 'S perceives that *x* is _____' is referentially opaque. There is some irony in a synthetic reductionist's committing this fallacy, the very fallacy of which reductionists often accuse G. E. Moore (see Harman 1977, p. 19; Putnam 1981, pp. 206–8).

38   Sturgeon (1985, pp. 52, 54, 65).

39   Moore (1992, p. 2517).

40   Sturgeon (1985, p. 66).

41   The electrolysis of water was discovered by William Nicholson in 1800. Lavoisier, Cavendish, and others had already argued in the 1780s that water is a compound of hydrogen and oxygen, on the basis of experiments in which combustion of hydrogen in oxygen produces pure water. I have focused on the electrolysis experiment in the text for its picturesque effect.

42   Sturgeon (1985, pp. 51–2).

43   I have slightly modified Sturgeon's (1991, p. 29) example.

44   The example is from Putnam (1975, pp. 295–7).

45   Moore (1992, pp. 2530–1); compare Railton (1998, pp. 179–80).

46   For the purposes of this argument, we may wish to restrict attention to *paradigm* evaluative properties, such as badness, and *paradigm* natural properties, such as weighing 130 pounds. These are properties whose status as evaluative or natural is clear and uncontroversial. In contrast, such properties as being pleasurable, being healthy, and being illogical are not paradigmatic; it is unclear whether they are evaluative, natural, both, or neither. The restriction to paradigms seems fair, since naturalists would undoubtedly like to reduce paradigm moral properties to paradigm natural properties.

47   Compare Searle's objection to the causal theory of reference (1983, pp. 249–50) and my (2001, pp. 54, 60–2). Bealer (1999, section 3) makes a related point, roughly to the effect that genuine understanding of a concept requires dispositions to have generally correct intuitions involving the concept. My view is that it is one's dispositions to have intuitions that are crucial to one's grasp of a concept, rather than actual intuitions or beliefs. However, beliefs may play a crucial role in one's reference to particulars.

48   Sturgeon (1986, p. 73). Railton (1986, p. 190) is an exception, proposing a quasi-utilitarian reduction of rightness.

## Chapter 5   Moral Knowledge

1   See my (2001, pp. 98–115) and (forthcoming). See BonJour (2004) for objections to the principle. The English 'phenomenon' derives from the Greek *phainomenon*, meaning 'appearance'; hence, Phenomenal Conservatism is a conservatism with respect to appearances. That is, it holds that we should avoid departing from the appearances unnecessarily.

2  The third one is a bit *odd*; normally, one would simply report that one has a headache. Reporting that one *seems* to have a headache is odd because of the conversational implicature that you are in a position to say nothing stronger. Nonetheless, though odd, I think the 'seems' report would be true. This need not mean that the appearance that one is in pain is a *separate* mental state from the pain; perhaps, rather, some mental states have awareness of themselves built in.

3  A person can believe what doesn't seem true by exercising self-deception or taking a leap of faith; see my (2001, pp. 108–10). But these ways of believing are epistemically irrational.

4  Compare Bealer's (1992, pp. 101–2) conception of intuition. This is not the only conception of intuition; in contrast to Bealer and myself, some philosophers see intuitions as a species of belief (Audi 2004, pp. 33–6).

   Note that I count unconscious and implicit inferences as a kind of 'reasoning', although I would not count information processing that is in principle inaccessible to reflection, such as the pre-conscious processing done by the visual system, as a form of 'reasoning'.

5  Fumerton (1990, p. 6) has 'no idea what these intuitions are supposed to be'. Ayer (1956, p. 31) says that to say someone knew something by intuition 'is to assert no more than that he did know it but that we could not say how'. See also note 8 below.

6  Tara Smith (2000, p. 24).

7  Whether the two 'if . . . then' statements should count as evaluative statements is a debatable, but merely semantic point; in any case, they would be of use in further reasoning in normative ethics.

8  Hudson (1967, p. 57; 1983, pp. 103–4); Brandt (1979, pp. 17, 20); Bennett (1995, p. 12).

9  Example 1 derives originally from James Rachels (in informal conversations in the 1960's) and is discussed further in Harman (1977, pp. 3–4). Example 2 is from Foot (1967).

10  Compare Smart (1973, pp. 69–72), confronting a similar example and admitting that some consequences of his utilitarianism are very unpalatable.

11  Popper (2001, pp. 49–50). The 'what we have seen to be true must indeed be true' remark is misleading; Popper could not be objecting to this, since it is a tautology, since 'see' is factive. Rather, what he doubts is that all intuitions count as seeing something to be true.

12  Among intuitionists, Moore (1960, p. x), Audi (1997, pp. 46, 55; 2004, pp. 30–2), Rashdall (1907, p. 85) and Lemos (1994, pp. 144–52) explicitly reject infallibility. Ross affirms the certainty of some moral principles (1988, pp. 29–30) but goes on to deny that judgments about particular acts are ever certain (pp. 30–1) and later allows that moral convictions sometimes need to be corrected (p. 41). Sterling (1994, pp. 130–1) claims that intuitions are necessarily true, since they are a kind of direct acquaintance, but that nevertheless, all ethical *beliefs* are fallible. Prichard calls ethical principles 'self-evident' but defines this only as meaning they

are not derivative (1957, p. 8); he allows the possibility of failures to see moral truths (pp. 9–10n). Shafer-Landau considers *some* moral principles unrevisable but denies that this is required for a principle to count as 'self-evident' (2003, p. 249).

13   Sinnott-Armstrong (1996, p. 10).

14   Stratton-Lake (2002a, p. xiii); Shafer-Landau (2003, pp. 247–50); Sterling (1994, p. 128).

15   These misunderstandings appear in Tara Smith (2000, pp. 25–6), who writes, 'The Intuitionists' assertion of the irrelevance of argument is plausible only as long as the examples invoked are carefully selected', apparently granting that *some* moral knowledge *is* plausibly regarded as intuitive.

16   But see above, note 12. I can find no intuitionist who claims moral infallibility.

17   The passage appears in 'Does Moral Philosophy Rest on a Mistake?' (Prichard 1957, p. 16), which, despite some exaggerated claims, is one of the most insightful papers in the field. Note that despite the sweeping 'self-evidence' claim I have quoted, Prichard maintains that certain 'preliminaries' may be required to see that one has a particular obligation in a particular case, which may include further gathering of non-moral information (pp. 7–8).

18   The idea that foundationalism requires incorrigibility is refuted by Audi (1983). Alston (1976) also refutes objections to foundationalism that depend upon this misunderstanding.

19   Tara Smith (2000, p. 24); Brandt (1996, p. 5).

20   Alston (1993) argues that it is impossible to give a non-circular argument for the reliability of sense perception. See especially (1993, pp. 115–19), where he applies the argument to all ways of forming beliefs.

21   For defenses of coherentism, see Davidson (1990) and BonJour (1985), but note that BonJour accepted coherentism only for empirical knowledge, not *a priori* knowledge (p. 193). For objections, see Foley and Fumerton (1985); Huemer (1997); and Fumerton (1995, pp. 144–7).

22   Hudson (1983, pp. 104–5); Ayer (1952, pp. 106, 118–20).

23   Sterling (1994, p. 79) makes the point about introspection. See my (1999, pp. 347–8) on the problem with memory. See Hume ([1758] 1975, pp. 32–9) on the problem of induction.

24   Thomson (1971).

25   Sinnott-Armstrong (1996, p. 10). Sextus Empiricus (1964, p. 74) levels the same charge against foundationalism in general.

26   Mackie (1977, pp. 38, 39).

27   As Sterling (1994, p. 67) observes.

28   See also my discussion of the argument from weirdness in section 8.1 below.

29   See BonJour's excellent *In Defense of Pure Reason* (1998) and Bealer (1992).

30   Crane and Piantanida (1983) claim to have produced sensory experiences of reddish green, or of a color that seems to be between red and green.

Some philosophers believe that this shows that one can have an experience of something being both entirely red and entirely green. For these philosophers, I note that '*x* is reddish' does not imply '*x* is red', nor does '*x* is between *A* and *B*' imply '*x* is both *A* and *B*'.

31  Essentially this point appears in Russell ([1912] 1997, pp. 72–4) and BonJour (1998, pp. 43–4).

32  As an aside, this criterion implies that typical 'analytic' truths such as 'All dodecahedrons have 12 faces' are *not* convention-dependent in any interesting sense. I think this is right. The *fact* that all dodecahedrons have 12 faces would remain even if we had no language, although the *sentence* 'All dodecahedrons have 12 faces' obviously would not. See Quine (1976) for related criticisms of the notion of truth by convention.

33  This is just what Mackie does (1977, p. 35).

34  Mackie (1977, pp. 35, 40); Joyce (2001, pp. 17–27).

35  Nelson (2003, pp. 76–7) makes a similar observation, inspired by Chisholm's (1982) remarks about the problem of the criterion, but Nelson grants that *both* arguments beg the question. My view is that *neither* does (insofar as begging the question is a fallacy). Chisholm similarly held that his own solution to the problem of the criterion begged the question, but excused this with the observation that every solution begs the question. Again, I would deny that any of the positions he discusses (particularism, methodism, and skepticism) begs the question. See my remarks about begging the question in section 4.2 above. James Rachels (1974, pp. 310-13) makes similar observations about 'begging the question' against ethical egoism.

36  The argument here is analogous to those found in Moore (1953, pp. 119–20), DePaul (1988, p. 85), and Huemer (2001, pp. 31–44). In the last, I argue that every form of philosophical skepticism is unjustified; the argument presented here is a special case of that argument.

37  Compare Chisholm's (1982) discussion of methodism and particularism, though Chisholm neglects the reflective equilibrium approach. The term 'reflective equilibrium' is from Rawls (1971, p. 48). DePaul (1988) defends this general approach to moral theory, which he calls 'coherentism'. In my view, the approach is not properly called coherentist, since some degree of foundational justification must be accorded to the initial appearances. See my (1997) and Olsson (2005) for the justification of this requirement.

38  This is something of a simplification of my view, however, since it implies that 'coherence' is an all-or-nothing property. A more precise statement would incorporate the notion of degrees of coherence, where these are partly determined by probabilistic relations among beliefs. In addition, the statement in the text implies that the absolute number of initially plausible beliefs that are held true is what matters. A more precise statement would take account of the fact that some pairs of initially plausible beliefs are so related that, if one of them is false, the other is almost certainly also false, so that giving up the latter belief

should not be counted as an *additional* cost of a theory that requires giving up the former belief. But I do not think these refinements are important for the present point, simply because nihilism on its face is so far from achieving any reasonable variant of reflective equilibrium.

39   This is a popular conception of epistemic justification; see BonJour (1985, pp. 7–8).

40   Compare Hare (1989, pp. 82–3).

41   See my (2001, pp. 11–16, 178–81); Hume ([1758] 1975, pp. 151–3). Global skepticism is the view that no one can be justified in believing anything.

42   A sensory experience of *x* is, roughly, the experience of seeming to perceive *x*; note that the having of such an experience does not entail that *x* actually exists. 'Memory experience' should be understood analogously.

43   My showing something to be true is of course compatible with *some* readers failing to see it. But if, upon reading my work carefully, most competent judges would not find that any of my premises seemed true, then, even if all my statements were in fact true, I would not count as having *shown* anything.

44   Nagel (1986, p. 146) appears to endorse this inferential conception of the role of ethical intuition: '[I]n ethics, one infers from appearances of value to their most plausible explanation in a theory of what there is reason to do or want.' This remark is, however, ambiguous; 'appearance' can refer either to the mental state of something's appearing to be the case or to the *content* of that mental state, that which appears to be the case. On one interpretation, Nagel counsels us to adopt the best explanation for why certain things *appear to be* valuable. On the other interpretation, he advises us to adopt the best explanation for why certain things *are* valuable, where these are the things that appear to us to be valuable. It is the former doctrine that I object to as a misunderstanding of the epistemological role of intuition.

45   Note that (1) may be a *reason why* belief in (2) is justified, in the sense of a condition that justification for believing (2) supervenes on, without being *one's reason* or even *a reason one has* for believing (2), in the sense of something from which one does or could legitimately infer (2). See my (2003, pp. 148–51) on this distinction.

46   Harman (1990) and Tye (2002) defend the transparency thesis. Reid (1983) provides an early form of direct realism. I elaborate and defend the view in my (2001). See especially pp. 81–5 on the skeptic's mistaken conception of the relationship between consciousness and its objects.

47   See my (2001, pp. 51–5) on the nature of awareness. Roughly, intuitions (sometimes) count as awareness of moral facts because (sometimes) moral facts correspond to the propositional contents of the intuitions, the intuitions represent their contents as actual, and it is non-accidental that these intuitions are true.

48   This follows if one accepts physicalism. But even mind/body dualists will probably accept that moral properties don't cause mental events. Note

that the arguments of this section should all be taken to concern fundamental moral facts, of the form 'F is good-making', 'G is wrong-making', and so forth.

49  In fact, I would prefer to regard them as principles about what are good-making, right-making, etc., features; see below, section 8.2.3.

50  Goldman (1967); Benacerraf (1973, p. 671). The present objection to moral knowledge is modeled on Benacerraf's objection to Platonism in mathematics.

51  See Nozick's (1981, pp. 172ff.) analysis of knowledge.

52  The objections I have in mind include the causal theory's difficulty in accounting for knowledge by induction, and the failures of closure implied by Nozick's theory. The alternative accounts of knowledge I have in mind include reliabilism, the defeasibility analysis, Plantinga's 'proper function' analysis, the relevant alternatives theory, and various forms of contextualism.

53  See Armstrong (1978a; 1978b) for more arguments in defense of universals and (1978a, pp. 60–1) on the difficulty sentences like (Y) pose for nominalists; but note that Armstrong accepts far fewer universals than I do. Bealer (1993) provides arguments supporting a premise analogous to my (2), concerning statements about the properties of propositions. But I doubt that either of these philosophers would agree with me that the existence of universals is a *trivial* truth.

54  Berkeley ([1710] 1965, introduction, sections 11–16); Hume ([1739] 1992, pp. 17–25). There are other forms of nominalism that I don't discuss here, particularly what Armstrong calls 'class nominalism' and 'resemblance nominalism'. I think they can be refuted similarly; see Armstrong (1978a, chapters 4, 5).

55  Similar views of a priori knowledge are provided by Bealer (1999) and Russell ([1912] 1997, chapters 9–10). I take Russell's notion of having 'acquaintance' with universals and Bealer's notion of possessing a concept 'in the full sense' to be essentially equivalent to my notion of 'adequately grasping' a universal. Lemos (1994, pp. 155–60) and Audi (1997, p. 28; 2004, p. 48) apply a similar conception of *a priori* knowledge to the case of ethics, but note that I do not, with Audi and Lemos, locate the justification for *a priori* beliefs in the understanding of their contents. Rather, I locate justification for belief in the state of something's seeming to be the case.

56  Since writing the remarks in the text, I have come to the conclusion that these conditions are necessary but not sufficient for adequate grasping of a universal, roughly because, for example, the concept of a simultaneously red and green object does not count as a grasp of any universal. I am uncertain as to what further conditions must be added.

57  In the philosophers' sense, a definition must state necessary and sufficient conditions for the application of a concept in all possible worlds.

58  But this does not require the existence of disjunctive universals. If one

disjoins two concepts, each concept may refer to a universal without the disjunction referring to one.

59  The 'cannot' adverts at least to all possible worlds whose intelligent beings are roughly like us psychologically. I suspect it applies to all possible worlds whatsoever—I reject the Humean supposition that 'anything can cause anything'. But I think the weaker modal claim is all that my account of *a priori* knowledge requires.

60  In other words, I take the Benacerraf problem to concern *warrant* in Plantinga's sense (1993, p. 3) rather than *justification*.

## Chapter 6  Disagreement and Error

1  Brandt (1996, p. 5); what he proposes to ignore is the idea that intuitions are reliable guides to moral questions about specific cases. Non-naturalism is dismissed in a few sentences on the preceding page. Among those who offer general theories of the nature of morality and ignore intuitionism are Joyce (2001), Blackburn (1993), and Harman (1977). James Rachels' (2003) excellent and widely used textbook contains no mention of intuitionism, though it includes sections on other metaethical theories. Liszka's textbook opines that 'the flaws with this approach are obvious' before glibly recounting the problem of disagreement (2002, p. 312). Jackson (2003, p. 562) observes, 'It seems that we know enough about what our world is like to know that there is no such property' as Moore's non-natural property of goodness; he gives no further elaboration. Jackson, Pettit, and Smith (2004, p. 221) dismiss Moore's non-naturalism as 'jejune', again with no further elaboration. However, intuitionism has gained renewed interest in some quarters in recent years (Stratton-Lake 2002b; Audi 1997 and 2004; Dancy 1993; Shafer-Landau 2003).

2  See Howard and Dunaif-Hattis (1992, pp. 314–15, 461, 573). Some anthropologists deny the authenticity of most alleged cases of cannibalism; see Arens (1979) and Howard and Dunaif-Hattis (1992, p. 489).

3  Rachels (2003, pp. 24–5).

4  Hare (1999, pp. 5–6) argues that because intuitions can differ, intuitionism entails relativism. But see note 5 below.

5  This is Hare's notion of objectivity (1999, p. 11).

6  Mackie (1977, pp. 36–8); Hudson (1967, pp. 58–60); Layman (1991, pp. 179–80).

7  Nowell-Smith (1954, pp. 46–7), Hudson (1967, p. 58), Liszka (2002, p. 312), Popper (2001, pp. 49–50), and Tara Smith (2000, pp. 25–6) all attribute the claim of infallibility to intuitionism. Smith explicitly attributes the claim of the irrelevance of reasoning, while the others seem to imply it. Claim (iii) is not explicitly mentioned but seems required by

the argument. Brandt (1944, p. 477) implies that intellectual insights must be infallible, under appropriate conditions.

8   See chapter 5, note 12. I can find no clear endorsement of the general infallibility claim in all of the intuitionist literature.

9   Clarke ([1705] 1964, p. 6). Quoted in Nowell-Smith (1954, p. 47). I have abridged the quotation.

10   Clarke ([1705] 1964, pp. 4–5). His other examples are similar, being generally along the lines of: it is better to help people than to cause misery and destruction for no reason.

11   Brandt (1944, p. 483).

12   Arens (1979); Mead (2001); Freeman (1983; 1999). See Gardner (1998) for a review of the cannibalism controversy. See Hellman (1998, chapter 10) for a review of the Mead-Freeman controversy. Hellman also reviews nine other great disputes in science.

13   Murray (1984).

14   See Newport and Strausberg (2001) on ESP and astrology and Gallup and Newport (1991, pp. 138, 141) on ESP, astrology, and telepathic experiences. Newport and Strausberg report that in 2001, 36 per cent of Americans believed in telepathy, though Newport and Strausberg did not determine how many believe they have actually had a telepathic experience.

15   Nowell-Smith (1954, p. 46); Hudson (1967, pp. 58–60).

16   See my (n.d.) on irrationality and bias.

17   This is the 'young Earth' position held by many creationists, such as Thompson (1999). The 6000 figure is arrived at by adding ages of people mentioned in the Bible, particularly in *Genesis*.

18   Compare Shafer-Landau (2003, p. 220).

19   Nowell-Smith (1954, pp. 44–6).

20   Sterling (1994, p. 130) and Brink (1984, p. 117) make similar points. For examples of rational arguments about abortion, see Thomson (1971), Tooley (1972), and Marquis (1989). Though these arguments have not succeeded in resolving the dispute to everyone's satisfaction, they are a step in the right direction.

21   Brink (1984, p. 116) argues similarly, though he seems to mistakenly think the point requires a coherentist theory of justification. My view resembles what Haack (1983) dubs 'foundherentism', but note that I do not, like Haack, assume that *all* foundational beliefs are fallible. Compare BonJour's (1985, pp. 26–9) notions of 'moderate' and 'weak foundationalism', both of which allow coherence to raise or lower the justification of foundational beliefs.

22   The point does not depend on witness dishonesty. Studies have found that the reliability of eyewitness testimony is greatly overrated, witnesses may be highly confident even when wrong, and many people convicted on the basis of such testimony have since been exonerated. See Wells and Olson (2003) for a review.

23  Sinnott-Armstrong (1996, pp. 26–7); Layman (1991, pp. 179–80); Ayer (1952, p. 106).
24  Nowell-Smith (1954, p. 47) purports to speak for intuitionists: '[T]hose who disagree with us on a moral issue must be insincere. It is force, not argument that they need.'
25  Singer (1993, pp. 169–73). He agrees that we 'should certainly put very strict conditions on permissible infanticide' (p. 173).
26  The latter principle is criticized by Stuart Rachels (1998), but I am unpersuaded.
27  Stuart Rachels (2003) lists nine ways of arguing for claims about intrinsic value, seven of which seem viable. None of the viable ones conflict with my thesis that intuition is the ultimate source of justification for all ethical claims.
28  Remarks to this effect are common; see Rawls (1971, p. 21); Timmons (1999, p. 7); Smith (1994, pp. 201–2).
29  This is Stevenson's (1963, pp. 26–7) explanation of moral disagreement.
30  Joyce (2001, chapter 6).
31  See Singer (1993, p. 327); Hare (1999, pp. 24, 58–9); Ruse (1998, p. 255).
32  Singer (1993, pp. 229–30). There is further discussion, of course, but the appeal to intuition is essential.
33  See above, pp. 145-7.
34  Singer and Posner (2001, opening letter). For further suggestions about our biases, see Singer (1974, p. 516).
35  Among anti-realists, only Scanlon seems to recognize this point: 'If, however, it is charged that our judgments about reasons for action *as a whole* are "merely" due to habituation, what conception of reasons backs up this "merely"? "Merely" as opposed to what? If the content of judgments about reasons suggested that they were supposed to reveal to us the facts about some "external" reality, then this charge might at least gain a foothold' (1998, p. 72).
36  The quotation is from Singer (1999, p. 316), referring approvingly to Peter Unger's arguments. Unger (1996, p. 101) gives several examples of obviously false moral claims that he thinks our intuitions depend on, though he does not claim that moral intuitions about cases are unreliable *in general* (p. 10). Singer (1999, p. 317) declares, 'These factors just cannot be morally significant'—end of argument.
      See also Singer (1993, pp. 232, 254) on the physical proximity bias. Singer (1974, pp. 516–17; 1999, p. 270) recommends that we rely on 'self-evident axioms' instead of intuitions about cases.

## Chapter 7   Practical Reasons

1  I use the term 'normative reasons' because I take it that the concept of rationality is a central normative concept. I take *moral* reasons to be a proper subset of normative reasons.

2  Hume ([1739] 1992, pp. 413–17). More precisely, in (a), we should read 'that you believe *A* will or might accomplish' as 'such that your subjective probability of its occurring given that you do *A* is greater than your unconditional subjective probability of its occurring'. In (b), we should read 'that you have reason to believe *A* will or might accomplish' as 'such that the epistemic probability, on your total evidence, of its occurring given that you do *A* is greater than the unconditional epistemic probability, on your total evidence, of its occurring'.

3  The argument derives from Hume ([1739] 1992, pp. 413–18, 455–70) and is discussed at length by Michael Smith (1994, esp. p. 12). One of the most popular arguments in all of philosophy, it has been endorsed by Mackie (1977, pp. 40–1), Gibbard (1990, p. 33), Hare (1999, p. 1), Nowell-Smith (1954, pp. 39–42), Joyce (2001), and Fumerton (1990, chapter 3), among others.

4  Kant ([1785] 1959) and Nagel (1970) reject the Humean Conception. McDowell (1978) rejects the Belief/Desire Gap. Ross ([1930] 1988, pp. 157–8, 163) rejects and Frankena (1958) calls into question the Magnetism of Values.

5  I take this to be true for any sense of 'should', not just the moral 'should'.

6  To have an available motivation for doing *A* is to have a mental state (possibly dispositional or subconscious) such that either it motivates one towards doing *A*, or one can bring it about that it so motivates one.

7  A variant is the idea that we should interpret others as having generally *true* beliefs (Davidson 1990, pp. 129–30); however, this version of the principle of charity is inferior to the one I discuss. We are justified in attributing false beliefs to others, provided that it would make the most sense for them to be holding those false beliefs. We are also justified in attributing false statements to others (including lies), when it would be most rational (perhaps for practical reasons) for them to make such false statements.

8  The term 'physical pleasure' is something of a misnomer—sensory pleasures are really no more physical than emotional pleasures. If physicalism in the philosophy of mind is true, both are physical; if dualism is true, both are non-physical.

9  Bentham ([1781] 1996, p. 11); Hume ([1739] 1992, p. 414). Compare von Mises' (1996, pp. 13–15) contention that all action aims at removing felt uneasiness and achieving happiness.

10  Compare the observation, in section 5.6, that our perceptions and intuitions are focused on the world. The mistake of treating awareness as being primarily directed at inner states is of a piece with the mistake of treating our goals as being primarily about inner states.

11  Hubin (1980, p. 75) deploys a similar example, to make the related point that self-interest does not consist in desire-satisfaction. See also Nozick's 'Experience Machine' example (1974, pp. 42–5), which shows that the objects of our desires are typically not internal states. Most people would not plug into the machine for the same reason they would not sell their

children into slavery: that would not get them what they want.

12 Compare Butler's ([1729] 1964, pp. 20–5) classic refutation of psychological egoism.

13 Michael Smith (1994, p. 114) treats desires this way. Nagel (1970, p. 29) suggests that we may ascribe a desire to someone *by virtue of* the fact that he is motivated in a certain way.

14 This need not amount to what Michael Smith (1994, pp. 104–111) calls the 'phenomenological conception of desire', since we need not assume that appetites and emotions must always have occurrent qualia. Compare: we can introspectively identify our beliefs, even though on the received view, beliefs have no qualia.

15 Few of the philosophers of this stripe would use the word 'intuition', or even the word 'obvious', in making this appeal. Rather, they would simply assert the Humean conception without argument, and it is this that leads me to construe them as relying on intuition.

16 Hume ([1739] 1992, p. 458).

17 The example is Anscombe's (1963, pp. 56–7). The 'direction of fit' terminology is from Searle (1979, pp. 3–4; 1983, pp. 7–9), who may have gotten it from J. L. Austin.

18 Michael Smith (1994, pp. 111–16).

19 Paraphrased from Michael Smith (1994, p. 116). Smith actually says that any mental state with world-to-mind direction of fit is a desire, and thus that motivation requires desire. I have slightly weakened Smith's claims to give the argument its best chance of succeeding.

20 Interestingly, Smith thinks that (2) is 'unassailable' and only (3) is open to challenge.

21 A normative reading of (2) is suggested by Smith's use of the phrase 'state with which the world *must* fit' (1994, p. 116; emphasis mine). However, since the argument concerns motivating reasons, rather than normative reasons, it seems that a descriptive reading is required. This reading is supported by Smith's remark that a state with mind-to-world direction of fit 'tends to go out of existence' when one perceives that the world fails to match it (p. 118). Shafer-Landau (2003, p. 35) argues that the notion of direction of fit *should* be understood normatively, along the lines of: a state with mind-to-world direction of fit is one that *ought* to go out of existence in the face of a perception that its content is unsatisfied. Note that the equivocation of which I accuse Smith in the text would arise whether one takes a normative or a descriptive interpretation of direction of fit.

22 Scanlon (1998, pp. 33–5) makes a similar claim, to the effect that a normative judgment can constitute a motivation, which I take to be roughly equivalent to the claim that making a normative judgment can constitute having a goal. The notion of 'having a goal' might, instead, be taken to require an *intention* to pursue the goal, but on that interpretation, Smith's argument would fail, since the presence of a

motivating reason to pursue *x* does not entail the presence of an intention to pursue *x*.

23 Hume ([1739] 1992, p. 458).

24 Hume ([1739] 1992, p. 416). As the context confirms, Hume's point is that no preference can be rationally criticized.

25 'Rational' is itself an evaluative term, about which a Humean might adopt an anti-realist theory (Gibbard 1990, pp. 6–7). It is natural to wonder how this would affect my subsequent arguments. The answer is that it should not affect them, provided the anti-realist view in question is plausible. For anti-realism about values is plausible only if it allows for the possibility of cogent reasoning, of roughly the sort that our actual discourse involves, about first-order evaluative questions. My arguments in the following sections about what is practically rational, then, would simply be instances of such evaluative reasoning.

26 Brandt (1996, pp. 51–3).

27 Brandt (1979, pp. 14–15); Williams (1981, pp. 104–5).

28 Michael Smith (1994, pp. 159–60). Smith considers himself an anti-Humean about normative reasons; I, however, call him a Neo-Humean.

29 Williams (1981, pp. 106–9).

30 Nagel (1970, pp. 39–41) takes this point to reveal a serious deficiency in the Humean account of practical rationality.

31 If a *large* set of beliefs is inconsistent, each individual belief may be sufficiently probable that one should not give it up. See Foley (1979).

32 Suppose, for example, that the atheist succeeds in showing that the concept of omnipotence is incoherent, that omnipotence is inconsistent with omnibenevolence, or the like.

33 Stuart Rachels (personal communication) suggests that it might be reasonable only to *wish* that world hunger would end, rather than to *desire* that it end. Perhaps there is a sense of 'desire' in which the having of a desire implies something like the belief that the object of desire has a reasonable chance of being attained. But I do not use 'desire' in such a sense here. I use 'desire' in a broad sense that includes wishes. On a similar note, my sense of 'desire' also allows one to desire what one already has.

34 BonJour (1985, pp. 169–79). See Olsson (2005) for criticisms of coherence on grounds of its inability to secure likelihood of truth.

35 I take epistemic justification to be a matter of likelihood of truth, in one sense of 'likelihood'.

36 Ryan (2003) defends such a position persuasively, though she is swimming against the current here.

37 Scanlon (1998, pp. 62–3). I have taken some liberties—where I speak of 'evaluative judgments', Scanlon speaks of 'conclusions about reasons' (which he takes as the most fundamental kind of evaluative judgment). This distinction does not affect my criticisms of him in the text.

38 I assume that '*x* is what makes *y* true' is transitive, so that if B is what makes A true, and C is what makes B true, then C is what makes A true.

The conditions become ever more complex as the series proceeds, since each condition mentions the previous one.

39   Unless ethical egoism is true.

40   Hume ([1751] 1975, pp. 285–6).

41   These individuals at least have Plato on their side. See the *Meno* (77d-e) and the *Protagoras* (345d).

42   Hume ([1739] 1992, pp. 399–407) rejects free will, as, I think, should anyone who holds his view of motivation.

43   One might also introduce, as a second factor determining the force of motivations, the confidence of the agent's belief that a given action will satisfy a given desire. The point made in the text will still hold, however, provided that the two factors can be combined into a single factor—for instance, by multiplying the degree of belief by the strength of the desire, as in standard expected-utility calculations.

Richard Fumerton (personal communication) suggests that features of desires other than their strength might be relevant to their motivational efficacy. Perhaps desires for immediate pleasures tend to have more motivational force than desires for distant benefits due simply to their content, rather than their strength. Though this is a theoretical possibility, it seems false introspectively: desires for immediate pleasures feel stronger than desires for comparable but more distant benefits, and this seems the most natural explanation for why the former desires often have more motivating force.

44   There is a large literature on whether that conflict is genuine, which I cannot go into here. See my (2000b) for more.

45   If a variable has a continuous infinity of possible values, then its probability of taking on any given one of those values must be zero; otherwise the total probability for all the possibilities would be infinite. So if there are continuum many possible degrees of strength, then the probability of any desire having any given exact degree of strength must be zero. Consequently, the probability of two different desires just happening to have the same degree of strength (assuming there is not some logical connection between them that requires them to have the same degree of strength) is zero.

Rather than saying the probabilities are zero, some people would wish to posit 'infinitesimal' probabilities here, where an infinitesimal number is one that is less than any real number but greater than zero. I do not believe in such quantities. Nevertheless, I take it that the fact that a theory implied that something which happens quite frequently has an infinitesimal probability of occurring would be extremely strong evidence against that theory, albeit perhaps not *quite* as strong as it would be if the theory implied that the event had probability zero.

46   Mackie (1977, p. 35).

47   Mackie (1977, chapter 5).

48   Mackie (1977, p. 43).

49   Ruse (1998, p. 253). Compare Joyce (2001, chapter 6). Ruse goes on to

express strong doubts that we could ever escape morality's influence. I do not know how to reconcile that with his remarks about the importance of the sense of objectivity to morality's function—unless he doubts (despite his own arguments) that we could ever accept anti-realism.

50  See Singer (1993, chapter 8); Unger (1996).

51  Singer (1993, chapter 12) in fact argues this way, several chapters after presenting his moral argument.

52  Admittedly, I have never given away the huge amounts of money that Singer requires. But I anticipate that the enjoyment derived from that would not be so much greater that that derived from donating smaller amounts.

53  Mackie (1977, p. 106) says this about our 'sense of justice'.

54  Dancy (1993, p. 29) and Scanlon (1998, pp. 33–5) defend this point.

55  See Butchvarov (1989, pp. 48–52). The view is traditionally ascribed to Prichard, though the attribution is hard to justify; see his (1957, pp. 111–12).

56  I do not here mean to rule out that moral philosophy may discover that traditional moral beliefs call for significant revision. In fact, I think moral philosophy has discovered precisely that. But for the sake of argument, suppose that the 'Why be moral?' question is asked in regard to a moral system that has already been subjected to the kind of reflection and criticism that a sophisticated intuitionist would endorse.

57  Fumerton (1990, p. 85) makes a related point: 'Why should I do $x$?' is a request for a reason to do $x$. But '$x$ is rational' just means that $x$ is what one has the most reason to do. So 'Why should I be rational?' amounts to a bizarre request for a reason for doing what one has the most reason to do.

58  Quinn (1993, pp. 236–7, 246–7) make a similar point, arguing that a mere urge unconnected to any tendency to see something as good does not provide a reason for action. Scanlon (1998, p. 38) denies that such an urge even qualifies as a genuine desire.

## Chapter 8   Further Objections

1  Mackie (1977, pp. 38–42). I have changed the argument's name from 'the argument from queerness' to 'the argument from weirdness'. Jackson's appeal to 'metaphysical plausibility' (2003, p. 562) is a version of this argument.

2  Other things commonly rejected on grounds of weirdness include: minds (if not identical with brains), universals, abstract objects in general, *a priori* knowledge, and libertarian free will.

3  In particular, Mackie finds 'queer' the connection between moral properties and non-moral ones, the motivating power of moral properties, and our knowledge of moral properties. I discuss these in section 8.2, chapter 7, and section 5.4, respectively.

4   Mackie (1977, p. 38).
5   Mackie (1977, pp. 31–5).
6   I have used the effort to define 'table' as an exercise in classes; no one has ever succeeded. Consider one initially plausible definition: 'A table is an item of furniture consisting of a flat, level surface and supports, intended to support other, smaller objects' (Rand 1990, p. 41). But a table need not contain supports: I once saw a table at Fallingwater attached directly to the wall. The table was supported, but no supports were part of the table. Suppose we modify the definition to say merely that the surface must be supported off the ground. The definition still implies that a bed or a stool is a table. Suppose we insert 'other than people' after 'objects.' Then the definition falsely implies that an operating table is not a table. It also implies (still) that desks and bookshelves are tables. Obviously, I cannot consider every possible modification, but this is enough to evidence that our understanding of the concept does not guarantee our ability to define it. Again, none of this gives me the least doubt that tables exist.
7   Supervenience (more specifically, 'strong supervenience') is usually defined as follows: $A$-properties supervene on $B$-properties iff: no two possible objects can differ in their $A$-properties without differing in their $B$-properties (Kim 1993, p. 65). However, the relation I intend to refer to in the text is stronger than this; I intend supervenience to also imply that $A$-properties *depend on* $B$-properties. Note also that we may want to weaken the thesis of the supervenience of the evaluative realm to a *global supervenience* claim: that the world as a whole could not have differed in the distribution of evaluative properties without also differing in the distribution of natural properties (Kim 1993, p. 68). For simplicity, I consider only strong supervenience in the text.
8   Mackie (1977, p. 41).
9   Ross ([1930] 1988, pp. 19–20).
10   Strawson (1949, pp. 29–30).
11   Gay (1985, p. 255) and Dancy (1993, p. 99) make similar observations.
12   Dancy (1993, pp. 100–4) discusses and criticizes this sort of analogy, but note that the analogy does not, as Dancy supposes, have anything to do with the propensity theory of probability (Newtonian physics makes no use of probabilities).
13   Most philosophers seem to agree with this, but see Stuart Rachels (2004) for interesting arguments to the contrary.
14   Dancy (1993, pp. 60–1, 102); McNaughton (1988, pp. 200–1).
15   Importantly, I am not seeking to refute particularism of the sort defended by Dancy or McNaughton. The 'liberalized' notion of *prima facie* rightness I have just suggested in the text is compatible with particularism, though it does not entail it.
16   For example, it makes sense to try to control the center of the board, since from there, one can attack more other places.
17   One qualification to this: the propriety of the rules depends on the players' calculating abilities. A player who could see the entire tree of

possible games and could calculate at unlimited speed could play a perfect game without recourse to these rules. I maintain nevertheless that the rules are necessarily correct in some sense: it is necessary that they approximate to how the perfect player would play. Perhaps something similar holds for an agent with perfect moral knowledge—perhaps there is a complete, precise moral theory that would obviate the need for principles of mere *prima facie* rightness. But if there is, we don't know it; hence our need for such principles.

Stuart Rachels has pointed out (personal communication) that what constitutes good play depends on the cognitive abilities of one's opponent, in the sense that, other things being equal, it is better to make a move that it would be more difficult for one's particular opponent to *see* an appropriate response to. I note, as an appeal to authority, that Rachels (1989 U.S. Chess Champion) has also endorsed my remarks about chess in the text.

18  More precisely, *N* is *A*'s maximal natural property—the property formed by conjoining all of *A*'s natural properties, including negative properties (such as 'not being red'), such that nothing with *N* can have any natural properties not entailed by *N*.

19  This is a composite of Blackburn (1993, pp. 114–19) and (p. 137).

20  Blackburn (1993, p. 137); compare p. 122, arguing that where we take an attitude towards something *because of* certain properties, we will take that attitude towards anything that has those properties.

21  Strictly, instead of 'total set of natural features', I should say 'maximal natural feature'; see note 18. If *A*'s *maximal* natural feature is good-making, then *A* is good *simpliciter*, since there can then be no other features that defeat *A*'s *prima facie* goodness.

22  There are two technical problems with this formulation of the argument: one, it assumes that either there exist infinitely long predicates, or there are only finitely many ways for a thing to be good; two, it assumes in any case that the possible ways for a thing to be good are countable. But we should waive these objections in order to get to more interesting replies to Jackson's argument.

23  Jackson (2003, pp. 562–3).

24  Jackson (2003, p. 565); see also (p. 562).

25  There is no consistent, complete formal system capable of deriving all the truths of arithmetic. This entails that there is no algorithm capable of generating all the arithmetical truths (without also generating contradictions). See Nagel and Newman (2001) for exposition of Godel's Theorem.

26  I owe this point to Richard Fumerton (personal communication).

27  Brandt (1996, p. 4) and Abraham (1933) raise this problem. The argument of this paragraph is from Abraham (p. 39).

28  Tara Smith (2000, pp. 27–8).

29  Hare (1989, p. 83) accuses Rawls of this sin, for Rawls' reliance on reflective equilibrium.

30  Nelson (1991) makes a similar point.
31  This objection was suggested to me by Brian Doherty and Bryan Caplan (personal communications).
32  Scientists have recently determined that the following is the world's funniest joke:

> A couple of New Jersey hunters are out in the woods when one of them falls to the ground. He doesn't seem to be breathing, and his eyes are rolled back in his head. The other guy whips out his cell phone and calls the emergency services. He gasps to the operator: 'My friend is dead! What can I do?' The operator, in a calm soothing voice, says: 'Just take it easy. I can help. First, let's make sure he's dead.' There is a silence, then a shot is heard. The guy's voice comes back on the line. He says: 'OK, now what?' (LaughLab n.d.).

However, I find my joke in the text funnier.
33  For more on these sorts of explanations, see Dawkins (1989, chapter 12), Wright (1995, esp. chapter 10), and Ruse (1998, pp. 218–22).
34  These arguments appear in Ruse (1985, pp. 237–8), Joyce (2001, chapter 6), and perhaps Wilson (2000, p. 562), though Wilson is obscure. See also Ruse (1998, pp. 252–4).
35  Compare Pinker's (2002, pp. 192–3) analogy between mathematics and ethics. Just as our evolved capacity to understand numbers leads us to correctly apprehend independently existing arithmetical truths, perhaps our evolved capacity to understand right and wrong leads us to correctly apprehend independently existing moral truths.
36  Nozick (1981, p. 345) makes this point. Compare James Rachels' (1990, pp. 78–9) example of 'mathobiology', a hypothetical field that would study the biological basis of mathematical thinking; this field would add nothing to mathematics. Ruse (1985, pp. 236–7) seems aware of the point but oddly unconcerned by it.
37  See above, p. 103.
38  See Ruse (1998, p. 222).
39  Allen et al. (1977, pp. 145–6).
40  Ruse (1988, chapter 6) discusses (without endorsing) this view.
41  Something like this explanation derives from David Friedman (informal communication). Friedman (1994) gives a similar account of the benefits of respecting rights.
42  Haidt (2001) and Haidt and Hersh (2001) present evidence of what I would call irrationality in moral judgment, though they do not describe it that way. Haidt and Hersh's evidence indicates that moral judgments are often caused more by emotions than by rational reflection and reasoning. As a case in point, about half of Americans believe that homosexual relationships are morally wrong (Haidt and Hersh 2001, p. 192; Gallup n.d.).
43  In 2005, 92 per cent of Americans thought that polygamy is wrong (Gallup n.d.).

44 Haidt (2001) reports that individuals confronted with a story involving harmless brother-sister incest commonly invent rationalizations for judging the action wrong (for instance, appealing to the dangers of inbreeding). When confronted with the falsity of their explanations (for instance, by being reminded that the story specified that the brother and sister used two forms of birth control), subjects commonly insist that the action is still wrong though they cannot explain why.

45 Ruse (1998, pp. 145–7).

46 See, for example, Richard Posner's contribution in Singer and Posner (2001): 'I do not feel obliged to defend this reaction; it is a moral intuition deeper than any reason that could be given for it and impervious to any reason that you or anyone could give against it. Membership in the human species is not a "morally irrelevant fact," as the race and sex of human beings has come to seem.'

47 Mackie (1977, pp. 36–7).

48 More precisely, it is determined by competent speakers' *dispositions* to apply the word—including applying it only in thought—to various possible things.

49 The last example is from Haidt, Koller, and Dias (1993), who have studied attitudes towards harmless, offensive actions such as cleaning the toilet with the flag, having intercourse with a chicken carcass, and eating the family dog when it dies. Haidt and Hersh (2001) have studied attitudes towards cases of harmless incest. In general, many judgments of moral wrongness seem to be based on emotions, are difficult to justify, and are unrelated to any harm done or believed to be done.

## Chapter 9 Conclusion

1 This objection assumes that the subjectivist endorses analytic reductionism. If the identity between wrongness and being forbidden by God is synthetic, then it would be *consistent* to think 'Stealing is wrong, but God does not forbid it'. Similarly, if the identity between wrongness and being forbidden by society is synthetic, then one could consistently think that polygamy is permissible but society forbids it, so two people could disagree about the permissibility of polygamy while agreeing that society forbids it. A similar point applies to individual subjectivism.

2 This argument assumes the principle of bivalence (every proposition is true or false) and the correspondence theory of truth (truth is correspondence to facts). There are important objections to bivalence, such as those deriving from vagueness and from empty names, but none of them are relevant here.

3 Van Inwagen (1983, p. 215).

4 See BonJour (1998, pp. 203–6) for a partial explanation of why this is so.

5 See Mackie (1977, pp. 30–5).

6 Joyce (2001).

7 See Stuart Rachels (2003, pp. 17–22) for further discussion of this point.

8 The move to an obligation not to harm others is controversial. See Parfit (1984, chapters 6, 7, and 9) and Nagel (1970) for more sophisticated defenses of this kind of move. But the simple thought in the text is what moves me.

9 Ross ([1930] 1988, pp. 21, 30–1).

10 See above, p. 103.

11 The following is a simplified version of one part of Davidson's views of the mental; see Davidson (1991).

# References

Abraham, Leo. 1933. 'The Logic of Ethical Intuitionism'. *International Journal of Ethics* 44:37–55.

Adams, Robert Merrihew. 1981. 'A Modified Divine Command Theory of Ethical Wrongness'. Pp. 83–108 in *Divine Commands and Morality*, edited by Paul Helm. Oxford: Oxford University Press.

———. 1999. *Finite and Infinite Goods*. New York: Oxford University Press.

Allen, Elizabeth, et al. 1977. 'Sociobiology: A New Biological Determinism'. In *Biology as a Social Weapon*, edited by Sociobiology Study Group of Boston. Minneapolis, Minn.: Burgess Publishing Co.

Alston, William. 1976. 'Has Foundationalism Been Refuted?' *Philosophical Studies* 29:287–305.

———. 1990. 'Some Suggestions for Divine Command Theorists'. In *Christian Theism and the Problems of Philosophy*, edited by Michael Beaty. Notre Dame, Ind.: University of Notre Dame Press.

———. 1993. *The Reliability of Sense Perception*. Ithaca, N.Y.: Cornell University Press.

Anscombe, G. E. M. 1963. *Intention*. 2nd ed. Ithaca, N.Y.: Cornell University Press.

Arens, William. 1979. *The Man-Eating Myth: Anthropology and Anthropophagy*. New York: Oxford University Press.

Armstrong, David. 1978a. *Nominalism and Realism*. Cambridge: Cambridge University Press.

———. 1978b. *A Theory of Universals*. Cambridge: Cambridge University Press.

Audi, Robert. 1983. 'Foundationalism and Epistemic Dependence'. *Synthese* 55:119–39.

———. 1997. *Moral Knowledge and Ethical Character*. New York: Oxford University Press.

———. 2004. *The Good in the Right*. Princeton, N.J.: Princeton University Press.

Austin, J. L. 1975. *How to Do Things with Words*. 2nd ed. Edited by J. O. Urmson and Marina Sbisa. Cambridge, Mass.: Harvard University Press.

Ayer, A. J. 1952. *Language, Truth, and Logic*. New York: Dover.
————. 1956. *The Problem of Knowledge*. London: Macmillan.
Bealer, George. 1992. 'The Incoherence of Empiricism'. *Proceedings of the Aristotelian Society* 66, supplement: 99–138.
————. 1993. 'Universals'. *Journal of Philosophy* 40:5–32.
————. 1999. 'A Theory of the A Priori'. Pp. 29–55 in *Philosophical Perspectives* 13: *Epistemology*, edited by James Tomberlin. Cambridge, Mass.: Blackwell.
Benacerraf, Paul. 1973. 'Mathematical Truth'. *Journal of Philosophy* 70:661–79.
Benedict, Ruth. 1934. 'Anthropology and the Abnormal'. *Journal of General Psychology* 10:59–82.
Bentham, Jeremy. [1781] 1996. *An Introduction to the Principles of Morals and Legislation*. Edited by J. H. Burns and H. L. A. Hart. Reprint, Oxford: Clarendon Press.
Berkeley, George. [1710] 1965. *Treatise Concerning the Principles of Human Knowledge*. Reprinted in *Principles, Dialogues, and Correspondence*, edited by Colin Turbayne. Indianapolis, Ind.: Bobbs-Merrill.
Blackburn, Simon. 1984. *Spreading the Word*. Oxford: Oxford University Press.
————. 1993. *Essays in Quasi-Realism*. Oxford: Oxford University Press.
————. 1998. *Ruling Passions: A Theory of Practical Reasoning*. Oxford: Clarendon Press.
BonJour, Laurence. 1985. *The Structure of Empirical Knowledge*. Cambridge, Mass.: Harvard University Press.
————. 1998. *In Defense of Pure Reason*. Cambridge: Cambridge University Press.
————. 2004. 'In Search of Direct Realism'. *Philosophy and Phenomenological Research* 69:349–67.
————. 2005. 'In Defense of the *a Priori*', 'Reply to Devitt', and 'Last Rejoinder'. Pp. 98–122 in *Contemporary Debates in Epistemology*, edited by Matthias Steup and Ernest Sosa. Malden, Mass.: Blackwell.
Borowski, E. J. 1980. 'Moral Autonomy Fights Back'. *Philosophy* 55:95–100.
Boyd, Richard. 1988. 'How to Be a Moral Realist'. Pp. 181–229 in *Essays on Moral Realism*, edited by Geoffrey Sayre-McCord. Ithaca, N.Y.: Cornell University Press.
Brandt, Richard. 1944. 'The Significance of Differences of Ethical Opinion for Ethical Rationalism'. *Philosophy and Phenomenological Research* 4:469–94.
————. 1979. *A Theory of the Good and the Right*. Oxford: Clarendon.

Brandt, Richard. 1996. *Facts, Values, and Morality*. Cambridge: Cambridge University Press.

Brighouse, M. H. 1990. 'Blackburn's Projectivism—An Objection'. *Philosophical Studies* 59:225–33.

Brink, David. 1984. 'Moral Realism and the Sceptical Arguments from Disagreement and Queerness'. *Australasian Journal of Philosophy* 62:111–25.

Butchvarov, Panayot. 1989. *Skepticism in Ethics*. Bloomington, Ind.: Indiana University Press.

Butler, Joseph. [1729] 1964. *Butler's Sermons and Dissertation on Virtue*. London: G. Bell & Sons.

Carson, Thomas. 2000. *Value and the Good Life*. Notre Dame, Ind.: University of Notre Dame Press.

Chisholm, Roderick. 1982. 'The Problem of the Criterion'. Pp. 61–75 in *The Foundations of Knowing*. Minneapolis, Minn.: University of Minnesota Press.

Clarke, Samuel. [1705] 1964. 'On Natural Religion'. Reprinted in *British Moralists*, vol. 2, edited by L. A. Selby-Bigge. Indianapolis, Ind.: Bobbs-Merrill.

Crane, Hewitt and Thomas Piantanida. 1983. 'On Seeing Reddish Green and Yellowish Blue'. *Science* 221:1078–80.

Dancy, Jonathan. 1993. *Moral Reasons*. Oxford: Blackwell.

Darwall, Stephen, Allan Gibbard, and Peter Railton. 1992. 'Toward *Fin de Siecle* Ethics: Some Trends'. *Philosophical Review* 101:115–89.

Davidson, Donald. 1990. 'A Coherence Theory of Truth and Knowledge'. In *Reading Rorty*, edited by Alan Malachowski. Cambridge, Mass.: Basil Blackwell.

————. 1991. 'Mental Events'. Pp. 247–56 in *The Nature of Mind*, edited by David M. Rosenthal. New York: Oxford University Press.

Dawkins, Richard. 1989. *The Selfish Gene*. Oxford: Oxford University Press.

DePaul, Michael. 1988. 'The Problem of the Criterion and Coherence Methods in Ethics'. *Canadian Journal of Philosophy* 18:67–86.

Dreier, James. 1996. 'Expressivist Embeddings and Minimalist Truth'. *Philosophical Studies* 83:29–51.

————. 2002. 'Troubling Developments in Metaethics'. *Nous* 36:152–68.

Firth, Roderick. 1952. 'Ethical Absolutism and the Ideal Observer'. *Philosophy and Phenomenological Research* 12:317–45.

Foley, Richard. 1979. 'Justified Inconsistent Beliefs'. *American Philosophical Quarterly* 16:247–57.

Foley, Richard and Richard Fumerton. 1985. 'Davidson's Theism?' *Philosophical Studies* 48:83–9.

Foot, Philippa. 1967. 'The Problem of Abortion and the Doctrine of the Double Effect'. *Oxford Review* 5:5–15.

Frankena, William. 1958. 'Obligation and Motivation in Recent Moral Philosophy'. In *Essays in Moral Philosophy*, edited by A. I. Melden. Seattle: University of Washington Press.

————. 1973. *Ethics*. Englewood Cliffs, N.J.: Prentice-Hall.

Freeman, Derek. 1983. *Margaret Mead and Samoa: The Making and Unmaking of an Anthropological Myth*. Cambridge, Mass.: Harvard University Press.

————. 1999. *The Fateful Hoaxing of Margaret Mead: A Historical Analysis of Her Samoan Research*. Boulder, Colo.: Westview.

Friedman, David. 1994. 'A Positive Account of Property Rights'. *Social Philosophy and Policy* 11:1–16.

Fumerton, Richard. 1990. *Reason and Morality: A Defense of the Egocentric Perspective*. Ithaca, N.Y.: Cornell University Press.

————. 1995. *Metaepistemology and Skepticism*. Lanham, Md.: Rowman & Littlefield.

————. Forthcoming. *Epistemology*. Blackwell.

Gallup Organization. n.d. 'Moral Issues'. (Most recent poll results dated May, 2005.) <http://www.gallup.com/poll/content/default.aspx?ci=1681>. Accessed 26 May 2005.

Gallup, George H., Jr., and Frank Newport. 1991. 'Belief in Paranormal Phenomena Among Adult Americans'. *Skeptical Inquirer* 15, 2: 137–46.

Gardner, Martin. 1998. 'Is Cannibalism a Myth?' *Skeptical Inquirer* 22, 1: 14–16.

Gay, Robert. 1985. 'Ethical Pluralism: A Reply to Dancy'. *Mind* 94:250–62.

Geach, P. T. 1965. 'Assertion'. *Philosophical Review* 74:449–65.

————. 1977. 'Again the Logic of "Ought"'. *Philosophy* 52:473–6.

Gettier, Edmund. 1963. 'Is Justified, True Belief Knowledge?' *Analysis* 23:121–3.

Gibbard, Allan. 1990. *Wise Choices, Apt Feelings*. Cambridge, Mass.: Harvard University Press.

Gilovich, Thomas. 1993. *How We Know What Isn't So*. New York: Free Press.

Glassen, Peter. 1959. 'The Cognitivity of Moral Judgments'. *Mind* 68:57–72.

Goldhagen, Daniel. 1996. *Hitler's Willing Executioners: Ordinary Germans and the Holocaust*. New York: Alfred A. Knopf.

Goldman, Alvin. 1967. 'A Causal Theory of Knowing'. *Journal of Philosophy* 64:357–72.

Haack, Susan. 1983. 'Theories of Knowledge: An Analytic Framework'. *Proceedings of the Aristotelian Society* 83:143–57.

Haidt, Jonathan. 2001. 'The Emotional Dog and Its Rational Tail: A Social Intuitionist Approach to Moral Judgment'. *Psychological Review* 108:814–34.

Haidt, Jonathan and Matthew A. Hersh. 2001. 'Sexual Morality: The Cultures and Emotions of Conservatives and Liberals'. *Journal of Applied Psychology* 31:191–221.

Haidt, Jonathan, Silvia Helena Koller, and Maria G. Dias. 1993. 'Affect, Culture, and Morality, or Is It Wrong to Eat Your Dog?' *Journal of Personality and Social Psychology* 65:613–28.

Hare, R. M. 1952. *The Language of Morals*. Oxford: Oxford University Press.

———. 1963. *Freedom and Reason*. Oxford: Clarendon Press.

———. 1970. 'Meaning and Speech Acts'. *Philosophical Review* 79:3–24.

———. 1989. 'Rawls' Theory of Justice'. In *Reading Rawls*, edited by Norman Daniels. Stanford, Calif.: Stanford University Press.

———. 1999. *Objective Prescriptions and Other Essays*. Oxford: Clarendon.

Harman, Gilbert. 1977. *The Nature of Morality: An Introduction to Ethics*. New York: Oxford University Press.

———. 1990. 'The Intrinsic Quality of Experience'. Pp. 31–52 in *Philosophical Perspectives* 4: *Action Theory and Philosophy of Mind*, edited by James Tomberlin. Atascadero, Calif.: Ridgeview Publishing Co.

Hellman, Hal. 1998. *Great Feuds in Science*. New York: John Wiley & Sons.

Hobbes, Thomas. [1651] 1996. *Leviathan*. Edited by Richard Tuck. Reprint, Cambridge: Cambridge University Press.

Horgan, Terence and Mark Timmons. 1992. 'Troubles for New Wave Moral Semantics: The "Open Question Argument" Revived'. *Philosophical Papers* 21:153–75.

Howard, Michael and Janet Dunaif-Hattis. 1992. *Anthropology: Understanding Human Adaptation*. New York: HarperCollins.

Hubin, D. Clayton. 1980. 'Prudential Reasons'. *Canadian Journal of Philosophy* 10:63–81.

Hudson, W. D. 1967. *Ethical Intuitionism*. New York: St. Martin's Press.

Hudson, W. D. 1983. *Modern Moral Philosophy*. 2$^{nd}$ ed. New York: St. Martin's Press.

Huemer, Michael. 1997. 'Probability and Coherence Justification'. *Southern Journal of Philosophy* 35:463–72.

———. 1999. 'The Problem of Memory Knowledge'. *Pacific Philosophical Quarterly* 80:346–57.

———. 2000a. 'Naturalism and the Problem of Moral Knowledge'. *Southern Journal of Philosophy* 38:575–97.

———. 2000b. 'Van Inwagen's Consequence Argument'. *Philosophical Review* 109:524–43.

———. 2001. *Skepticism and the Veil of Perception*. Lanham, Md.: Rowman & Littlefield.

———. 2003. 'Arbitrary Foundations?' *Philosophical Forum* 34:141–52.

———. n.d. 'Why People Are Irrational about Politics'. <http://home.sprynet.com/~owl1/irrationality.htm>. Accessed 28 May 2005.

———. Forthcoming. 'Compassionate Phenomenal Conservatism'. *Philosophy and Phenomenological Research*.

Hume, David. [1751] 1975. *Enquiry Concerning the Principles of Morals*. Reprinted in *Enquiries Concerning Human Understanding and Concerning the Principles of Morals*, edited by P. H. Nidditch. Oxford: Clarendon Press.

———. [1758] 1975. *Enquiry Concerning Human Understanding*. Reprinted in *Enquiries Concerning Human Understanding and Concerning the Principles of Morals*, edited by P. H. Nidditch. Oxford: Clarendon Press.

———. [1739] 1992. *Treatise of Human Nature*. Reprint, Buffalo, N.Y.: Prometheus.

Hurka, Thomas. 1980. 'Geach on Deriving Categorical "Oughts"'. *Philosophy* 55:101–4.

Jackson, Frank. 2003. 'Cognitivism, A Priori Deduction, and Moore'. *Ethics* 113:557–75.

Jackson, Frank, Graham Oppy, and Michael Smith. 2004. 'Minimalism and Truth Aptness'. Pp. 233–51 in *Mind, Morality, and Explanation*, edited by Frank Jackson, Philip Pettit, and Michael Smith. Oxford: Clarendon.

Jackson, Frank, Philip Pettit, and Michael Smith. 2004. 'Ethical Particularism and Patterns'. Pp. 211–32 in *Mind, Morality, and Explanation*, edited by Frank Jackson, Philip Pettit, and Michael Smith. Oxford: Clarendon.

Joyce, Richard. 2001. *The Myth of Morality*. Cambridge: Cambridge University Press.

Kant, Immanuel. [1785] 1959. *Foundations of the Metaphysics of Morals*. Translated by Lewis White Beck. Reprint, Indianapolis, Ind.: Bobbs-Merrill.

Karmo, Toomas. 1988. 'Some Valid (but no Sound) Arguments Trivially Span the "Is"-"Ought" Gap'. *Mind* 97:252–7.

Kim, Jaegwon. 1993. 'Concepts of Supervenience'. Pp. 53–78 in *Supervenience and Mind*. Cambridge: Cambridge University Press.

Kripke, Saul. 1972. *Naming and Necessity*. Cambridge, Mass.: Harvard University Press.

Layman, C. Stephen. 1991. *The Shape of the Good: Christian Reflections on the Foundations of Ethics*. Notre Dame, Ind.: University of Notre Dame Press.

LaughLab. n.d. <http://www.laughlab.co.uk/>. Accessed 27 May 2005.

Lemos, Noah. 1994. *Intrinsic Value*. Cambridge: Cambridge University Press.

Lewis, David. 1986. *On the Plurality of Worlds*. New York: Blackwell.

Liszka, James Jakob. 2002. *Moral Competence: An Integrated Approach to the Study of Ethics*. 2$^{nd}$ ed. Upper Saddle River, N.J.: Prentice Hall.

Mackie, John L. 1977. *Ethics: Inventing Right and Wrong*. New York: Penguin.

Maitzen, Stephen. 1998. 'Closing the "Is"-"Ought" Gap'. *Canadian Journal of Philosophy* 28:349–66.

Marquis, Donald. 1989. 'Why Abortion Is Immoral'. *Journal of Philosophy* 86:183–202.

McDowell, John. 1978. 'Are Moral Requirements Hypothetical Imperatives?' *Proceedings of the Aristotelian Society* 52, supplement: 13–29.

McGrath, Sarah. 2004. 'Moral Knowledge by Perception'. Pp. 209–28 in *Philosophical Perspectives* 18: *Ethics*, edited by John Hawthorne. Malden, Mass.: Blackwell.

McNaughton, David. 1988. *Moral Vision: An Introduction to Ethics*. Oxford: Blackwell.

————. 2000. 'Intuitionism'. Pp. 268–87 in *The Blackwell Guide to Ethical Theory*, edited by Hugh LaFollette. Oxford: Blackwell.

Mead, Margaret. 2001. *Coming of Age in Samoa*. New York: HarperCollins.

Moore, G. E. 1947. *Ethics*. London: Oxford University Press.

————. 1953. 'Hume's Theory Examined'. Pp. 108–26 in *Some Main Problems of Philosophy*. London: Allen & Unwin.

————. 1960. *Principia Ethica*. Cambridge: Cambridge University Press.

Moore, Michael S. 1992. 'Moral Reality Revisited'. *Michigan Law Review* 90:2424–533.

Murray, Charles. 1984. *Losing Ground: American Social Policy, 1950–1980.* New York: Basic Books.

Nagel, Ernest and James R. Newman. 2001. *Godel's Proof.* Revised ed. New York: New York University Press.

Nagel, Thomas. 1986. *The View from Nowhere.* New York: Oxford University Press.

———. 1970. *The Possibility of Altruism.* Princeton, N.J.: Princeton University Press.

Nelson, Mark. 1991. 'Intuitionism and Subjectivism'. *Metaphilosophy* 22:115–21.

———. 2003. 'Sinnott-Armstrong's Moral Scepticism'. *Ratio* 16: 63–82.

Newport, Frank and Maura Strausberg. 2001. 'Americans' Belief in Psychic and Paranormal Phenomena Is up Over Last Decade'. The Gallup Organization. June 8. <http://www.gallup.com/poll/content/?ci=4483&pg=1>. Accessed 26 May 2005.

Nowell-Smith, P. H. 1954. *Ethics.* Baltimore, Md.: Penguin.

Nozick, Robert. 1974. *Anarchy, State, and Utopia.* New York: Basic Books.

———. 1981. *Philosophical Explanations.* Cambridge, Mass.: Harvard University Press.

Olsson, Erik. 2005. *Against Coherence: Truth, Probability, and Justification.* Oxford: Clarendon Press.

Parfit, Derek. 1984. *Reasons and Persons.* Oxford: Clarendon.

Pigden, Charles. 1989. 'Logic and the Autonomy of Ethics'. *Australasian Journal of Philosophy* 67:127–51.

———. 1991. 'Naturalism'. Pp. 421–31 in *A Companion to Ethics,* edited by Peter Singer. Oxford: Basil Blackwell.

Pinker, Steven. 2002. *The Blank Slate: The Modern Denial of Human Nature.* New York: Penguin.

Plantinga, Alvin. 1993. *Warrant: The Current Debate.* Oxford: Oxford University Press.

Plato. 1996. *Plato's Euthyphro, Apology, and Crito.* Edited by S. W. Emery. Lanham, Md.: University Press of America.

Popper, Karl. 2001. 'Facts, Standards, and Truth: A Further Criticism of Relativism'. Pp. 32–52 in *Moral Relativism,* edited by Paul Moser and Thomas Carson. Oxford: Oxford University Press.

Prichard, H. A. 1957. *Moral Obligation.* Oxford: Clarendon Press.

Prior, A. N. 1976. 'The Autonomy of Ethics'. Pp. 88–96 in *Papers in Logic and Ethics,* edited by P. T. Geach and A. J. P. Kenny. London: Duckworth.

Putnam, Hilary. 1975. 'Philosophy and our Mental Life'. Pp. 291–303 in *Mind, Language and Reality*. Vol. 2 of *Philosophical Papers*. Cambridge: Cambridge University Press.

—————. 1981. *Reason, Truth and History*. Cambridge: Cambridge University Press.

Quine, W. V. 1976. 'Truth by Convention'. Pp. 77–106 in *The Ways of Paradox*. Revised ed. Cambridge, Mass.: Harvard University Press.

Quinn, Philip. 2002. 'God and Morality'. In *Reason and Responsibility*, 11th ed., edited by Joel Feinberg and Russ Shafer-Landau. Belmont, Calif.: Wadsworth.

Quinn, Warren. 1993. 'Putting Rationality in Its Place'. Pp. 228–55 in *Morality and Action*. Cambridge: Cambridge University Press.

Rachels, James. 1974. 'Two Arguments against Ethical Egoism'. *Philosophia* 4:297-314.

—————. 1990. *Created from Animals: The Moral Implications of Darwinism*. Oxford: Oxford University Press.

—————. 2003. *The Elements of Moral Philosophy*, 4th ed. Boston: McGraw-Hill.

Rachels, Stuart. 1998. 'Counterexamples to the Transitivity of *Better Than*'. *Australasian Journal of Philosophy* 76:71–83.

—————. 2003. 'A Defense of Two Optimistic Claims in Ethical Theory'. *Philosophical Studies* 112:1–30.

—————. 2004. 'Six Theses About Pleasure'. Pp. 247–67 in *Philosophical Perspectives* 18: *Ethics*, edited by John Hawthorne. Malden, Mass.: Blackwell.

Railton, Peter. 1986. 'Moral Realism'. *Philosophical Review* 95:163–207.

—————. 1998. 'Moral Explanation and Moral Objectivity'. *Philosophy and Phenomenological Research* 58:175–82.

Rand, Ayn. 1964. *The Virtue of Selfishness*. New York: Signet.

—————. 1990. *Introduction to Objectivist Epistemology*. 2nd ed. New York: NAL Books.

Rashdall, Hastings. 1907. *The Theory of Good and Evil: A Treatise on Moral Philosophy*. Oxford: Clarendon.

Rawls, John. 1971. *A Theory of Justice*. Cambridge, Mass.: Harvard University Press.

Reid, Thomas. [1788] 1983. *Essays on the Active Powers of Man*. Selections reprinted in *Inquiry and Essays*, edited by Ronald Beanblossom and Keith Lehrer. Indianapolis, Ind.: Hackett.

Ross, W. D. [1930] 1988. *The Right and the Good*. Reprint, Indianapolis, Ind.: Hackett.

Ruse, Michael. 1985. *Sociobiology: Sense or Nonsense?* Dordrecht: D. Reidel.

Ruse, Michael. 1988. *Homosexuality: A Philosophical Inquiry.* Oxford: Basil Blackwell.

————. 1998. *Taking Darwin Seriously.* Amherst, N.Y.: Prometheus.

Russell, Bertrand. [1912] 1997. *The Problems of Philosophy.* Reprint, Oxford: Oxford University Press.

Ryan, Sharon. 2003. 'Doxastic Compatibilism and the Ethics of Belief'. *Philosophical Studies* 114:47–79.

Scanlon, T. M. 1998. *What We Owe to Each Other.* Cambridge, Mass.: Harvard University Press.

Searle, John R. 1964. 'How to Derive "Ought" from "Is"'. *Philosophical Review* 73:43–58.

————. 1969. *Speech Acts.* Cambridge: Cambridge University Press.

————. 1979. *Expression and Meaning: Studies in the Theory of Speech Acts.* Cambridge: Cambridge University Press.

————. 1983. *Intentionality: An Essay in the Philosophy of Mind.* Cambridge: Cambridge University Press.

Sextus Empiricus. 1964. *Scepticism, Man, and God.* Edited by Philip Hallie and translated by Sanford Etheridge. Middletown, Conn.: Wesleyan University Press.

Shafer-Landau, Russ. 2003. *Moral Realism.* Oxford: Clarendon.

Shandley, Robert R., ed. 1998. *Unwilling Germans? The Goldhagen Debate.* Minneapolis, Minn.: University of Minnesota Press.

Singer, Peter. 1974. 'Sidgwick and Reflective Equilibrium'. *The Monist* 58:490–517.

————. 1993. *Practical Ethics*, 2nd ed. Cambridge: Cambridge University Press.

————. 1999. 'A Response'. Pp. 269–335 in *Singer and His Critics*, edited by Dale Jamieson. Oxford: Blackwell.

Singer, Peter and Richard Posner. 2001. 'Animal Rights: Debate between Peter Singer and Richard Posner'. *Slate Magazine*, June 11–15 <http://slate.msn. com/id/110101/>.

Sinnott-Armstrong, Walter. 1996. 'Moral Skepticism and Justification'. Pp. 3–48 in *Moral Knowledge? New Readings in Moral Epistemology*, edited by Walter Sinnott-Armstrong and Mark Timmons. Oxford: Oxford University Press.

Smart, J. J. C. 1973. 'An Outline of a System of Utilitarian Ethics'. In *Utilitarianism: For and Against* by J. J. C. Smart and Bernard Williams. Cambridge: Cambridge University Press.

Smith, Michael. 1994. *The Moral Problem.* Oxford: Basil Blackwell.

Smith, Tara. 2000. *Viable Values.* Lanham, Md.: Rowman & Littlefield.

Sterling, Grant. 1994. *Ethical Intuitionism and Its Critics.* New York: Peter Lang.

Stevenson, Charles L. 1963. *Facts and Values: Studies in Ethical Analysis*. New Haven, Conn.: Yale University Press.

Stratton-Lake, Philip. 2002a. Introduction to *The Right and the Good*, by W. D. Ross. Oxford: Oxford University Press.

————, ed. 2002b. *Ethical Intuitionism: Re-evaluations*. Oxford: Oxford University Press.

Strawson, P. F. 1949. 'Ethical Intuitionism'. *Philosophy* 24:23–33.

Sturgeon, Nicholas. 1985. 'Moral Explanations'. In *Morality, Reason and Truth*, edited by David Copp and David Zimmerman. Totowa, N.J.: Rowman & Allanheld.

————. 1986. 'Harman on Moral Explanations of Natural Facts'. *Southern Journal of Philosophy* 24, supplement: 69–78.

————. 1991. 'Contents and Causes: A Reply to Blackburn'. *Philosophical Studies* 61:19–37.

Sumner, William Graham. 1907. *Folkways*. New York: Ginn and Company.

Thompson, Bert. 1999. 'The Bible and the Age of the Earth'. *Reason and Revelation* 19, 8: 57–63.

Thomson, Judith Jarvis. 1971. 'A Defense of Abortion'. *Philosophy and Public Affairs* 1:47–66.

Timmons, Mark. 1999. *Morality without Foundations: A Defense of Ethical Contextualism*. New York: Oxford University Press.

Tooley, Michael. 1972. 'Abortion and Infanticide'. *Philosophy and Public Affairs* 2:37–65.

Tye, Michael. 2002. 'Representationalism and the Transparency of Experience'. *Nous* 36:137–51.

Unger, Peter. 1996. *Living High and Letting Die: Our Illusion of Innocence*. New York: Oxford University Press.

Vallentyne, Peter. 1996. 'Response-Dependence, Rigidification and Objectivity'. *Erkenntnis* 44:101–12.

Van Inwagen, Peter. 1983. *An Essay on Free Will*. Oxford: Clarendon Press.

Van Roojen, Mark. 1996. 'Expressivism and Irrationality'. *Philosophical Review* 105:311–35.

Von Mises, Ludwig. 1996. *Human Action: A Treatise on Economics*, 4th ed. Irvington-on-Hudson, N.Y.: Foundation for Economic Education.

Warnock, Mary. 1966. *Ethics Since 1900*. 2nd ed. London: Oxford University Press.

Weatherson, Brian. 2003. 'What Good are Counterexamples?' *Philosophical Studies* 115:1–31.

Wells, Gary and Elizabeth Olson. 2003. 'Eyewitness Testimony'. *Annual Review of Psychology* 54:277–95.

Westermarck, Edward. 1960. *Ethical Relativity*. Paterson, N.J.: Littlefield, Adams, & Co.

Williams, Bernard. 1981. 'Internal and External Reasons'. Pp. 101–13 in *Moral Luck: Philosophical Papers 1973–1980*. Cambridge: Cambridge University Press.

Wilson, Edward O. 2000. *Sociobiology: The New Synthesis*. Cambridge, Mass.: Harvard University Press.

Wright, Crispin. 1992. *Truth and Objectivity*. Cambridge, Mass.: Harvard University Press.

Wright, Robert. 1995. *The Moral Animal*. New York: Random House.

Zaibert, Leo. 2003. 'Intentions, Promises, and Obligations'. Pp. 52–84 in *John Searle*, edited by Barry Smith. Cambridge: Cambridge University Press.

# Index

a priori knowledge, 111–15; and
  Benacerraf problem, 123–7
abortion, 46, 47, 125, 129, 138–9,
  142–3, 145, 213
Abraham, 261n18
Abraham, Leo, 281n27
abstract objects, 124–5, 210
abstractness, as cause of error, 139
accidentalness, 123
accosting, 258n28
Adams, Robert, 57, 59, 255n5,
  261n12, 261n16, 261n19
addiction, 189
adequate grasp, 125–6
adultery, 21–2, 55
aesthetic realism, 211
affirmative action, 129
agreement, in ethics, 130–1. *See also*
  disagreement
Agrippina, 21, 226
alcoholism, 243
algorithms, 137, 209
Alston, William, 268n18, 268n20
altruism, 214, 218, 250
ambiguity, test for, 37
analytic truths, 125, 112–13, 206,
  269n32
analytic reductionism, *see* reductionism
anomalous monism, 252
Anscombe, G. E. M., 276n17
anthropology, disagreements in,
  135, 136
anti-realism, defined, 4; difficulty of
  explaining moral disagreement,
  148–9; inconsistent attitudes
  towards, xxii–xxiv; insincere,
  xxiii; metaphysical, 12–13; and
  moral methodology, 152–4; ni-

hilism most forthright form of,
  249; popularity of, xxii; three
  forms of, 4–5; undermines morality, 192–6, 248–50; about
  weirdness, 200–1. *See also* subjectivism; non-cognitivism; nihilism
appearances, 99–101, 232; initial,
  101–2; intellectual, 100–1; logical, 101
appetites, 161–2
appropriateness of desires, 178,
  182, 235
approval, and moral belief, 49–50
arbitrariness, and divine command
  theory, 60, 227; and ideal observer theory, 63; and relativism,
  52, 227; and Rossian intuitionism, 250–2; and subjectivism, 50,
  64, 213, 227; of morality on
  Humean view, 187–8, 234
Arens, William, 135
argument from disagreement, *see*
  disagreement
argument from interpretation, 159–
  61
arguments, assessing strength of,
  116
Armstrong, David, 256n1, 271n53,
  271n54
assertions, marks of, 20–1, 225–6;
  Timmons' view of, 40
assertoric non-descriptivism, 39–44;
  differentiated from moral realism, 42–4; as differing only verbally from non-cognitivism, 40
astrology, 135
Audi, Robert, 267n12, 268n18,
  271n55

about heat, 83–5, 87; about sound, 83, 94–5; synthetic, 6, 83–94, 228, 229–30; about water, 83–5, 89–90, 94–5
reference, correctness requirement, 95, 130; purported vs. successful, 256n6; and speaker's intentions, 208; and usage, 207–8, 221
reflective equilibrium, 117, 269n38
Reid, Thomas, 270n46
relativism, *see* cultural relativism
reliability, of intuitions, 107–8, 134; as requirement for knowledge, 123
religion, as basis for morality, 54; disagreement about, 135; as source of bias, 144–5; unreliability of, 141
reputation effects, 214
revisability, of moral beliefs, 105–7; of perceptual beliefs, 107
revisionary ethics, 219–23
rigidifying move, 53
Ross, W. D., 250–2, 267n12, 275n4
rules of inference, evaluative, 264n16
Ruse, Michael, 192–3, 217, 278n49, 282n34, 282n36
Russell, Bertrand, 271n55
Ryan, Sharon, 277n36

Sabbath, 55
Samoa, 135
sanitation engineers, 243
Satan, 58
Scanlon, T.M., 183–4, 262n2, 274n35, 276n22, 277n37, 279n57
schizophrenia, 139
science, as atypical form of knowledge, 251; contrasted with ethics, 245; disagreements about, 135–6; as revisionary, 219–20
scientism, 244–5
Searle, John, 74–6, 257n12,

264n20, 266n47, 276n17
second law of thermodynamics, 131
seeming, *see* appearances
selective attention, 138
self-image, as source of bias, 140
self-deception, 267n3
self-evidence, 106
self-interest, and morality, 186; as source of bias, 140; as source of motivation, 162–3
semantic disputes, 8–9
semantic questions, 1
sensory experience, 270n42
sex, 55
sexiness, subjectivity of, 2, 211, 214
Sextus Empiricus, 268n25
Shafer-Landau, Russ, 268n12, 273n18, 276n21
shape, objectivity of, 2
showing claims to be true, 120
signs of external facts, 118–19, 121–2
Singer, Peter, 145, 150, 151–2, 193–4, 274n36, 279n51
Sinnott-Armstrong, Walter, 268n25, 274n23
skepticism, 12, 107–9, 118–19, 121–2, 232, 236, 252–3, 256n12, 258n12
slavery, 54, 55, 129, 153; selling children into, 163
Smart, J. J. C., 267n10
Smith, Michael, 168–71, 176, 182–3, 257n10, 262n1, 272n1, 274n28, 275n3, 276n13, 276n19, 276n21, 277n28
Smith, Tara, 106, 267n6, 268n15, 268n19, 272n7, 281n28
social welfare programs, disagreements about, 135
sociobiology, 214–19, 242
Socrates, 114
spirit of the age, 242–5
square pegs and round holes, 92–3
statue/clay example, 166